In Search of the Maquis

In Search of the Maquis

RURAL RESISTANCE IN SOUTHERN FRANCE, 1942–1944

H. R. KEDWARD

CLARENDON PRESS · OXFORD

Oxford University Press, Walton Street, Oxford OX2 6DP
Oxford New York
Athens Auckland Bangkok Bombay
Calcutta Cape Town Dar es Salaam Delhi
Florence Hong Kong Istanbul Karachi
Kuala Lumpur Madras Madrid Melbourne
Mexico City Nairobi Paris Singapore
Taipei Tokyo Toronto
and associated companies in
Berlin Ibadan

Oxford is a trade mark of Oxford University Press

Published in the United States
by Oxford University Press Inc., New York

First Published 1993
Paperback first Published 1994

British Library Cataloguing in Publication Data
Data available

Library of Congress Cataloging in Publication Data
Kedward, H. R. (Harry Roderick)
In search of the maquis: rural resistance in southern France, 1942–1944/ H. R. Kedward.
p. cm.
Includes bibliographical references and indexes.
1. World War, 1939–1945—Underground movements—France, Southern.
2. Forces françaises de l'intérieur. 3. France, Southern—History. I. Title.
D802. F8S675 1993 940.53'448—dc20 92–23270

ISBN 0–19–821931–8
ISBN 0–19–820578–3 pbk.

Printed in Great Britain on acid-free paper by
Bookcraft (Bath) Ltd., Midsomer Norton, Avon

Preface

THE wide steps leading up to the terrace of Loubejac are still there, under the moss and the wild violets, but not even a shell of the château remains. The lichen has covered the signs of the fire by which the Germans destroyed the building, used as a winter base by the local armed Resistance, some twenty kilometres south of Cahors in the Lot. By the time the Germans arrived the maquis had dispersed. The Germans fired the château but stopped short of murderous reprisals in the village. No monument tells the story of the maquis either at the château or in the locality where they were fed and protected during the cold month of February 1944. In apparent contrast, just to the north of Cahors a sombre monument close to a railway bridge carries the names of villagers seized at random in the commune of Gourdon and shot at that point on the road from Boissières to Calamane. The inscription reads, 'Here fell 22 martyrs from Gourdon shot by the German barbarians on 30 June 1944.' But there is nothing on the monument to connect this event with all the maquis activity in the area. Even here the history of the Resistance is implicit. In both places the presence of the maquis has to be discovered, by questions to which fewer and fewer people are able to offer an experiential answer.

Tombstones are designed to outlive the transience of memory, but by tradition they carry names and dates rather than interpretations or even narratives. They are signposts to history, though they have an iconography and history of their own. In some parts of rural France the monuments to the maquis are more explicit and informative, and stand proudly at a busy crossroads or on a mountain plateau beside explanatory texts. Elsewhere they are barely visible in the overgrown verges of a country road. Their style, lettering, and choice of words have only some of the rich variety of the monuments to the vastly more numerous dead of the First World War, but where they exist, their siting at the points of ambush, combat, or reprisals does suggest something of the diversity of maquis location, and allows the imagination to glimpse a history whose paths radiate out from these focal points into the villages and countryside beyond. By following such paths, both literally and metaphorically, this book sets out to discover the maquis.

The aim is not a military or strategic history of the maquis, or more generally of the Forces Françaises de l'Intérieur (FFI). It is not another history of the Liberation of France, nor does it attempt to analyse the purges, reforms, and political struggles which accompanied and followed the Liberation. These subjects were researched in local detail for the thirtieth anniversary in 1974, and will be even more discussed in 1994. If this book marks the fiftieth anniversary it is of the embryonic and growth period of the maquis in 1943 as well as the months of combat that followed. The winter of 1943–4 is pivotal. It revealed the essential structures of the maquis and it lies at the core of this study. The aim of the book is to investigate the nature and life of the maquis, to explore the maquis experience. What life? Whose experience? These questions are at the very heart of the search.

From its origins through to its imagery in memory and retrospect, the maquis was always more than a military phenomenon. These other aspects figure prominently in the pages of this study. All wars of liberation against occupying forces are, to varying degrees, the wars of civilians. Alongside the irregular soldiers, known variously as francs-tireurs, guerrilla fighters, maquisards, and partisans, there are what might be called the irregular civilians. Extending the term still further one could speak of irregular places: several villages, towns, and public institutions such as hospitals were given the 'médaille de la Résistance'. It is this wider notion of irregularity, indeed the whole concept of transgression, which opens up the possibility of a deeper and more exploratory search. Sadly the geographical limitations are many: only some areas have been researched to any depth. Some expansive horizons had to remain unreached, horizons not only of space but also of time. At Caniac-du-Causse, one of two villages in the Lot to be 'médaillé' (the other was Terrou in the Ségala), there was a medieval tower, dating from what continues to be known as 'the English Occupation' of Aquitaine in the thirteenth and fourteenth centuries. It fell down shortly after the Germans had gone, and its stones were used to level the village square. There are so many layers of possible comparative history contained within those broken stones. Specifically, there are still many maquis locations which await serious historical investigation. That is the excitement of the subject: so much to explore, so much still to be discovered.

The maquis is analysed here both as a choice and as a necessity in the face of increasing German pressure and demands. Its development led to polarities within French society, but its history is not offered as a simple exemplar of what are currently labelled 'les guerres franco-françaises'. Such a civil-war image may reflect the open conflict between the maquis and the Milice, but it over-simplifies the complex dynamics between Vichy and the maquis. Much of this book is devoted to their relationship, and there is plurality within Vichy no less than in the experience of the maquis. Their histories were interwoven. Both central and local Vichy authority gave shape and substance to the maquis. Conversely it was the maquis which determined much of the final history of Vichy.

This book now forms the second volume of what hopefully will be a three-part study of Resistance in the southern zone of Occupied France. It continues my preoccupation with Resistance as a mosaic of distinctive movements created from below, an image I set out to project in my study of motivations and ideas in the south, published in 1978 as *Resistance in Vichy France*. That study, which was limited to the early years of Resistance, 1940–2, was town-based, for that is where the movements of protest and resistance began and developed. With this volume on 1943–4 there is a shift to rural areas, and it might seem as if the concurrent expansion of Resistance in the towns has been marginalized. That is far from my intention, and I have already started research for a final volume in which urban themes will be reintegrated into the whole.

For this second study I have not rehearsed the facts and interpretations of the first, and undoubtedly some knowledge of the early years of Resistance is taken for granted. But the book stands on its own in the sense that the maquis was a fundamentally new departure in 1943, so that origins and beginnings are once again the subject of the opening chapters. There is also a continuity of method and approach linking the two books, in so far as I chose to pursue the same forms of oral research and presentation, while yet responding to the opening of the archives. Even now there are many relevant dossiers in the archives which remain closed, or are only available in selected extracts, but the belief that the archives of the Vichy period should be open to research now happily inspires the decisions of archivists, politicians, and administrators who at one stage appeared to have decided that the cost of revelations would always be too high. Since much of the official documentation which can now be studied originated in oral testimonies, particularly in the case of police reports, there is a double dependency here on what people thought or wanted others to think. I do not believe that any study of the Resistance, whether urban or rural, can fully escape from the prevalence of opinion, imagery, and representation. Oral testimony, even fifty years after the event, suggests hypotheses, provides personal details, reveals local colour, facilitates insights, and preserves individuality in a way that historians of an under-documented area of history cannot easily afford to ignore. Oral transmission of history from one generation to another continues with or without the attention of historians. History continues to be written with or without oral testimonies. But in many subtle ways the two processes are more interrelated than their separation appears to suggest. The presentation of oral evidence within the text of this book attempts to make this interrelationship overt. More radically it affirms that people have their own history to tell. In doing so they also tell the history of others. The resulting checks and balances create intricate patterns of memory and analysis. Realities are fractured and pluralized, but they are rarely eclipsed.

At all stages of my research I was conscious that the period of the maquis was one of those disputed points in French history round which knots of wise and knowing heads collect as they do round a game of boules under the plane trees in the evening sun. Wherever I went to investigate the maquis I found it a subject on which comment was personal and passionate but which relied on several received truths and conventional constructs to give authority to an individual point of view. Like an outsider initiated over and over again to the alternative or complementary merits of *tireurs* in boules, who go for the instant strike, and *pointeurs* who specialize in positional play, I was insistently introduced to the differences in the maquis between 'action immédiate' which struck wherever possible, and 'action à terme' which prepared for the major action at Jour-J (D-Day). I was told continuously that statistics showed that only a small percentage of the young men who refused to be drafted for labour service in Germany (*réfractaires*), actually became combatants in the maquis. I found repeatedly that it was presumed that I would be interested more in the celebrated areas of maquis history, in the Ain, the Glières, the Vercors, the Limousin, and at Mont Mouchet, and could learn little of importance from anywhere less prestigious or unfamiliar, and I was assured authoritatively that the effectiveness of the maquis could only be judged by whether or not it liberated a particular town or region.

My reaction throughout has been not to deny the validity of these constructed priorities in the understanding of the maquis, but rather to present them in other perspectives. To do so I established my own centre of operations in the forests, hills, and plateaux of the southern Massif Central, from the Cévennes across to the Quercy, looking mainly at the *départements* of the Gard, Lozère, Hérault, Aveyron, Aude, Tarn, and Lot. This dictated my choice of archives, and inevitably my analysis is influenced by the selectivity of these areas, though I have attempted a number of narrative sorties into the better-known territories of maquis history which lie outside my archival and oral base. There are always stories within stories and mine is one of deepening involvement in the history of the localities in which I have worked, and a concern that ordinary people and out-of-the-way places should be named. Detailed maps were essential tools in my research: the maps in this book are no less essential to the text. The place-names can be valued as poetry for purely evocative sounds, but I would also hope that some of their resonance will now have a ring of familiarity in the ever-widening history of the Resistance.

My thanks and acknowledgements for the parts played by so many people during the preparation of this book start with Pat Kirkpatrick whose speed and accuracy in the typing of the manuscript were accompanied by numerous helpful suggestions. This extra involvement in the text was greatly appreciated both as the expression of professionalism and of friendship. To undertake the research over periods of leave in 1982 and 1991 I acknowledge with gratitude the grants generously provided by the ESRC, the British Academy, the Nuffield Foundation, and the Twenty-Seven Foundation, while for my shorter visits to France I have been considerably helped by research grants from the University of Sussex. This gives me an opportunity to thank students and colleagues at Sussex over many years for all the ideas they have supplied, most especially Siân Reynolds whose frontier work in putting women back into the history of modern France has been of outstanding importance both to me and to all those in contemporary French studies. She has been warmly supportive at many decisive moments.

Across the UK many friends and fellow historians have been constantly encouraging with their interest, comments, and advice, in particular Roger Austin, Richard Cobb, Bill Halls, John Horne, Douglas Johnson, Maurice Larkin, John Simmonds, and Hilary Footitt. The historian of SOE, Michael Foot, has been the most instructive friend and mentor in all matters pertaining to the presence of British agents in the French Resistance, and such is the authority of his book that I have not attempted any reassessment of their role, nor looked with any depth at their activity, though I was given numerous new insights by those of SOE who kindly agreed to be interviewed, notably H. M. Despaigne, Yvonne Cormeau, Maurice Buckmaster, and, over a long, fascinating day in his remote house in the Drôme, Francis Cammaerts. I also listened on many occasions to the personal history of Harry Rée, whose modest and whimsical accounts have achieved a classic status in the canon of Resistance memoirs.

From the beginning of my research I have been fortunate to experience the kindness and support of François Bédarida as Directeur of the Institut d'Histoire du Temps Présent in Paris. Thanks to his recommendations my relationships with the archives were always easy and positive, and in that respect the contribution of Madame Bonazzi at the Section Contemporaine of the Archives Nationales was also fundamental in the rapid location of sources. She has been a real friend to all historians of modern France. I also wish to thank Jean-Pierre Azéma for inviting me to try out my ideas on the culture of the outlaw at one of the Institut's seminars, and he and others at the Institut, Claude Lévy, Dominique Veillon, Françoise Mercier, Marianne Ranson, Michel Rauzier, and more recently Henry Rousso and Denis Peschanski, have done much to make me feel welcome in the collective enterprise aimed at understanding every aspect of French life under the German Occupation. As part of this huge historical reconstruction I am equally grateful to Pierre Laborie, Jean Sagnes, and originally Gérard Bouladou, for revealing so much of the south to me, and suggesting numerous ideas and lines of approach. My debt in this respect to all the local historians mentioned in the bibliography is enormous.

My particular gratitude goes to all those I interviewed, together with local archivists and experts of various kinds. I could not have written this book without them, and although individually they may decide that their memoirs, interpretations, and expertise should have figured more prominently in my account, I do hope they will not feel any sense of abuse. I remember all our meetings with appreciation and respect, and with a multitude of pleasurable sensations. Over the many months of oral research I was treated only once to a stressful event, and then it was not intentionally so. An ex-maquisard in the Cévennes whose age and health were cause for concern took me to a perilous pathway above Saint-Jean-du-Gard, which he had used many times in descents for food and other necessities, and while I went on ahead at one point he suddenly disappeared. My frantic shouts only echoed across the valley, and I scrambled in every direction looking for signs of his fall. It must have been twenty minutes, which seemed like hours, before he emerged triumphantly from a cave totally hidden behind a cleft in the rock, delighted to have demonstrated that this ancient hiding-place which they had used in the maquis was still undetectable to the uninformed, and even desperate, searcher. This was unusual: most of my memories of memories are associated with hours or days of hospitality which passed like minutes. The archives too seemed to eat up the time, and when I was pressed I was especially grateful to the local archivists who steered me through the material which was still largely uncatalogued.

Many were the friends who provided food and accommodation, and I particularly want to thank Nora and Denis Knight for the use of their home at Piboulède, a village with only a handful of inhabitants on the Causse de Limogne in the Lot. Their deep attachment to the people and history of the locality was inspirational, and through them I encountered the generosity of Micheline Bismes, Irène Marty, and the Pinsard and Espitalié families. My warm thanks go also to Amelia and Teddy Brett for the loan of their house at la Borie Basse surounded by vineyards under the Monts de l'Espinouse close to the mining areas of the Hérault which were still relatively active in 1943. Many nights and days have been happily spent over the years with Paulette and Philémon Pouget at la Paillade in Montpellier and in the hilltop village of Montjézieu in the Lozère, and it is from Paulette and Philémon that I have learned most of what I know about culture and community in Occitanie. It is they who knew others, who knew others, who made up one of the *boules de neige* in the Montpellier region by which oral contacts were first established. In Paris my friends Jean Gordon and Bernard Frévaque have kept me colourfully in touch with the shifts and undercurrents of French political life, and have always held out a warm and human welcome, while nearer at home my close friend and fellow historian, Antony Copley, has been unfailingly supportive and intellectually challenging by bringing wider dimensions of culture and history constantly into view.

Even more personally, I am only too aware that colleagues, friends, and family, and the medical staff of King's College Hospital, London, and the Royal Sussex County Hospital, Brighton, did more than I can possibly imagine to bring me through heart surgery and the two years of recuperation which came at the moment when I had hoped to draw together my research and start writing in 1986. It all had to be started again, as if from scratch, and I can never thank my family enough for their wonderful care, humour, and love. To my wife, Carol, and my son and daughter, Joshua and Jessica, I owe everything.

H.R.K.

Brighton, 1992

Contents

Maps

Note. The Index of Place-Names indicates the number of the maps in which the places can be found as well as the pages in the text where they are mentioned.

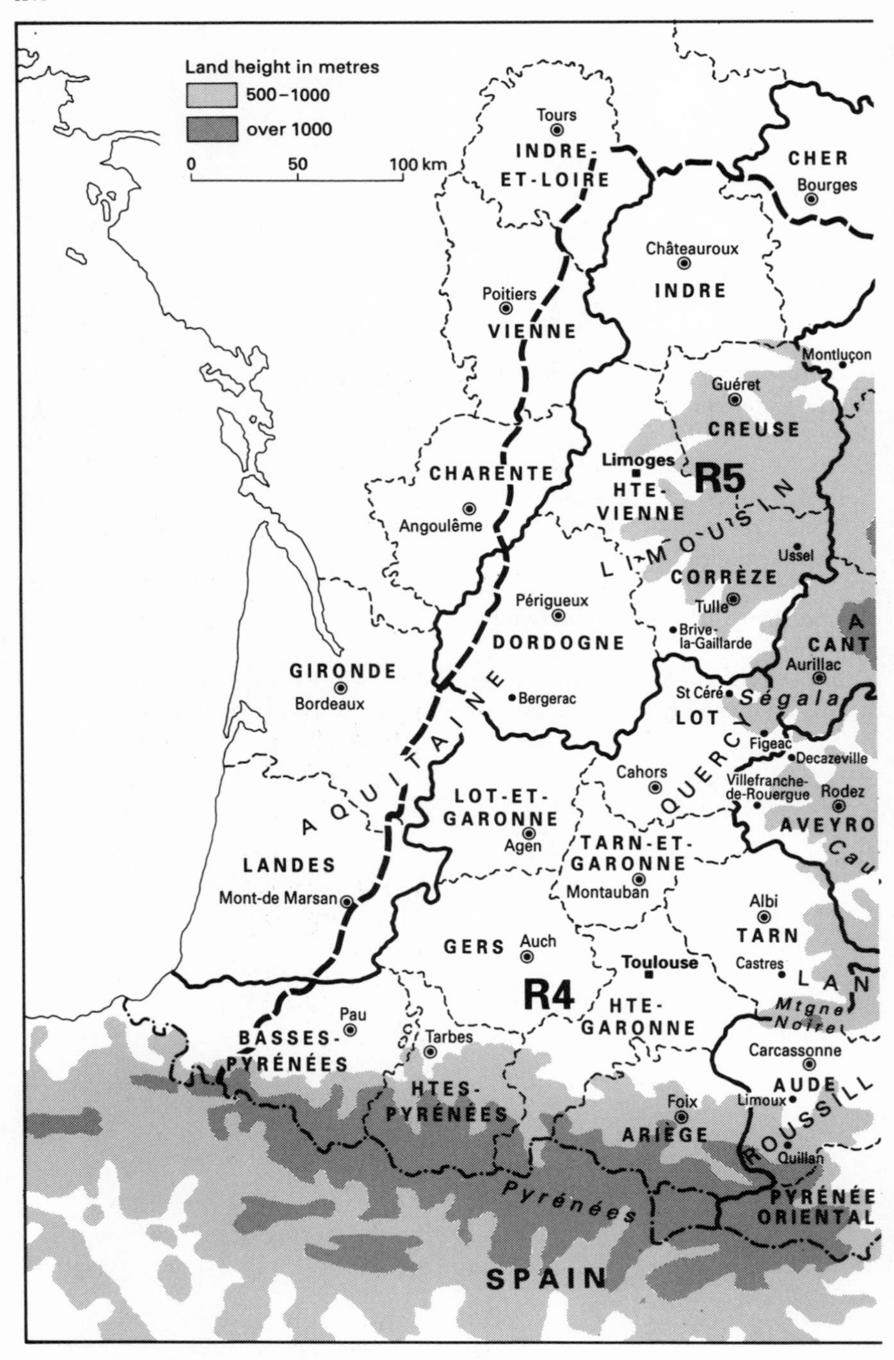

1. South of France, November 1942–August 1944

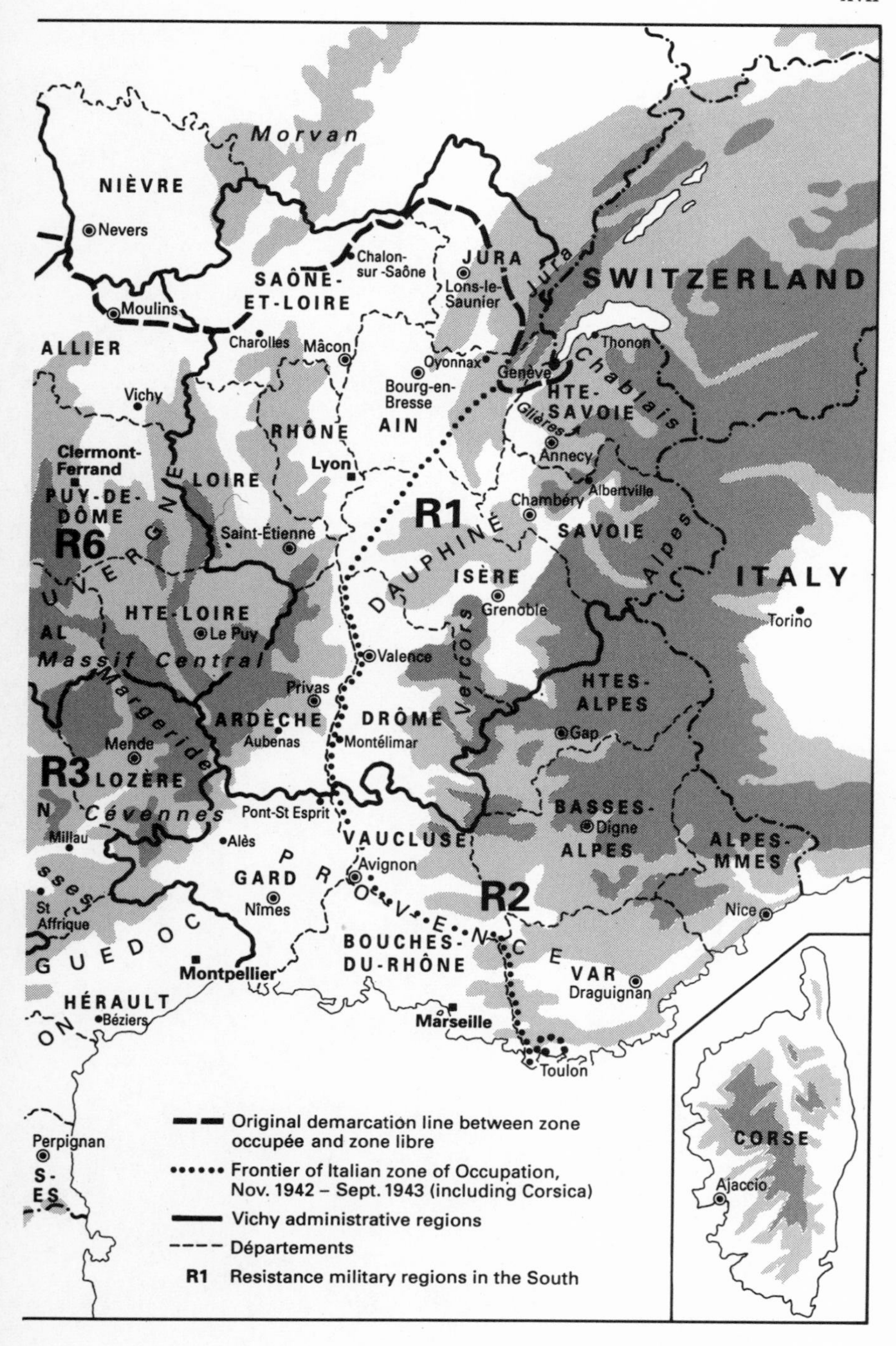
Morvan
NIÈVRE
Nevers
Chalon-sur-Saône
JURA
Lons-le-Saunier
SWITZERLAND
SAÔNE-ET-LOIRE
Moulins
ALLIER
Charolles
Mâcon
Thonon
Oyonnax
Genève
Chablais
Bourg-en-Bresse
HTE-SAVOIE
Vichy
RHÔNE
AIN
Glières
Clermont-Ferrand
Annecy
Lyon
LOIRE
Albertville
PUY-DE-DÔME
R1
Chambéry
R6
Saint-Étienne
DAUPHINÉ
SAVOIE
Alpes
ISÈRE
ITALY
HTE-LOIRE
Grenoble
Torino
Le Puy
Vercors
Massif Central
Valence
Margeride
Privas
HTES-ALPES
ARDÈCHE
DRÔME
Aubenas
Montélimar
Gap
Mende
R3
LOZÈRE
Cévennes
Pont-St Esprit
BASSES-ALPES
Digne
Millau
Alès
VAUCLUSE
ALPES-MMES
Avignon
GARD
PROVENCE
Nîmes
R2
St Affrique
Nice
BOUCHES-DU-RHÔNE
VAR
Montpellier
Draguignan
HÉRAULT
Béziers
Marseille
Toulon
CORSE
Ajaccio
Perpignan
Original demarcation line between zone occupée and zone libre
Frontier of Italian zone of Occupation, Nov. 1942 – Sept. 1943 (including Corsica)
Vichy administrative regions
Départements
R1 Resistance military regions in the South

I

Resistance and Refuge, 1942

EXPERIENCE of the Occupation is normally measured in terms of the German presence. That seems to declare the obvious and to defy contradiction. In 'Paris under the Occupation' written in 1945, Jean-Paul Sartre starts by describing how life adapted to the occupiers, and states that Parisians and the Germans were 'hustled along and tossed together in the stream and swirl of urban existence'. He sets out to dispel melodramatic images of Germans striding, revolvers in their hands, through streets of cowed and terrified civilians, and yet it is the constant German presence which haunts the city and dictates the patterns of experience. But that is only a starting-point. Gradually the darker, malignant side of this presence began to be felt by the sudden disappearance of a friend, or the distinctive ring of a telephone in an empty flat, and in these ways it was absence which came to mark the impact of the Occupation most acutely.[1]

Sartre's interest in the paradox presented by the almost tangible feel of absence may ultimately be philosophical, but it is grounded in the realities of the historical situation. The defeat of 1940 brought Germans into France; by the same token it took over a million and a half French soldiers into the Reich as prisoners of war, and the Occupation as it developed was equally both presence and absence. By 1942 the fact, threat, or fear of enforced absence extended to increasing numbers of individuals, groups, and localities as the German presence intensified.

Pierre Laval's second term of power gave this interrelationship of presence and absence a sharp and unexpected twist. Facing the insistence of Fritz Sauckel that the occupied countries of Europe should provide labour for the Reich within Germany, Laval parried with the inventive scheme of the *Relève*, which traded specialist workers for prisoners of war. He thus accepted a shared responsibility for the absence of those French who could be induced

[1] Jean-Paul Sartre, 'Paris under the Occupation', in J. A. Weightman (ed.), *French Writing on English Soil* (Sylvan Press: London, 1945), 124.

to go to Germany, and imposed a moral pressure on the families at home to accept that absence as part of their national duty. The *Relève* introduced a new range of possible experiences for the ordinary French person, family, or industry. Absence was now something which could be volunteered, and the German presence in France would be mitigated by the returning presence of fathers, brothers, and sons from the Stalags of the Reich.[2]

Laval announced his scheme on 22 June 1942, setting it within his belief in the opportunities afforded by the New Europe, and coupling it with his wish for a German victory to preclude the triumph of Bolshevism across the continent.[3] The *Relève* was accepted in principle by Sauckel in his capacity as Reich Minister of Labour, but the collaboration of Vichy France in the recruitment of volunteers did not predispose this bullying, doctrinaire Nazi to any flamboyant concessions. The first contingent of returning prisoners did not arrive until 11 August,[4] and throughout the summer Sauckel reiterated his impatience at the slow progress of worker recruitment. On 22 August he stipulated that all men and women between 20 and 65 within occupied Europe would be considered mobilized for labour service, and Laval's instinct for barter and exchange was yet again stimulated into making a proposal of French co-operation. By the Vichy law of 4 September 1942 the *Relève* was given a conscriptive character, and all French men between 18 and 50, and single women between 21 and 35, were made eligible for labour at the state's discretion. It was less sweeping than Sauckel's ordinance and kept some initiative and most of the responsibility within Vichy's domain.

In itself this was a hollow victory: it could only be given substance if benefits were seen to result at the popular level at which Vichy's propaganda and financial inducements were aimed. Success or failure at this level was signalled by the monthly prefects' reports to the Ministry of the Interior, an index of public opinion supplemented by the Contrôle postal, by means of which hundreds of thousands of letters were opened weekly and their contents annotated under themes of current concern for the government, such as the popularity of Pétain, the problems of *ravitaillement*, and, now, the workings of the *Relève*. Both sources of information indicated widespread apprehension about the scheme. In certain rural areas a cautious acceptance

[2] The *Relève* is introduced and discussed in its earliest forms in H. R. Kedward, *Resistance in Vichy France* (OUP: Oxford, 1978), 224–8.

[3] 'Je souhaite la victoire allemande, parce que, sans elle, le bolchévisme demain s'installerait partout.'

[4] See Yves Durand, *La Vie quotidienne des prisonniers de guerre* (Hachette, 1987). On p. 199 he describes the scene at Compiègne where Laval in person welcomed the returning prisoners, and he states that the contingent was made up of '900 cultivateurs, 40 soutiens de famille, 30 veufs, quelques "sanitaires", quelques spécialistes, plusieurs "services rendus" et notamment une vingtaine de P. G. désignés par les Allemands au dernier moment en vue de faire de la propagande en France'.

is evident from the intercepted letters, but the reports showed a new, and for the administration, disturbing degree of disbelief and hostility.[5]

The possibility of rural sympathy for the *Relève* had been nurtured by Vichy's argument that the return of prisoners, who were overwhelmingly from the agricultural sections of French society, would start to redress the town–country imbalance of national sacrifice, and conversely, Vichy officials expected any opposition to the *Relève* to be urban based. But the tenor of prefectoral reports suggests that the antagonism they had encountered to the *Relève* constituted a surprisingly widespread rebuke for the government in both town and country, a final collapse in the credibility of the already unpopular Laval, and a worrying decline in the public estimation of Pétain, whose message on 17 June 1942, the second anniversary of his assumption of power, was depressed and disappointing in tone.

On 4 August the Prefect at Avignon reported that a tenacious Germanophobia gripped the population of the Vaucluse, and they were unconvinced by Laval's claim that the government could pursue no other policy.[6] From Albi the Prefect sent reports which constantly stressed the rural conservatism of the Tarn, but at the end of July he not only reported that Laval's speech had been a failure but also that opinion was convinced of 'la défaite allemande qu'elle souhaite', a backhanded inversion of Laval's own words of 22 June. He acknowledged that the peasants recognized the potential of the *Relève* to compensate for some of their sufferings, but he could see little sign of a wave of volunteers, not least because the workers were just as attached to their locality as the peasantry, often possessing a small parcel of land which kept them rooted to the area. The fact of a Prefect proclaiming that the average worker was 'fermement attaché à son clocher' as if that might be seen as a moral weakness in mid-1942, when 'retour à la terre' had been a prime ideological theme within the *Révolution Nationale*, carried a heavy irony which cannot have been lost on ministers at Vichy.[7] The message was echoed throughout the southern zone. From Marseille there came the observation that the local employers were unenthusiastic about the *Relève*, fearing a loss of valuable workers at a time of labour shortage, and from Grenoble the Prefect expressed the scepticism of the local population who suspected that workers would go to Germany but that no prisoners would return.[8] Only from two prefects was there any suggestion that Laval's

[5] For an excellent article on the Contrôle postal, see Roger Austin, 'Surveillance and Intelligence under the Vichy Regime: The Service du Contrôle technique, 1939–45', *Intelligence and National Security*, 1/1 (1986). Lengthy instructions were sent by Laval to prefects on 24 Aug. 1942 at which time he stipulated that it was 'un organe d'information et non un service de police'; AD Lozère VI. M2. 19.

[6] AN F1C III. 1195, Vaucluse, report of 4 Aug. 1942.

[7] AN F1C III. 1193, Tarn, report of 31 July 1942.

[8] AN F1C III. 1143, Bouches-du-Rhône, report of 4 Aug. 1942; and F1C III. 1158, Isère, report of 5 July 1942.

speech and the *Relève* were acceptable commodities. In Mende at the heart of the most sparsely populated *département* in the south, the Prefect told Vichy that the Lozère was receptive to Laval's mid-summer broadcast, while from Nîmes the Prefect of the Gard said that Laval's words had been a profound shock to local people, but that the *Relève* held out hopes for the families of the prisoners of war, even if there were no volunteers in view. Both prefects made it clear how closely they personally supported Vichy's policy towards the occupiers.[9]

Historians agree that by the end of 1942 Sauckel's first demands for 250,000 men had more or less been met, but mostly from the more populous and industrialized *zone occupée* where the impact of the German presence was immediate, or from compulsion throughout the two zones after the law of 4 September. Statistics, used outside the context of all other indicators, point therefore to the success of labour conscription in 1942, but this image of success, even after September, is not sustained by official reports from the southern prefects, nor was it tantamount to the success of the *Relève*. The name of the scheme highlighted not the departure of workers but the return of prisoners, and on that criterion it was widely felt to be a miserable failure. The unfavourable ratio of one prisoner for every three specialist workers, which Laval had been forced to accept, meant the scheme was always on the defensive in any public debate, and Vichy could barely mobilize enough liberated prisoners to testify to the benefits of the scheme when the coercive law of 4 September made its positive propaganda even more vulnerable. Paul Creyssel, Director-General of Propaganda, urged his regional representatives to maximize the display of compliant prisoners in a co-ordinated assault on public opinion between mid-September and mid-October, but the impact does not appear to have been significant.[10] It was departure, conscription, and deportation which became the keywords of the last few months of 1942, not return, relief, or compensation. Vichy was becoming identified with Germany as a predatory force, responsible for absences.

The use of the word deportation was a powerful rendering of the way people came to experience the *Relève*; it was also the product of intensive pamphleteering by the Resistance, and a daily campaign by the BBC describing Laval's scheme as a treasonous slave-trade and Laval himself as the slave-trader selling French workers for personal gain and ideological ends. There is also little doubt that Vichy prefects told the government in no uncertain terms that the *Relève* was a blunder. Vichy's propaganda, said the Marseille Prefect in October, was a total misreading of French psychology, and two months later he declared that the *Relève*, to all intents and

[9] AN F1C III. 1165, Lozère, report of 4 July 1942; and F1C III, Gard, report of 3 Aug. 1942.

[10] 'Circulaire aux délégués No. 85', AD Bouches-du-Rhône M6. 11094, kindly made available to me by Lucy Jaffé.

purposes, was dead.[11] But the meaning of deportation in the last months of the year went well beyond a polemical description of the *Relève*. However persuasive the BBC and the Resistance press were in producing a language of deportation and slave labour, it was the cumulative impact of three events which gave the words such emotive power: first the *Relève* itself, secondly the mass deportations of Jewish men, women, and, particularly, children, and thirdly the effect of the Nazi occupation of the southern zone.

The savage round-up and deportation of immigrant Jews in August and September 1942 provoked impassioned objections from individuals, and gave a new moral urgency to Resistance, both of which have been analysed elsewhere.[12] Substantial protests and expressions of outrage were received by Vichy administrators, as the squalid scenes of brutal hounding were enacted by German and French police in the occupied zone and by French police alone in the *zone sud*. The deportation of Jews revealed the essence of Nazism and the moral degradation of Vichy, but it would be a falsification of the situation to say that the French people, any more than any other nations involved in the war, were as horrified as they should have been. The corrosion of exclusive nationalism and dehumanizing legislation had severely weakened many people's willingness to identify racism and resist it. Nevertheless, as the trainloads of victimized people were shunted across the south into the occupied zone, there was a discernible hardening of opposition to Vichy, and the deportations gave a new irony to the term *zone libre* two months before the German invasion of the south on 11 November destroyed its meaning altogether.

The German occupation of the *zone sud* was in response to the Allied landings in North Africa, but it had clearly been anticipated, to judge from the rapidity of Vichy's reaction, with its flood of rationalizations and repressive measures. The extended German presence was to be called an *opération* not an *occupation*, and in an urgent instruction to prefects in what he still called the *zone libre* Laval emphasized that all police activities were to be carried out directly and exclusively by the French under their own responsibilities and according to French law. At the same time, prefects were to set up as frequent contacts as possible with the German authorities with a view to resolving difficulties by personal conversations.[13] But in the light of the Armistice settlement, Vichy went on to redefine the duties of southern prefects to include close police co-operation with the Germans in the arrest of German deserters, and dual responsibility for the pursuit of anyone engaged in attacks or acts of sabotage directed against the German presence. As a postscript, orders were given that searches and arrests effected in the course of enquiries should be handled by the French police alone, whose

[11] AN F1C III. 1143 Bouches-du-Rhône, reports of 7 Oct. and 5 Dec. 1942.
[12] See Kedward, *Resistance in Vichy France*, 164–84.
[13] AD Gard CA 367, telegram of 13 Nov. 1942.

'essential duty in these circumstances is to put all its efforts into protecting the national community'.[14]

This role of 'protector', together with the Armistice obligation to provide security for the German forces, involved a major extension of the mechanisms of repression and control, directed at the minorities in the south defined as suspect or dangerous. High on the list were Spanish republican activists, anti-fascist refugees from Central Europe or Italy, all immigrant Jews who had avoided the deportations of the summer, and all known communists and anarchists. Lists of suspect Spaniards had been drawn up in September 1942 in compliance with a Vichy circular from Henri Cado in the general secretariat for police, and the same official issued urgent warnings in December that communists liberated from Algerian prisons by the Allied victories would be recirculating in the southern zone and should be rigorously controlled. To aid the local police he included the home addresses of all those previously interned in North Africa in a booklet which ran to thirty-four tightly printed pages, half of which were given to those of French nationality, mostly registered as communist militants, and half listing internees from Germany, Armenia, Austria, Bessarabia, Spain, Hungary, Poland, Romania, Russia, Czechoslovakia, Turkey, the Ukraine, and North Africa. The Poles, filling four pages, were mostly described as old members of the International Brigades, and in the five pages given to those with Spanish origins the nomination was most frequently 'anarchist', 'member of the POUM', or just 'extremist'.[15]

The bulging police files to which these details were added already contained many hundreds of names 'à rechercher', in particular immigrants who had escaped from camps at Gurs and Rivesaltes, among others.[16] The files were a mixture of imprecision, which can only have hampered detection, and meticulous biographical information, which served to highlight or exaggerate a particular individual's subversive potential. Prefects were compelled to jostle for commendation by outbidding each other in the number of arrests and internments, and a protracted file kept by the Regional Prefect Honteyberie at Montpellier testifies to Vichy's almost daily concern to tabulate, count, and verify all foreigners in the south. The police worked closely with the organization of foreign labour, Travail Étranger (TE), and at the heart of the file lies a Vichy telegram dated 18 November 1942 instructing Honteyberie to arrest all foreigners of subversive potential, and to let the camps and labour centres act as sorting stations later on. A subsequent telegram asserted that only French authorities were to have access to the prisons and camps, but in apparent contradiction to this

[14] AD Hérault 18W 19, secret circular from the Ministry of the Interior, Nov. 1942.

[15] AD Hérault 18W 14, circulars dated 1 Sep. and 15 Dec. 1942, the latter containing the booklet of addresses.

[16] AD Hérault 18W 8–18W 10.

assertion of independence a series of instructions gave prefects the authority to communicate to the Germans all names of internees whose origins lay outside France in the rest of occupied Europe.[17] It is difficult for a historian to give a coherent picture of the pressure put on local Vichy authorities in the months following the total occupation of the south, but a picture which is too coherent would miss the feeling which runs through these official archives that the police were hopelessly over-stretched and ultimately confused by the barrage of instructions.

The pressure of the *Relève*, the racial persecutions, and the investigations and arrests after November, brought the language of deportation and the facts of authoritarianism into village squares and rural towns which had existed since 1940 in relative isolation from the German Occupation and from state interference. Rationing restrictions had been as close as most people had come to experiencing the increased power of government, and both contemporaries and historians differ radically on whether the frustration and defiance produced by food controls were related to a growing spirit of resistance or not. The significant increase in the regulation of people's labour and lives was a different matter. In December 1942 for the first time since 1940, the evidence provided by the intelligence network of the Renseignements Généraux gave a clear indication that the 'population bourgeoise' and the 'paysans' who had figured so consistently as sympathizers of the government, were no longer reliable. The Prefect in Cahors, summarizing the situation in the Lot, reported that the term *Révolution Nationale* was now greeted with nothing but laughter: the population had abandoned the internal politics of the government.[18] The Lozère now provided disappointing conclusions for the Prefect who had given the government encouraging news in the summer. By the end of December,

> The majority of people in the Lozère, indoctrinated by the foreign radio broadcasts and too exclusively attached to their locality, remain systematically hostile to the policy of collaboration and refuse to understand the requirements of the day.

In the lightly industrialized town of Saint-Chély-d'Apcher, he continued, the workers, and still more important, the employers are obstinately opposed to the *Relève*, and resistant to the Prefect's attempts to persuade them of its benefits.[19] Other *départements* carried a similar or more substantial story of general disillusionment. The *zone sud* was turning its back on the regime which had appeared, somewhat miraculously in 1940, to have guaranteed it a privileged immunity from the war and from the everyday presence of threats and fear. A hostile distance between Vichy and the populace had

[17] AD Hérault 18W 8, Ministry of the Interior to Regional Prefect, 18 and 27 Nov. 1942; AD Hérault 18W 19, Ministry of Interior to Regional Prefect, 1 Dec. 1942.

[18] AN F1C III. 1163, Lot, report of 5 Dec. 1942.

[19] AN F1C III. 1165, Lozère, report of 5 Jan. 1943.

been ascribed to working-class opinion in many areas since mid-1941: in the winter of 1942–3 it was steadily extending to all classes. It was a distance which had been measured verbally in expressions of resentment or disillusion. It was now a distance which began to announce itself spatially. A new form of absence makes its appearance in the official reports. Individuals, and among them many immigrant Jews, are reported missing but still in the locality, hidden by sympathizers. Absence could be a symptom of revolt.

The early history of Resistance can point to many individuals who moved from one hiding-place to another, and includes several others who were not themselves pioneers of Resistance but were nevertheless sought by the police for political reasons, were forced to hide, and found themselves part of the disparate opposition to Vichy. Being clandestine did not necessitate staying hidden in one place, but involved a way of life which relied on a number of safe places in more than one town. Finding, offering, and running such places was a central part of the infrastructure of Resistance. The geography as well as the *vie quotidienne* of Resistance from 1940–2 was essentially urban, and Resisters became adept at manipulating the possibilities that towns provided for cover and sustenance, and for the production of newspapers, pamphlets, forged documents, and explosives. A safety in urban numbers had also allowed considerable scope for public demonstrations of protest and assertiveness, which continued even after the occupation of the south. Thus, in Limoges in early December, the Prefect signalled to Vichy that there had been a silent gathering of 3,000 people in one of the town's squares in protest against the *Relève*, a level of collective action that matched those on the days of traditional public affirmation such as 1 May and 14 July.[20]

It was the function of the *Relève* to recruit the kind of urban, industrialized workers whose skills had kept them away from the fighting front in 1940, and the posters designed by Vichy to advertise the scheme made no secret of this fact, while yet avoiding the explicit statement that urban loss would be rural gain. Workers were tempted by high wage promises and secure employment, and the posters used the time-honoured icon of wife and children wishing a dutiful farewell to the responsible husband, thus adding strong moral and patriotic pressure to the financial inducements. Given the marked development of urban Resistance throughout 1942, the posters rarely survived intact without some defacement or counter-slogan, and the struggle to dominate the walls reflected the struggle within the factories, where the clandestine trade unions, often only reconstituted on a theoretical basis, were given new substance by the *Relève* and the attendant police activities. Urged not to go to Germany by these unions, by the Resistance press, and by the

[20] AN F1C III. 1197, Haute-Vienne, report of 3 Dec. 1942. For demonstrations against both Vichy and the occupiers on days of fête, see Kedward, *Resistance in Vichy France*, 210–28.

BBC, the workers who did refuse had no easy alternative, and of those who went into hiding with friends and relatives elsewhere in their own town, many were unable to sustain their individual rebellion. There was no ready-made and coherent strategy for this kind of absence: it went beyond the familiar challenge of hiding leaders as they moved from place to place, which Resistance movements had met for over two years.

Very few Resisters in the last months of 1942 imagined that the countryside might contain a solution to the changing needs of those in opposition to Vichy and the occupiers. Vichy had flattered the peasantry and exalted country life by its recapitulation of Barrèsian themes of 'le pays réel' and 'la terre et les morts', and drastic food shortages in the towns meant there were sound economic reasons for placating the agricultural producers and encouraging them to work in harmony with the Ministry of Provisions. Vichy's theories of regionalism, the interest in local customs and folklore which prefects were encouraged to promote, and the care for prisoners of war and their families which Pétain was seen to personify, all pointed to the regime's preference for rural values, which urban Resisters took to be reciprocated by peasant acceptance and docility in the face of growing Vichy collaboration. In this light the *Relève* was doubly suspect to the Resisters, both as compromise with the occupiers and as a further divisive step in the polarization of town and country. The existence, since the Armistice itself, of *passeurs* on whose local knowledge the *réseaux d'évasion* depended for crossing both the demarcation line and the national frontiers, had not successfully established a pattern of rural Resistance to offset the negative image of a submissive and egoistic peasantry. The cupidity of a minority of the *passeurs* was more often referred to than the skills and time given selflessly by the majority. It was during 1942 that money began to be seen as a vital factor in Resistance, a fact acknowledged by both the British and the Free French, and yet even as Jean Moulin, among others, distributed money to Resistance leaders for logistic necessities and clandestine survival, it continued to be a subject of denunciation and criticism that rural *passeurs*, in offering a safe passage and even incidental shelter and food, should expect to be paid. The 'mythe noir du passeur' was already widespread by the end of 1942. It did much to undermine any nascent ideas that the countryside might be hospitable to impecunious workers avoiding the *Relève*.

Understandably, such workers and urban Resisters generally could have had little knowledge of the shifts in rural opinion about which the prefects' reports were so suggestive. Where urban attitudes were grouped round a mixture of envy and anger at the control which peasants were perceived to exercise over *ravitaillement*, the reports register the other side of that control, the mounting disaffection of a peasantry which saw itself crucially deprived of labour, seed, fertilizers, and animal foodstuffs, and was determined to sell direct rather than submit to Vichy's regulations and imposed food prices.

The Prefect of the Tarn, who had warmly embraced Vichy regionalism, and had welcomed Carcopino's permission in December 1941 for schools to teach the Langue d'Oc, was far from supportive of Occitan peasants when it came to the economy, accusing them of making veritable fortunes and meeting the food inspectorate with denials of hoarding. They were also reported as putting the blame on German requisitions for any food shortages.[21] Clearly the peasants had a vested interest in pointing to the Germans as responsible for the nation's *ravitaillement* problems, but in so doing they were nearer to the truth than town dwellers who continued to blame 'la cupidité paysanne'.

In the nearby *département* of the Lot a letter from the mayor of Pomarède to the Prefect on 20 July 1942, headed 'le problème paysan', itemized what local peasants really expected from Vichy: pensions for all agricultural workers; subsidies for young couples looking for land; insurance against loss and injury; extensive loans, and a defence against millers, bakers, the spinning and weaving industries, distillers, and sawyers. The Prefect sent it on without comment as an appendix to his report that the peasantry was basically uninterested in politics, an urban definition which denied the mayor's letter its potential political content.[22] Put into fuller context, the economic demands and frustrations of the peasantry, all too easily dismissed as self-regarding by the urban authorities, make it much easier to understand why rural opinion was more cautious towards the *Relève* than Vichy anticipated. In addition there was a multiplicity of local particularisms which insulated certain areas from the blandishments of Vichy and made them suspicious of authority, foremost among which were the Protestant Cévennes, where sympathy for refugee Jews caused increasing concern to Vichy from August 1942 onwards.

On the first Sunday in September 1942, the annual Protestant assembly at the Musée du Désert near Mialet in the Cévennes provided effective cover for a collective action to bring over 100 Jews into the area and to conceal them in the valleys and villages of the mountains. The action was organized by the CIMADE, the Protestant Comité inter-mouvements auprès des évacués, which had distinguished itself by its relief work in the harsh and degrading conditions to which Jews were subjected in Gurs and other camps in the south-west of France.[23] Mobilizing *pasteurs* and their wives, social

[21] AN F1C III. 1193, Tarn, reports of 31 Jan., 28 Feb., 3 May 1942.

[22] AN F1C III. 1163, Lot, report of 3 Aug. 1942.

[23] In a report from the Renseignements Généraux on 18 May 1943 to the Ministry of the Interior, the following figures are given for deportations from Gurs: 1,000 on 6 Aug. 1942, 700 on 8 Aug., 500 in Sept., 925 in Feb. 1943, 770 in Mar. 1943. The report absolves the camp authorities of all cruelty, and when detailing the conditions of the deportations states, 'Sans doute, il s'agissait de wagons de marchandises. Mais est-il nécessaire d'ajouter que les réfugiés français au cours de leur exode de juin 1940 n'ont pas toujours été aussi bien partagés.' AN F7. 15312.

workers, and teachers, and backed by Pastor Boegner at the head of the Reformed Church, the CIMADE had successfully created escape routes via the Cévennes, and the village of le Chambon-sur-Lignon in the Haute-Loire in particular, to the Swiss border.[24] The action at the Protestant assembly was on a grand scale: it marked a significant escalation of Protestant civil disobedience in the area north of Nîmes and Alès.

The willingness of the Protestant inhabitants of the Cévennes to assimilate individuals, couples, and extended families wanted by the Vichy police and the occupiers, lay in their ethic of sympathy for religious minorities victimized by unacceptable authority, and their cultural pride and folk memory of the Camisard rebellion against the forces of King and Catholic Church in the early eighteenth century. The suitability of the area for successful concealment lay in the facts of steady depopulation, which had left isolated houses, farms, and outbuildings abandoned but in solid structural condition, and the region's mixed agricultural economy in smallholdings which provided relative immunity from the severe food problems experienced in the towns. These explanations are presented and analysed in the detailed study of the area, published as *Cévennes, terre de refuge 1940–1944*, a powerful documentation of the welcome and assistance extended by the Cévenols to Jews and anti-fascist immigrants, refugees, and escapees. It is clear from the careful research carried out from village to village that even within this apparently homogeneous Protestant area, which stood in stark contrast to the neighbouring Catholic area of the Haute-Lozère, there were nevertheless still more specific particularisms which made, for example, Saint-Germain-de-Calberte or the valley of la Mimente much safer for refugees than the localities of Florac and Meyrueis, where there was 'a hard core of Pétainists and collaborators who did not hesitate to act as informers to the authorities'.[25]

The people of the Cévennes were not alone in 1942 in helping to bring rural action out of the margins of Resistance history and edge it closer to the centre. In his report for the turn of the year, the Prefect of the Haute-Savoie specified that in his *département* the rural communities in particular 'demeurent hostiles à la politique de collaboration'.[26] In the Alpine mountain range of les Bornes which encompassed the plateau des Glières,

[24] See *Les Clandestins de Dieu, CIMADE 1939–44* (Le Signe Fayard, 1968), and *Le Plateau et l'accueil des Juifs réfugiés, 1940–45* (Chambon-sur-Lignon, 1981).

[25] *Cévennes, terre de refuge*, textes et documents rassemblés par Philippe Joutard, Jacques Poujol, et Patrick Cabanel (Presses du Languedoc: Montpellier, 1987), 144. This thorough and sensitive work is a mine of local information, as well as giving sharp insights and excellent interpretations. On 30 Nov. 1942 the President of the local Commission of the Contrôle postal summed up letters in the Lozère about the arrival of Jewish refugees, by saying that local people saw it as a real invasion, and were very hostile. This almost certainly refers to the Haute-Lozère and not to the part of the Lozère in the Cévennes; AD Lozère VI. M2. 19.

[26] AN F1C III. 1187, Haute-Savoie, report of 4 Jan. 1943.

farms were already, by the beginning of winter, sheltering a few individual workers who had refused the *Relève*, and claims that the local authorities, including the gendarmerie and Catholic clergy, were sympathetic do not seem exaggerated. The local peasantry, wrote François Musard, were cautious and secretive, but resistant to the political pressures of Vichy: 'The vast horizons have given them the taste of freedom. They have an innate sense of justice, and once they have offered their friendship that gift has the value of a sacred pact that nothing can break.'[27] The Alpine borders of France had not been invaded or defeated in June 1940 and there were groups of Chasseurs Alpins dispersed in the region who began to talk of possible military action at the time of the occupation of the *zone sud* when the Armée de l'Armistice was dissolved and all units ordered to surrender their arms. Reliance on the rural communities was taken for granted.[28] This trust could not be generalized across the whole of the countryside of the *zone sud* nor, indeed, throughout the Haute-Savoie. Mostly it was a question of single villages or individual farms which initiated a degree of resistance in 1942, and even in those areas, rural secretiveness and suspicion in neighbouring communities often worked against strangers and refugees rather than in their favour. This was true even in the Forêt de Châteauneuf in the Limousin where the communist *instituteur*, Georges Guingouin, had been sheltered by individual farmers on many occasions since he went into hiding in mid-1941. His rural resistance had to be built very selectively in the first two years.[29]

What further complicated the map of rural attitudes in late 1942 was the highly localized significance of immigrant labour. As Vichy organized its Travail Étranger (TE) and moved much of the work-force out of the big concentrations such as Gurs into small mountain and forestry camps where the labour shortage was acute, so it unintentionally set up structures for the retention and concealment of those whose deportation was ordered or contemplated in August or after. It was by maximizing this system that the CIMADE enabled many Jews to secure Vichy permits for rural labour, the first stage in their escape or disappearance into hiding. The Spanish republicans, for whom the big camps had originally been intended, before being replaced by Jewish immigrants, were particular beneficiaries of the TE dispersal, finding themselves deployed across the southern region of the Massif Central and in the Pyrenees in labour camps where their work was valued and protected by authorities and local community alike. Fred Plisner, a young Jewish refugee from Austria, has described his situation as Travailleur Étranger in the region of Pau between 1940 and 1942, as one of

[27] François Musard, *Les Glières* (Éditions de Crémille, 1971), 44.
[28] Louis Jourdan *et al.*, *Glières, Haute-Savoie, 31 janvier–26 mars 1944. Première bataille de la Résistance* (Association des rescapés des Glières: Annecy, 1946), 12–13.
[29] Georges Guingouin, *Quatre ans de lutte sur le sol limousin* (Hachette, 1974), 36–44.

opportunism and survivalism, but also of continuous dependence on the individual decisions of persons in the locality:

Our *maire.* He was a *paysan.* A man of the land. He slogged away at his various scattered fields taking one day at a time. He was no hero and he was no giant, but not one to cave in to other people's demands. He was the elected mayor of Riupeyrous, a hamlet of about forty farms, because he was the natural selection. And he took his office seriously . . . And when the gendarmes came and told him that in accordance with procedure they would be rousing him at four the next morning to take them to where we lived, he acquiesced.

But he would be damned if he was going to assist the Vichy government in their dirty dealings. It was the end of August. And the end of the easy times. We had returned from our wood-felling job . . . and there was the *maire* talking to mother. He told us what was about to happen. It was for us to decide what to do in the light of his disclosure. But he stuck around and helped us . . . [30]

The Plisner family owed their escape to the mayor's defiance of Vichy, but it is of interest in Plisner's account to see how Vichy was given great credit for the successful ways it had created work for immigrants caught up in the defeat of France and the *exode.* For all its reactionary nature, he argues, the regime had enabled such workers to find employment and food, and by such achievements it set up positive relations between immigrants and rural communities in a considerable number of areas. When it came to Laval's heightened co-operation with Sauckel's demands and his determination to deport all immigrant Jews, such positive working relations were often the basis for protective rural action, the assimilation of absence.

The stirring of civil disobedience in the countryside in the second half of 1942 should not be exaggerated and certainly not generalized. But it should be emphasized. It was the prerequisite for any extension of urban revolt and it was itself an enlargement of the nature of Resistance. If industrial action in the towns, involving go-slows, absenteeism, sabotage of goods earmarked for Germany, and the manipulation of labour statistics to protect workers from the *Relève*, can be claimed as part of the ways in which an expanding minority of French people in 1942 expressed their resistance to the German Occupation and Vichy collaboration, then the isolated incidents of rural obstruction of Vichy authority, the widespread retention of foods which were subject to requisitioning, the localized assimilation of immigrant and Jewish refugees, and the plurality of *filières* across the borders must be given the possibility of similar status. A vast amount of detailed local research could alone determine the extent of such actions in 1942, but the presumption should not be automatic that the typology of rebellious town and submissive

[30] Mr Fred Plisner very kindly showed me a copy of his unpublished autobiography in 1988, and has generously allowed me to use this extract.

country, current in popular discourse in 1942 and perpetuated in so many historical accounts, was accurate even in general terms.

Henri Cordesse and Aimé Vielzeuf, two excellent historians of local Resistance, who know their areas of the Lozère and the Gard through their own Resistance experience as well as through research, both acknowledge the slow response of established Resistance organizations to the idea of moving into the countryside. In the Lozère the first generation of Resistance leaders, Bourillon, Peytavin, Lyonnet, and Grasset, were sceptical of rural action throughout the winter of 1942–3, while Vielzeuf recounts the difficulties of a young Nîmois, Marcel Adam, in making contact with Resisters in either Nîmes or Marseille who would know where he could hide once he had decided not to go to Germany for the *Relève*: 'Hélas! Fin 1942–3 rien n'est organisé dans notre région.'[31] The mounting pressure by the BBC and the clandestine press on workers not to respond to the *Relève*, and the escalation of calls to Resistance were creating problems within the major towns just at the time when German garrisons were installed after the occupation of the *zone sud*, accompanied by the whole machinery of Gestapo infiltration which extensively used networks which were enmeshed with the urban black market. The uncertainties of the towns were finally heightened at this point by the creation of the Milice at the end of January 1943. The *zone sud* was now beginning to experience the full rigour of Occupation which the northern zone had been forced to endure for over two years. The south had unevenly benefited from easier communications and greater freedom of organization and expression; they were benefits which had produced a considerable degree of complacency, but also an expectation that such relative freedom could and should be maintained, if not by Vichy itself, then by anti-Vichy action. .

A ministerial recognition that the *zone sud* was protecting itself from Vichy's restrictions on the freedom of labour, and doing so successfully, came on 11 December 1942 in a letter from Lagardelle, Bichelonne, and Bousquet to regional prefects, giving facts and figures about the *Relève*. They remonstrated that whereas the *zone occupée* had furnished 130,000 skilled workers for Germany, the *zone sud* had provided only 2,500. In order to avoid an even heavier requisition in the north, Vichy had decided to demand an urgent provision of 15,000 skilled workers from the south, by a basic levy of 20 per cent of all specialists in all industries except mining, the railways, bauxite, and the postal services, together with a selected few others which were protected. The instructions went on to say that industries which had no economic priority could be required to surrender up to 100 per cent of their skilled work-force. Unskilled workers were to replace all

[31] Henri Cordesse, *Histoire de la Résistance en Lozère* 1940–44 (Cordesse, n.p., 1974), 52, and evidence from H. Cordesse, 22 Mar. 1982; Aimé Vielzeuf, *On les appelait 'les bandits'* (Éditions de Crémille: Geneva 1972), 16.

those recruited.[32] This urgent demand put local authorities under direct pressure to intervene in the process of labour requisition and intensified the bitterness in the towns. In the Vaucluse only three skilled workers out of 76 designated had left during November, and although these brought the number of specialists provided by the *département* up to 100 the Prefect was clearly on the defensive in presenting his record, and by early 1943 he was declaring that the figures of skilled departures had improved, and in all there had been a total of 700 volunteers, which he considered very appreciable for a dominantly agricultural area.[33] Letters monitored in January 1943 in the Lozère describe the sending of workers to Germany as 'cruel', 'deplorable', 'sad', and 'disgraceful', and compare the departures with the deportation of convicts. There were few illusions about their voluntary status. One letter from a woman in Saint-Chély-d'Apcher on 5 January showed how a shortage of tacks in a carpentry workshop was used as an excuse to lay off workers: 'You can easily guess why: a week later they sent off fifteen workers—all volunteers of course! They're already preparing further lists.'[34] This was the working of the December instructions in a *département* where the Prefect was assiduous in meeting his obligations. In such circumstances any public belief that Vichy could assure the south a continued insulation from the Occupation was difficult to sustain, and the number of threatened workers, particularly from the smaller towns, who began to go into hiding with relatives in farms and villages, dramatically increased.

In the Lot four such workers hid with sympathetic relatives near Arcambal, 15 km. east of Cahors, during the month of December, and were soon joined by others from neighbouring communes. Marie Pouget, on the nearby farm of le Poujoulat, was already sheltering and feeding workers on the run, and went on to provide them with 15 francs a day from collections she made in the vicinity.[35] The needs of the Occupation economy had increased the value of lumber industries throughout France, and the Lot, as elsewhere, saw a mushroom growth in forestry camps. Many of these provided a refuge for Resisters in the last months of 1942, and their owners are specifically named in the local history *Ombres et espérances en Quercy*: MM Mangieu, the mayor of Boissières, Bordes of Dégagnac, Teulat of le Vigan, Raymond Mousset of Figeac, Alfred Rougié of Saint-Céré. Many provided work and pay as well as shelter.[36] It was a recurrent pattern throughout the south: labour

[32] AD Hérault 161W 69, Largardelle, Bichelonne, and Bousquet to regional prefects, 11 Dec. 1942.

[33] AN F1C III. 1195, Vaucluse, reports of 5 Dec. 1942, 5 Feb. 1943.

[34] AD Lozère VI. M2. 23, Mme X from Saint-Chély, 5 Jan. 1943.

[35] AN 72. AJ 157, 'Vie des maquis dans la commune d'Arcambal', and evidence from Marie Pouget's son and daughter, André Pouget and Élise Jouclas, 5 Mar. 1991.

[36] Raymond Picard and Jean Chaussade, *Ombres et espérances en Quercy 1940–45* (Éditions Privat: Toulouse, 1980), 62.

contracts marked many of the first Resistance actions bringing town and country together.

Just how many arrangements of this nature there were at the turn of the year cannot easily be quantified, but the process gathered momentum through personal contacts and the structures of extended families which existed around most of the smaller towns. It only needed the spring weather to make country life more comfortable, and there was the reasonable hope that those in hiding could survive the Occupation untouched, until the Allies carried out what some already thought to be an imminent invasion from North Africa. Had certain country areas not already embarked on civil disobedience, town workers seeking an unmolested life might have encountered the hostility and incomprehension that many urban people attributed to the entire peasantry. But on the contrary the point to be made is that by January 1943 certain individuals from the larger towns were discovering for themselves the growing ambivalence of parts of the countryside towards the authority of Vichy, and their experience was instructive enough to force others to recognize that a new stage in the Resistance had begun. Tentatively the town was rediscovering and reappraising the country. The discourse of incompatibility was weakening. Absence from the towns for a small number had come to mean presence in the country, and in many areas there was no incompatibility at all.

The small town of Aubenas, overlooking the river Ardèche, is flanked to the north and west by thickly wooded hills, and stands at a crossroads of winding routes from Provence to the centre of France, and from Languedoc to the Rhône valley. The German garrison after November 1942 was relatively inconspicuous and the town quickly became established as one of several in the south from which refugees, people on the run, and deserters from the German army were directed into farming and forestry where their labour was welcomed and their provisioning assured. Michel Bancilhon, an architect in the local administration of Ponts et Chaussées, saw the urgent necessity of seeking out safe places and equipping the refugees with false identity papers and ration cards, and he emphasizes the slow but cumulative nature of his clandestine *intendance*. He stressed that Aubenas was less a town with its distinct urban or industrial identity, despite its silk workshops, than a *gros bourg* integrated with the surrounding agriculture and forestry.[37]

Further to the south, the much larger mining and industrial town of Alès, on the edge of the wild crests and valleys of the Cévennes, but under 50 km. from the urban elegance of Nîmes, was inseparable from the rural villages which encompassed it. Alès, la Grand' Combe, and Bessèges formed a mining complex for coal, lead, zinc, and asphalt which stretched up the valleys formed by the rivers Gardon and Cèze, and gave peasants and

[37] Evidence from Michel Bancilhon, 5 July 1982.

workers a linked social and familial identity. The strong Protestantism of the area, interlocked with material resources, produced a web of intricate communal help and interdependence, in which the communists who had dominated the political development of the town in the 1930s could count on structures of refuge, solidarity, and secrecy in resisting both Vichy and the heavily armed German presence in the town itself.

In the mining community of Decazeville, at the border of the Lot and Aveyron; in the market town of Saint-Affrique on the edge of the Larzac plateau; in Figeac in the fertile valley of the Célé at the centre of le Quercy Noir with its dense forests of chestnuts rivalling those of the Ardèche; in Quillan approaching the foothills of the Pyrenees and close to the fortress of Montségur where the Cathar revolt ended in 1244; in the Savoyard town of Albertville at the confluence of the rivers Arly and Isère under the Alps; in Ussel in the Corrèze and in nearby Neuvic, where Léon Moneger's garage was at the centre of a network of refuge in the surrounding country, dotted with small villages; in Oyonnax and Brénod in the Ain; Thônes in Haute-Savoie; Lasalle, Valleraugue, and le Vigan in the Cévennes; Villard-de-Lans and Pont-en-Royans, from where the first refuge was organized in the Vercors mountains close to Grenoble; in all these towns Resisters have emphasized similar interconnections between town and country which facilitated the creation of rural hiding-places in 1942–3. Although there can be no surprise that certain towns and their immediate localities shared patterns of labour, marketing, and culture, this identity of interest needs to be stressed as a corrective to the widespread assumptions about town–country polarities under the Occupation. Such polarity may have seemed the norm to those most affected by food shortages in the larger towns, but once outside the big urban centres the major differences were more between one area and another rather than between town and country. Furthermore, it was already evident in the winter of 1942–3 that in those areas where towns and countryside formed a cohesive unit sympathetic to developments in Resistance, few questions were asked about the provenance of those taken into hiding. Anti-fascists and Resisters from Eastern Europe, from Spain, from Alsace, from Lille, and Paris, as well as from the southern conurbations, were hidden almost as readily as those from the immediate vicinity. In early 1943 the most that many peasant farmers demanded of those on the run was a readiness to work. The arrangements initially concerned separate individuals, or groups of two or three, and the problems of housing them were not acute. So many outbuildings, farms, and even whole hamlets were disused or depopulated in the upper regions of the southern zone that a dry, solid stone building as a hiding-place was not a luxury.

The numbers involved at the beginning of this hiding process were small, yet the achievements were considerable. But just as impressive uplands are described as foothills to the larger mountains to which they give rise, so the hiding and care of those on the run in 1942 came to be seen as the prehistory of the drama that followed, such was the impact of the Service du Travail Obligatoire.

2

Refusal and Revolt, Spring 1943

THE law defining the Service du Travail Obligatoire (STO) was enacted on 16 February 1943, but was subject to endless refinements and classifications. It required all young men born between 1920 and 1922 to register at the local *mairies*, and, by listing several categories of workers, divided them into those who were exempt, those who would be liable for compulsory service in Germany, and those who would have to work for German industries within France. The most notable categories of exemption were for those working in agriculture and in the mines, and there were deferrals until September for students. Women of the same age-groups were not immediately affected by the law but remained subject to the labour directives under the legislation of September 1942

In early January Sauckel had demanded that, in addition to those who had left in 1942, a further 250,000 workers should be sent to Germany by mid-March, and it was to meet this demand that Vichy enacted the law of 16 February. STO did not replace the obligations laid down in September 1942, but by formalizing a registration process made it far more difficult for those designated for Germany to find reasons for not complying. The three years, or *classes*, were those who had missed military service due to the defeat, but many had done eight months of service in the Chantiers de la Jeunesse, or were in the process of doing so, and Vichy received immediate reactions of anger that they should be summoned so soon for a second period of enforced labour. Comparisons were made with those born in 1922 who had not yet been called to the Chantiers, and Vichy showed itself sensitive to these arguments by reducing the number of exemptions available for this particular year, to the point where exemption no longer applied automatically to all agricultural workers or students born in 1922. This did not become clear for nearly two months, by which time Sauckel had demanded a second contingent, this time of 220,000 workers, a figure Laval finally accepted on 9 April with a deadline for the end of June. The same three years were still the target age-group, but to these were added those born in the last quarter of 1919 who had not been mobilized in 1939.

This rolling programme of registration and redefinition of categories carried with it a weight of administration which put prefects, mayors, and their staff under intolerable pressure, and the urgency with which Laval himself supervised the second period of STO with almost daily enquiries and exhortations directed at local administrators, showed how conscious Vichy was that the system was permanently close to breakdown. The Prefect of the Lozère was not one of Vichy's reluctant authorities; he had enthusiastically promoted the round-up of Jews in hiding in his *département* and had called for police reinforcements from Montpellier to make it more effective. But the numbers required from the Lozère for STO were such that even this zealous practitioner of Vichy policies felt the need to protest, asking in early March 1943 whether Vichy could either reduce the numbers or take them in small batches over a longer period. If not, he argued, the effect on the only four towns with a population of over 2,000 would be drastic.[1] In the far more populous and industrialized Bouches-du-Rhône the Prefect in Marseille also complained, but less about the numbers exacted than about the mere three days allowed between the first registrations and the first departures, which gave no time for a careful investigation of claims for exemption. Most were given the benefit of the doubt and the result was that exemptions totalled over 50 per cent of those registered.[2] If this sounded like an excuse for sending fewer workers to Germany than Vichy had anticipated, it was no more than one of many used throughout the south, as almost every authority found something in the February law to query, reject, or use as a rationalization for lower numbers. And yet official figures show that the required numbers were both found and sent. For all its unpopularity and cumbersome machinery STO was sharply focused: it had a cutting edge and purpose which the measures of 1942 had lacked. From February to April it appeared that it was not easily avoided or delayed.

Yet what was reported in these first months of STO does suggest a very considerable degree of refusal. The pioneering actions of individuals and groups in hiding Jews and Resisters during 1942, and the reputation of certain areas as willing reception centres, had created a patchwork of local possibilities which those determined to avoid STO began to exploit. In Vichy's administrative parlance they were *défaillants* or *insoumis* and were threatened with instant dispatch to Germany once they were caught, a threat which almost amounted to an official recognition that STO in Germany was punitive and could be administered as *de facto* deportation. The terms

[1] AN F1C III. 1165, Lozère, report of 5 Mar. 1943. An indication of the dominance of agriculture in this *département* is given by the fact that of the 1,861 men aged 20–23 who were registered in the Lozère, 1,400 were exempt as agricultural workers.

[2] AN F1C III. 1143, Bouches-du-Rhône, report of Apr. 1943.

were soon reinforced by the stronger word *réfractaire*, but this carried positive resonances in certain Catholic circles, signalling resistance by priests to the Civil Constitution of the Clergy at the time of the Revolution, and involved questions of historical and pastoral identity. Parish priests were still important authority figures for the local population, alongside primary schoolteachers, and they were immediately caught between the public exigencies of Vichy on the one hand and the private requests for counsel on the other.[3]

Between February and mid-May the word *défaillant* entered against a name in the local records was far from a precise categorization. It could mean that the person in question had moved house, was ill at the time of the summons, thought he was exempt, was away from home for any of a large number of reasons, had failed to attend the obligatory medical examination, had eventually, but not initially, been given exemption, was a student, was still in the Chantiers de la Jeunesse, or had only recently been discharged.[4] Regularizing the situation was as much the problem of the administration as it was of the *défaillant* in question, and once the category had been more narrowly defined there was still the problem of how to pursue the *défaillant* and with what degree of rigour. An instruction from Vichy in April 1943 insisted that *réfractaires* should be located by the local gendarmerie and not by the more militarized police units, the Groupes Mobiles de Réserve (GMR), and that prefects should take over hotels close to the railway station in which to keep the workers prior to departure. These *camps d'hébergement* became a feature of all major towns, but the severity of the supervision varied wildly from place to place, and within individual places from week to week.[5]

It is clear that the local authorities tried, and largely succeeded, to do three things in the wake of STO. First, they complied by producing the required number of departures for Germany; secondly, they demonstrated in report after report that STO was provoking attitudes and scenes of public hostility, unprecedented since the Vichy regime was established; and thirdly, they tried somewhat ambivalently to mediate the law with a degree of leniency towards the *défaillants*. An incident at Mazamet in the Tarn in March was thoroughly documented by the Commissaire de Police and was symptomatic of the ambivalence which STO had occasioned. Mazamet, a small but important textile centre at the foot of the Montagne Noire, where sheeprearing was as traditional as in the Cévennes further east, was hit hard by the first STO conscription, and 116 young men were scheduled to leave for Germany on 11 March. Violent scenes of remonstration by parents and

[3] See ch. 4. For a full discussion on the relationships of the Catholic Church to STO see the scholarly work by W. D. Halls, *The Youth of Vichy France* (Clarendon Press: Oxford, 1981), 357–94.

[4] AD Hérault 17W 163–8.

[5] AD Hérault 17W 8, Correspondence Ministry of Labour and Regional Prefect, Apr. 1943.

friends marked the departure, with crowds estimated at 2,000, at least a sixth of the town's population. Singing 'La Marseillaise' and 'L'Internationale', and shouting 'A bas Laval' and 'Police à la Relève', they were eventually broken up by an overstretched gendarmerie who arrested twenty-eight men and women. Of these presumed ringleaders several detailed descriptions were given in the report, which argued for clemency towards the protesters. Gabrielle Ferret, aged 46, without children, was a spinner and was described as a woman of excellent reputation and high morals, but disputatious and rebellious. Juliette Iche, a housewife with one child, was noted as even more troublesome, and had been observed at the centre of previous food demonstrations, encouraging others to protest; otherwise her character was given as unimpeachable. Eugène Escande, leather worker and father of one of the men scheduled for Germany, was thought to be the instigator of the demonstration, but he, unlike many of the others, was not described as 'Gaulliste' or one of the 'organisateurs de la Résistance' and was obviously seen by the police as a protester of circumstance, provoked by STO into actions not previously contemplated. When an inquiry was finally carried out on 23 March by the Commissaire de Police de Sûreté, this was the character given to the rising as a whole, a spontaneous incident sparked by a shortage of vouchers available for equipping those due to depart. If there were political motives they were supplied by 'a few communists and Spaniards in the crowd who found it easy to provoke the demonstrators', and a decision followed to imprison four of these so-called political activists. The overall feel of both the report and the inquiry is that protest and refusal were an understandable public reaction to the excessive exactions of STO.[6]

It was not as if STO was the only pressure on the French labour force. Several workers designated for Germany, reported the Regional Prefect of Montpellier, were being kept back to work for the Germans in France, and although he claimed to have negotiated their release, his protest to the Germans was only the beginning of protracted negotiations with Organisation Todt (OT). The attitude of OT, the main German labour organization within France which specialized in constructions of a military nature, was crisp: a letter at the end of June 1943 from the Groupe Ouest of OT stated categorically that the STO office had no right to move French workers from OT to any other work whatsoever.[7] To accommodate this insistence Vichy ultimately agreed that deserters from STO or from the immigrant labour force, Travail Étranger, who found work with OT, would not be pursued by the Vichy police.[8]

[6] AD Haute-Garonne 1769/98, Report of Commissaire de Police, Mazamet, 15 Mar. 1943. Inquiry by the Sûreté, 23 Mar. 1943.

[7] AD Hérault 161W 51, OT Groupe Ouest to Prefect, 30 June 1943.

[8] AD Hérault 18W 65, TE groupement no. 3 to Regional Prefect, 14 Sept. 1943.

Alongside OT the Germans also demanded intensive labour investment in policing the railways, forcing Vichy to recruit *gardes des voies* with increasing compulsion and desperation as Resistance attacks on the railways escalated.[9] Vichy was also looking for more miners to step up production at the coal face, but in this case the volunteers were readily found, since miners were exempt from STO, and 15,000 were enlisted throughout France between March and June. As this number was exceeded, the Prefect of the Tarn made the observation in June that men with money had come from outside his *département* to work at the Carmaux mines north of Albi, suggesting that they were probably *réfractaires*.[10] Crossing the boundaries of the *départements*, still more of the administrative regions, was to become one of the surest ways of delaying detection; enlisting in the mines one of the surest ways of gaining protection. But by far the most pressing labour shortage was in all aspects of agriculture where a standstill in mechanization, but a growth in demand and exactions, necessitated a manual input higher than the depleted peasantry could provide.[11] Peasant women had always been as integral to the rural work-force as men; they were not a reserve pool of labour waiting to take over when the men were away, and although they took on an exceptional range of work which had previously been shared, the need for extra labourers was intense. It was therefore catastrophic both for agriculture and for Vichy's credibility in the countryside when Laval lifted the exemption from STO for agricultural workers born in 1922. In this attempt to appease some of the objections raised by industrial workers born between the end of 1919 and 1921, who had already served in the Chantiers de la Jeunesse, the whole system of conscription lurched into a phase of complications and contradictions from which it never recovered. Commissions to decide who was and who was not an agricultural labourer were formed, but while these were working out their criteria, a telegram from Vichy on 18 May provided an *ad hoc* basis for definitions. It listed five major categories and twenty subdivisions which encompassed all from peasant proprietors to hired sawyers and drivers of lumber lorries. No worker from any of these categories would now be exempt if born in 1922, and for *agriculteurs* born in the other years to qualify for exemption there had to be proof that they had been in their jobs at least since 1 October 1942.[12]

Anger in the countryside at the inclusion of *agriculteurs* in a labour scheme which had, in the first stages of the *Relève* promised a return of rural labourers, threatened to give the *réfractaire* from whatever source a new status and a new security.[13] Local Renseignements Généraux began to report that

[9] AN F1C III. 1186, Savoie, report of 24 Apr. 1943.

[10] AD Haute-Garonne 1769/5, Prefect of Tarn to Minister of Labour, 4 June 1943.

[11] Ibid.

[12] AD Hérault 18W 63, telegram from Commissaire général du STO, 18 May 1943.

[13] The report of the Prefect of the Haute-Vienne was typical: 'A la terre l'émotion causée

the secrecy and silence of the peasantry was closing round the *réfractaires*, and the situation for the Vichy administration and police, already acute, became intractable. The Regional Prefect at Montpellier commented at the end of May 1943 that STO would have been possible to administer only if there had been no exemptions at all, just a total mobilization of all fit young men who had not done their military service.[14] As it was, the plethora of exemptions, reprieves, special cases, and changes in the categories had created a dense, tangled thicket which was impenetrable.[15] The Prefect in Dijon, in the old *zone occupée*, spoke for all rural areas when he complained to Vichy that the conscription of *agriculteurs* born in 1922 would hit the peasantry just as the summer months were beginning. And it was not just the farm labourer that would be missed; almost as serious was the loss of rural artisans.[16] In the Haute-Vienne round Limoges there was talk of 'doléances paysannes' recalling the Cahiers presented in 1789, and itemizing not only hostility to STO but also a fear that rural *boulangeries* would be forced to close after instructions that small millers should surrender their reserves of corn to the larger milling companies. Rises in agricultural prices had lagged behind those of industrial products, and the Prefect's conclusion was that there was a scandalous margin of profit by urban food retailers, particularly in the *boucheries*.[17] With an earlier report on the destruction of a pillar of the railway viaduct in the country at Bussy-Varache on the Limoges–Ussel line, by 'un communiste dangereux, Guingouin, Georges, en fuite', and concurrent statements in June of increased 'terrorism', growing German oppression, and a rise in *défaillants*, the message from the Haute-Vienne could not be lost on Vichy that the peasantry might have good economic reasons for sympathizing with communist or other Resistance activists in the countryside.[18]

Guingouin himself claimed that by mid-1943 he was beginning to be the protector of peasant interests against both STO and the German requisitions, and the attack on the viaduct was occasioned by the imminent departure for Germany of a contingent of local workers including three men from the

par l'annonce toute récente du départ sans exceptions admises de la classe 1942 est déjà très vive.' AN F1C III. 1197, report of 4 June 1943. From the Tarn came a report on 31 July saying that peasants were very hostile to STO: 'Non seulement, disent-ils, on ne nous rend pas les prisonniers, paysans en majorité, mais on nous enlève la main d'œuvre.' AN F1C III. 1193.

[14] AD Hérault 18W 63, Regional Prefect to Commissaire général du STO, end May 1943.

[15] An example of the various categories for exemption before the further complications of May comes from Marseille on 1 Apr., where 250 out of the 486 present at the medical were declared exempt for the following reasons: inaptes temporaires (65), inaptes définitifs (45), jeunes gens travaillant pour les autorités allemandes (91), père de famille (11), plus d'un an de service militaire (9), Milice (7), étudiants (7), agriculteur (1), électricité (2), PTT (2), Trésor (1), Juifs (2), déjà parti pour l'allemagne (1), DAT (1), SNCF (1), étranger (1), marin (1), industrie protégée (1), sans motif apparent (1); AD Bouches-du-Rhône M6. 11094.

[16] AN F1C III. 1148, Côte-d'Or, report of 4 June 1943.

[17] AN F1C III. 1197, Haute-Vienne, report of 4 June 1943.

[18] Ibid., reports of 6 Apr. and 4 June 1943.

small commune of Bussy-Varache, two 'cultivateurs', and a 'bûcheron'. All three had decided not to go, and Guingouin organized the attack to underline the growing disaffection of the rural areas round Eymoutiers, where he had been a schoolteacher before taking to the woods. He knew the peasantry well, both as *instituteur* in the commune of Saint-Gilles-la-Forêt, and as secretary to the communist section at Eymoutiers. Faced with certain arrest by Vichy for political activities, he went into rural hiding in February 1941, moving from farm to farm in the Corrèze and Haute-Vienne before returning to his own neighbourhood and starting to organize groups of *réfractaires* from both towns and countryside. The pressure on rural labourers was crucial in enlarging the cover afforded by the Limousin peasantry: from the spring of 1943 Guingouin could depend on more collective support rather than the maverick sympathy of individuals which had earlier ensured his survival.[19]

In the Lozère, another conjuncture of communist action and the arrival of *réfractaires* was judged by the police and Prefect to be particularly threatening to rural stability. Twenty-six communists escaped from the prison of le Puy on the night of 24–5 April and split into three groups, one of which took refuge in the hills to the east of the Margeride massif at Chambon-le-Château, where they were joined by a number of *défaillants*, some from Saint-Étienne and Roanne and some from the locality. The Commissaire de Police reported a successful raid which caught 15 of the communists and 19 *défaillants*, but he warned the Prefect that the attitude of the population in this border area of the Lozère and the Haute-Loire was one of 'une sourde hostilité' to the policies of Laval. Most people, he stated, had known of the existence of the *défaillants*, and they were well received in the farms and villages where they had the passive sympathy of the three local mayors, a local president of the Légion, and the local gendarmerie. Only the arrival of the communists 'loosened tongues and persuaded people to talk'. But even so, the communists were still able to 'play on the patriotism of the peasantry and their Germanophobia'.[20]

The arrival of *réfractaires* in another rural area, already known for its complicity with refugees and Resisters on the run, created rumours of armed bands in well-established camps long before this was a reality. In March

[19] The claim by Guingouin to have been the first maquisard in France is clearly based on his long rural odyssey from 1941 onwards. There were others in hiding as early as 1941, but very few who then went on to become major maquisard leaders. See Guingouin, *Quatre ans de lutte sur le sol limousin*, 33–75. The Prefect in his report of 4 June referred again to Guingouin, this time as the 'communiste Guingouin, excitateur des défaillants de la Relève et condamné à mort par contumace'; AN F1C III. 1197.

[20] The Commissaire de Police said that the *défaillants* were 'd'inspiration étrangère'; AD Lozère R. 7049. See also the May 'synthèse' of interceptions by the Contrôle postal, which stated that the communists and *réfractaires* together had 'mis en effervescence les paisibles populations du nord de la Lozère'; AD Lozère VI. M2. 19.

1943 the Swiss Radio began to transmit news of a 'rising in the Haute-Savoie' of several thousand *réfractaires*, a story which Maurice Schumann embellished on the BBC, by celebrating the 'Légion des Montagnes' and referring to 'les irreductibles, les réfractaires de la France des Alpes, portrait de tout un peuple'. The broadcasters quickly received a cautionary warning from André Philip not to give such 'risings' any legitimacy, but as Jean-Louis Crémieux-Brilhac perceptively concludes, 'for the first time the connection between revolt against STO and the eventuality of armed popular resistance had been explicitly made.'[21] This was just the connection that Vichy reports were trying to deny, though the Alpine rumours were not without substance. Early in March the Prefect of the Haute-Savoie had signalled to Vichy the existence of several hundred *réfractaires* in the mountains, and described it as a very serious situation, since the men were said to have arms and ammunition. But the measure of how unwilling the Prefect was to polarize the situation lay in his proposed solution: he had asked the gendarmerie to let him have the precise locations and he would go there in person and explain to the *réfractaires* just how much trouble they were causing for the *département*.[22] Two months later he claimed that the *réfractaires* had already become disillusioned and bored with inaction: some who had been caught revealed that they had been misled into believing everything had been arranged for them in the mountains, whereas in fact they had found nothing.[23] The local history of the Francs-Tireurs et Partisans (FTP) of the Haute-Savoie has given the 'risings' retrospective credibility by claiming that from 1 March a camp for more than 200 *réfractaires* had been established in the Mont de Draillant in the Chablais hills above Thonon, and that on 9 March one unit of *réfractaires* captured the Regional Prefect Angeli from Lyon who was on a visit of inspection to the area, and held him for several hours. Two days after his release the area was swarming with motorized police, whose threatening presence forced many of the *réfractaires* back into the towns.[24]

In the neighbouring *département* of Savoie, the Prefect drew attention to a Resistance tract found locally with a map of the hills, roads, and rivers of the canton of Aime, designed to help *réfractaires*, but he claimed he had arrested a group of 22 in the region of Chindrieux, 12 in the commune of Monthion, and had located a further 13 in a region where there was still a metre of snow, making an expedition to arrest them impossible. In all there had been 260 *défaillants* out of 580 called for STO and these had the 'complicité totale de toute la population'.[25] A subsequent report on 1 July

[21] J.-L. Crémieux-Brilhac, 'Radio et information au maquis', in *Colloque sur les maquis* (22 and 23 Nov. 1984), 125–6.
[22] AN F1C III. 1187, Haute-Savoie, report of 4 Mar. 1943.
[23] Ibid., report of 3 May 1943.
[24] *R.I.3. Francs-Tireurs et Partisans de la Haute-Savoie* (Éditions France d'Abord, 1946), 25–7.
[25] AN F1C III. 1186, Savoie, report of 24 Apr. 1943.

continued to underline that young men from the *département* were simply refusing to go on STO, but nevertheless he wished to correct all stories of organized groupings of *réfractaires* both in and outside his region, claiming that intensive police operations had revealed that such groupings were extremely few, if not non-existent.[26] It had been one thing for local authorities to demonstrate eagerly that STO was a disaster in terms of public opinion, and to make the most of evidence which emphasized the hostility and refusal of the conscripts and their families. But to suggest, in mid-1943, that police control was insufficient to prevent the grouping and arming of *réfractaires*, or any other persons in hiding, was a different matter, and reports in the early summer abound in assurances to Vichy that a combination of refuge and refusal did not amount to revolt. The Prefect of the Lozère, a staunch supporter of strong action against any form of popular disobedience, was content to play down signs of mounting rejection of STO in the local Chantiers de la Jeunesse even when the postal censorship revealed that at Groupe 6 'no one wants to work any more. They no longer salute their leaders. It's worse than a routed army.' The Prefect sent this information on to Vichy but added, 'I am sure that everything will soon return to order.'[27]

Whenever possible, the blame for incidents described as ugly or threatening, or for any kind of organization of the *réfractaires*, was placed on communists first and foremost, Spaniards secondly, and Gaullists thirdly, but in all cases on political activists 'cynically exploiting family and local resentment'. Whether at Mazamet in the Tarn, the Haute-Savoie, or Chambon-le-Château close to le Puy, to mention only three of the many 'events' which had similar characteristics throughout the south, Vichy authorities worked hard to suggest that tough measures against the *réfractaires* would be counter-productive. But from May onwards, with the rural population more and more implicated in specific areas, the delicate balance of law enforcement on the one hand, and clemency towards the *réfractaires* on the other, was seen to be inadequate. Under pressure from Sauckel's second package of demands and Laval's daily instructions, the authorities were forced to pursue the *réfractaires* more strenuously, to introduce threats of fines and even imprisonment for parents encouraging *défaillance*, and to police the areas of refuge more assiduously. It looked as if the act of refusing STO was to

[26] Ibid., report of 1 July 1943.

[27] AD Lozère VI. M2. 19. The Prefect was well supported in his campaign to see STO respected in his *département* by the Bishop of Mende, Mgr. François-Louis Auvity, whose episcopal letter of 2 July 1943 addressed to young men eligible for STO contained the sentence, 'A cette question précise que vous me posez, "Qu'avons-nous à faire? Vaut-il mieux partir?" je réponds, Votre intérêt et la sagesse demandent que vous partiez.' He argued that if they did not go, other compatriots would be constrained to go in their place, the *Relève* scheme would be undermined and their families would get into severe trouble. See AN 72. AJ 159 for the full text of his letter, which carried considerable weight in the clerical areas of the Haute-Lozère, but far less influence in the Protestant regions of the Cévennes, in the south of the *département*.

become harshly criminalized by these measures, and some authorities moved very close to this position. If they were diverted from this path, it was not because of the demonstrable success of sensitive policing or administrative clemency, it was due to the emergence of the mystique and discourse of 'le maquis'.

The first *réfractaires* in the Lozère, recounted a local Resister Marcel Pierrel in a report after the Liberation, were found an individual refuge with peasant farmers either in the plateau of Aubrac or in the Cévennes, but it was evident to leaders of the Resistance in the *département* that this solution could be no more than provisional for two main reasons: first, outside the harvest season the peasantry had no economic reason for accepting the extra labour and the *réfractaire* would become highly conspicuous in a thinly populated community, and secondly, the isolation of individual *réfractaires* had a debilitating effect on their morale.[28] Near Aubenas in the Ardèche, Monsieur Montcouquiol, himself an *agriculteur*, found it easy to hide individuals among the local peasantry, which he claimed were 90 per cent sympathetic; but peasants who adapted easily to the concealment of individuals were not infrequently wary of any collective escalation which would draw the attention of the police to their vicinity.[29] Whatever the level of general sympathy for *réfractaires*, the risk of being denounced was felt to be a compelling reason for increasing the secrecy and inaccessibility of the refuge, and ultimately that could only mean specially constructed camps in the dense forests or remote hills, and the rediscovery of hillside caves and isolated and disused farm buildings, such as *bergeries*, which were dotted among the depopulated hills of the southern Massif Central. In March, René Rascalon, an artisan plumber and socialist and a member of the Armée Secrète (AS) in Nîmes, organized what was initially known as a 'pouponnière' for *réfractaires* above the commune of Saint-André-de-Valborgne in a remote farm, and other pioneer groupings were known as 'camps' or 'réduits' when they were referred to at all. The first strategy was to avoid any mention that would alert informers, not least because most of the early camps in 1943 contained not only *réfractaires* but also anti-fascists and Resisters wanted already by the police.[30] These were seen at best as an uncomfortable presence by the rural population, except in the areas where acts of refuge throughout 1942 had established a positive complicity with those on the run. Small groups of Spanish and Central European political refugees had spontaneously formed

[28] AN 72. AJ 159, M. Pierrel, 'Chronologie sommaire des évènements'. Marcel Pierrel was deported in Aug. 1943.

[29] Evidence from Édouard Montcouquiol, 6 July 1982.

[30] Lucien Maury writes of a 'maquis' known as the 'Maquis d'En Bec', originally established in 1941, between Quillan and Saint-Louis-et-Parahou in the hills of the Aude, which contained several ex-members of the International Brigades and Otto Klepper, who had been Prussian Minister of Finance in 1931. Lucien Maury, *La Résistance audoise* (Comité d'Histore de la Résistance du Département de l'Aude: Quillan, 1980) i. 43.

after the occupation of the southern zone, and their early history is of mobility and fragmentation as they searched for secure concealment. For them STO and its widespread unpopularity meant a surge of interest from Resistance groups which had led a parallel existence to their own, with only minimal contact. The first refusals by French youth were concurrent with a sharp acceleration of desertion by immigrants from TE camps, and by escapes from *chantiers* run by OT or factories serving the German military economy. The first organized group hidden by the Resistance in the Haute-Lozère was at Bonnecombe in the Aubrac in March 1943, and consisted of five immigrant workers from the TE camp at Chanac who were conscripted to work in factories at Saint-Chély-d'Apcher and were constantly harassed for political reasons, several of them having fought with the International Brigades. It was barely the end of winter and the snow still lay on the hills where the makeshift camp was constructed. The life was hard: the problems of provisioning acute.[31]

Such a small camp contrasts strongly with the first camps in the much publicized Savoyard region, where local *réfractaires* clearly outnumbered those from the north or outside France. Whatever the degree of exaggeration in the Resistance and BBC reports of '5,000 réfractaires' prepared for an armed rising, local historians emphasize that the école d'horlogerie at Cluses, not far from Bonneville in Haute-Savoie and the reservoirs and hydro-electric works at the lac de la Girotte further south furnished *réfractaires* in considerable numbers.[32]

The interest of these first two months of refusal of STO and the embryonic camps and groupings that resulted lies in this plurality of local initiatives which cannot be reduced to a single formula. Individuals who found a 'planque' in a working farm or a disused building, groups of politically motivated anti-fascists and immigrant workers on the run, mixed groups of raw *réfractaires* and veteran fighters from the Spanish Civil War, there was no single normative development. But during April, out of a period of both determined and tentative refusal, there grew an aggressive movement, a combative discourse, and a romantic mystique of rural revolt. 'Prendre le maquis', 'le maquis', and 'le maquisard' entered the history and language of Resistance with an effect which it is difficult to exaggerate.

It is far from established how the Corsican term arrived on the mainland. The Italian-derived word 'maquis', used as a common description of woods and scrubland on the island, evoked an all-encompassing image of woods and mountains, whereas the more limited word 'garrigue' used in the South of France indicated a rebarbative and inhospitable terrain, and the words 'bois', 'forêt', and 'montagne' were too bland. As for words for fighters within

[31] Cordesse, *Histoire de la Résistance en Lozère*, 52, and evidence from Henri Cordesse, 22 Mar. 1982.

[32] See e.g. Abbé Ploton, *Quatre années de Résistance à Albertville* (Ploton: Albertville, 1946), 48.

the woods, 'franc-tireur' and 'groupe franc' were words with a long historical pedigree and were generic terms which could have assumed the general role of 'maquis' and 'maquisard', but both were already defined within town-based Resistance. The strength of the term 'maquis' was that it could indicate both the bands of fighters and their rural location. What is certain is that the image of 'maquisard' as a committed and voluntary fighter out in the woods, a *combattant*, as distinct from the more negative connotations of *réfractaire*, began to emerge in April 1943 and quickly established a hold over the imagination of all those involved in revolt. By mid-summer the term 'maquis' was being used for Resistance activity in isolated woods in the plains of northern France, in the undulating hills of the Morvan, Brittany, and Normandy, as well as on the high Alpine and Pyrenean slopes and in the mountainous woods of the Massif Central: its origins and exact moment of appearance were swallowed up in the ubiquity and rapidity of its usage. Post-war claims by certain Resisters to have formed the first maquis in France, or by certain historians to have located it, are invariably tendentious. The concept did not exist in January 1943; it was everywhere by June.

Vichy was far from a passive spectator in the development of what became a new Resistance discourse. It was dialectically involved. From the first stirrings of protest from local authorities at the speed and size of the recruitment demanded by Sauckel, there developed unofficial mechanisms of delay and obstruction within the local administrations which counted on some degree of connivance by the prefects at the top and by the gendarmerie throughout the *départements*. STO was never embraced by Vichy personnel with the illusory expectations which had marked the *Relève*: it was quickly seen for what it was, an obligation forced on the vanquished by the victors, and in that light *défaillance* could be interpreted in the town halls and prefectures and among the gendarmerie as a patriotic act. It could not be allowed, but it could be acknowledged, and this created difficulties in knowing how strictly and how speedily to enforce the law. Relief from this predicament was provided by the emergence of the mystique of the maquis and its combative discourse. Since June 1941 the clear existence of communist Resistance throughout France had enabled Vichy to make distinctions between 'dangerous, treasonous, political subversion' on the one hand, ascribed to communism, and Resistance of a more understandable 'patriotic' nature on the other, often referred to generically as 'Gaullism'. Now in the early summer of 1943 the emergence of the maquis as a combative or 'terrorist' force played the same role, enabling the latent sympathy for *défaillance* to coexist more easily alongside the duty of repression. In this way Vichy played a formative part in the investment of the word 'maquis' with combative, insurrectionary meanings. It allowed the word 'réfractaire' to carry more openly the notion of a well-intentioned, though wayward, action. It was a distinction which was inconsistently effective, but which became almost a coherent principle of action by the late summer, and was eventually, but belatedly, endorsed by Laval.

It seems reasonable to conclude from the many excellent local histories of the Occupation that most *réfractaires* were only too happy to lie low, but that a substantial minority were, by June and July, enthused by the new discourse and were in search of the maquis. In the rolling woodlands of the Dégagnac region of the Lot, north of Cahors, twelve *réfractaires* were arrested at dawn on 8 July 1943 by the gendarmerie. Aged between 20 and 27, with one older man aged 40, five came from the Lot itself, including four from the *chef lieu* Cahors, four from neighbouring *départements*, two from the Paris region, and one from the Pyrénées-Orientales. Four had been employed in agriculture, the two from the Seine were both drivers, the older man was a furniture dealer, and the others were butcher, bookshop assistant, hairdresser, and two *fonctionnaires*. What the head of the Renseignements Généraux in Cahors was keen to point out was that they were not in contact with anyone else, they had no arms, they had received no newspapers. They had arrived there by word of mouth which said they should jump from the train as it came into Cahors and follow the tracks into the Dégagnac woods. They were, he stressed, only wanting to escape STO, not to engage in 'résistance armée'. He concluded, 'The truth is, they are fed by the people of the village, who have looked after them well . . . and they are smoking locally-produced tobacco.' In all, this was not a group 'd'inspiration communiste'.[33] A few days earlier the police had arrested seven men in the upland forest of Hautaniboul in the Montagne Noire, west of Mazamet in the Tarn and some 80 km. due east of Toulouse, and from the details gathered, the seven were clearly waiting for something to fulfil their expectations after using a password 'Y a-t-il des truites dans le ruisseau?' to reach the mountainous forest where they had been living for several days. There was a cache of arms containing 18 'mousquetons' and 10 kgs. of ammunition, but the group claimed to know nothing about it. Their occupations were: baker's assistant, two students, a hairdresser, an agricultural worker, a miner, and an electrician, but only the first four were *réfractaires*. The miner would not have been liable, and the other two were only 17, and had gone to the woods, the agricultural worker perhaps because he was Jewish, and the electrician 'par esprit d'aventure'.[34]

These arrests were a few among many in the early months of STO, and the police reports continue the lenient tone prevalent from February to April, but the half-organized groups which they found are very much the mark of the mid-summer months, May to July. There is the feeling in the police comments that with a little more leadership and sense of purpose these men on the run could have been turned into maquisards, even if evasion was the

[33] AD Haute-Garonne 1960/6, report from Renseignements Généraux, Cahors, 12 July 1943.
[34] Ibid.

affirmed aim of the majority. Their youth, their ready response to what had been the vaguest of directions, their easy rapport with the local population, and their sense of expectancy, make them typical of hundreds of cases across the southern zone. The degree of their organization corresponds to the stage that many local Resistance groups had reached in encouraging and directing *réfractaires*. After tentative starts with individuals in farms and lumber camps, they had moved on to groupings of five or six, to as many as thirty, and had moved from village buildings into the woods and mountains. The twelve in the Dégagnac woods were living in a hut made of bracken and branches, the seven at Hautaniboul in the entry to an old mine.

In fact the state of organization in certain areas should not be underestimated. Many early *réfractaires* did find or create their maquis. In the mountains enfolding the valley of the Aude, *réfractaires* found shelters at le Roc Blanc built of branches and earth, but they also found an experienced Resistance organization directed by Ernest Zaugg, an engineer in charge of the hydro-electric station of Usson, who had received people on the run from the occupied zone. Originally of Swiss nationality, he became leader of the AS at le Donézan, and directed his energies and those of some twenty *réfractaires* at creating a safe escape route into Spain.[35] Several early camps had a military purpose from the start, however scarce the arms and ammunition. In the Haute-Corrèze the valley of the Dordogne had been a refuge for Huguenots, refractory priests, and men escaping conscription into the armies of Napoleon. Here *réfractaires* were formed into one of the first maquis of the area, constituted in March to April as the armed 'camp de Chambon' on the initiative of members of the AS of Ussel, Neuvic, Tulle, and Lapleau. It was carefully envisaged and planned, and Louis le Moigne and Marcel Barbanceys, two of its originators, and the historians of the maquis of the Haute-Corrèze, describe it as almost a model construct, invested with 'romantic' expectations and illusions. On 15 June the maquis was surprised at dawn by the forces of the Groupes Mobiles de Réserve (GMR) and shots were fired wounding two of the maquisards, while two others were arrested. 'This unfortunate experience', wrote le Moigne and Barbanceys (himself one of the injured) 'taught us that we had to make a complete change in our concept of a maquis camp. At Chambon . . . security was thought to be ensured by isolation. This was not the case . . . we had to think of camps in regions less wild and more open to information so that they could be moved more quickly . . .'[36] The Maquis de l'Estibi, a small hamlet close to Villefranche-de-Rouergue in the Aveyron gorge, received its student *réfractaires* at the end of May after not only the camp but also a training school had been meticulously planned by members of the AS in

[35] Maury, *La Résistance audoise*, 236–9.

[36] Louis le Moigne and Marcel Barbanceys, *Sédentaires, réfractaires et maquisards. L'Armée secrète en Haute-Corrèze 1942–1944* (Amicale des Maquis de Haute-Corrèze, 1980), 66–77.

Toulouse led by Jean Capel. A cavalry officer, Christian de Roquemaurel, had agreed to act as the training instructor, and by 25 July the camp contained thirty-five maquisards, all of them French, an unusual phenomenon at a time when the percentage of Spanish and other anti-fascists among the French activists was so high.[37]

On the high, dramatic plateau of the Vercors, rich in beech and coniferous forests, and cut by deep gorges, *réfractaires* from nearby Grenoble and Romans were grouped into a camp at Ambel and numbered over eighty by March. Initiated by socialists of the movement Franc-Tireur in Grenoble and Villard-de-Lans, it was organized locally by Victor Huillier whose bus company plied between Grenoble and Villard, bringing recruits who had been screened by Eugène Chavant, a café owner in Grenoble. The camp's activity, both as cover and much-needed daily occupation, was forestry, and it was slowly provided with light arms. It served as a model for further camps created in the spring and summer until some 400 *réfractaires*, together with anti-fascist Italians, Czechs, Romanians, and others, were structured as maquisards of the Vercors, financed by Yves Farge of the MUR in Lyon, and supplied and sustained by a doctor, Eugène Samuel in Villard, a headteacher, Benjamin Malossane in Saint-Jean-en-Royans, and Georges Clergé, owner of a small factory making wooden soles at la Chapelle-en-Vercors, a business described by Paul Dreyfus as a 'véritable pépinière de maquisards'.[38] Closer to the main road and railway between Grenoble and Romans, the FTP set up a camp for *réfractaires* and hunted communists at Malleval, called 'Camp En-Avant'. Organized in April, it was typical of the many small camps which started when a place of refuge, in this case a peasant farm owned by the brothers Marand, which hid two communists Paul Billat and R. Périnetti, became a focus for *réfractaires*. Another location and more space was found, tents were procured from Cognin, and the camp eventually became a selection camp for FTP maquis throughout the Dauphiné.[39]

No amount of examples should be allowed to dull the image of inventiveness and unpredictability that the early maquis threw on to the screen of Resistance. Local initiatives, already so high in promoting the richly diffused movements and networks of 1940–2, now operated to produce a surge of independent action just at a time when the earlier Resistance was beginning

[37] R. Maruéjol and Aimé Vielzeuf, *Le Maquis Bir-Hakeim* (Maruéjol et Vielzeuf: Nîmes, 1947), 16. The *nom de guerre* of Jean Capel was Commandant Barot.

[38] Paul Dreyfus, *Vercors, citadelle de liberté* (Arthaud, 1969), 35. Paul Silvestre, in his superbly analytical article on the maquis in the Isère, has estimated that although *réfractaires* numbered some 2,000 in the *département* and were 56% of those summoned for STO, no more than 10% of the *réfractaires* became maquisards. 'STO, maquis et guérilla dans l'Isère', *Revue d'histoire de la deuxième guerre mondiale*, 130 (1983), 7–8.

[39] Paul Billat, *Levés à l'aube de la Résistance dauphinoise* (Les Imprimeurs Réunis: Sassenage, 1978), 140–1.

to be more centrally organized and led. The combative maquis discourse enshrined belligerent assertiveness right from the start, not least because ordinary Resisters felt the pace of action against the occupiers suddenly quicken in the summer of 1943. There was widespread expectation of an imminent Allied landing in the West after the successes in North Africa and the Russian victory at Stalingrad, and many Resisters took their cue from the feverishly excited tone of the BBC in its promotion of the Savoyard 'rising' in March. It gave added momentum to those who had already envisaged the Armée Secrète (AS) as a fully-fledged fighting unit, or the Francs-Tireurs et Partisans (FTP) as a combat force. The dominant language soon became one of armaments, training, ambushes, skirmishes, battles even, and a long-prepared clandestine consciousness of a volunteer army at war with the occupant appeared to have broken into the open. The transition in a few months was startling, and the discourse far outran the immediate possibilities, but the existence of the small groups of experienced anti-fascists forged in the heat of the Spanish conflict, and the availability of French officers living in a vacuum after the dissolution of the Armée de l'Armistice in November 1942, fuelled linked, but contrasting, military expectations. The seasonal factor of spring in the calendar of revolution and revolt, merged into summer months which made life in the countryside more feasible. Taking to the maquis gave a Resistance meaning to pastural transhumance.

The first general circulars from Michel Brault, newly appointed by the MUR at national level to direct maquis operations, made powerful contributions to the early identity of the maquisard as someone special, set apart from the rest of society. The circulars were issued on 25 May, several weeks after the creation of a Service National du Maquis by the Comité Directeur of the MUR which had met in early April, galvanized by both the number of *réfractaires* and the fast developing groups at local level. 'Individual initiatives', stated Henri Frenay 'have occurred, often without us. Groups have constituted themselves and have taken to the hills.'[40] Brault, a lawyer by profession working for Lloyds, had been mobilized in 1940 as a captain in the air force, had tried unsuccessfully to get a boat to England at the time of the defeat, and had worked in several *réseaux* in the Paris region before being forced to cross into the *zone sud* in early 1942. There he was given the job of forming the Service de Renseignements of Combat, before Frenay suggested him for the urgently needed role of maquis co-ordinator and national leader. Addressing his second circular to 'tous hommes des Maquis de la Résistance Unie' he issued ten clear instructions, the first of which established the definition of 'any man who seeks entry into a maquis' as 'not only a *réfractaire* . . . but a volunteer franc-tireur and an auxiliary of

[40] Quoted by F. Marcot in 'Les Maquis dans la Résistance', in *Colloque sur les maquis* (1984), 13.

the Armée Secrète of the Forces Françaises Combattantes, commanded by General de Gaulle and the Comité National Français'. As such he was to submit to 'the very tough discipline of the maquis'; to obey all orders from his appointed leader; to renounce all links with family and friends until the end of the war; to expect no regular wage or certainty of arms; to respect the private property and life of the population, not least because 'the men of the maquis are the élite of the country' who must set an example; to prepare for 'opérations de pillage' directed against Vichy's police supplies; to respect opinions and beliefs of his comrades, whether Catholic, Protestant, Muslim, Jew, atheist, royalist, radical, socialist, or communist, and to surrender all egoism and individualism for the common cause. 'All men of the maquis', specified the final instruction, 'are the enemy of Marshal Pétain and the traitors who obey him.'[41]

It is indisputable, as François Marcot argues in a highly perceptive article on the maquis in the Resistance, that the maquis were born outside the initiative of the national leaders of the Resistance,[42] but Brault's conception of the men of the maquis as disciplined fighters in organized camps was a very early bid to provide a forceful structure to the combative maquis discourse which was forming at the grass roots. The word 'maquisard' does not appear in the circular, the more military 'homme des maquis' being the term used throughout, but what le Moigne and Barbanceys called the romantic mystique of the maquis is sketched in Brault's expectation that the men would be able to cut themselves off from their homes and insulate themselves from their previous lives in their 'refuges de la résistance'. Here was the pure vision of a new kind of mobilized *combattant*, as detached from his home as the fighter at the front in a conventional war. It was a vision which became a model construct, hiding the realities of maquis history as it actually evolved, but a vision which gave a positive military justification to men whose refusal and whose refuge might have seemed largely negative and evasive. The creation of a national body to locate, train, and co-ordinate the groups which had spontaneously formed, mirrored the initiative already taken by leaders of the Resistance at local level, but it gave a strategic authenticity to the operation, which maquisards of all descriptions were quick to invoke.

The Front National and the FTP were no less conscious of the dynamic of STO in the development of Resistance. A report on 'Déportation' on 10 March 1943 accredited to the FN, stated that 'the central French drama is no longer *ravitaillement*. It is deportation.' Men were being deported every day, it continued, and figures claiming that *réfractaires* were running at 60–70 per cent were certainly exaggerated. In some *ateliers*, it said, almost all the

[41] AN 72. AJ 63, Brault 'Circulaire No. 2', 25 May 1943.
[42] Marcot, 'Les Maquis dans la Résistance', 13.

workers had been taken for work in Germany.[43] The urgency of the situation, highlighted by this report, was equally conveyed in the language of local communist tracts, in the special numbers of *France d'Abord* in March devoted to the STO and in repeated calls in subsequent issues for *réfractaires* to join the FTP either in 'les forêts, les montagnes, les landes, les marais', or in the towns and villages. A local tract, typical of many, came from a group of metal workers of the Aude and Hérault and called on workers threatened with STO to refuse by all possible means, which includes leaving for the country and taking refuge with friends, but 'better still, join the ranks of the valorous Francs-Tireurs et Partisans'.[44] Roger Bourderon, in an excellent account of the origin of the maquis FTP, notes how the word 'maquis' was not initially employed in these early calls for an extension to the FTP. The term preferred was 'groupe de combat' so that no separate generic category was given to groups in the countryside, unlike the decisions of the MUR which had specifically identified the maquis as different in nature from the 'groupes francs' originated by Renouvin in the Montpellier area, which constituted the commando units within the AS.[45] When the MUR set up its Comité d'Action contre la Déportation (CAD) alongside the Service Maquis, a letter from the Front National dated 1 July 1943 to the CFLN in Algiers, offered the support of the FN and the clandestine trade unions to the CAD and went on to repeat its claim of 10 March that trainloads of young people were still leaving for Germany, often because they had no friends in the countryside, did not know how to find the 'réduits de partisans', and did not have the material resources to live without a job. Given this, the FN appealed for 'réduits de réfractaires' to carry out 'daring acts' to protect the peasantry against Vichy's food exactions, and suggested that every *quartier* and every village should have its Comité de la France Combattante to collect money, food, clothes, and equipment for the *réfractaires*. In summary, the FN called on the CFLN to aid groups of *réfractaires* already established, to send money to France, and to support them by tracts and radio which would make information about the FTP available to all French people.[46]

Once again the word 'maquis' is not used, and throughout the summer, instructions from the leaders of the FTP continue to employ such terms as 'groupes de combat' or 'petits groupes' when urging the incorporation of

[43] AN 72. AJ 63, Comité directeur du Front National to CFLN, 1 July 1943.

[44] 'Lettre ouverte aux jeunes ouvriers, ouvrières du Gard, de l'Aude et de l'Hérault', Mar. 1943; AD Gard CA 328. Note that in the Nîmes and Alès area a wider-based tract emanating from le front patriotique des jeunes français made out a strong case for equating Francs-Tireurs with 'la nouvelle armée nationale', claiming that 'soon the exploits of the army of "Francs-Tireurs français" will be as famous as those of the Serbian partisans of General Mikailovitch'; AD Gard CA 328.

[45] Roger Bourderon, 'Les Maquis F.T.P.: la mise en œuvre particulière d'une conception globale du combat clandestin', in *Colloque sur les maquis*, 87–98.

[46] AN 72. AJ 63; see n. 43 above.

réfractaires into their ranks, while the official FTP language for the maquis as terrain or location was 'un camp FTP' within a proliferation of rural words—'montagnes', 'forêts', 'régions peu peuplées', or simply 'la nature'. Aimé Vielzeuf, meticulous in his description of maquis origins in the Gard, credits a communist shoemaker, Couderc, from Pont-Saint-Esprit, with creating the first FN group of *réfractaires* in an abandoned farm near Méjannes-le-Clap at the beginning of March, while a Catalan, Roger Torreilles, was the pioneer of various groups on the border of the Gard and the Lozère, the eventual location of the first fully-structured maquis FTP in a disused farm at Figuerolles on 27 July. He refers to one of the first FTP ventures in the Cévennes as being known as 'camp No. 4', while in the Corrèze the first major FTP grouping of *réfractaires* and anti-fascists started its existence in March to April 1943 as 'le camp Vincent Faïta' named after the FTP activist in Nîmes who had shortly before been arrested and was executed by Vichy on 22 April. This first name of the camp appears, however, to have been used interchangeably with 'Maquis de la Tourette' and neither Vielzeuf in his local history of the Gard, nor the FTP accounts in the collective evidence assembled as *Maquis de Corrèze*, make substantive comment on the difference between the various terms.[47]

Nevertheless what was achieved by the FTP language in the first months of STO was a sense of escalating struggle as the FTP spread into the countryside, and a commitment to unity of action between rural and urban FTP. The FN image of the rural Resister as another volunteer partisan of a citizen army, an irregular soldier, joined with the image, sanctioned by Brault and the Service Maquis, of the mobilized *combattant* in a disciplined encampment. The two images merged, but they could be kept or forced apart. Where they came together was in the development of the maquis discourse away from a concentration on the process of *défaillance* and towards the image of combat. Refuge and refusal were necessary to this discourse but they were not enough. Fugitives had to become fighters; well-intentioned absence had to be turned into a committed presence. There had to be revolt.

The shift in evaluation of the *réfractaire* brought about by the emergent maquis was evident well before the middle of the year. It became apparent that the intentions of many *réfractaires* were ones of avoidance more than revolt, and for many Resisters and anti-fascists who had already embarked on acts of Resistance before STO, the term *réfractaire* never quite lost a sense of 'sauve qui peut' or self-regarding evasion. There began a value-laden contrast of *réfractaire* and maquisard, which has led to separate histories, as the percentage of *réfractaires* who started or joined a maquis is calculated in

[47] Aimé Vielzeuf, *La Résistance dans le Gard* (Vielzeuf: Nîmes, 1979), 14; *Maquis de Corrèze* par 120 témoins et combattants (Éditions sociales, 1971), *passim*.

some regions as only 6–10 per cent, and rarely in any region over 50 per cent. Maquisards can be found who minimize or even deny their original status as *réfractaires*; and maquis groups developed who were suspicious or even contemptuous of those whose first motivation was the avoidance of STO. In this contrast of meanings, no falsification of history is involved if it is merely a question of deciding, on the one hand, how many *réfractaires* were passively assimilated into the rural economy, or regularized their position and returned to their homes, and on the other, how many forged a new identity for themselves as combative fighters. But falsification is involved when the maquis discourse hides or marginalizes the huge amount of collective and community action involved in the history of the *réfractaires*.

The history of the opposition to STO is the history of those who refused to go, but it is just as much the history of those who encouraged, organized, and sustained that refusal. Although the decision which led to *défaillance* was ultimately an individual one, it was located firmly within extensive collective action. A tract, 'Jeunes de France', found in Nîmes and Alès in January and February, conjured up a revolt against the *Relève* and STO which encompassed the worker, his comrades at work, the whole factory and workplace, indeed the whole working population. It urged:

> In the event that a worker does not have time to escape and they come for him in his home, he and his family should rouse the whole building, the street, the *quartier*, and all French people to run to his rescue and force them to release him. If, despite everything, workers are rounded up, it is the duty of their mothers, their wives, their fiancées, their relatives and friends, and all patriots to go to the station, to demonstrate and prevent the train from leaving as was done at Montluçon on 6 January.

Behind the tract lay a common front called le comité des forces unies de la Jeunesse, comprising jeunesses communistes, jeunes de Combat, jeunes des Francs-Tireurs, and the front patriotique des jeunes.[48] The image of collective refusal was not merely the result of such a wide-based alliance. A month later a tract attributed to Combat alone used very similar language:

> Wives and mothers, exhort your husbands and sons to show their courage. If they are arrested, go with them, and take your children and relatives, go all the way to the gendarmerie. Demonstrate with cries of 'Liberty! Death to Laval,' and 'Police on our side!' Doctors, fail as many young people at the medical as possible! Police and gendarmes, refuse to be the grave-diggers of French youth! . . . In every town, every village, help those who are threatened: hide them, feed them, employ them. If they are arrested, form yourselves into a group, demonstrate, reclaim them, organize their escape . . . Allons, enfants de la patrie![49]

[48] AD Gard CA 328, tract 'Jeunes de France', Jan.–Feb. 1943.
[49] Ibid., tract 'Debout contre l'esclavage', Feb.–Mar. 1943.

The March edition of *Le Populaire* under its heading 'Résistez à la déportation' made *défaillance* the activity of everyone: 'All the people of France must take up the struggle. Peasants! Welcome them, feed them, hide them. Administrators! Steal and destroy the registration documents, fill them with mistakes. Police! Sabotage the search for *réfractaires* . . .'[50]

However propagandist and polemical these tracts, they were not illusory in trying to mobilize the whole community. STO came close to unifying previously disaggregated sections of the population, including substantial sections of the administration: the Prefect of the Savoie spoke for many levels of the state and local bureaucracy when he reported on 27 February that 'STO has been very badly received by the whole population and the administrators and officials are humiliated by the job they are forced to do.'[51] In this collective reaction, the leading role of women was particularly promoted by the Resistance press and noticed in the Vichy police reports. It was women who were reported as preventing a train from leaving Saint-Étienne, just one of many places where they lay down on the tracks or demonstrated at the station;[52] there were women thought dangerous enough to public order to be arrested and investigated at Mazamet in the Tarn,[53] and the same story was enacted in many other small and large towns, while in the countryside women in numbers and name as yet unresearched had a final say in who was sheltered, fed, and given work. For example, the *institutrice*, C. Brunet, at Arcambal near Cahors in the Lot, who was involved from the start in the support for *réfractaires*, drew attention to Marie Pouget as 'the woman proprietor of le Poujoulat' who had made the farm a 'refuge, a rest-house, and an infirmary' for Resisters of all kinds.[54] Another *institutrice*, Mlle Salvignol, enabled Raymond Fournier to escape STO on 4 May 1943 at Saint-Affrique in the Aveyron, and Madame Prades from Ganges in the Gard organized the false identity card and ration tickets for her husband when he became a *réfractaire* in the Cévennes.[55] They were far from exceptions.

The whole process of *défaillance* involved collective, or collusive, action at every step. But at the same time the mystique of the maquis and its combative discourse took the maquisards into a world of their own, where they developed the language of a vanguard army at the front, a camaraderie of men, an image of 'les purs', uncorrupted by the necessary compromises of the towns and villages they had left behind, even if only for a day and night, or a week, at a time. In so doing, the community role in the revolt

[50] *Le Populaire*, 10 (Mar. 1943).
[51] AN F1C III. 1186, Savoie, report of 27 Feb. 1943.
[52] AD Lozère VI. M2. 23, intercepted letter, Mende, Feb. 1943.
[53] See Ch. 1.
[54] AN 72. AJ 157, report by C. Brunet, 6 Jan. 1950.
[55] Evidence from Raymond Fournier, 23 Mar. 1982, and from Monsieur and Madame Prades, 4 Feb. 1982.

against STO could all too easily become separate from the life of the maquis, surviving within the discourse merely as a support system or a network of aid. It was much more structural than this, and although it has clearly been acknowledged as essential to the maquis, many accounts of the maquis have been written without it.

It is essential to keep the history of collective action against STO and the history of the maquis as interwoven as possible, while accepting that they could, and did, diverge at many points. Stressing the importance of community involvement in both histories is one way of underlining the fact that the years 1940–4 were not just the years of the German Occupation, they were also the years of Vichy État. Being a *réfractaire*, or a maquisard, or both, has to be analysed as much in terms of civil disobedience against authority and police control as in terms of military resistance. Dr Hermes, head of the German censorship in Paris, said on 2 March 1943 that 'the departure of the French work-force to Germany would, by itself, disorganize the army of resistance'. By the middle of the year the irony of this prediction was obvious, and Sauckel was being widely referred to as the recruiter, *par excellence*, for the army of the maquis. In either case the emphasis is on the men who did or did not go, and on the armies which, according to Dr Hermes, would be decimated, or, as it happened, were swollen by the numbers involved. Had Dr Hermes thought more about the effect of STO on families, friends, and co-workers, and on the reaction of the *quartier*, the village, or the whole area, he might have paused before making his remark. Furthermore, a generation in the future, less affected by war, or less enthused by it, might be more interested in the ways people found of extracting themselves from authoritarianism and legal obligations, and living a hidden, alternative existence. Such an approach might lead to a more pluralistic notion of revolt. Both refusal and revolt were keywords in resistance to STO and they remained keywords in the history of the maquis. They direct us towards the continuing and escalating acts of civil disobedience by people who were never considered to be maquisards. Without such acts the maquis could not have survived, unless it had been armed and supplied from the start by the Allies and imposed on the population as a strategic necessity, a scenario which some Resisters would have preferred. As it was, the multi-layered refusal and complicity which STO provoked and which mobilized far more people in opposition than any other single act by Vichy, meant a community involvement which developed into an integral part of the history of the maquis. The search for the maquis, whether by *réfractaires* or police, led not just to the men in the woods, but also to the intricate structures of Resistance of which they were part. The search for the maquis by historians has at least the same paths to follow.[56]

[56] See Ch. 4. One history of the maquis makes this explicit at the outset in the title of the book, *Sédentaires, réfractaires et maquisards*, by Louis le Moigne and Marcel Barbanceys. It is an educative title.

It is instructive that the Protestant Pastor, Georges Gillier of Mandagout in the Gard, close to le Vigan, begins his story of the maquis he helped to create with a detailed account of how he fabricated false identity cards two or three days after receiving the first *réfractaires* at his presbytery in the Cévennes:

Ah, the identity cards, what a job! It was difficult for me locally to buy twenty or so cards at a time without attracting attention . . . so I used a trip to Anduze where a friend ran a bookshop, in order to buy a stock. As for the licensing stamps I got friends in le Vigan to buy them for me one by one . . . but the most difficult thing was to find a suitable rubber stamp. I tried initially to make one by trimming an erasing rubber with a razor blade, but the result was very poor.

It was then that Monsieur Salliège of le Vigan gave me one with an image of the Republic in the centre and the name of the Caisse d'Épargne du Vigan. With a razor blade I lifted off the words without destroying the individual letters, and with other letters from other old rubber stamps I composed 'Mairie de Nîmes—Gard' and stuck them on with solution from a puncture repair outfit. It wasn't perfect, but I was able to stamp over 100 false identity cards with it, several of which enabled people to get out of tight corners.[57]

It is not that false identity cards are in any way new to the history of the Resistance in mid-1943, but that here in a small village in the Cévennes, as in so many places, the process of outwitting the authorities should begin at the same *ad hoc* level as working out a basic code, misdirecting a German convoy, hiding a clandestine tract, falsifying quantities of produce, fly-posting at night, or any of the other practical acts for which no specialist knowledge or ability was required. The maquis was as dependent on these day-to-day initiatives as the first movements of Resistance had been in 1940–2. By their very nature they lay within the capacity of people who had no military pretensions and no thought of long-term strategies of resistance. But every such act was a dissolvent of Vichy authority, and in rural areas where anything or anybody unusual was immediately conspicuous, it was almost impossible to indulge in acts of civil disobedience without local collusion. Gillier's fabrication of a suitable rubber stamp was already a collective act, dependent on the active contribution of some, and the passive connivance of others. The dissolution of Vichy authority is a variable but cumulative motif in maquis history. It did not occur everywhere or evenly, but it was essential for the origins of the maquis, for its growth and for its survival.

STO, therefore, was a mobilizing force in terms of men, women, and communities. Its impact was far more than statistical. Its side-effects were immediately felt by immigrant labour; it forced a disturbing breach in the

[57] Georges Gillier, *Les Corsaires* (Éditions du Hublot: Toulouse, 1945). The booklet is not paginated. The extract is from what would be p. 4.

institutional loyalty of Vichy officials; the extent of refusal provoked a discovery and an extension of rural refuge, and the collective opposition became a structure of initiatives and actions which carried Resistance into a new stage. The refusal was a forcing-house, a dynamic at local and national levels, pushing Resisters into a widespread organization which might have been no more than patchy at best had those on the run been limited to those already sought by the police, such as Spanish Republicans and other anti-fascists. But in their turn these anti-fascists, hardened in partisan struggle, were there to add a vital dimension of experience to the combative discourse of the maquis as it gathered momentum in the late spring and early summer.

As the notion of combat developed and the maquisard became a special kind of *réfractaire*, a 'réfractaire encadré' to use Pierre Mermet's term,[58] so there was a shift in the nature and the dangers of refuge. Safety was not automatically assured by place alone as the destruction of the camp de Chambon in the Corrèze had shown. Yet in June 1943 there were few places that seemed as secure as the place known as 'la baraque du Bidil', a large wooden hut close to an isolated forester's house at Aire-de-Côte in the forests of Mont Aigoual at the heart of the Cévennes. Over a hundred *réfractaires* were grouped there by the middle of June, as the *pouponnière* of René Rascalon had rapidly grown during May, and there was an extensive network of organization and supply which included an officer of the gendarmerie at le Vigan who agreed to warn the leader of the group if there was to be an attack from the Vichy police. But the attack was mounted not by Vichy but by German forces from Alès, and the poorly armed camp was easily destroyed in a single action on 1 July. The maquis had been betrayed by a Belgian called Paulus, who had been a fractious member of a group of men who had hidden several months before in la baraque du Bidil. Three maquisards were killed in the attack, 15 wounded, and 43 were taken prisoner and deported to Germany, including the forester, Berrière, and the mayor of the village of Saumane, Fernand Borgne, one of the organizers of the camp.[59] Of the thirty-two young *réfractaires* who originated from the Gard, seven were from Nîmes and four from Alès, but most were from smaller towns and local villages. The bodies of two of those killed were dumped from the back of a lorry in the main street of Saint-Jean-du-Gard as the German forces sped through on their return to Alès, and their burial was forbidden by the German authorities.[60]

[58] Pierre Mermet, 'Du Service du Travail Obligatoire (STO) au maquis', in *Colloque sur les maquis*, 63.

[59] Aimé Vielzeuf, *On les appelait 'les bandits'*, 15–74. Less than half of those deported survived.

[60] No German troops were stationed in the Gardois valleys of the Cévennes, but on 1 Dec. 1942 there were 1,500 at Alès, 2,158 at Nîmes, and 6,237 in 29 other communes of the Gard; AD Gard CA 367.

Several reports from the Renseignements Généraux to the Prefect at Nîmes commented on the reaction which the attack provoked in the Cévennes, and although there was some local criticism of the *réfractaires* themselves, there was mostly an intensification of bitter hostility to STO, Vichy, and the Germans. 'The local population', said one report, 'remains favourable to hiding the young *réfractaires*, but it seems that farmers would hesitate to take responsibility for groups hidden as isolated units.'[61] On 5 July the evidence given by one of those who escaped from Aire-de-Côte, and who gave himself up to the police, identified four persons by name and many by occupation, and added that 'several thousands' were lying hidden in the Aigoual 'waiting for the Allied landing'. He testified that the local population was 'devoted to the *réfractaires* who had easily found hospitality when they were in difficulty', but he himself 'regretted what he had done and promised not to escape again'.[62]

Here was one *réfractaire* who could certainly not be credited as a maquisard, but as the historian of Aire-de-Côte, Aimé Vielzeuf, has shown, the attack of 1 July revealed just how helpless *réfractaires* or maquisards were at that time without arms or precise military function. Despite the fact that those at Aire-de-Côte had an excellent relationship with the community and the gendarmerie, it was easy for a unit of German paratroopers to surround the camp and destroy it, once the betrayal had been carried out in such malevolent detail.[63] Refuge did not equal security: if *réfractaires* could find the maquis, so too could *voyous*, infiltrators, the Vichy Renseignements Généraux, the Groupes Mobiles de Réserve, the Milice, and the German forces. There was no easy answer to this vulnerability. The maquis, however constituted and in whatever location, were essentially on the run or at bay. They had a combative discourse which they were impatient to actualize. The hunt, for most maquisards, was to be their initiation into combat.

[61] AD Gard CA 763, report from the Sûreté to the Sub-Prefect in le Vigan on a mission into the villages of Camprieu and Saint-Sauveur-des-Poureils, 5 July 1943.

[62] Ibid., evidence contained in a report from the Renseignements Généraux to the Prefect, 6 July 1943.

[63] Vielzeuf, *On les appelait 'les bandits'*, 15–20.

3

Hunters and Hunted, Summer–Autumn 1943

THREE weeks before the German attack on Aire-de-Côte in the Cévennes, a gendarme from Mende, *chef-lieu* of the Lozère, wrote to his parents in the Nord, and told them: 'Lots of young people are just taking off: it makes us run around after them. I don't know how they're managing to hide, but there's no way of collaring them. It's odd.'[1]

It was just one letter out of thousands opened in Mende by the Contrôle postal, noted, and sent on to its destination. Many others at the time spoke just as openly about the climate of revolt, escape, and pursuit, and several young letter-writers confided their ideas of possible flight into the hills to parents, relatives, or friends. One such letter from a youth at the Collège de Mende was noted by the Contrôle as saying, 'I might be going to hide somewhere . . . I'll be forced to change my handwriting and use a pseudonym to put those looking for me off the scent. For your part, you mustn't reveal my hiding-place to anyone.' The extract was filed with a note from the Prefect ordering light surveillance of the writer 'in case he carries out his intention to leave'.[2]

In the weeks following Aire-de-Côte, police in the Gard were dispatched in larger numbers to locate and hunt down those known to be hiding in the *département*, and one report refers to fifty *réfractaires* hiding in abandoned farms on the isolated, wooded plateau of Méjannes-le-Clap, and gives details, clearly obtained from an informant, of a Yugoslav Povilitch from Bagnols who was organizing their food, and two Spaniards from Uzès and a Frenchman from Nîmes who were helping him, all three workers at a forestry camp owned by the Société Willers.[3] The official image of police efficiency given by the precision of the numbers, names, and locations in this report

[1] AD Lozère VI. M2. 23, letter from Monsieur X, Mende, 9 June 1943. Cf. the report from the Prefect of the Isère which stated that the Italians were finding the *défaillants* elusive, despite intensive searches; AN F1C III. 1158, Isère, report of 28 June 1943.

[2] AD Lozère VI. M2. 23, letter from pupil at Collège de Mende, 25 May 1943.

[3] AD Gard CA 763, report from Renseignements Généraux, 3 July 1943.

becomes a regular feature of the hunt for *réfractaires*, aimed at reassuring Vichy and, more importantly, the Germans that all was being done. The Prefect of the Vaucluse, writing from Avignon in early June, did not minimize the problem to Vichy, reporting that those nominated for STO 'slide out of it' by all possible means and are supported by the population. But that had merely fired his enthusiasm for rounding them up and fulfilling the quotas for the *département*. A massive hunt had been staged in the Luberon hills south of Apt, where ancient dry-stone huts known as 'bories' were thought to offer a base for the *réfractaires*, and the Prefect claimed several arrests in the area, just after the occupying Italian troops had seized ten *réfractaires* in a separate 'hunting' excursion. He praised the devotion of the Milice, who regarded him as one of their local leaders, and had told the municipal authorities in his charge that they would be judged on the numbers of *réfractaires* in their area. He was, he reported, determined not to have any dissident camp in his *département*.[4] In the neighbouring Var, Resisters had evidence that the police were persuading local peasants to reveal the little-known springs in the hills, so that they could concentrate the hunt on hiding-places within easy reach of water, and drive the *réfractaires* into the arid parts of the region.[5]

All such reports seem to run counter to the tenor of the gendarme's letter from Mende, but his concluding comment, 'It's odd', suggests that the efficiency of the police ought to have yielded results. A similar expectancy informs the official reports throughout the early summer. Where detection was thwarted, the prefects and police invariably blamed the local population for its sympathy for the *réfractaires*, but what increasingly emerges from the reports as the summer progresses is that the embryonic maquisards were rapidly learning from the hunt, and that their enforced mobility was becoming a tactical skill.

Escape and refuge were to remain two of the permanent characteristics of the maquis. They were not just the first chronological stages in its history: they remained structural to its continuance and development, and the language of combat adapted to this necessity. The theme of escape from Vichy detention, from prison camps, or from STO is perpetuated within the maquis in strategies of retreat and policies of dispersion. The skills used in going absent from work, home, or supervision, were redeployed over and over again in the day-to-day survival of the maquis. The language of flight might theoretically appear negative, but within the maquis it was given a new sense of purpose. But it had to be learned.

Throughout the summer and autumn of 1943 the nature of many maquis locations was governed more by circumstances created by Vichy's hunt for *réfractaires* than by anything resembling military logistics. It was not a simple

[4] AN F1C III. 1195 Vaucluse; reports of 5 June and 31 July 1943.
[5] Christian Durandet, *Les Maquis de Provence* (France-Empire, 1974), 128.

matter of expanding the first places of refuge. Because many of these had been linked to agricultural or forestry labour, offered illegally by peasant farmers or even organized lumber camps, an afflux of volunteers or *réfractaires* could wreck the delicate balance of needs and provisions on which these arrangements were based.[6] Rethinking the whole operation to avoid a breakdown of local trust and benevolence was an urgent necessity for all those who had pioneered the early stages of refuge. The search was for abandoned farm buildings, mountain chalets, or disused forestry camps which would allow a maquis to develop with a degree of security from the hunt, but in an area where food was available and occasional employment could be obtained. There was little initial consideration of easy access to potential military targets. In the Haute-Savoie, one of the many parish priests to have joined the maquis, Abbé Étienne Chipier, described the first grouping as one with no possibility for attack or defence, some twelve or more *réfractaires* from Paris, Marseille, Bordeaux, Toulouse, and local parts of the Chablais, living in a chalet with one stove, a few candles, and hardly any clothes. They had no alternative but to run when the GMR arrived.[7] M. Roche from Sète on the Languedoc coast was one of twelve *réfractaires* who were grouped in the spring of 1943 in a *colonie de vacances* near Lacaune in the Tarn. Most were easily arrested by the Vichy police after a month of inactivity, and were brought to trial in Montpellier on 4 September, but the sentences were minimal and some returned to their search for a viable grouping in the Tarn after only a few days' detention.[8] In the south of the Aude a provisional maquis, behind the village of Artigues, was the first grouping of *réfractaires* who arrived by bus from Quérigut, Axat, and Quillan; it was a four-hour climb from there to the maquis on Roc Blanc in the Pyrenees, organized by Ernest Zaugg, and most of the first few months were spent moving between the two camps and looking for food. In September 1943 five maquisards were surprised by a German patrol as they were skinning a stray sheep, caught on their way back from Andorra. The provisional maquis, so useful as a first staging-post, was forced to disperse.[9] A German attack on 21 July 1943 in the Bois Noir of the Lot, east of Cahors, forced the Maquis 'France' into several months of insecurity in which it nevertheless survived as a group. Formed by Jean-Jacques Chapou, who had become chef départemental of Libération (sud) in 1942,[10] this early maquis

[6] Henri Cordesse pointed out that some *réfractaires*, who were 'bien placés', opposed the creation of maquis groups in their locality, for fear of attracting the attention of the authorities. Cordesse, *Histoire de la Résistance en Lozère*, 62.

[7] Abbé Étienne Chipier, *Souffrances et gloires du maquis chablaisien* (Reflets de notre temps: Thonon-les-Bains, 1946), 50.

[8] Gérard Bouladou, *Les Maquis du massif central méridional*, thèse de doctorat, Montpellier, 1974 (Lille, 1975), i. 146. The evidence given by Bouladou is from M. Roche from Sète. Bouladou's thesis was a pioneering work in local research into the maquis.

[9] Maury, *La Résistance audoise*, i. 242.

[10] See Kedward, *Resistance in Vichy France*, 162–4.

was serviced by people from the village of Arcambal, including the *institutrice* C. Brunet, Marie Pouget at her farm, Abbé Gauch, and the restaurant *patronne*, Mme Jouve, and consisted initially of only three or four men. When Chapou joined it, and adopted 'Philippe' as his *nom de guerre*, he brought the complement to eight—but its arms and ammunition were almost non-existent and there was no possibility of avoiding retreat and continuous movement.[11]

This nomadic existence, described in numerous accounts of events in 1943, was more than the conditioned reflex to attack or betrayal, it was also a vital part of the process of discovering the possibilities and limitations of the rural areas in which the maquis found themselves. Monsieur P. Lafargue described the lessons rapidly learnt by the maquis of the Lot in the summer of 1943:

> In the absence of organized requisitions, the maquisards had to be fed without alienating the local population on whom we depended for support. We therefore began to ambush lorries of corn, flour, and livestock, particularly if they were part of German convoys—and in that way we could recover some of the French goods exacted as tribute by the occupying forces. We also learned to make demands on collective concerns rather than individuals, but at the same time to gain help or skills from individuals according to their jobs and patriotic motivation. Millers, bakers, butchers, and garage mechanics were located and enrolled to help us . . .[12]

The period in which the maquis was most unstable was thus the period in which two vital discoveries were made: the importance of keeping a group together by tactical mobility, and the need for a sensitive mixture of dependence on the local community and self-reliance. By encountering differences from one village to another and from one valley to its neighbour across the hills, the maquis adjusted its life not only to the varying rigour of the hunt but also to the shifts and variations in local response. By the end of the year few maquis groups had any excuse for underestimating the ruse, guile, and instinct for self-preservation on which the hunted depend.

The problems created by instability varied in degree from maquis to maquis, but there is no easy way of concluding that one type of maquis was more affected than another, or that one of the two dominant organizations of the maquis, the AS and the FTP, suffered less or more from the predicament of the hunted. Lieutenant Mars argued in his post-Liberation report on the Cévennes that lessons of poor leadership and organization were learnt from the destruction of Aire-de-Côte on 1 July 1943, and that as a result leaders of the Resistance looked to the FTP of the Ardèche as a model: 'small and compact numbers; high mobility; easily able to disperse; targets chosen well away from the base camp; tight investigation of recruits

[11] Georges Cazard, *Capitaine Philippe* (Coueslant: Cahors, 1950), 90. [12] Ibid. 348.

before they were taken on . . .' but he has to add that the FTP units constructed in the Lozère by Monsieur Pantel, a communist from Saint-Michel-de-Dèze, and based on this model, were forced to move, regroup, and purge themselves several times in order to deal with infiltrators, poor sites, or distance from food supplies.[13] The account produced by Éditions France d'Abord in 1946 of FTP action in the Haute-Savoie does not minimize the high dispersal rate of the early units, and says there was a constant interaction with AS organizations in attempts to escape the effective Italian and GMR forces. The camp at Montfort which was attacked by the Italians on 10 August is reported as comprising forty-seven men of the AS and FTP, all of whom were arrested.[14] In the Gard, writes Aimé Vielzeuf, the remnants of Aire-de-Côte came together with a group of maquisards organized by Guy Arnault and Robert Francisque near Lasalle to form the embryo of the 'Maquis AS de Lasalle', more purposeful in intent, but nevertheless forced to move on at least forty times through a series of *bergeries* and abandoned farms.[15] In the same month (July) the first fully structured maquis FTP of the Gard was formed at Figuerolles on the border with the Lozère, but its early life too was dominated by the need to keep on the move for reasons of security.[16]

It was therefore an exception in the summer of 1943 for maquisards to nurture an image of stability. Yet this exception existed in a distinctive form of maquis organization and development. The so-called 'rising' of *réfractaires* in the Haute-Savoie in March 1943, over-dramatized by the BBC but none the less causing a flurry of anxiety within the Vichy administration, announced a military possibility which the maquis groupings in the Vercors, at Ambel and elsewhere, had also envisaged. In January 1943, before the Vercors camps were created, Pierre Dalloz, architect, writer, and passionate devotee of mountain life, had confided his long-prepared ideas of a Resistance citadel in the Vercors to Yves Farge in Lyon, and in the six months that followed this vision was formulated in military terms by Capitaine Alain le Ray, himself a skilled Alpine climber. At the same time it was piloted by Farge and Jean Moulin through the political maze of Gaullist relations with mainland Resistance and entrusted to General Delestraint, the head of the AS, designated by de Gaulle. Delestraint's inspection of the Vercors in April confirmed the vision as both viable and desirable as military strategy. To all intents and purposes what was later known as 'le plan montagnards' had

[13] AN 72. AJ 159, Lieutenant Mars, 'Rapport sur la Résistance active dans les Cévennes', 24 Mar. 1945.

[14] *R.1.3. Francs-Tireurs et Partisans de la Haute-Savoie*, 40. The account continues: 'Les prisonniers seront déportés de l'autre côté des Alpes, jugés par un tribunal militaire, et contraints au travail pour l'ennemi. La défaite italienne les trouvera dans le département des Alpes-Maritimes d'où beaucoup d'entre eux regagneront la Haute-Savoie et prendront de nouveau une part active à la Résistance.'

[15] Vielzeuf, *La Résistance dans le Gard*, 12.

[16] Ibid. 14.

been accepted, though it has never been precisely established who, in London or Algiers, accepted what, or to what extent, if any, the Allied High Command was involved. Nor is there any certainty that the plan rejected mobility; on the contrary, both Francis Cammaerts, the SOE agent in the south-east, and Paul Silvestre, the historian of the maquis in the Isère, emphasize its commitment to mobile tactics in the build-up to the expected *débarquement*.[17] We shall return to the Vercors later in the book, but what is important for the early months of the maquis is that the image of a rising presented by the March events in the Haute-Savoie, and the plan montagnards for the Vercors, both represent a significant current of military thinking which saw an opportunity to create outposts of a regular army behind and within enemy lines. The maquis groups assembled during the summer of 1943 in the Vercors knew little of these high-level plans, but the idea of a fortress in the hills was canvassed widely among professional army officers. General de Lattre de Tassigny had perhaps envisaged this when, alone, he had tried to defy Vichy's dissolution of the Armée de l'Armistice in November 1942 by heading for the Montagne Noire; General Giraud had created a resurgent French army within Algeria and was known to favour a new role within France for officers from the disbanded Armée de l'Armistice in preparation for a landing in Languedoc, and in November 1942 a number of these officers formed the Organisation de Résistance de l'Armée (ORA), aimed at the reconstitution of regular army bases within the south.[18]

It was in pursuit of this aim that Commandant Vallette d'Osia and fellow officers of the 27e Bataillon de Chasseurs Alpins, centred at Annecy, had looked to the foothills of the Alps as a natural fortress for a Resistance army, and in the winter of 1942–3 had set in motion a clandestine plan of recruitment, training, and liaison, which created most of the first groups of the AS in the Haute-Savoie. The connection between this embryonic army and the flight of *réfractaires* into the mountains in March 1943 was not exactly cause and effect, though d'Osia became widely acknowledged as the leader of the groups of AS maquisards which formed in the months after the so-called 'rising'. His military conception of a stable and regular army base in the mountains influenced both the recruitment and outlook of the maquis in this area, but his arrest in November 1943 disrupted the development of his strategy. It led to doubts about its practicality, though his initial plan for an internal army, primed to strike in co-ordination with the French and Allied *débarquement*, continued to be shared by the proponents of the plan

[17] Evidence from Francis Cammaerts, 18 Mar. 1991; Silvestre, 'STO, maquis et guérilla dans l'Isère', 13.

[18] See Georges Roidot, 'Les Maquis de l'Organisation de Résistance de l'Armée', in *Colloque sur les maquis*, 99–115.

montagnards, and by officers of the ORA, both within the Alpine regions and in other mountainous areas of the south.[19]

This strain of thinking within the early maquis was more the product of planning 'from the top' rather than the discovery of possibilities 'from below', but it does not follow that it created an élite within the maquis or that other maquis groups, preoccupied with avoiding the hunt, ignored the questions of combat and military strategy. In the Ain, the *département* which flanked the Haute-Savoie and comprised the mountainous regions of le Bugey and the lower regions of la Bresse, Henri Petit (Romans), an army captain, organized a network of camps in the dense forests of the uplands, according to rigorous military thinking, but without establishing a single 'camp retranché' or 'fortress maquis'. His concept of guerrilla warfare was unusually advanced, and the principles on which the camps were constructed gave primacy to isolation from all habitation but also to sites which permitted a hasty retreat. The views from the hills were extensive, neutralizing the element of surprise attack, but despite the care with which Romans-Petit inculcated the principles of liaison between multiple camps, tight security, and readiness to withdraw, he was later prepared to state that 'Our intelligence was often insufficient, and we too often neglected the fundamental principle of mobility. Several camps occupied the same site for several months, in defiance of our own elementary rules which we had established from the beginning . . .'[20]

The early movements of the Maquis de l'Ain, argued Romans-Petit, created a psychosis of fear within the enemy. Whether mobility was planned, enforced by surprise attack, or discovered through day-to-day needs of food, shelter, and clothing, it rapidly became associated not just with survival but with ubiquity, giving an impression of numbers and strength which was more illusory than real. In the struggle for control of rural areas, illusion as much as fact was the basis of power. Maquisards in their role as the hunted gradually made the terrain of the hunt unpredictable for the hunters. Eventually it became inhospitable to the enemy, and finally dangerous.

For Vichy the primary aim of the hunt in the summer of 1943 was less to seek out and destroy any maquis presence in the countryside, than to locate and capture the absent *réfractaires*, whom local officials were desperately trying to keep within the law. The number of 220,000 workers demanded by Sauckel by the end of June had not been met, and the shortfall noted in July was between 50,000 and 60,000. It was already a major source of complaint from the prefects in the old *zone occupée* that the *zone sud* had furnished only a fraction of those who had left for Germany, and now it

[19] See Jourdan *et al.*, *Glières*, 21–9.

[20] H. Romans-Petit, 'Quand je commandais les maquis de l'Ain', *Le Journal de la France*, 54 (1972), 1494–6.

seemed clear that the bulk of the *réfractaires* were finding it easy to hide in the hills and forests of the south. The southern prefects were faced with quotas which forced them to choose between draining the small towns of almost all available skilled workers and wrecking their economy, or mounting extensive man-hunts and recovering the 40–60 per cent of those eligible for STO who had gone missing since May. With Laval requiring daily bulletins throughout June, but still insisting that *réfractaires* were to be located by the gendarmerie and not the GMR, the local police had to arrive at strategies for hunting down those in hiding without forcing them into acts of subversion or alienating the local communities in which the gendarmerie had to function. Any area thought to harbour *réfractaires* was subjected to intensive search and questioning, and the gendarmerie relied heavily on informants to discover any weaknesses in the cover provided by the local population. The result was a mountain of reports, sampled and summarized by the prefect, whose reflex reaction to Vichy enquiries was to insist that the outlaw presence or threat was slight.[21]

Within the Montpellier region, encompassing the Languedoc plain of the Hérault and the Aude, the Catalan *département* of the Pyrénées-Orientales, and the plateaux (Causses) of the Aveyron and the Lozère, the police and prefectoral reports reveal both the meticulous rigour of the search and its severe limitations imposed from within and without. Already at the end of May the gendarmerie of the Aveyron had established what became one of the norms for the reports. Using an informant who had posed as a would-be *réfractaire*, they discovered both the place of refuge in a farm near Rivière-sur-Tarn, and two men, Alfred Bousquet and Léon Célié, who were deemed to be organizing the reception of *réfractaires*. But despite the hard evidence acquired, the police did not intend to issue criminal proceedings, but proposed to have the two men confined to their residence until they could perhaps be designated themselves for work in Germany.[22] Both men were over the age targeted by STO, but would nevertheless count as two more towards the quota for the *département*.

Another norm was established in the report from the Prefect of the Lozère on 10 June which simply stated:

> From certain information received, it appeared that young men escaping STO were hiding in the region of Barre-des-Cévennes.
>
> On 5 June the gendarmerie carried out an active search in this area. At 6 a.m. several hamlets were surrounded and the identity of the inhabitants checked. Everyone questioned was in order, and no *défaillant* was discovered.

[21] AD Hérault 18W 13. Laval's instructions were conveyed in a circular of 1 June 1943, Telegram 07323, AD Hérault 18W 63.

[22] AD Hérault 18W 13, report dated 28 May 1943 from the Millau section of the gendarmerie to the Regional Prefect.

I would add that the questioning did not result in any confirmation of the information I had received. Still further, once the main operation was over, several farms in the region, both occupied and deserted, were searched, but again with no result.[23]

This particular norm of protracted investigations leading nowhere, despite the advantage of reliable information in advance, is repeated over and over again throughout the region, and after his report of 10 June, Dutruch, the Prefect of the Lozère, tried to secure the greater investigative and deterrent powers of the GMR before Vichy had officially sanctioned it.[24] In the Gard an equal proponent of collaboration, the Prefect Chiappe, turned to the Milice, but in neither case were the results significantly different. Dutruch admitted on 26 June that extensive investigations into the massif de l'Aigoual had been fruitless,[25] and his failure undoubtedly helps to explain why the Germans stationed at Alès took matters into their own hands and launched their attack on Aire-de-Côte. Further indication of the Prefect's frustration came on 12 July, when Dutruch signalled a major escalation of *défaillance*: the *instituteurs* of six communes had failed to report at Mende for the scheduled departure to Germany. The implication of his note to the Minister of the Interior was that teachers, as public employees with a strong local influence, would give a powerful endorsement to the revolt against STO.[26]

July was the first of two particularly active months for the Vichy police throughout France, and the government was keen to impress on the Germans the extent of their operations. In a table of figures at the end of July, summarizing police achievements since Sauckel's second demand of the year (for 220,000), 10,637 arrests are claimed for the *zone nord* out of 46,959 police operations, and 3,389 for the *zone sud*. Vast police searches, involving anything from 300 to 1,500 men, were said to have been carried out in all the mountainous areas, and the report's final statistic of 250,000 identity checks in stations, trains, towns, and rural communes testifies to the scale of the hunt.[27] But the local information passed from police to prefects and tailored by the prefects to suit their own relationship with the government suggests that a successful operation was an increasing rarity in August and

[23] AD Hérault 18W 13. The report was sent to the Ministry of the Interior.

[24] In Jan. 1943 the Prefect of the Lozère had sought Vichy's permission to hand over all the addresses of foreigners resident in his *département* to the German authorities in Mende. Vichy stalled, but eventually allowed him to make the list known to the Milice; AD Hérault 18W 19. Letters written by Jews in his *département* referred to being 'bêtes traquées'; AD Lozère VI. M2. 19. The Lozère contrasts with the Aude where the Prefect was dismayed at the German hunt for Jews, saying in February 1943, 'Ils cherchent à se dissimuler dans les campagnes. De nouvelles rafles ont accru l'inquiétude de ceux qui restent encore libres.' In March he referred to 'rafles monstres' which had brought support for the Jews from the most diverse sections of society, 'Catholiques, corréligionnaires, jusqu'à un officier allemand'; AD Aude M. 2656.

[25] AD Hérault 18W 13, Prefect of the Lozère to Minister of Interior, 26 June 1943.

[26] Ibid., Prefect of the Lozère to Minister of Interior, 15 July 1943.

[27] AN F7. 14889, statistics provided by the Préfet délégué du Secrétaire général à la Police, 29 July 1943.

September. The Regional Intendant de Police in Montpellier on 7 August starts a long report on the hunt for *réfractaires* with a recognition that 'les organisations de réfractaires' move from place to place and slip from one region into another, meaning either across the Cévennes into the Marseille region or north into the region of Clermont-Ferrand. He specifies two centres of *réfractaire* activity, the massif de l'Aigoual where the Germans had taken over the hunt, and the borders of the Aude and the Tarn in the Montagne Noire. It is here that he reports a unanimity of support for the *réfractaires* among the dispersed population, who dupe the informants and infiltrators sent by the Milice with false rumours, and exhaust the police in fruitless investigations. The local Chantiers de la Jeunesse, in which the majority of the leaders and almost all the 'jeunes' are known to be 'Anglophiles et antigouvernementaux', provide regular recruits to the 'petits groupes de réfractaires', and he concludes that the recent events in Italy give the *réfractaires* good reasons to hold out in the 'maquis'.[28] This use of the word maquis in inverted commas is clearly inserted to show that the official use of the term 'petit groupe de réfractaires' was a euphemism. A reference to a parachute drop of arms in the region of Puivert west of Quillan on the lower slopes of the Pyrenees, which had 'excited the imagination of the local population', confirms the report as an implicit warning to Vichy of the evolution of *réfractaires* into *combattants*.[29] Vichy policy in August hinged on preventing this evolution.

Keeping *réfractaires* and maquis apart; pursuing both, but helping the former to accept their 'patriotic duty' was the message of an Instruction issued to the Languedoc gendarmerie at the end of August. It summarized policy as follows:

> Inform, counsel, guide, and persuade each individual that it is in the interest of all to submit. Treat *réfractaires* as those who have gone astray, not as criminals. Most of them have left their homes and find themselves in the hands of outlaw leaders, many of whom are common criminals or enemies of society who hold them at their mercy and incite them to violence. Work through their friends and families to try to make them face the truth that they are being duped. But whenever faced with a group, avoid disaster by being cautious, and give the impression of being out in force and well armed.[30]

[28] AD Hérault 18W 13, Intendant de Police to Regional Prefect, 7 Aug. 1943. Contrast this reference to the attitudes of the leaders of the Chantiers with evidence below, pp. 82–3. In the Haute-Corrèze the leaders of the Chantiers at Lapleau betrayed the whereabouts of a depot of arms belonging to the former Maquis de Chambon. They informed Capitaine de Pontbriand of the gendarmerie who delivered it to the Germans; evidence from Jean Marut, in Le Moigne and Barbanceys, *Sédentaires, réfractaires et maquisards*, 173–4.

[29] AD Hérault 18W 13, Intendant de Police to Regional Prefect, 7 Aug. 1943.

[30] AD Hérault 18W 64, instruction from the commander of the Légion de gendarmerie du Languedoc, 31 Aug. 1943.

This was a clear example of Vichy's new shield philosophy in the making, protecting the French, including the *réfractaires* themselves, from the maquis, but, like the previous report quoted, it could be read as a covert acceptance that the distinction between harmless *réfractaires* and armed 'bandits' was becoming questionable.[31]

At the top, the government was still concentrating on making up the numbers for the second contingent of STO, not least because Sauckel's reaction to the shortfall was to demand a further 500,000 workers for Germany which, for the first time, would include women. Laval conveyed this fact to the regional prefects in a meeting at Vichy in mid-August, and told them that he had refused categorically to allow women to go to Germany, and that he was deep into negotiations with Sauckel to block the new demand. To strengthen his position, the prefects were given new deadlines for making up the previous shortfall, and were instructed to maximize the hunt for *réfractaires*. For the Marseille region the new quota was set at 3,000 extra men by 5 September, a figure the Regional Prefect said he was 'absolutely incapable of providing', and his statement was echoed by all other regional prefects in the *zone sud*.[32]

In all ways, August 1943 was a crucial month of re-evaluation, negotiation, and redefinition of Vichy policy. The sense of crisis underlies all official documents: to the problem of *réfractaires* was added that of 'retardaires', the name given to those prisoners of war who had been transferred to work within Germany as 'travailleurs libres', who had been allowed home to France on leave and who had failed to return to Germany. The level of this new kind of *défaillance* was running at 50 per cent and the Germans were threatening the suspension of all leave.[33] On women's labour, Laval succeeded in keeping it within France but at the expense of a final and total collapse of Vichy's family and work policy, trumpeted in the speeches of Pétain and the measures of the Révolution Nationale, but already severely undermined by the obligations on women imposed in September 1942.[34] Now, in August 1943, prefects were urged to employ women in preference to men in all branches of their administration, and to encourage women into industrial jobs by a rise in wages. The only restriction was that their jobs should permit them to return home every evening.[35] It was a last valedictory gesture towards the high moral ground of the early Vichy.

[31] See Kedward, 'The Maquis and the Culture of the Outlaw', in R. Kedward and R. Austin (eds.), *Vichy France and the Resistance: Culture and Ideology* (Croom Helm: London, 1985), 242.

[32] AD Gard CA 763, undated report from the Regional Prefect to prefects in the region. No date is given for the meeting of Laval and the regional prefects, but it would seem to be sometime between 17 and 29 Aug. 1943. [33] Ibid.

[34] For Vichy's policies towards women, and an analysis of their centrality to the Révolution Nationale see Miranda Pollard, 'Femme, Famille, France: Vichy and the Politics of Gender. 1940–1944' (Trinity College, Dublin, Ph.D. thesis, 1989).

[35] AD Gard CA 763. Laval's instruction is contained in the Regional Prefect's report mentioned in fnn. 32 and 33 above. The Prefect of the Haute-Vienne told the Minister of the

The final summer hunt for *réfractaires* in the five *départements* of the Montpellier region produced derisory results. In a last surge, 853 *réfractaires* were individually pursued from a list drawn up at the end of August, but of these only one was discovered. Information of a negative kind was discovered for a further 158, but of the other 694 there was no trace. Out of the fifteen major operations mounted by the gendarmerie since June, eleven had yielded no result, and although the other four had produced over thirty arrests for suspected communist activity and sheltering *réfractaires*, they had not succeeded in recovering the *réfractaires* themselves.[36] The energy spent in the long and fruitless searches must have seemed doubly wasted to the hard-pressed gendarmerie, when they learned in October that Laval had shifted his ground and was now promoting an amnesty for all *réfractaires* with a promise that they would not be sent to Germany if they gave themselves up and regularized their position with the authorities. It was a promise which undermined the moral argument of fairness and responsibility with which the supporters of STO had belaboured the *réfractaires*, and protests poured in to the prefectures from parents whose sons had submitted to the departures.[37] *Réfractaires* were now to be offered the comparative security of a job within France, which had been denied to those who had fulfilled their legal obligations. The irony was not lessened by the news that Laval had negotiated a cessation of all departures to Germany from mid-October until the end of the year, an achievement which Vichy circulars said was to be used to convince the public of Laval's skilful handling of the labour issue ever since the *Relève*. To that end a summary of the history of the *Relève* and STO was sent by the Ministry of Labour to the regional prefects. It claimed that Sauckel had made total demands of 1,200,000 in contingents of 250,000 in 1942, 250,000 in January 1943, 220,000 in April, and 500,000 in July, but

Interior on 25 Oct. 1943 that female labour was gradually replacing male where departures for STO were affecting the availability of labour; AN F1C III. 1197.

[36] AD Hérault 18W 64, report from the Commissaire de Police, 20 Nov. 1943. An overview sent to the Regional Prefect on 19 Sept. 1943 by the Ministry of Labour's regional office at Montpellier stated that the Lozère, the Aude, and the Aveyron were the most *défaillant*, whereas the Hérault and the Pyrénées-Orientales had met their targets for the first and second contingents of 1943. It added that the percentage of *défaillants* in the region had leapt from 5% to 70% at the fall of Mussolini and to 98% at the news of Italy's turn to the Allies; AD Hérault 18W 63. In the Haute-Garonne the police researched 241 names of *réfractaires* from Toulouse during October 1943. 43% of the investigations led to addresses of relatives often as far away as Paris or Marseille. 57% led nowhere, or returned the answer 'parti à une destination inconnue'; AD Haute-Garonne 2008/88.

[37] An example of this protest is a letter sampled by the Contrôle postal at Mende in the Lozère from the mother of a young worker who had left for Germany on STO. Dated 30 Jan. 1944 it reads, 'Il a appris non sans amertume qu'aucun de ses camarades n'est parti pour travailler en Allemagne. Ils se sont bien cachés; maintenant ils réapparaissent sans encourir de sanction. Bien mieux on leur offre un emploi payé. Ils se moquent de ceux qui sont partis: des c—— disent-ils. Voilà qui ne servira pas le gouvernement actuel. Cela se retrouvera un jour.' AD Lozère VI. M. 2. 23.

that on 15 October 1943 only 670,000 Frenchmen had gone to Germany. In return, 110,000 prisoners had returned and 250,000 had been transformed into 'travailleurs libres' within Germany. In percentage terms Vichy concluded that 1.6 per cent of the French population had been sent to Germany compared with 6.6 per cent from Belgium, and on this comparison the Ministry rested its explicit defence of the government's policy.[38]

Laval's amnesty for *réfractaires* was not without its appeal for the hesitant and undecided, but it was too late to have any fundamental effect on the growth of the maquis or on the communities which had become identified with the men on the run. Vichy's drive to uncover the *réfractaires*, whatever its successes or failures, had alienated increasing sections of the rural population. The emphasis on figures, quotas, and contingents should not obscure the less quantifiable nature of the hunt. Identity checks by the gendarmerie, the Milice, and occupying authorities had become increasingly baroque, with elaborate sets of papers to be scrutinized. Civil disobedience, which had started with delays and failures to register for STO, escalated in the middle months of the summer into a complex mix of evasion, bluff, cover, and fraudulence. The net of public control tightened with every week, as new regulations were issued, and it was soon necessary for all men of working age to carry a work permit stamped with 'exemption' from service in Germany or 'unfit', as well as a normal identity card. Both had to be presented to secure ration cards or any other public amenity, and anyone found with an unstamped permit, or without a permit at all, was liable to immediate enlistment.[39] Notices on every *mairie* asked, 'Êtes-vous en règle?' and gave tables of exemption and those eligible for temporary reprieve, and the local Vichy press regularly carried notice of the regulations and sanctions.[40] By such means the whole population was caught up in the mechanisms of the hunt. The active collusion with the hunted by a steadily growing minority was backed by the passive collusion of the majority, and stood diametrically opposed to the denunciations and betrayals by a significant few. Nothing polarized French society under Vichy as much as the intensive hunt for *réfractaires*, nothing undermined the fabric of the law so systematically. Previously law-abiding citizens, and increasing numbers of officials and gendarmes, found themselves taking the first steps towards what must be recognized as an outlaw culture: the belief that natural

[38] 'Précisions pour les départs pour l'Allemagne', Ministry of Labour 29 Feb. 1944; AD Hérault 17W 10.

[39] AD Haute-Garonne 1867/268, Laval to all mayors, 13 July 1943. For four days, 17–20 July 1943, mayors were to carry out this 'pointage' of all 'cartes de travail' for those years subject to STO, and during these four days Vichy offered an amnesty for all *défaillants*.

[40] Ibid. The posters made it clear that those born in 1922 were not exempt even if they were agricultural workers, members of the gendarmerie and other police formations, railway guards, or miners. Nevertheless, many Vichy authorities at local level continued to think of all of these categories as exempt, and confusion was widespread.

justice and moral rectitude can no longer be equated with the official process of the law and can only be found outside it. After three years of occupation, and following a year in which positive support for Vichy had dwindled into the conspicuous prejudices of a small minority, the outlaw culture began to afford patriotic reassurance, personal justification, and, not insignificantly, a pleasurable satisfaction at outwitting the zealots of the hunt. The felt need to do anything to 'narguer les Allemands' had created a 'petite histoire' of resistance. Banal or improvised many of the actions were, but in the last six months of 1943, these individual strands of defiance formed their own maquis of impenetrability. Police reports leave no doubt about this: they are a record of small actions which blocked or misled the hunters, and which, in the recent passion for de-mythologizing the Resistance, have been mistakenly ignored. Questions of who was delaying what and who was being obstructed by whom are implicit in all protracted correspondence within and between the *départements*, even the most routine, such as these two examples between October and December. On 20 October the Intendance régionale de police at Marseille writes to the Regional Prefect in Montpellier asking him to look for two men called Garcia, recently living in Marseille and now thought to be at Frontignan, not far from the Languedoc port of Sète. On 8 November the Prefect writes to the Commissaire de police at Frontignan ordering their arrest. On 20 November the police write back saying they are unknown at Frontignan and a letter to this effect is drafted to Marseille. In the second example the Prefect of the Tarn, *within* the Montpellier region, asks the Prefect of the Hérault on 17 November to look for a *réfractaire* Albert Arnaud believed to be visiting his Aunt at Capestang. The Prefect writes to the gendarmerie, the gendarmerie visits the Aunt and reports back on 3 December. The Prefect conveys their report to the Prefect of the Tarn on 9 December: the Aunt had seen him in the summer, had later had a postcard saying he was leaving for Germany, but had received no further news. In both instances a whole month or more is taken over a simple request from one *département* to another, even within the same administrative region. The delays either passively reflect, or deliberately contribute to, the difficulties of the hunt: it is not easy to say which.[41]

[41] AD Hérault 161W 51. On 12 June 1943 a huge printed list of hunted names, totalling over 1,300 was sent from the region of Limoges to Toulouse. It went to the bottom of a pile in Toulouse, already stacked with names from within the local region; AD Haute-Garonne 1769/4. In addition to the hunt for *réfractaires* there was also the continued supervision of potential terrorists, identified on two lists which circulated within the *zone sud* and were constantly updated. On the lists dated 6 Sept. 1943, 309 names of 'dangerous characters' were signalled as living in the Montpellier region, 71 in the Aude, 85 in the Aveyron, 82 in the Hérault, 15 in the Lozère, and 56 in the Pyrénées-Orientales. All appeared on 'Liste S', and were to be arrested immediately there was any sign of insurrection. A much longer catalogue of names and addresses formed 'Liste S^1', signalling those whose arrest was to follow if a second preventative operation

From mid-summer onwards the borders between *départements* where the hunt had been intensified received not only search parties from the gendarmerie, but undercover surveillance by police from the Sûreté and the Renseignements Généraux, and the high-profile operations of the GMR. After a top-level meeting of police from the regions of Toulouse, Clermont-Ferrand, and Limoges at the end of June 1943, it was decided on a discreet infiltration of all canteens and sleeping quarters at forestry camps on the borders of the Cantal, the Lot, and the Corrèze, deep in the Massif Central. The insistence on strictest secrecy was emphatic.[42] No less secret were the planned operations of five Groupes Mobiles de Réserve into the Montagne Noire on 17 July, on the borders of the Aude, the Haute-Garonne, and the Tarn, but in both cases any information on *réfractaires* was to go through the departmental channels of the local gendarmerie.[43] It was this restriction that those Vichy officials, who marked themselves out as the determined hunters of the maquis, were to bypass increasingly as the summer progressed, denying in practice the distinctions between *réfractaires* and maquisards which they were obliged to accept in theory. At various levels they came to suspect or to know that the gendarmerie in many areas was affected by the popularity of the revolt against STO. Henri Romans-Petit went as far as to say that the gendarmerie of the Ain was sympathetic to the maquis right from the start.[44] This could not easily be substantiated in detail either for the Ain or for any other area as early as the spring of 1943, but late in June de Brinon in Paris informed Pierre Laval that he had evidence that local police were helping *réfractaires* escape, by warning the rural *mairies* of the approaching 'battues', yet another of the recurrent hunting terms which proliferate in official communications. He specified Annecy, Albertville, Ugine, and Thonon in the Savoyard region, and the *départements* of the Cher, Maine-et-Loire, and Seine-et-Oise in the *zone nord*. He demanded an immediate enquiry, which Vichy carried out at speed, exculpating the police in Maine-et-Loire and Seine-et-Oise, blaming shortage of personnel on the problems in the Cher, but finding the Savoyard police 'suspect' but not proven, adding that the mountainous terrain made the hunt for *réfractaires* especially difficult.[45] Laval had already sent a stern warning to all government officials threatening immediate dismissal and transportation to Germany for anyone who, in any way, undermined the working of STO, and more elaborate warnings and regulations followed with regularity throughout the summer.[46] The gendarmerie,

was deemed necessary. 90% of all names were communists, the other 10% covering anarchists, libertarians, one or two Gaullists, and those merely referred to as Spanish refugees; AD Hérault 18W 19.

[42] AD Haute-Garonne 1960/6, report from Renseignements Généraux, Cahors, 29 June 1943.
[43] AD Hérault 18W 13, Intendant de Police to Regional Prefect, 15 July 1943.
[44] Romans-Petit, 'Quand je commandais les maquis de l'Ain', 1492.
[45] AN F7. 14889, report prepared for Laval, 28 June 1943; no authorship given.
[46] Ibid. Laval to all police authorities, 1 June 1943.

like all essential government agencies, including the Milice, was mainly protected from STO, but by the autumn there were the first indications that gendarmes, as well as municipal authorities, would be held responsible by German officers for the more overt actions of maquisards and would be summarily dispatched to Germany.[47]

As Henri Cordesse has argued for the Lozère, many gendarmes carried out their Vichy duties while helping the local Resistance, but it was often difficult to know exactly which of the two positions was cover for the other.[48] Such ambiguity is probably nearer the norm in 1943 than either the overt collaborationism of the Chef de la section at Ussel in the Haute-Corrèze, who arrested *réfractaires* and led attacks on maquis camps with brutal efficiency, or the Resistance of the Chef de brigade at le Malzieu in the Lozère, adjudant Cazals, who helped hunted Jews and *réfractaires* escape and set up an embryonic maquis at Brassaillères in the heart of the Montagne de la Margeride.[49] The strength of the gendarmerie in the *zone sud* was 14,900 in December 1942, over 5,000 short of its theoretical establishment of 20,186, and the SS General Oberg, head of the German police, was insistent that arms should not exceed one *pistolet* per gendarme.[50] By November 1943 the complaints to Vichy from the regions listing inadequate staffing, ineffective weaponry, harassment of gendarmes by German authorities, and loss of morale throughout the forces of law and order, were a commonplace.[51] Friction between Germans and gendarmerie erupted dramatically on 7 December at Sainte-Foy-la-Grande on the border of the Gironde and the Dordogne: German soldiers, housed nearby, entered the gendarmerie, asked a number of questions, then declared, 'The comedy is over,' and machine-gunned the personnel. Two gendarmes were killed and two severely injured.[52] It was not an isolated incident. By the end of the year the stable base from which the search for *réfractaires* had been launched was visibly crumbling.

[47] Over the winter of 1943–4 the Germans exerted increasing pressure on Vichy to permit the recruitment of established police and police administrators for work in Germany. Vichy responded with categoric refusals, but police reports in AN F7. 14889 show that members of the police at local level were increasingly drafted against their will. Note that members of the police born in 1922 were theoretically *not* exempt from STO (see n. 40 above).

[48] Cordesse, *Histoire de la Résistance en Lozère*, 84.

[49] Le Moigne and Barbanceys, *Sédentaires, réfractaires et maquisards*, 139; Cordesse, *Histoire de la Résistance en Lozère*, 84.

[50] Oberg's regulations were reaffirmed in November 1943, and he ordered that all arms seized by the gendarmerie should be handed immediately to the Germans. He conceded that local emergencies might result in permission for the gendarmerie to carry heavier weapons, but only on a temporary basis; AN F7. 14893.

[51] The Regional Prefect at Marseille blamed excessive German demands and duties outside the region for the extreme difficulties in the execution of all police duties; AD Gard CA 764 (Nov. 1943).

[52] AN F7. 14898, 'Incidents provoqués par les troupes d'occupation', dossier from all *départements*.

The role played by the developing maquis in the destabilization of Vichy authority was an active one. The hunt was always two-way. The maquis were both hunted and hunters; the police, or more widely Vichy and the occupying authorities, both predators and prey. Where the first clandestine tracts against STO in February and March had urged workers to escape by whatever means, those circulating in June and July had begun to assert that escape was not enough. In the Isère, one such tract declared:

> So you want to escape to the maquis? Well, you may think the maquis is just a hide-out, the ideal place where you can happily wait until the end of it all, a real easy life.
>
> Think again!
>
> Going to the maquis means a solemn commitment to the Resistance army . . . it's sleeping rough, going hungry and submitting to iron discipline . . .[53]

In the Gard a tract in July headed 'La déportation, c'est la mort' rehearsed the persuasive argument that workers on STO in Germany were liable to be killed by Allied bombings, and concluded,

> The risks are fewer and the honour greater if you open yourself to adventure within France . . . join the maquis, form Groupes Francs and groups of FTP. Victory will go to those who fight. Deportation is the final ordeal. It will not weaken our resolve for vengeance.[54]

The call to stand and fight, to round on the pursuers and exact revenge, puts an end to the earlier language of flight and evasion, and embraces the combative language of the maquis discourse. The maquis was defined in the Resistance press as 'those who are already fighting back'. In this way, 'Prenez le maquis' became a summons to the ranks, a rally to the colours, a call to the hunt.

The means by which the maquis inverted the hunt were in large part an extension of direct action already pioneered by groupes francs of the Armée Secrète (AS) and by urban units of the FTP. This extension posed no problems for the FTP, for whom all combative and subversive action, whether in the towns or in the countryside, fell into one category, commonly referred to as 'action immédiate', or direct action. But the MUR had created problems for its activists by an over-elaborate division of Resistance action into several different categories, which theoretically kept the groupes francs of the AS and the maquis apart. The combative identity of the groupes francs was an inheritance from the first flamboyant actions by Jacques Renouvin and others in 1940–1 which had mainly been directed against the property and institutions of collaborators.[55] By 1943 the groupes francs had grown into the core of the AS in several areas, notably in the Marseille

[53] AN72. AJ 63, tract quoted in report on the maquis by the CFLN, early 1944.
[54] AD Gard CA 328, tract 'La déportation c'est la mort', July 1943.
[55] See Kedward, *Resistance in Vichy France*, 68–9, 143–4.

area, and in the Lot where they constituted the Groupes Vény, named after their leader the socialist Jean Vincent (Colonel Vény). The groupes francs were the only paramilitary sector of the MUR before the maquis, but there were other sectors, specifically Résistance-Fer and eventually Action Ouvrière, dedicated to sabotage. The maquis were distinguished from all these by the role ascribed to them in the more obviously military struggles of the Liberation which were expected to coincide with the Allied invasion, an event which was impatiently anticipated for the very near future. Their main brief, therefore, within the MUR was to train and prepare for this eventuality. But whereas this separation of functions might have made administrative sense when Brault's Service National du Maquis was created, it became less and less meaningful as the conflict between hunters and hunted fluctuated and developed. For many maquis groups, organized and supported by the AS, the debate between 'action immédiate' and preparation for the armed struggle, known as 'action à terme', became an academic exercise, unrelated to a reality which made the two both necessary and unavoidable.[56]

There was also the dynamic of boredom. In August 1943 Robert Noireau (Georges), a communist and trade-unionist teacher from Paris, escaped through the effluent of a German prison close to Rodez in the Aveyron, and was put in contact with the maquis of the Lot. Describing himself as 'hunted game' he arrived at the AS 'Maquis de la Pergue' in the forest of the Ségala above Figeac. 'It was a camp of nomads. No arms except for two or three hunting rifles . . . everyone seemed very well behaved . . . The core was made up of young local peasants, *réfractaires* from STO, but there were also refugees from the east, a few Parisians, and five or six Jews on the run, older than the rest of the group.' He revelled in the feeling of freedom, but soon it was boredom which most accurately characterized the life of the camp. Before long he had become leader, and took responsibility for organizing a 'coup de main'. 'If we wanted to be taken seriously we had to cause some sort of material damage.' The objective was chosen. They would derail a train, a small and simple action carried out with railway tools and not explosives, but one which, although 'anodin', raised the morale of the whole camp, 'satisfying the thwarted anger of some, and fulfilling hopes which had been suspended for too long'. In November they decided to raid the Chantiers de la Jeunesse at Maurs in search of clothing, after two deserters from the Chantiers had joined the maquis and brought inside information on the stocks available. For this they needed transport, and in the first act of commandeering a lorry they were met by a group of

[56] Picard and Chaussade, *Ombres et espérances en Quercy*, 70–1. See also Madeleine Baudoin, *Histoire des Groupes Francs (M.U.R.) des Bouches-du-Rhône* (PUF, 1962), and Jean Delmas, 'Les Maquis: action immédiate ou action à terme', in *Colloque sur les maquis*, 49–58.

gendarmes. 'We were shot at like rabbits,' and one maquisard was taken prisoner. Although the gendarmerie at that stage were not to be relied on, he added, the Germans were not yet worried about the maquis, so a *coup de main* against the Chantiers raised no real difficulty. The raid was successful and the 'bag' plentiful: hundreds of clothes and twenty new recruits from the camp itself.[57]

Noireau's account, with its hunting language deployed deliberately throughout, could represent the first actions of many maquisards throughout the south: a strike against a railway or electrical installation, already the regular objectives of the most active groupes francs, and a raid on a local Chantiers de la Jeunesse, an action more specific to the maquis, providing them with the clothing, tents, tools, and supplies necessary for life in the woods.

The FTP companies based on Annemasse and Bonneville in the Haute-Savoie combined on 15 October in a particularly flamboyant raid on a Chantiers depot close to Bonneville, using a lorry with false German police number plates, and a driver dressed in GMR uniform. They neutralized the guards, filled the lorry with clothes and shoes, and negotiated a check-point of *gardes-voies* by giving orders in German. The raid was one of several organized by René Naudin, an employee of the SNCF at Annemasse, celebrated within the FTP for his combination of bravura and meticulous organization.[58] The units involved were not technically the maquis, but rather those known as 'sédentaires', or in some places as 'statiques', operating from their homes, not from a rural camp, but the action was designed to equip the FTP camps in the Chablais, Aravis, and Glières regions as well as the more town-based commando units. The interpenetration of FTP units in town and country makes it difficult to decide which FTP *coups de main* were maquis actions. The advantage of this co-ordinated structure was that it gave the FTP their capacity to strike at targets within, or close to, towns and then disperse either into the camps in the hills or back to their homes. The mining area of the Cévennes centred on Alès and la Grand' Combe could be described as the *chasse gardée* of the FTP and the constant attacks mounted there on pylons, transformers, bridges, and railway lines forced local authorities and employers permanently on to the defensive, with a major increase in armed guards in September 1943, despite the great difficulty experienced by the engineers and directors of the mines in finding security personnel. At la Grand' Combe itself guards were increased from seven to forty, but shortly afterwards there was a major sabotage of the transformer serving the mines there.[59] In October the Sub-Prefect of

[57] Robert Noireau (Colonel Georges), *Le Temps des partisans* (Flammarion, 1978), 95–8.

[58] *R.1.3 Francs-Tireurs et Partisans de la Haute-Savoie*, 51–2. Evidence also from Jean Vittoz, 19 May 1969.

[59] AD Gard CA 662, report by Sub-Prefect of Alès, 22 Sept. 1943.

Alès suggested weeding out all Spanish miners suspected of a history of combat in the Spanish Civil War and sending them to bauxite works in the Var, and there were frequent arrests and surveillance of known communists in the area.[60] On 14 October an armed robbery of a post-office employee carrying 1,300,000 fr. to the Mining Company of Molières was reported by the police as carried out by a band of 'malfaiteurs' and 'terroristes' who disappeared into the woods in the commune of Courry. In an exchange of fire one of the band, Gabriel Mourier, was killed by the gendarmerie: he was aged 19, from Firminy in the Loire, and on 2 November his grave in Courry was decorated with flowers bearing the message 'Ici repose un patriote: mort pour la France. Tu seras vengé.'[61] In a summary of 80 major *attentats* carried out in the Gard between November 1942 and December 1943, excluding railway sabotage, the police categorized 15 as directly affecting German troops, 43 as sabotages or thefts of ration tickets or money, and 22 as against persons or places associated with collaboration.[62] Yet again, these *attentats* cannot simply be labelled maquis action, since so many did not derive from camps located in the woods and hills. But in the Corrèze, where AS *sédentaires* and maquis, and FTP units and camps were all involved in direct action, the Prefect had no compunction in ascribing the 285 *attentats* listed between 1 October and 30 November 1943 as 'committed by *réfractaires* in the maquis Corrézien'.[63]

All these actions, however minor their effects and however unrelated to larger questions of military strategy, reversed the hunt and carried it into German and Vichy territory. It was not only the material damage that was important: much more significant was the pressure exerted on policing, surveillance, and security. The mobility of the maquis and direct actions of *sédentaires* and maquis groups forced Vichy to provide increasing numbers of reluctant volunteers, or enlisted recruits, to guard railways, mines, electrical installations, food and clothes depots, public buildings, and all industries working for the German war effort or supplying the day-to-day needs of the occupying forces. In the Savoie the Prefect reported in September that all accessible points of the *département* had been checked and alpine organizations interrogated, and he was satisfied that 'armed and organized groups no longer exist in the Savoie'.[64] But his next report, dated 27 October 1943, contradicts what was clearly no more than wishful thinking, with a heading of 'Attentats' under which he states that 'the crimes of armed and well-organized bands are expanding', and after a list of sabotage involving mostly

[60] Ibid., report by Sub-Prefect of Alès, 21 Oct. 1943.

[61] Ibid., reports by Sub-Prefect of Alès, 15 Oct. and 3 Nov. 1943.

[62] Ibid. There were also two other *attentats* listed; by collaborators against the Jewish synagogue in Nîmes.

[63] AN F1C III. 1147, Corrèze, report of Dec. 1943. He reported that 390 *réfractaires* had recently regularized their situation, but that the numbers still living illegally were far higher.

[64] AN F1C III. 1186, Savoie, report of Sept. 1943.

pylons and railways he announced that he had ordered all employers to set up protection squads to guard their factories, hoping to secure authorization for them to carry arms.[65]

Such extra surveillance was not just an intolerable pressure on the labour supply: the diversification of law enforcement created endless friction with the local authorities, and between Vichy administrators and the Germans; it opened up ever more possibilities for subversion and sabotage within the ranks of security guards and part-time police, and it raised the contentious issue of who should be armed and at what level. On this issue the Germans were caught between rigid refusal to arm French civilians for any reason, knowing that such arms could easily be purloined by the maquis, and alarm at the incapacity of unarmed guards to protect vital German interests. Freedom feeds on the paradoxes of repression, and maquis freedom thrived as law enforcement expanded beyond its capacities. For many areas, particularly the Haute-Corrèze, the months of August to October were the first of several dark periods of repression, when embryonic maquis and their support structures were broken, and many individuals arrested, killed, or deported,[66] but even the statistics of loss were interpreted by the maquis as the measure of their local significance, and such a calculation became an integral part of the maquis discourse as it constructed its own balance sheet of achievement.

The legendary nature of the maquis was not a post-war invention or nostalgia. It was structural to its growth, implanted at the time, and cultivated with every action. It was essential to create a climate of mystery and force, and particularly vital to use any explosives available for this purpose.[67] The most diffuse and apparently contradictory tactics and strategy adopted by different maquis meet at this point: the creation of an instant legend. The essential ruse of fugitives who round on their pursuers is to maintain the initial impression of an unexpected resilience and strength, while yet avoiding the direct confrontation which would show that strength to be inadequate or illusory. Finding ways of asserting this power was akin to an ontological search, looking for means of proving the legend and making it real. Among many acts of inversion it meant literally hunting the hunters, pursuing individual members of the police and the Milice, and tracking down the informants and infiltrators. For the FTP this was a particularly self-assertive area of activity. In their circulars to all members of the police forces towards the end of the year, the FTP proclaimed that a gendarme's sympathy for certain kinds of Resisters would be no protection if he continued to treat

[65] Ibid., report of 27 Oct. 1943.

[66] See Le Moigne and Barbanceys, *Sédentaires, réfractaires et maquisards*, 159–64.

[67] Evidence from Henri Cordesse, 22 Mar. 1982, and Francis Cammaerts, 18 Mar. 1991. The latter points out that certain acts of sabotage could have been carried out more effectively without explosives.

communists, socialists, and trade-unionists of the FTP as terrorists. 'Patriots will accept no discrimination. An attack against one is an attack against all.'[68] General warnings were supplemented by threats to named individuals, normally within the gendarmerie where names were more easily available to local maquisards, and where ambivalence towards Vichy was known to be more widespread. Playing on that ambivalence was part of the strategy of threat and pursuit: a tract widely disseminated in December stated: 'We know that there are large numbers within the police force who on many occasions have given help to the FTP and to *réfractaires* . . . and we know that most of you are in agreement with the huge majority of the French population, and, by extension, with the CFLN [Comité français de Libération Nationale] . . . Do all you can to sabotage the actions imposed by Vichy.' There followed four specific instructions on how to warn the FTP of imminent operations against them, stressing that, in any confrontation, the gendarmes should allow themselves to be disarmed at the first command from the FTP.[69]

To this classic reversal of roles, the maquis added a touch of provocative celebration, the image of a world turned upside-down, if only for a day or a few hours. On 11 November 1943 the maquis of the Ain 'occupied' the town of Oyonnax, a town described by the Prefect in 1941 as 'un fief communiste' and 'cité ouvrière'.[70] Like other celebrated *journées* in French history, the occupation of Oyonnax was almost immediately given a symbolic status, but the difference from other comparable days is that it was consciously designed as such. A deliberate stroke of maquis propaganda, aimed to show the population that the maquis were not the rabble of foreign bandits portrayed by Vichy propaganda, it was carried through with a military control and precision which contrasts vividly with the flood of emotions it unleashed. It was the idea of Henri Romans-Petit, leader of the AS maquis in the *département*, but it was even more his design and execution. There were no German troops in Oyonnax, and the gendarmerie was sympathetic to the maquis, allowing itself to be immobilized. The immediate risks were calculated, but the repercussions were unknowable. It was a gamble, a bluff, a *coup de théâtre*. Almost 300 maquisards, dressed as a uniformed company with officers wearing their decorations, took over the town at midday, staged a military procession, laid a wreath at the *monument aux morts*, and sang the 'Marseillaise', joined by the unbelieving population in scenes of deep emotion. 'A sea of warmth and affection engulfed us . . . people cried out

[68] AD Hérault 18W 13. The circulars were headed, 'Un avertissement aux policiers qui arrêtent des patriotes, les torturent et les livrent à l'ennemi'.

[69] Ibid. The FTP circular came from the 'Haut commandement des F.T.P.F. zone sud. En opération le 10 décembre 1943'. See also a child's account of the disarming of a gendarme at Gramat in the Lot, below, p. 269.

[70] AN F1C III. 1135, Ain, report of 3 Feb. 1941.

"Thank you, thank you, France". We were assailed with poignant gestures of devotion . . .' The withdrawal was as disciplined as the arrival, and the company dispersed to their various camps in the hills. A small flotilla of lorries had been used. Existence, identity, presence, and mobility were all equally asserted, and the text of the wreath summarized the historicity of the act and the power of the actors. 'Les Vainqueurs de Demain à Ceux de 14–18'. The maquis of the Ain had already successfully raided a depot which stocked every kind of clothing material for the Chantiers de la Jeunesse, and on 28 September had repeated the operation more audaciously in Bourg, under the eyes of a strong German garrison, seizing a large quantity of provisions from an army depot. 'We now had enough stocks for nine months,' concluded Romans-Petit, 'even if our numbers substantially increased.'[71]

The occupation of Oyonnax, relayed throughout France by the clandestine press and praised by de Gaulle, became an instant symbol of the emergent maquis, of the hunted turned hunters. Westwards across the Massif Central, on the same day, there was another occupation, procession, and the laying of a wreath in the small village of Marcilhac in the Lot. The occupiers were the Maquis 'France', whose leader was Jean-Jacques Chapou (Capitaine Philippe). Numbering between thirty and forty, the maquisards were offered a wealth of presents by the population, blankets, shoes, jars of food, and cakes, before they returned to the woods. The Prefect mentions no retaliation either by the Vichy authorities or the German.[72] Gabrielle Boudet lived in a house overlooking the *monument aux morts* at Marcilhac and remembered the excitement of the event. She said that most of the village supported the maquis, but not all. Her brother was influenced to the point of joining the maquis straight from the Chantiers de la Jeunesse, and other young people were similarly impressed. The maquis did not stay very long; they were clearly on edge and left quickly.[73] A wreath was also laid by the local AS maquis in the village of Sainte-Féréole in the Corrèze: Pierre Merlat, a maquis instructor who had started his resistance in Amiens and Paris, described the 'profound impression it made on the civilian population, many of whom burst into tears'.[74]

There was no immediate German reaction to the occupation of Oyonnax, but just over a month later the larger, nearby town of Nantua was devastated by the arbitrary round-up and deportation of over a hundred men, and the arrest and shooting of Doctor Mercier, an AS organizer, and the first local head of the Service de Santé which was to become one of the most successful infrastructures of the armed Resistance. The Prefect had no doubt that the events of Oyonnax and Nantua were interconnected, and claimed that the

[71] H. Romans-Petit, *Les Maquis de l'Ain* (Hachette, 1974), 31–4.
[72] AN 72. AJ 157 and AN F1C III. 1163, Lot, report of 5 Dec. 1943.
[73] Evidence from Gabrielle Boudet, 7 Mar. 1991.
[74] AN 72. AJ 112, Témoignage de Pierre Merlat, 19 Apr. 1945.

population of both towns were living in equal fear of the maquis and the Germans. Official relationships with the German authorities, he reported to Vichy, were 'severely strained by the effects of terrorist action, and the number of raids and armed thefts carried out by the maquis'. The Germans had embarked on a reign of counter-terror with the conviction that the raids would cease only when the population feared the Germans more than the maquis. Like all prefects across the *zone sud*, he made the almost gestural request for an increase in police strength to protect the 'terrified local populace'.[75]

The noticeable shift in local Vichy reports towards the language of protection, within the ongoing calls for pursuit, marks the extent to which the poorly armed Resistance in 1943 was successfully imposing its combative identity. A touchstone of this change within Vichy is the mounting attention given to the crisis in the *garde des communications*, the service which provided *gardes-voies* to patrol and protect railway works, turntables, lines, tunnels, and viaducts. By the end of the year it was close to collapse in many areas. Created by a succession of laws and decrees in 1941–2, the *garde* was a uniformed branch of the police under the Ministry of the Interior, and in March 1943 numbered approximately 2,900 in the *zone sud*. Increases were agreed by the German authorities during 1943, but a tight control was exercised over the level and availability of arms. For certain duties they were allowed a hunting rifle or a revolver, but these had to be handed in at the end of the patrol, and arms were by no means in regular use in all areas.[76] In addition there were 'requis civils', requisitioned by prefects to supplement the overstretched official personnel, and the prefects could require any men to stand in as *gardes-voies* as a form of national duty. These 'requis' were crucial to the system, but they were also a serious liability. In the Gard, the lines between le Teil and Alès, and Alès and Nîmes, had been regularly sabotaged in the summer of 1943 by FTP town-based units and Résistance-Fer, and between 25 August and 24 December twenty-one major attacks on the railways were listed by the Prefect's office, though smaller attacks occurred three or four times a week.[77] Many of the *gardes-voies* tried to find ways of being busy elsewhere when the attacks were mounted, particularly if they were themselves accomplices from within, but the success of the attacks increasingly exposed them to punitive arrest by the German security forces. Two such arrests were made in the Gard after a sabotage on 28 August and a further one on 19 September, whereupon the Intendant de Police warned the Prefect that such interventions by the Germans threw the whole French policing system into turmoil.[78]

[75] AN F1C III. 1135, Ain, report of 4 Jan. 1944.

[76] AN F7. 14894, General Perré, 'Historique de la garde', May 1943.

[77] AD Gard CA 664, 'Attentats voies ferrées 1943'.

[78] Ibid., letter from Intendant de Police to Prefect, 1943. The Prefect, Chiappe, had earlier accepted the inevitability of the arrests and had earmarked the Milice for the central role in the maintenance of order in his *département*, AN F1C III. 1153, Gard, report of 4 June 1943.

It is important to reiterate that the rural-based maquis were not the main perpetrators of derailments and other attacks on the railways in 1943, though they became so in the summer months of 1944. Most of the early attacks were the responsibility of groupes francs, FTP units from the towns, Action Ouvrière, and Résistance Fer, the organization within the railway workers themselves. But the very existence of the maquis was a useful cover for employees of the SNCF suspected of sabotage or dereliction of duty: they could talk vaguely of 'surprise attacks from the hills by armed men' or still further make intricate reports in language and detail likely to impress the authorities. As a result of such reports 'model reconstructions of terrorist attacks' were circulated by the Prefect of the Gard to police and *gardes-voies*, unwittingly providing a basis on which further credible accounts could be fabricated by those who needed cover for their active collusion. The model specified 5 a.m. as the preferred hour of the attackers, when workers would be on their way to the day's work, providing a crowd in which the saboteurs could lose themselves. The Prefect also stated that saboteurs were well paid for their sabotage and that workers carrying large sums of money should immediately be suspect.[79] Ironically, with every elaboration of Vichy's security and protection, new ways were created for the armed Resistance to profit from the measures taken and to refine as well as diversify its activity. The very defensiveness of Vichy was a continuous justification of direct action.

Above all, the unannounced, unregulated, and unpredictable incursion of German forces into Vichy's dwindling sphere of police autonomy was the most significant effect of the mounting *attentats* and *coups de main* of 1943. Vichy's policy towards German assertiveness was based on a Franco-German agreement reached by René Bousquet, head of the French police, on behalf of Vichy in April 1943. The central principle was that German policing should extend only to securing the safety of the German army and civilians, and that all other policing should be done by the French. When the German head of labour recruitment in the Aveyron, Hundmeyer, suggested in December 1943 that parents of *réfractaires* could and should be arrested, the Prefect not only rejected the proposal as totally against French law, but also told the Germans that if they proceeded unilaterally they would be breaking this established principle.[80] Both the Vichy Ministry of the Interior and the

[79] AD Gard CA 666. This unusual handbook for action against 'terrorism' was entitled 'Attentats terroristes sur les voies ferrées'. It included basic instructions to the hunters: 'En chasse, ne pas parler, ne pas fumer, marcher sans bruit, s'arrêter fréquemment et se dissimuler. Attendre dans l'immobilité absolue chaque fois un temps assez long et observer . . . Ne pas faire usage de lampes électriques au moment critique de l'observation . . . Par nuit claire, les silhouettes se profilent en terrain découvert sur une distance de 300 mètres.'

[80] AD Hérault 18W 64, Prefect of Aveyron to Regional Prefect, 4 Dec. 1943. In his speech to Oberg on 16 Apr. 1943 Bousquet talked of France rediscovering its place 'dans une Europe qui prend conscience de son unité' and affirmed the necessity of fighting 'contre des adversaires

Regional Prefect at Montpellier backed the Prefect to the hilt on this issue, and ramifications of the principle can be traced in many other defensive letters and reports by Vichy personnel against German encroachments.[81] But the vital interests of the Germans in labour supply as a matter of war economy carried the sphere of German policing into the hunt for *réfractaires*, and into all regulations affecting German-related industries. Bousquet moved quickly to keep the policing of all strikes theoretically within French control, after the Germans had arrested thirty-five striking workers at Romans on 20 September 1943 and a further twenty-five in Lyon at a strike in a Citroën factory on the same day. In an immediate circular he urged all regional prefects to act extremely fast against strikers in order to assert French power and autonomy. Nevertheless all strikes and potential strikes were to be reported at once to the German authorities.[82]

It was by this kind of arrangement, autonomy of policing but a flow of information to the Germans, that Vichy tried to negotiate a *modus vivendi* with the occupying forces. It was never easy in theory. It proved impossible in practice. At any point, the Germans could justify their intervention, if they bothered to do so, by referring to the French failure to complete the last contingent of STO or to the suspected connivance of any Vichy official with the outlaws. Every outlaw action which left the perpetrators free was interpreted by the Germans as a sign of weakness or collusion by the Vichy police, and any other relevant body. The Intendant de Police in Marseille made the consequences of this deduction clear to police chiefs and prefects of the region on 27 August 1943. The local German commander, Lieutenant-General Niehoff, he told them, was disposed to act directly against any police officials he believed to be failing in their duty. Only the most convincing display of sedulous policing could avert this punitive action.[83] In the Gard, where the Prefect and the occupying forces were on cordial terms, the German authorities passed on information to help the French police in the location of maquisards. The SS leader Hauck in Nîmes told the Prefect on 6 September that English airmen were coming and going in the area of Saint-Jean-du-Gard in the Cévennes, and that a bus, full of fuel, and a crowd of young *réfractaires* under communist leadership, were ready

communs, et notamment en matière de répression terroriste'. He said that given the similar interests of Germans and the Vichy government in the pursuit of terrorists, communists, Jews, Gaullists, and foreign agents, the Germans should not interfere with the course of French justice once such individuals had been caught. Finally at the end of the speech, directly addressing Oberg, he concluded that he wanted the French police to be both 'loyale envers vous, et active dans la mission qui lui est confiée par le gouvernement français'; AD Gard CA 367.

[81] e.g. AD Hérault 18W 19, circular from Laval, 8 Apr. 1943, saying that postal workers have no authority to hand over post to the German authorities.

[82] The agreement negotiated by Bousquet is in AN F7. 14897, and a copy of Bousquet's circular is in AD Gard CA 367.

[83] AD Gard CA 367, Intendant de Police, Marseille, 27 Aug. 1943.

to blow up bridges and railways. 'I have given you the facts,' concluded the German officer, 'I now expect you to do what is necessary.'[84] The consequence cannot have reassured him. The Sub-Prefect at Alès investigated the issue and denied all the alleged facts; there was no sign, he reported, of any English airmen, the buses were owned by two individuals who had 'no time for extremists', only five *réfractaires* were on official lists in Saint-Jean-du-Gard and their whereabouts were unknown, and finally there was no sign of any arms. He prefaced his report with the observation that Saint-Jean-du-Gard was Protestant and Gaullist in sympathy, but that did not mean it was in favour of terrorism or would get involved in any extremist action.[85] This was exactly the kind of temporization that the Germans read, often rightly, as complicity with the outlaws. It is probable that the bus in question was the one celebrated by Aimé Vielzeuf as 'the bus belonging to "Cévennes-Cars", driven by M. Vacarès, which the majority of *réfractaires* hidden in the Cévennes knew extremely well', and it was in Saint-Jean-du-Gard that the German forces had dumped two of the bodies of ambushed *réfractaires* from Aire-de-Côte on 1 July.[86] The Sub-Prefect's denial, and several more from the Cévennes in the following months, undoubtedly contributed to the ferocity of the German reprisals there in February 1944.[87]

With clear signs of ambivalence within its gendarmerie and local authorities, and growing instances of German intervention in law and order matters, Vichy officials at the end of 1943 had to decide whether to let the situation deteriorate to the point where the occupying forces would regard the French administration as no more than a façade covering the Resistance underneath, or whether to try to move back to the active hunting of the mid-summer months, only this time with full military action against the maquis. At the top, Bousquet, Darnand, and Henriot adopted the latter position, with Laval endorsing their belligerence, but at regional level there was every position from covert support for the maquis to full-scale repression. The dissolution of Vichy policing accelerates as the two paths diverge, noticeably as the gendarmerie resents the ever-increasing power of the

[84] Ibid., Hauck to Prefect, 6 Sept. 1943.

[85] Ibid., report of Sub-Prefect of Alès, 20 Sept. 1943.

[86] A. Vielzeuf, *Épopée en Cévenne* (Vielzeuf: Nîmes, 1976), 23. For Aire-de-Côte, see Ch. 2.

[87] See Ch. 5. The German authorities in the Gard had been particularly incensed by a bomb attack on 20 Feb. 1943 on a brothel in Nîmes reserved exclusively for German soldiers. Three German soldiers had been killed and five wounded. Fifty arrests were made by the French police, but on 22 Feb. the German commander in Marseille told the regional Intendant de Police that he wanted massive arrests of Jews, communists, and Gaullists throughout the *département*. Vice-Admiral Platon, on behalf of the French government, set himself against this course of action, arguing to the Germans that the investigation was yielding results and it was difficult to justify collective arrests when individual perpetrators could be found. The Germans did not actively pursue the notion of reprisals at the time, but by late winter 1943–4 they were far less inclined to leave the internal policing to the French; AN F7. 14888.

Groupes Mobiles de Réserve (GMR). Established in April 1941 and described as 'brigades fortes', the GMR were put at the disposition of Regional Prefects. Each group totalled 217 men, divided into 16 brigades, well armed and equipped with considerable transport. In 1943 they were separately administered from the rest of the Police Nationale, and given greater mobility between regions. In October 1943 there were four groups for the region of Clermont-Ferrand, five for Limoges, six for Toulouse, four for Montpellier, seven for Marseille, two for Nice, and nine for Lyon.[88] All groups were given names to indicate a specific regional identity, but this never became rooted in local sympathy. Thus the four groups in the Montpellier region were called Maguelone, Bitterois, Minervois, and Roussillon. It was a formalistic reference to the regionalism of Vichy ideology, which became highly ironic as the maquis took root in communities at the very heart of these regions.

The Germans inspected GMR equipment and armoury, with a suspicious attention to any new request, and it took Bousquet five months to secure Oberg's agreement for skis and other special equipment for the three GMRs he designated to patrol the higher mountain areas of the Savoyard region.[89] Both Oberg and Knochen were adamant against any major combination of GMRs, imposing disabling restrictions which ultimately baulked the more fervent police chiefs, such as Marty, Intendant de Police at Montpellier from October 1943 to April 1944, and his successor, Hornus, in their attempts to eradicate the maquis.[90] Nor were the GMRs, or even the Milice, universally confident in their role. From the Pyrénées-Orientales on 5 November 1943 came a letter from the local head of the Milice to his superior in Vichy saying that 'we are nearing the end. Supporters of the Milice are a small minority, hundreds of threats are being received by those who are still the leading members of the population, and magistrates are reluctant to prosecute either communists or Gaullist factions.'[91] The Prefect of the Corrèze claimed in December that the morale of the police, 'especially the GMR', was deplorable, and in the Aude the head of the gendarmerie was investigating a clutch of resignations from the GMR on 12 October, and further defections a fortnight later.[92]

[88] AN F7. 14894, list of GMR for the *zone sud*, 14 Oct. 1943.

[89] On 12 Aug. 1943 Bousquet wrote to Laval saying that 'les événements récents de Savoie et de Haute-Savoie ont montré la nécessité de disposer d'unités de maintien de l'ordre aptes à poursuivre des opérations en haute montagne.' After asking many questions Oberg agreed on 13 Jan. 1944; AN F7. 14894.

[90] See Ch. 5.

[91] AD Pyrénées-Orientales, Fonds Fourquet. A letter from the Prefect of the Pyrénées-Orientales to the Regional Prefect on the same day (5 Nov. 1943) stated that most of the gendarmerie had received written threats; AD Hérault 18W 25.

[92] AN F1C III. 1147, Corrèze, report of Dec. 1943; AD Hérault 18W 15 report from the Prefect of the Aude, Nov. 1943.

Despite these signs of local nervousness and the limitations imposed by German regulations, the GMR and Milice were a powerful offensive force, empowered by Vichy to make no concessions to the maquis, whatever the level of tolerance openly proclaimed by the régime towards repentant *réfractaires*. When Joseph Darnand, head of the Milice, and Philippe Henriot, the skilful radio propagandist, moved into the Vichy government at the end of the year, the hunt for *réfractaires* was turned into a military campaign against the maquis. The autumn months, when the hunt had faltered through ambivalence and concessions, quickly disappeared into a distant past. Although the amnesty for *réfractaires* who surrendered to the authorities was extended by Laval in the new year, the policy of trying to distinguish *réfractaires* from the maquisards among those caught in the woods was largely abandoned. The repression by GMRs and the Milice was modelled on German policing: the maquis were to be pursued relentlessly by both, acting jointly in several instances. Had this ruthlessness been employed in the spring and summer of 1943 against the *réfractaires* the maquis might have been destroyed at birth, though the cost would have been an earlier and greater risk of civil war within France. As it was, the months of popular rejection of STO and of ambivalence within Vichy had seen the implantation of the maquis as a diffuse, but effective force, and its successful inversion of the hunt. It now had its own power base in rural communities. The greater repression of Vichy and the Germans was to reveal how deep-rooted this was. So too was the onset of winter, when much of the history of the maquis became bound up with the dynamics of sheer survival.

4

Structures and Communities, Winter 1943–1944

UNFULFILLED expectations or hopes are invariably called illusions in retrospect. In the France of 1943 hopes ran high for an imminent Allied landing, first in the spring after the Russian victory at Stalingrad; then even more expectantly in the three months that followed the invasion of Sicily and the fall of Mussolini in July. The collapse of the Italians, reported the Prefect from Avignon, made people feel the war was nearly over: all the more reason, he added, for young men to go into hiding to avoid STO.[1] The uprising of the Corsican Resistance in September and the final liberation of the island in early October fuelled the belief in the south that the landing would be from the Mediterranean, and much of the confidence in the early maquis discourse stems from the constant recharging of this belief from May through to October. It would be difficult to understand the enthusiasm of Dalloz, Delestraint, Farge, and Moulin for the 'plan montagnards' without reference to the excitement generated by the idea of an impending Allied arrival on the coast of the Midi.[2]

In August Pastor Gillier took his first *réfractaires* from his presbytery at Mandagout up a steep winding path, frequented only by goats, to a shepherd's hut in the Aigoual massif. The view, he said, was magnificent: they could just make out the Mediterranean coast. 'We'll have balcony seats for the Allied landing,' said one of the *réfractaires*, who came from Lorraine.[3] Such expectations could be dysfunctional, projecting answers before even the most basic questions had been formulated, but they were also a structural element in the military projects formulated by the Service National Maquis and even more by the Organisation de Résistance de l'Armée (ORA). What was often ignored by maquisards in the FTP, who were the fiercest critics of any military strategy which implied waiting for the Allied invasion, was that the expectations were a vital part of the atmosphere within which all

[1] AN F1C III. 1195, Vaucluse, report of 31 July 1943. [2] See Ch. 3.
[3] Gillier, *Les Corsaires*, 3.

maquis groups were created between STO and the onset of winter. For example, one of the first maquis in the Pyrénées-Orientales, in the area of Caixas, was created, armed, and sustained by the communists and the FTP leaders in Thuir during March and April 1943, only to be betrayed by a Spanish charcoal burner and attacked by the police on 27 April. The two communist organizers, Pierre Mach and Gilbert Mestres, were arrested, but the maquisards themselves eluded the police with the help of an expectant local population.[4] The Vichy intelligence in Perpignan reported that 'almost all the population of the Pyrénées-Orientales look forward to an Anglo-American victory, and for over a month now have lived in hope of a landing'.[5] Throughout France such widespread hopes worked constantly in favour of the emergent maquis, whether FTP, AS, or ORA in origin.

By the end of the year the hopes appeared to be an illusion. The Prefect in Limoges, empathizing with the majority opinion, declared in early December that the optimism of the summer had given way to deep despondency. The Allied progress in Italy was slow and the air raids on French towns had caused considerable dismay. People were now less prepared to use the term 'liberators' to describe the English and the Americans, and reports from other *départements* also mentioned the lassitude of Anglophiles.[6] People who talk of the long, cruel winter of 1943–4 are invariably referring to the depressed mentalities as well as the specific, climatic conditions. 'Le débarquement' became a term used to indicate the future that never comes, a bitter joke in the face of mounting German repression and Vichy collaboration, an ironic promise at a time of increased shortages and deprivation. The cleverly angled broadcasts of Philippe Henriot, powerfully delivered and insidiously persuasive, played on this disillusionment, and called the *débarquement* not an illusion but a delusion: if it came, he argued, it would only bring Bolshevik terror in its wake; the western Allies, he argued, were no more than vassals to the all-powerful communism which threatened to engulf civilization.[7]

The influence exerted by Henriot was a symptom of the volatile public opinion during the winter, and some local authorities believed they could detect a general re-emergence of sympathy and understanding towards Vichy. Certainly the amnesty for *réfractaires* and the suspension of departures to Germany had taken some of the heat out of STO in the last two months of 1943. In almost all areas there were scores of *réfractaires* who emerged from hiding-places and left the partial employment which had been provided by hard-pressed peasants and sympathetic relatives, though few prefects were prone to exaggerate the importance of their return to legality. The report

[4] Georges Sentis, *Les Communistes et la Résistance dans les Pyrénées-Orientales (1939–1947)* (Institut des recherches marxistes, Comité d'Histoire de la Résistance catalane: Perpignan, 1985), ii. 26–7.

[5] AN F7. 14904, report from the Renseignements Généraux, 24 May 1943.

[6] AN F1C III. 1197, Haute-Vienne, report of 12 Dec. 1943.

[7] See P. Henriot, *Et s'ils débarquaient?* (Inter-France, 1944), 16–18.

from the Corrèze which had referred to the November upsurge of 'attentats commis par les réfractaires dans le maquis Corrézien',[8] went on to say that 'numerous youths who were camping in the maquis have come back to the towns: 390 have regularized their situation, but the number of others who have just gone home or have been taken in by friends is far higher.'[9] Letters from Vichy's Ministry of Labour to regional officials told them to promote the amnesty in a major drive to recover some measure of public support, and a ministry circular on 15 December promised that any *réfractaires* who reported before the end of the year would be assured of a placement not just in France but within their local area. At the same time, as a measure either of Vichy's confidence in the amnesty, or of desperation at its limited success, the ministry extended it on 31 December into the New Year.[10]

There seems little doubt that this 'mesure de bienveillance', as it was termed, would have been perceived as a fundamental rethinking of STO had it not been contradicted by almost all the other measures emanating from the Ministry of Labour. Despite the suspension of departures to Germany, the medical examinations of those on the register had continued, and those marked fit for service in Germany (*apte Allemagne*) knew they would be the first to go if the Germans renewed their pressure. Still further, as the class of 1943 became eligible for what would have been military service, they were added to the older classes already mobilized for STO, and their registration set in motion. On 15 December and the following few days some 2,447 agricultural workers were summoned to medicals in Montpellier, and the same process elsewhere made it clear that STO was still central to Franco-German collaboration.[11] Submission or *défaillance* was therefore a very real choice for those in line, even after the amnesty.

It was even more of an issue for certain key groups who had benefited from the complications of exemptions and suspensions during the spring and summer. By 20 August 1943 students qualifying for exemption had been whittled down to those in medicine, other than those authorized to stay in France to sit competitive examinations. All other students were to be considered as available for STO.[12] Young men still serving their eight months in the Chantiers de la Jeunesse were next to be targeted. The intake who finished their period of service on 10 October were ordered at the end of the month to report back to their original base during the first week of

[8] See above, p. 63.

[9] AN F1C III. 1147, Corrèze, report of Dec. 1943. The local historians, Le Moigne and Barbanceys, write, 'L'amnistie offerte aux réfractaires du S.T.O. par Laval . . . amena une diminution spectaculaire des effectifs des maquis de l'A.S. en Haute-Corrèze. En particulier les jeunes de la région en profitèrent pour se faire embaucher dans les entreprises locales.' *Sédentaires, réfractaires et maquisards*, 159.

[10] AD Hérault 17W 1, circulars from Ministry of Labour, 15 and 31 Dec. 1943.

[11] AD Hérault 17W 231, handwritten list of 'agriculteurs convoqués', n.d.

[12] AN 72. AJ 9, Laval circular, 20 Aug. 1943.

November to be re-equipped for work within France, 500 to go to each of the regions of Limoges, Clermont-Ferrand, and Montpellier, 1,000 to the regions of Toulouse and Marseille, and 1,500 to Lyon. There were certain exceptions, but essentially the net was widely cast and resentment correspondingly high. It was now clearly apparent to the French population that the Chantiers were being used as an organizational annex to STO.[13]

Those employed within France went mostly to Organisation Todt (OT) or to the protected industries designated by Albert Speer, whose plans for using French labour within France conflicted with the deportation preferences of Sauckel. The number of these Speer-Betriebe industries grew with every month and Laval was under severe pressure to make sure they had the necessary qualified labour. Simultaneously OT was pressing for increased numbers of workers with experience in the lumbering and construction trades who would be put to work on German sea defences both on the Channel coast and on the Mediterranean, and Laval knew that such experience was largely available among immigrant workers employed by Vichy in forestry camps. Between the end of December and the beginning of February 1944 Vichy set out to redeploy thousands of these workers, organized in Travail Étranger (TE), into Organisation Todt, and on 9 February 1944 Boyez, secrétaire-général à la Main d'œuvre, announced to his regional underlings that 'After discussions with the German authorities, the Vichy government acknowledges the current demands of the European struggle and will make every effort to accommodate them . . . and to put the greatest possible numbers of foreigners at their disposal.'[14]

Within six months, therefore, from late summer 1943 to early spring 1944, Vichy pressurized students, the *jeunes* of the Chantiers, and immigrant workers, the very categories that local Vichy officials acknowledged were 'easy prey' for agents recruiting for the maquis and the Resistance.[15] Tracts

[13] Ibid., circular from Robert Weinmann of Ministry of Labour, 28 Oct. 1943. For further details of the Chantiers de la Jeunesse and STO see Halls, *The Youth of Vichy France*, 386–94. In early Feb. 1944 Bichelonne, the Industry Minister, announced that the new regulations on STO effectively deprived the *jeunes* of the Chantiers of their freedom after their period of service. 'En conséquence, à la date qui marque la fin de leur stage légal dans les Chantiers, les jeunes ne sont pas libres de s'embaucher dans une telle entreprise de leur choix ou de reprendre leurs études. *Ils sont requis* dans leur affectation actuelle, ou dans celle qui sera fixée par mes soins . . .' Letter from Bichelonne to the Director of the Chantiers, 7 Feb. 1944; AD Hérault 17W 10.

[14] AN 72. AJ 9. Organizers of TE were far from universally compliant in the loss of their labour force. Many argued that qualified foreigners were of more use to the French economy than certain categories of French workers, and the organizer of TE in Montpellier clearly had specific trades in mind when he argued, 'Comme actuellement nous ne pouvons *utilement* faire des cultivateurs, des mineurs, des bûcherons, de tous nos garçons de café, de tous nos coiffeurs, de tous nos marchands, nous devons tout faire pour tenter de conserver le maximum possible de cette main d'œuvre étrangère devenue maintenant spécialisée.' Letter to Vichy from the Chef du Groupement 3, Montpellier, 6 July 1943; AD Hérault 18W 64.

[15] AD Lozère R 5902, Rispoli, head of the Renseignements Généraux to the Prefect of the Lozère, 3 Jan. 1944.

distributed in the Cévennes during the winter specifically addressed the foreign workers:

in your own countries, as in France, the struggle grows. In the mountains and in the towns your brothers are rising up and arming themselves to drive out the invader . . . The Soviet army, the soldiers led by Tito, the Polish partisans, Italian patriots and Francs-Tireurs in Norway form a single army along with the French maquis. This army calls on all patriots: your place is with them. Join the maquis . . . [16]

To stop the steady drift of all these threatened categories into hiding or the maquis, Vichy employed extended fines, imprisonment, and force, and it is in the context of this accelerated repression that the disillusioned hopes of an Allied landing, the seduction of the amnesty, and the effective casuistry of Henriot need to be set.[17] In particular the law of 20 January 1944, setting up courts martial to judge and execute anyone caught 'in the act of terrorism', was symbolic of Vichy's new militancy, and in February Darnand and Laval pressed for its extension to cover anyone merely found within an armed group.[18] The conflict between hunters and hunted now had all the trappings of internal warfare.

The propaganda aspects of this war against the maquis hinged on the accusation that the *coups de main, attentats*, and sabotage by armed bands were producing a reign of terror which directly victimized the French population itself, especially the peasantry. The official press and radio had the ambivalent task of accentuating the numbers of thefts, attacks, and explosions while reassuring the public that the situation was under control and that the perpetrators were being caught and brought to justice. The same balancing act had to be performed in all communications with the German authorities. In December 1943 the Regional Prefect in Montpellier, for example, sent a summary of all arrests for 'terrorisme' since 1942 to Colonel Distler, commander of the German forces in the town, and followed this with a fortnightly index of all clandestine operations in the region provided by Marty, the Intendant de Police. A regular format for the fortnightly lists from the end of December to the end of February, 1943–4, makes it possible to break down the *attentats* into the following categories:

4 attacks on mairies for ration tickets
4 on public depots of food, clothing, and petrol
16 burglaries or thefts on private persons or retailers
12 explosions or attacks on collaborationist centres, buildings, or clubs
4 attacks on police buildings

[16] Tract headed 'Travailleurs Étrangers'; AD Gard CA 328.

[17] On 1 Feb. 1944 Laval promulgated a law imposing heavy fines up to 100,000 fr. for any employer who obstructed the labour directives of the Main d'œuvre; AD Hérault 17W 13.

[18] AN F7. 14892, report from Laval and Darnand, 6 Feb. 1944.

11 assassinations or attempts against presumed collaborators
4 direct attacks on German personnel and buildings
11 acts of sabotage against pylons and other electrical installations
20 such acts against the railways
11 other acts of industrial sabotage, chiefly against mining machinery and hydroelectric plant

No attack on banks or other financial buildings was listed and only one against a depot supplying the Chantiers. Despite the accompanying notes asserting that enquiries and prosecution were proceeding, the lists mention only a handful of arrests, and if the overall tone is reassuring it is because of the matter-of-fact way in which each *attentat* is described, and the understanding that many of the thefts and assaults might be the work of individuals unconnected with Resistance. It also becomes clear from other lists compiled within each *département* that these regional summaries cover only a quarter or even a fifth of the *attentats* reported locally.[19]

Despite their incompleteness, these lists for the Languedoc-Roussillon region allow certain relative conclusions to be drawn on the most recurrent types of action in this area, in mid-winter. If acts of sabotage, and attacks on collaborators, police, and German personnel and property are put together in a single category labelled 'military', they account for 73 out of the 98 incidents, a high percentage, which reports from elsewhere often, but not always, substantiate. In the Dordogne a breakdown in January of 'acts of terrorism' revealed a much higher proportion of raids and thefts: out of 188 incidents, there were

23 acts of railway sabotage
17 burglaries
26 vehicle thefts
23 thefts of petrol
32 thefts of tobacco
21 raids on mairies
11 individual assaults, including 5 assassinations
35 'other' types of attacks

The report states that the 'terrorists circulate in the northern part of the *département* as masters of the land' and those sympathetic to the maquis feel more and more confident. For example, an armed band openly attacked Périgueux station at 7.30 one evening, and transport loads of livestock and vegetables were being 'brazenly seized in many places'.[20] In the region of Marseille, the Gard provides an enormous number of reported incidents for January and even more for February. Thefts and assaults occur with such frequency in the Cévenol areas of le Vigan, Saint- Hippolyte-du-Fort,

[19] AD Hérault 18W 25, fortnightly reports, Regional Prefect to Colonel Distler.
[20] AN F1C III. 1151, Dordogne, report of 9 Feb. 1944.

Lasalle, and Alès, that the police are seen to be totally helpless.[21] In the Savoie 95 *attentats* were reported by the Prefect for December compared with 53 for November, and he specified a particular rise in thefts from the Chantiers de la Jeunesse and in individual killings. He pointed to the valley of the Tarentaise and the valley of the Isère between Albertville and Moûtiers as the areas most affected, with factories in the Tarentaise heavily sabotaged, and he described the Resistance in this corner of the Savoie as 'a dissident organization perfectly informed with remarkably well-armed bands of 20 to 100 individuals': a train had been attacked in broad daylight, a manifestation of their confidence.[22] Attacks on railways were highlighted in the Toulouse region in January and February, and the police echoed the comments in the Savoie by estimating that the attacks were carefully organized and the attackers well equipped, notably on the Toulouse–Paris line passing through the forest of Montech in the Tarn-et-Garonne.[23]

Taken generally, these selected reports for the two main winter months do not suggest that Vichy intelligence and police enquiries were co-ordinated to fuel Henriot's propaganda of maquis bands intent on terrorizing the peasantry as primary objects of revolutionary action. Henriot's propaganda was not in search of the maquis, but was constructed ideologically to undermine its base in the countryside by persuasive misinformation. By contrast the official reports give a much more accurate picture of the plurality of maquis actions and objectives.

This relative accuracy had its limitations. It cannot have escaped the compilers of the reports that the ascription of the incidents to a particular Resistance group was at best extremely vague but mostly non-existent. No history of the different actions and relative successes of groupes francs, FTP, maquis AS, Action Ouvrière, or Résistance-fer, could start from these reports, or be quickly illuminated by them. The blanket terms 'bandes armés', 'groupes de terroristes', 'bandits', and 'jeunes gens masqués' confound and confuse the distinctions which historians would like to make. It was not that the authorities were ignorant of the different strands of Resistance: the police files contain considerable information, particularly on the FTP whose communist pedigree and consistent policy of direct action made them more prone to pursuit and arrest.[24] The generalized terms suggest, rather, that evidence given to the police after most incidents was insufficient to allow any precise formulation of possible suspects and there is much to support the notion that, despite Vichy's attempts to drive a wedge

[21] AD Gard CA 667, police file of 'attentats' for Feb. 1944.

[22] AN F1C III. 1186, Savoie, report of 25 Dec. 1943.

[23] AD Haute-Garonne M 1526[4], Intendant de Police, Toulouse, Apr. 1944.

[24] For example, the Prefect's report from the Savoie of 25 Dec. 1943 contained specific information on the FTP structures in Chambéry, obtained after the arrest of two local FTP members; AN F1C III. 1186.

between the local populations and the armed Resistance, people were mostly as unhelpful to the police in their reactions to *attentats* of all kinds as they had been in their reaction to *défaillance*. A linked hypothesis is that some of the gendarmerie and much of the populace came to see the *attentats* and *coups de main* as a logical, even if disquieting, consequence of maquis existence and as necessary to maquis survival, so that a bland tone of inevitability pervades many of the first-hand accounts, not least those detailing the thefts of food, clothing, and other daily necessities.

As winter approached and set in, a violent mood of anger and protest against food shortages and problems of distribution swept through the regions and alarmed most of the local authorities. The Resistance press gave headline coverage to hunger: 'Arrière les Affameurs', proclaimed a Languedoc-Roussillon edition of *Combat*, and an abundance of tracts carried the accusation that Vichy was deliberately and callously starving the population.[25] One mordant tract, signed by 'Un révolutionnaire', held Pétain responsible:

> My grandfather had an ass (well before the war): he left it for 15 days without food. The ass got used to it: my grandfather was very happy.
>
> Unfortunately the ass died on the 16th day. What a pity. If it hadn't died it could have lived without eating.
>
> The Maréchal is doing the same with the French: perhaps they'll get used to it.[26]

The Provençal *département* of the Var was one of the least favoured areas in terms of *ravitaillement*. Except in wine, salt, and oil it was utterly dependent on other regions, and during the summer, the Prefect complained, the other *départements* had not fulfilled their obligations. There was consequently no meat, hardly any fat or eggs, and a severe shortage of milk products. People who travelled came back from areas where meat was eaten twice a day and where eggs and milk abounded. Seeing or hearing of the disparities, the report continued, the local people believe it must be the government's intention to starve the Var, and they are reported as very close to violence. At the same time, after the collapse of Italy, considerable numbers of Italian soldiers had been taken in by the maquis in the hills, to whom the Italians brought arms and ammunition. The Prefect acknowledged that the French, and not the Germans, should deal with this situation, but he concluded that in both respects 'we are up against the population', and in December he added that the food problems were at crisis point.[27]

Even in a more favoured area within the old *zone occupée*, the Côte-d'Or, centred on Dijon, the message from the December report was similar. 'Terrorist groups', declared the Prefect, 'range through the countryside and

[25] *Combat du Languedoc et du Roussillon*, 2 (Dec. 1943).
[26] AD Gard CA 328, tract, 'Une Idée', n.d.
[27] AN F1C III. 1194, Var, reports of 1 Oct. and 1 Dec. 1943.

hold peasants in isolated farms to ransom.' He pointed to more and more 'criminal acts with little political motivation', but then added that a main reason was that all people were afraid of the winter and were ready to resort to theft and violence.[28] It was in the Monts Auxois of the Côte-d'Or that the Maquis Bernard set up its own structure of local taxation by which money or goods were demanded from peasants on a sliding scale of estimated collaborationism or hostility to the Resistance. The maquisards agreed that this caused initial hostility but that in most cases it was gradually accepted.[29]

Certainly the problems of food, clothing, and equipment were a dynamic in the history of all maquis groups, and in some cases proved insoluble. In the densely wooded hills of the Aude, south of Carcassonne, in the area of Puivert and Chalabre, the first Maquis des Roudiés, created by the local AS, faced crippling hunger and cold. One of the maquisards, Edmond Roudière, remembered living for eight days on a few large onions, and all the members of the maquis became thin and emaciated before the eventual dispersion of the group in late January 1944. Lucien Maury, historian of the Resistance in the Aude, commented that this experiment with a small unarmed maquis deprived of all means of survival was quite unsatisfactory. It served only as an important negative lesson for those, led by himself, who went on to create the Maquis de Picaussel nearby. 'We knew we had to get together the means to survive and to fight *before* organizing the maquis. That was a simple necessity if we were to create an effective maquis which went beyond simply hiding unarmed *réfractaires*.'[30] Raymond Fournier has written a telling description of the acute problems of a small maquis formed near Millau on the edge of the Sévérac plateau in the Aveyron, called alternatively the Maquis Bochetto, in memory of an Italian killed in Montpellier after attacking the Gestapo, or the Maquis des Lacs. It was formed in October 1943 by two anti-fascist Italians, Antoine Marcolin and Serge Forcolin, both members of the Communist Party in Millau, and the maquisards, numbering eleven, lived in a cave for most of the winter, fed by the efforts of a local farmer Roger Maury and communist comrades from Millau. It moved eventually to a shepherd's hut at 900 m. altitude, at least three hours' walk from the nearest habitation. Inaction, fear, boredom, biting cold, and extreme hunger were their daily experience throughout January and February before they were warned of an imminent attack and began a series of moves across country, eventually joining the active and effective FTP Maquis d'Ols in the area of Capdenac on the border with the Lot.[31]

[28] AN F1C III. 1148, Côte d'Or, report of 1 Dec. 1943.
[29] *La Vie d'un maquis d'Auxois* (Association du souvenir de la Résistance: Dijon, n.d.), 9.
[30] Lucien Maury, *La Résistance audoise*, i. 392–3, and evidence from Lucien Maury, 24 June 1982.
[31] Raymond Fournier, *Terre de combat*, 135–56.

These two examples indicate that long after the first experiments with camps of *réfractaires*, and the spread of the maquis discourse and mystique, there were groups of self-declared maquisards who were still essentially looking for the maquis. In their state of utter dependency for food and clothing they were unable to find or impose their identity. They constituted a noticeable, but minority, sector of the French maquis during the winter of 1943–4.

The norm was to forge an identity out of the very necessity of survival, so that survival and action became interchangeable. As a result, raids for food and necessities became as structural to most of the maquis as the idea of armed resistance itself. The larger and more professionally organized maquis which became a feature of the spring and summer 1944 had their own *intendance* to look after food, so that many individual maquisards never took part in *coups de main* for provisions. But many of the smaller and evolving maquis, which dominated the middle period of maquis history, created themselves as active and combative units partly through the necessity of raids for day-to-day survival, which underpinned their actions of a more obviously military nature. A lengthy and amazingly well-informed report on the maquis in the Lot, compiled in July 1944 by local Vichy intelligence and police, had a section on supplies which listed not only major maquis attacks on the largest food depots in the *département* and frequent thefts of rationing cards from the *mairies*, but also action against egg collectors, food trucks at stations, abattoirs, wine producers and distributors, tobacco wholesalers, clothes shops, particularly those with several branches in the *département*, Chantiers de la Jeunesse, petrol stations, post offices, banks and savings banks, and tax offices. The list concludes with the observation that 'the principal suppliers of the maquis are the maquisards themselves'.[32]

The raids on the Chantiers de la Jeunesse were the most recurrent in this predatory action, and the overwhelming success of the maquis in these attacks was symbolic of the shifting balance of power in the countryside. The Chantiers were the most significant ideological representations of Vichy in the hills and forests of the *zone sud*, which the maquis were beginning to claim as their own. Any local respect the Chantiers had gained in 1941–3, for the labour they supplied at harvest times and the stimulus they gave to the area's economy, was largely dissipated during 1943 by the readiness of the national leader, General de la Porte du Theil, and the leaders of many of the individual Chantiers to promote the acceptance of STO as part of the corporate discipline, Pétainist patriotism, and public morality, which the Chantiers were held to personify. Roger Austin's study of the Chantiers in the Languedoc region relates how the transfer further inland of camp 24, from Lodève in the Hérault to Saint-Affrique in the Aveyron, and camp 25 from le Bousquet-d'Orb in the Hérault to Mauriac in the Cantal, exposed

[32] AN 72. AJ 157, Renseignements Généraux, 22 July 1944.

them to suspicious and hostile local opinion as early as April and May 1943. He relates that, in November, when camp 19 at Meyrueis in the Lozère was attacked by maquisards, 'the camp leader accused his men of cowardice because they had refused to defend the camp', and that by mid-winter the transformation of the Chantiers into mere 'holding camps for STO' made the gap between leaders on the one hand, and the *jeunes* of the Chantiers and the local population on the other, unbridgeable.[33] It was logical that these centres of Vichy indoctrination should be undermined from within and attacked from without by the alternative discipline, patriotism, and morality represented by the maquis, and the transfer of food, clothes, equipment, and recruits which resulted from the desertions and the raids confirmed in a material way the transfer of credibility from Vichy to the Resistance. Nowhere were the inversions in authority effected by the maquis so obviously apparent as in this shift of legitimacy literally from one camp to another.

The growing vulnerability of both the Chantiers, and the related organization Jeunesse et Montagne, was reflected in the defensive moves by the Ministry of the Interior in September and October 1943, when the more isolated Chantiers were regrouped in less exposed camps, a measure particularly protective in the *départements* of Haute-Savoie, Savoie, and Isère in the Lyon region, and the *départements* of Corrèze and Creuse in the region of Limoges, all areas where the ministry had registered a growing number of attacks. With the regrouping went a major reorganization and relocation of the Chantiers' supply depots, which the ministry estimated, in its secret circular to regional prefects, stocked 'enough food and material to supply 1500–3000 men, i.e. about the size of a regiment'. All the relocated depots were to be heavily guarded and no depot was to be restocked once it had been raided.[34]

What the government could not do was to guard all the depots *and* all the manufacturers who made the clothes and equipment destined for the Chantiers, and it was one major manufacturer, the Paulhan factories in Saint-Jean-du-Gard in the Cévennes which fell victim to a maquis raid on the night of 15 January 1944. The company produced clothes and tents for a whole range of military purposes as well as for the Chantiers, and the raid yielded 1,980 pairs of khaki shorts, 1,455 khaki jackets, and 1,640 tent canvases, besides overalls and forestry jackets, the whole, calculated by the police, worth over 800,000 francs.[35] The raid was planned as a collective venture by several maquis groups located in the deep, winding Cévenol valleys which ran on either side of the Corniche des Cévennes, valleys in

[33] Roger Austin, 'The Chantiers de la Jeunesse in Languedoc, 1940–44', *French Historical Studies*, 13/1 (Spring 1983), 123–5.

[34] AD Hérault 18W 13, circular of 27 Sept. from the Secrétaire-Général à la Police, and telegram of 4 Oct. 1943 from Secrétaire-Général du Gouvernement.

[35] AD Gard CA 668, Prefect to Minister of Interior, Jan. 1944.

which almost every hamlet was implicated in maquis activity. In the event, the leading role in the raid was taken by a maquis which did not originate in the Cévennes, but had started its mobile and turbulent life in the Aveyron gorge as the Maquis de l'Estibi, initiated by Jean Capel (commandant Barot) and the AS of Toulouse.[36] Just a year after the first major victory of the Free French at Bir-Hakeim in Libya, the maquis adopted the name of the battle as its own, and moved first into the gaunt and rocky hills near Bédarieux in the Hérault, then westwards to a disused Chantiers camp on the western end of the Pyrenees, before making an arduous trek across the Languedoc to the east of the Gard and the plateau of Méjannes-le-Clap, some 30 km. north-east of Alès, recruiting more *réfractaires* and other volunteers from the Hérault and the Gard *en route*. The Maquis Bir-Hakeim had its own commando vanguard in the form of motorized corps francs which ranged across considerable distances to carry out their raids. In the autumn they had secured two tons of equipment and food from the Chantiers depot at Labruguière just north of the Montagne Noire in the Tarn, one of the depots subsequently moved by the Ministry of the Interior in its September reorganization.[37] The Paulhan raid in the Cévennes substantially reinforced the tough and flamboyant reputation of the Maquis, which ran ahead of its exploits, though the success of the raid was also due in part to the inside co-operation provided by the manager of the factory, Monsieur Janel, who had been won over by maquisards from the local area.[38] His contribution is a particularly striking example of the inside collusion which was becoming typical throughout maquis country in shops, depots, and, above all, *mairies*.

It was to the escalating thefts of ration tickets that Vichy turned after its concern for the Chantiers and their supply depots. In mid-December the regional Intendant of Police at Montpellier, Marty, wrote a memorandum to the Prefect detailing the haphazard way in which ration tickets were delivered, kept, and distributed in the Cévennes, the area Marty was personally determined to penetrate and purge in order to demonstrate to the German forces at Alès and Mende the equal resolution of the French police under his command. At Florac, he stated, tickets were carried by an unarmed employee of the *mairie* to and from his home; at Bassurels they were locked in a cupboard in the *mairie*, and although two gendarmes were present at their distribution, the postal worker who delivered them to the *mairie* was unarmed; at Moissac they were taken by the unarmed mayor from an unarmed postal worker and kept initially in his bedroom, and in these and other communes the monthly process of distribution took several days due to the widely dispersed population. Marty recommended more

[36] See Ch. 2.
[37] AD Hérault 18W 13, Minister of Interior to regional prefects, 27 Sept. 1944.
[38] Maruéjol and Vielzeuf, *Le Maquis Bir-Hakeim*, 36.

arms and the installation of safes, but his reports clearly suspected the mayors of calculated negligence, since on 12 February 1944 Darnand wrote to the Regional Prefect to remonstrate at the high number of thefts of ration tickets in the region, and to threaten sanctions against mayors whose lax procedures he held to be responsible.[39] Darnand had already noted a few days before that in the old *zone occupée* some thirty *mairies* were attacked every day for ration tickets, so the Prefect in Montpellier was in no way alone in his predicament.[40] He could not easily deploy more gendarmes to guard the tickets, since Marty had already complained that 104 *gardiens de la paix* out of a total of 200 in Montpellier alone were tied up in the protection of tickets for over sixteen days every month, so that the only alternative was to pressurize the mayors themselves.[41] This pressure, from Vichy on one side and the maquis on the other, imposed a necessity on the mayors to initiate any ruse which might cover them from the sanctions threatened by Darnand, and the unpredictable intervention of the Germans. An elaborate scenario was therefore devised to accompany maquis raids, by which officials allowed themselves to be seized and bound and even roughly handled to simulate maltreatment by the maquisards. This became a structural device within maquis activity, designed to achieve maximum protection of the sympathetic mayor, shopkeeper, or guard, and maximum reverberations in the local community from the exaggerated accounts of maquis numbers and arms which the 'assaulted' officials would give.[42]

The reason for calling this artifice structural to the history of the maquis is that it represented a basic form of contract between the armed resistance and the population. It acknowledged that the risks and consequences of a *coup de main* were shared by both the attackers and the attacked; it welcomed the complicity of members of the community in the fundamental provisioning of the maquis without necessarily requiring a full-time commitment from them; and it endorsed the plurality of means by which the Resistance had to be waged, and the disparate skills and positions of authority which had to be safeguarded if they were to be of recurrent use. In so far as it was a stratagem based on camouflage and cover it enlarged the figurative meaning of the word maquis as the undergrowth of people and practices within which the maquisards could effectively operate. In the Lot the persistent thefts of ration tickets came to have a semi-official status: the secretaries at several *mairies* waited regularly at the end of each month for the maquisards to

[39] AD Hérault 18W 13, Darnand to Regional Prefect, 12 Feb. 1944.

[40] AN F7. 14895, note by Darnand on thefts from *mairies*, 31 Jan. 1944.

[41] AD Hérault 18W 13. Thefts of tickets were not only from *mairies*. See e.g. the theft of 25 kilos of tickets from the Chambéry–Albertville train related in Abbé Ploton, *Quatre années de Résistance à Albertville*, 36–7.

[42] Colonel Sarda de Caumont, appointed by the Service National du Maquis to organize the Toulouse region, said that the local leaders of the Chantiers de la Jeunesse often co-operated with raids in this way, offering to be tied up and gagged; AN 72. AJ 63.

come and burgle them.[43] Robert Noireau (Colonel Georges), eventually one of the leaders in the Lot, also claimed that the thefts of cattle were normally staged after the peasants had been paid by the Vichy authorities, but before the cattle were loaded for transportation. The maquis then handed some back to the peasants and some to the local population.[44] On one occasion in the autumn of 1943 the Prefect of the Lot, Loïc Petit, personally appealed to the maquisards to return a stock of baby clothes stolen in a raid on the Red Cross at Cahors along with 8–9 tons of foodstuffs, and the Maquis France, led by Jean-Jacques Chapou, acceded to his request. It was shortly before the brief occupation of Marcilhac by the Maquis France on 11 November, and the population's enthusiasm was in part a response to the group's sensitivity to public opinion. Maquisards and their rural providers in the Lot are adamant that Chapou (Capitaine Philippe) punished any maquisard who stole from the peasantry, and local villagers still distinguish between the genuine maquis and those individuals dubbed 'faux maquisards' who used the situation as a licence to rob and pillage.[45] Certainly the agreed scenarios only occurred when the maquis were known to the villagers and mayors and their cause both understood and supported.

At Durfort in the Cévennes the *mairie* was raided at the end of November 1943, and when questioned on the attack the mayor was said to have replied, 'Well, what about it? They have to eat don't they?' The police took the investigation further but could only substantiate the mayor's excellent record in local affairs and his eminent respectability. The problem they reported was a community one—all the villagers were strongly anti-Vichy and their pastor had already been fined for hiding Jews and giving them false identity cards.[46] The police chief, Marty, from Montpellier discovered for himself just how tangled the undergrowth of persons protecting the maquis could be, when he led a reconnaissance into the Cévennes on 11 February 1944. He reported that the gendarmerie formed the thickest part of the cover. At Saint Germain-de-Calberte, which had featured in almost every report on *réfractaires* and maquisards in the area, he found the gendarmerie unanimous in their denials. To his insistent questioning they answered, 'No maquisards in the whole region. Absolutely nothing to report.' Yet in the neighbouring hamlet of la Fare, wrote Marty to Darnand, the maquisards took so little

[43] AN 72. AJ 157, 'Les Maquis du Lot', post-war report from several different Resistance sources, n.d.

[44] Pierre Bertaux, *Libération de Toulouse et de sa région* (Hachette, 1973), 39–52. See also Robert Noireau (Colonel Georges), *Le Temps des partisans*, 156, where Noireau also claims that after the Liberation 'nombreux furent ceux qui prétendirent soit avoir été pillés, soit avoir égaré les bons de réquisition délivrés par le maquis'.

[45] AN 72. AJ 157, 'Les Maquis du Lot'. The raid was on 17 Oct. 1943. See evidence from Maurice Darnault, 7 Mar. 1991, and Joseph Nodari, 28 Mar. 1991, insisting that Jean-Jacques Chapou was adamant in opposing thefts from individuals.

[46] AD Gard CA 662, report from the Renseignements Généraux to the Prefect, 10 Jan. 1944.

trouble to hide themselves that they had even installed electricity in their camp, rerouting the power lines which served several houses in the vicinity. What specifically enraged him was the overt complicity of one gendarme who was allocated to Marty as a guide. He 'took us by the most roundabout, implausible routes to reach a given objective, and this slowed up our operation considerably, removing the element of surprise which we had intended for our visit'.[47] The personal humiliation suffered by Marty on this occasion helps to explain some of the brutality with which he planned and carried out his return to the area two weeks later.[48]

The maquis *coups de main* for food and other essentials produced a model of relationships between the maquis and the population which cannot easily be labelled either fact or fiction. It sustained the image of tough and resolute groups of fighters 'out there', descending on their chosen objectives in surprise attacks before disappearing back into the woods as mysteriously as they had come. This image gave substance to the adventurous mystique of the outlaw as it was positively rendered in the maquis discourse, and it also provided the mix of fact and fantasy with which Vichy fashioned its negative portrait of the outlaw, as a terrorist victimizing the law-abiding rural society. But as Marty and scores of police in the Renseignements Généraux throughout the south were discovering, the model by itself was inadequate as a representation of reality. Alongside it, or, in more structural terms, underneath it, was the model of the maquis as the armed embodiment of ever-widening popular and rural resistance. From the first places of refuge and the first waves of revolt in 1943 the maquis had been a symptom of 'collective' and 'community' resistance. The words have to be chosen and used with care. 'Community' implies locality and corresponds to the terms 'du coin' and 'du pays', and from the earliest tentative moves into the maquis there were indeed whole villages, hamlets, and valleys committed to maquis action and survival, but where that was not the case the construction and preservation of maquis units still had a 'collective' base within the local population, if only consisting of loosely aggregated individuals providing supplies, in an otherwise unresponsive, or even hostile, environment. The winter months of 1943–4 saw both the outlaw model and the rural resistance model assume greater solidity, and only a subtle and shifting blend of the two, adjusted to the particularities of different regions, could create a realistic image of the maquis in this period. Even as the number and extent of the *coups de main* radically increased, giving credence to the statement in the Lot report that the maquisards were their own providers, at the same time the community and collective structures of the maquis were reinforced, in many instances by the common experience of repression shared by maquis and population alike.

[47] AD Hérault 18W 25. The report is dated 21 Feb. 1944.

[48] See Ch. 5.

Human undergrowth or infrastructure, 'maquis d'hommes', or 'intendance', the action of people who protected, supported, fed, clothed, and cared for the maquis, intensified and enlarged the popular revolt which had started with STO. The search for the maquis lay, and still lies, through and within these structures, within the fundamental interconnections between the maquisards and the local population. A history of the maquis purely as 'the men in the woods' cannot do justice to the rural revolt. Exposed to the exigencies of winter and the offensive repression and reprisals of both Germans and Vichy, the more or less *ad hoc* arrangements of the summer and autumn crystallized into logistic dependencies. Although no stage of the maquis development is more significant than any other, it is the entrenchment of the winter period that fully established the maquis as an essentially local phenomenon over which many localities expressed some kind of proprietary claim. There was widespread use of the terms 'nos maquis' and 'nos gars' linking parental sentiment to pride in the admixture of local topography, culture, and history of which the maquis experience was comprised. In this sense, during the months from October to the end of February the maquis, however mobile within its region, showed just how rooted it was. In most areas maquisards were forced by the winter to make their descent on sympathetic local farms, or into friendly local villages, a more frequent occurrence. For many this was a temporary return to the bonds of their own homes, for others a new bonding with unknown but willing sympathizers, who were drawn into the orbit of the maquis experience and became subject to its associated risks and dangers. The denser the cover provided by the supportive structures, the more protected was the precise locality and movements of the maquisards, but also the more exposed was the local community to the frustrated vengeance of the repressors.

In the Haut-Limousin, in the area known as la Montagne, with its dense woods and bocage and a thinly scattered population, the plateaux formed a countryside ideal for the mobile maquis units identified with the initiative of Georges Guingouin. Whereas in the summer they could disperse into the woods leaving little trace, in the winter tracks would be left in the snow, and Guingouin counselled an entrenchment in supportive communities such as his own village Saint-Gilles-la-Forêt on the border with the Corrèze, where he established a training camp for his 'shock troops' in the Château de la Ribeyrie, vacated by its owners during the winter, and where the farm, run by the family Dujacques, was a sympathetic home to the maquisards. Throughout January the training in weaponry and tactics was pursued in this inhabited location without infiltration or betrayal, but some 25 km. to the north near the town of Eymoutiers a maquis group occupying the Château de Farsac was betrayed by the château's owner. The group was linked to Guingouin's and was provisioned by the Périgaud family on the château's farm. It was surrounded on 5 February 1944 by SS troops from Limoges, and to three maquis deaths and a large number of injuries was added the deportation of Marcel Périgaud and his mother and the burning of their farm. Most of the population of Eymoutiers attended the funeral of the young maquisards, mounted as an affirmation of local complicity in the culture of the outlaw.[49]

To the south-east of the Limousin in the Haute-Corrèze, Resisters in the towns of Ussel, Neuvic, Égletons, and the village of Lapleau sustained the reduced number of local maquisards in their winter entrenchment after successive waves of repression had decimated the embryonic AS maquis of the area in October and November. The German parachute brigade stationed at Ussel patrolled the neighbouring countryside in force, judging that the villages were mostly committed to supporting the maquis, and that the winter would force those involved more into the open. On 18 December, at the village of Chaveroche, 8 km. above Ussel, they intercepted a group of young men collecting for the maquisards, and an exchange of fire led the Germans to seize five men at random from houses in the village and execute them summarily in the village street. Two of the victims were on a visit from Paris to their uncle, the local mason.[50] In such ways throughout maquis areas the fate of specific villages represents an extension of maquis history beyond the action of the maquisards themselves. When the enemy entered a village hunting for the maquis, the front was where the enemy was, and at Chaveroche and Farsac as in many areas at other times, it was the men and women of the locality as much as the men in the woods who were exposed to attack. The distinctions between home front and fighting front become blurred in the community history of the maquis.

The incursions of German forces, GMR, and Milice into villages known to be sympathetic to the Resistance, placed a particular stress on women villagers who were left to cover for the maquis. The Vichy hunt for men to fill the STO quotas, and the arbitrary German round-ups, left women as the dominant occupiers of public space, such as streets, shops, and railway stations, and the main, or in some areas the only, responders to the knock on the door. The woman at the doorway, and the woman intercepted in the square or street and told to account for the whereabouts of husband, son, brother, or other male villagers, are recurrent images in any reconstruction of the period through memory or archives. In both situations, doorway or street, women had a role for which there was no *école des cadres*, no training encampments, and no traditional store of expertise, beyond the villagers' inherent suspicion and caution towards representatives of urban

[49] Guingouin, *Quatre ans de lutte sur le sol limousin*, 138–52.
[50] Le Moigne and Barbanceys, *Sédentaires, réfractaires et maquisards*, 167.

authority. This role has its history and its sociology, which has yet to be fully researched, but its crucial importance in the structures of cover and provision cannot be overestimated.[51] Police and German troops were significantly delayed, misled, and rerouted on countless occasions by a doorway response, allowing time for documents to be disposed of, for men to leave the village for the forests and hills, or for the network of liaisons to come into operation to warn encampments of the approaching forces. The women villagers or peasant proprietors, managing smallholdings on their own, had to make instant decisions on the possible identities and objectives of men knocking for food, clothing, and shelter. Abbé Ploton in his memoirs of the maquis in the area of Albertville in the Savoie pays homage to the importance of women helpers, 'the anonymous auxiliaries', whose numbers were large and who worked 'unknown and in silence',[52] but the image is too quietistic. Women had shown in their vociferous presence at demonstrations against STO that they were a discomforting force for the authorities, and although women at the doorway and women as providers employed the strategies of silence and discretion to a high degree, their names were well known at local level and their confrontations with the incursive units of Germans and French involved assertiveness as well as evasion. Their pre-eminence as liaison agents was due to their ability to use the relative freedom they possessed to travel confidently through public spaces and across huge distances, and to manipulate the idealized image of women fostered by Vichy's family propaganda and legislation. Shopping baskets and bags, children's necessities and equipment of all kinds, and the proprieties of imminent or recent motherhood, provided a cover for transportation and movement sanctified by the familial and natalist priorities of the regime. But there was nothing automatic or inevitable about women's use of this cover. Like any other strategy of resistance it was a result of choice and decision.

The pioneering work of Madame Marie Granet in interviewing women Resisters after the Liberation resulted in the first emphases on women's role in the collective history of the maquis. At the château and farm of Bordas in the Corrèze, Mlle Sylvie-Anne de la Gueronnière became 'patronne' of local maquisards who established their command post in her property. The farm's produce fed the maquis, but in a region of valleys and woods, where self-sufficiency was high and small-scale stock breeding and rearing, particularly of pigs, was widespread, food was not a great problem. The role and skill of Mlle de la Gueronnière was to front and protect the maquis, whose use of the château involved the storing of arms and supplies parachuted into the region. Constantly questioned on the maquis by police and GMR she successfully stalled their enquiries until a German attack in the spring of

[51] The article by Paula Schwartz, 'Partisanes and Gender Politics in Vichy France', *French Historical Studies*, 16/1 (Spring 1989) is a pioneering step in mapping out areas for this research.
[52] Abbé Ploton, *Quatre années de Résistance à Albertville*, 51.

1944 led to the destruction of the château.[53] The area fell within the organizational region of the Limousin (R5) whose co-ordinator for the Service National du Maquis in 1943 until January 1944 was Georgette Gérard (pseudonym Claude). Her report, given in an interview with Madame Granet in 1950, emphasized the complicity of the local population in feeding and protecting the estimated 5,000 maquisards mobilized by November 1943, and she stated that the *agents de liaison* were often little known to the maquis leaders themselves. Anonymity was a structural necessity at the time, and is not just a product of historical neglect, but the absence of local names and precise locations from her own testimony, whether intentional or not, unfortunately preserved the imprecisions of clandestinity.[54]

The names can be found, but it needs a generation of researchers to put them back into history. A start has been made by certain local historians who are concerned that no one should be omitted. The local history of Raymond Fournier gives a chapter to one of the *agents de liaison* in the Tarn and Aveyron, Michèle Domenech, written in a telegramese style, highlighting action, movement, the rapid heart-beat, and the sharp intake of breath. Her vital and creative achievements led to the formation of structural support for the FTP across the two *départements* in both towns and countryside, and her arrest in September 1943 was one of hundreds experienced by women involved in similar actions throughout France. Her successful escape from a guarded hospital was organized by the Albi FTP and she continued her organization of the comités féminins into the spring and summer of 1944. Hers was a decisive part in sustaining FTP activity, and her *points d'appui* and networks featured Madame Carrel, Maria Lacan, and Paulette Calpéma in Rodez, Madeleine Capus in the coal-mining area of Decazeville, which nurtured large numbers of FTP and maquisards, and Yvonne Maraville who eventually became the departmental secretary of the Union des Femmes Françaises (UFF), the women's movement from the time of the Paris Commune of 1871, relaunched by the Communist Party as a broad front for Resistance women in 1944.[55] With a more measured style, but similar concern, Le Moigne and Barbanceys have produced an account of the Haute-Corrèze, which successfully recreates the community history of the maquis by allowing the structures of support to be seen as no less inventive and adventurous than the exploits of the maquisards themselves. The concerted move by Germans and Miliciens against the Corrèze maquis in October and November 1943 threw the role of women into sharp relief. At Ussel the leading organizer of the AS, Louis Le Moigne, was hiding a

[53] AN 72. AJ 112. Evidence from Mlle Sylvie-Anne de la Gueronnière collected by Marie Granet, 25 Feb. 1950.

[54] AN 72. AJ 63. Evidence from Madame Georgette Gérard (Claude) collected by Marie Granet, 31 Jan. 1950.

[55] Fournier, *Terre de combat*, 49–60, and evidence from Raymond Fournier, 23 Mar. 1982.

number of ration cards destined for the maquis when the Gestapo raided his house. In his absence his mother-in-law, Madame le Bars, successfully prolonged an intense interrogation, while the *femme de ménage* stowed the documents in a shopping bag, filled it with potatoes and sent it out of the house with Nicole, Le Moigne's 9-year-old daughter, who hid them in a nearby meadow. Madame le Bars was taken to the *mairie* for further questioning but revealed nothing, while Le Moigne was safely elsewhere in the town, and Madame Le Moigne, who had gone to Tulle, was alerted to the Gestapo's raid by a woman friend meeting her at the station. On the same day the Gestapo raids in the neighbouring town of Neuvic forced the Monéger family to leave the area. The family had sustained local maquisards throughout the summer. It was Suzanne Monéger who had said in the spring of 1943, 'We've got to prevent our young men from being taken; we're going to start a maquis. Will you help us feed them?' She was speaking to Madame Deprund, the local butcher who was running the shop in her husband's absence as a prisoner of war. Madame Deprund became involved.[56] The event was typical of thousands, as indeed was the courage shown by Madame Reynier of Crest in the Drôme, in the face of Milice brutality, recounted by Francis Cammaerts in his oral evidence.[57]

Another local history, of the Maquis Paul Claie and the AS of the sud-Aveyron, goes further than most maquis histories by giving a number of potted biographies of women Resisters alongside those of the maquisards. The brief portraits are prefaced by Odette Bessières, the 'responsable départementale' of the Service Social de la Résistance, which was constituted officially in the struggles of the Liberation, but represented work done with the families of *réfractaires*, maquisards, political and racial victims, deportees, and all others caught up in the sacrifices demanded of Resisters, which had started as early as Resistance itself. Odette Bessières herself had been organizing hide-outs for those persecuted for political or racial reasons well before 1943. Her tribute to her fellow women Resisters emphasizes both the fulfilment and the transcendence of gender stereotypes. They waged war, but as women they also 'softened the rigours of warfare': they were soldiers, and 'I saw the gleam in your eyes of fierce resolution and unshakeable will'.[58] Unlike the Yugoslav partisans there were very few women who fought in

[56] Le Moigne and Barbanceys, *Sédentaires, réfractaires et maquisards*, 162–3.

[57] See Ch. 7, Oral Memories.

[58] Henri Barthes, *Histoire de l'Armée Secrète du Sud-Aveyron et le Maquis Paul Claie* (Bardou: Espéraza, 1988), no pagination. The book has an additional title, *Moïse ne savait pas nager. De Roquefort à Montpellier.* It is yet another example of excellent local work using oral and written memoirs, photographs, and maps. Another local work which devotes a full chapter to women Resisters, giving a number of oral recollections, is Paul Billat, *Levés à l'aube de la Résistance dauphinoise*, 50–62. The women featured are: Irma Naime, Marguerite Monval, Claudine Scorzione, Germaine Vallier, Yvonne Bontoux, Monique Rolland, Suzanne Paillard-Boyer, and Simone Ortolland.

the French maquis, but liaison work and the organization of shelter and supplies put women at the nerve-centre of the growth and development of the maquis. By linking maquis camps not just to the Resistance structures of command but also to the local people in farms, villages, and towns, they personified the community nature of the maquis, to the point where many maquisards remember women rather than other men as the epitome of what they mean by 'local' Resistance. Odette Belot, a hotelier at Saint-Pons in the Hérault just east of the Montagne Noire, was seen in this way as the 'patronne de la Résistance locale', and references to women who were known as the local 'mère du maquis' abound. Madame Teulon, who kept a grocery in the village of Valleraugue in the Cévennes, sheltered the local leader of the Maquis d'Ardaillès, Pastor Olivès, for three months after the devastating German attack at the end of February 1944, while continuing to supply the maquis with provisions secured by ration cards given to her clandestinely by the *mairie*. Here is one action among many evocatively presented in memoirs by Janet Teissier du Cros, a young Scotswoman with three small children, who became actively involved in support for the maquis in the locality of the massif de l'Aigoual. There are few memoirs of the period which so effectively recreate the intricate patterns of private and public life in the period of the maquis. Although the maquisards in these valleys and villages of the Cévennes are clearly portrayed as men with lorries, guns, and grenades, she vividly captures the enabling power of bicycles, food, shelter, local information, and above all the tenacity of Resistance conviction, which led many women to choose to be at the centre of the community history of the maquis.[59]

It might be argued that all the acknowledgements made by maquisards of the essential role of women merely tends to camouflage the traditional separation of men, as the activists and the fighters, from women, as the carers and providers. But while this is true of many, if not most, maquis accounts, it needs to be remembered that many maquisards in the woods experienced the same kind of anxiety for their womenfolk exposed to German reprisals as women traditionally felt for the fighting men at the front. For example, the Occitan poet Max Allier, who was not a combatant, but on several occasions took to the woods with the maquis in the Cévennes, was under no illusion that his wife left in the village was the one exposed to the enemy.[60] In addition maquisards knew that women *agents de liaison*

[59] Janet Teissier du Cros, *Divided Loyalties: A Scotswoman in Occupied France* (Canongate: Edinburgh, 1992), 280–322. This book was originally published in 1962, and I am greatly indebted to Amanda Mackenzie Stuart for introducing me to it when she was writing a film script based on the experiences of Janet Teissier du Cros. The tribute to Odette Belot in Saint-Pons came from Armand Calas and Dr Joseph Bec, 18 June 1991, while Maurice Darnault referred to Élizabeth Roques as 'la mère du maquis' in Loubejac in the Lot, 7 Mar. 1991.

[60] Evidence from Max and Madame Allier, 26 Mar. 1982.

were not only an infrastructure of communication, helping to prop up and service their activity: they also knew that the work brought a degree of knowledge, a scale of mobility, and a level of danger, which gave many women an activist status conventionally credited only to men. Joseph Rohr, a maquisard in the Lot, speaks of Simone Selves, the ubiquitous liaison agent in the area of Figeac, Gramat, and Saint-Céré, as the embodiment of all that was heroic and adventurous in the maquis.[61] Such perspectives carry an egalitarian force in the history of Resistance, challenging initial gender assumptions. They cannot be said to have brought substantial changes in sexual politics within French society, even though the women's vote in 1945 appeared briefly to hold out some promise in that direction, but it would be a misrepresentation of a great deal of oral evidence to ignore the felt equality between women and men Resisters expressed in many *témoignages*.[62] The main problem in overcoming the imbalance in historical accounts that still exists is that many women's choices under the Occupation are so often held to be natural and unexceptional that they are denied the quality of a historical decision, heavy in consequences, that is given to a man's choice to take to the maquis.

The search for the maquis, then and now, reveals much about the 'unexceptional', or the daily norms of rural 'vie quotidienne', but at the same time it is a process which questions the way in which the concept of daily life is used. The notion of 'vie quotidienne' implies that 'life goes on underneath it all'. That predictability could not be taken for granted under the Occupation, first in the towns and then increasingly in 1943 in the rural areas. To a large extent the concept of daily life in urban and industrialized France had been seen to be threatened well before the war by strong movements of change and disruption, and it was partly, if not mainly, as a reaction to this supposed 'loss of equilibrium' in the pattern of daily life that the abstract and mythologized images of rural existence as harmony, peace, and continuity were proliferated between the wars. Not all is discourse in the construction of *mentalités*, but the discourse of 'la terre' as a paradigm for an authentic France was unusually powerful in the formation of both Pétainism and the *mentalités* of Vichy État, carrying with it unquestioning assumptions about the unchanging nature of the peasantry. Well before the imposition of STO, reports from all areas of France, from prefects and Renseignements Généraux, were showing just how much the economic values of the peasantry were impinging on these abstract idealizations, and throughout 1943 the adjustments to the Vichy ideal saw the re-emergence

[61] Evidence from Joseph Rohr, 3 Apr. 1991.

[62] For example, evidence from Françoise Maury, 24 June 1982, Simone Conquet, 22 Mar. 1991, and Yvonne Cormeau, 22 Jan. 1991. For an original local study of women, based mainly on extensive oral evidence, see Hanna Diamond, 'Women's Experience During and After World War Two in the Haute-Garonne, 1939–1948: Choices and Constraints' (University of Sussex D.Phil. thesis, 1992).

of much older urban prejudices about the egoism, insularity, and stubbornness of the peasant, but still couched in the language of permanence, continuity, and predictability. It is into this imagined community of undisturbed tranquillity, on the one hand, and grasping self-centredness on the other, that the maquis experience is often set, or indeed into which many *réfractaires* or Resisters from the towns believed they had arrived. Those who were responsive to the real communities in which they found themselves discovered a much greater unpredictability and a much more fractured daily life than they had been led to expect, and it is something of that agitated quality of rural life in 1943–4 that a study of the maquis experience must evoke.

An account of a conventional hunt that mentioned only hunters and hunted would be guilty of neglecting its effect on the countryside through which it passed, an effect which could vary from negligible to devastating. The hunt for *réfractaires* and maquisards, which broke all conventions, and the inverted hunt which turned the tables on the pursuing authorities, brought effects which were rarely negligible, and from December 1943 onwards varied only at one end of the scale, between considerable and catastrophic. The dislocation to patterns of everyday life could come from a road-block or identity check, producing panic and anxiety, or from indiscriminate reprisals plunging whole communities into terror and tragedy. But whatever the scale of disturbance which the dual presence of maquis and repressive forces brought to a specific area, dislocations were already by the end of 1943 a significant aspect of rural experience due to shifting combinations of labour shortages and economic restrictions, controls, and evasions.

A profitable return to atavistic habits was how many prefects described the adjustments made by the peasantry, and this was how many urban people perceived it. An unpredictable economy oscillating between crippling government interference, which had to be resisted, and alternative markets, which had to be explored, was how most peasants experienced it. A combination of untroubled productivity and high profit was extremely rare, though inhabitants of towns, where shortages were acute, could be excused for imagining that this was everyday rural life. Where their analysis was correct was in the fact that the producers of food were indeed intent on keeping the prices high, by avoiding market controls wherever possible. This very process kept the peasantry in a state of defiance, illegality, and nervousness, which organizers of *réfractaires* and maquisards were able to use to their advantage. They realized during the summer and harvest period of 1943 that peasants who were prepared to alleviate their labour problems by taking on *réfractaires* or hiding food had taken a critical first step in the direction of the outlaw culture. The maquis were less hampered by abstract notions of the peasantry, whether idealized or prejudiced, than the Vichy authorities. They showed a bargaining strength which exploited the peasantry's hostility to Vichy and German requisitions and profited from the breakdown of controls.

Statutory food prices, enforced by Vichy *collecteurs*, were acknowledged by prefects throughout 1943 as universally unacceptable to the peasantry, and it was argued by some that the peasants, no less than the urban population, were affected by expectations of an imminent landing and an end to the war, making them even more 'unwilling to surrender goods to the Ravitaillement Général which they believe will soon be dismantled'.[63] The local Corporation Paysanne, complained the Prefect of the Dordogne, was defending the interests of the peasantry and failing to give the administration the support it needed. An article he quoted from *L'Agriculteur du Périgord* stated, 'They speak to us of our duties . . . let them pay more attention to our rights,' and the Prefect acknowledged this was symptomatic of peasant attitudes throughout his area.[64] The Prefect of the Haute-Vienne in August 1943 had remonstrated to Vichy that the prices of pork, corn, and poultry were set far too low, with the result that peasants were open to unofficial offers from individuals,[65] and at some stage in the summer and autumn most other prefects made similar points. In the Dordogne the statutory price for a kilo of potatoes stood at 2 fr. 20 in October 1943 whereas black market prices reached an astronomical 15 fr., and peasants were either selling to individuals at retail level, or to companies from outside their *département*. The Prefect said he was trying to stop this, but it was impossible to put 'an inspector behind every peasant's door and to place a gendarme at every fork in the road'.[66]

The growing presence of even a poorly armed maquis in the countryside did, however, make an alternative, outlaw system of regulation and control a possibility, and in the Limousin this had already been initiated by Georges Guingouin during the summer of 1943. In the hills and forests south-west of Eymoutiers, the maquisards 'allowed' the peasants to charge higher prices than those imposed by Vichy, but combined this incentive with threats of punishment if the producers demanded prices that went even higher. Lists of these maquis-controlled prices were fly-posted on walls and trees in the villages near Saint-Gilles-la-Forêt and signed 'Le Préfet du Maquis', a title written in Guingouin's own handwriting which, he asserts, was immediately recognized by the inhabitants of Saint-Gilles as belonging to the ex-*instituteur* and 'secrétaire de mairie'.[67] The posters, and individual letters sent to producers who contravened the regulated prices, bore the heading 'Armée

[63] AN F1C III. 1151, Dordogne, report of 27 Sept. 1943.
[64] Ibid.
[65] AN F1C III. 1197, Haute-Vienne, report of 6 Aug. 1943.
[66] AN F1C III. 1151, Dordogne, report of 27 Sept. 1943.
[67] Guingouin, *Quatre ans de lutte sur le sol limousin*, 106.

Nationale des Francs-Tireurs et Partisans' and declared that any fines exacted would go to the Resistance. News of these outlaw controls was carried inadvertently by the regional daily paper *Le Courrier du Centre* on 5/6 December 1943, and prefectoral reports for the Haute-Vienne and its neighbouring *départements*, Corrèze and Dordogne, all highlight the mixture of fear, respect, and enthusiasm with which the peasantry and the inhabitants of small towns were responding to the maquis threats and subversion. The Prefect of the Haute-Vienne referred to the emergence of a 'Préfet du Bois' in two villages north of Limoges, some distance from the centre of Guingouin's operations, and he also reported that a 'bande de terroristes' calling themselves 'Groupe des Rhinocéros' visited nine communes in the area of Eymoutiers during December and told the *maire* and the *adjoint* in each to resign. All did so.[68] These details testify to the strength of Guingouin's maquis groups in the area, which had taken names of wild animals as an operational code, Ours, Tigres, Loups, Lions, Éléphants, Pumas, and Rhinocéros.[69] The effect of their threats, persuasion, and protective activities was to make the smooth running of Vichy administration an impossibility: the population had become irrevocably enmeshed in the networks of alternative power. The Prefect of the Dordogne suggested a state of anarchy with his conclusion at the end of November that 'no one trusts anyone or anything any longer',[70] but in December it is much clearer to the authorities in Périgueux that what was happening was less a total collapse of all authority than a transfer of power from Vichy to the maquisards. Two examples were given of the loyalty which the maquis now inspired. At Terrasson 150 people witnessed a theft of ration tickets, but refused to give the gendarmes any details of the car used in the operation, and at la Coquille the population stood by and applauded a group involved in a similar theft. It may have been a sign of some sympathy for popular protective action when the Prefect went on to announce that he himself was stopping all exports of potatoes to other *départements* after a weak crop, threats to collectors, and intransigeance by the Corporation Paysanne had led to the collection of only 5,000 tons out of the imposition of 14,000.[71] This is just one of many indications that the peasantry, whether threatened by the maquis or not, were successfully undermining the impositions of the Ravitaillement Général. Peasants needed little persuasion from anyone else to claim that the bulk of the impositions at the low, authorized prices were

[68] AN F1C III. 1197, Haute-Vienne, reports of 12 Dec. 1943, 17 Feb. 1944.

[69] Guingouin, *Quatre ans de lutte sur le sol limousin*, 104–6.

[70] AN F1C III. 1151, Dordogne, report of 29 Nov. 1943. Compare the Prefect's report of Jan. 1944 from the Corrèze which stated, 'La population des campagnes vit dans une atmosphère de crainte et a perdu toute confiance dans les forces de police . . . Néanmoins il est certain que la majorité des bandes qui tiennent le "maquis" ont la sympathie de la plus grande partie de la population.' AN F1C III. 1147.

[71] AN F1C III. 1151, Dordogne, report of 31 Jan. 1944.

intended for Germany: for well over a year they had justified their non-co-operation with the regime on these grounds.[72]

It was through a positive understanding and encouragement of this peasant recalcitrance that most maquis groups imposed their prices and made their own requisitions. Where Vichy called the non-co-operation peasant egoism and greed, the maquis were prepared to call it patriotism, though few maquis groups could divorce themselves entirely from the suspicion of peasant motivations, rife in most of the towns. Abbé Chipier was attached to FTP groups in the Haute-Savoie, with their urban base at Thonon-les-Bains on Lac Léman and rural refuge in the hinterland of the Chablais hills, and after the war he wrote that *ravitaillement* was always a problem, though, improbable as it seemed to him at the time, the Service de Renseignements of the FTP at Thonon received a regular and sizeable supply of ration tickets directly from someone in the Vichy *ravitaillement* office at Annecy. Peasants themselves, he said,

> often keep their heart and their purse very close to each other; but the FTP introduced them to the larger issues. The FTP decided on the prices to be regulated and posted them in public places. But would the peasants obey? The maquis were in close surveillance, in the thick of the markets, under the inquisitorial eye of the Germans. If a peasant demanded prices above those agreed we 'pinched' his goods and a maquis van stood by to carry away this fine imposed on the recalcitrants.

By similar means they exacted meat from farmers who were hoarding stocks, and made sure that threshing-machines got to farms where they were needed. In short, he concluded, 'the maquisards acted as police, and the Germans never understood a thing'.[73] By the end of the winter, the same tactics were being widely employed throughout FTP territory. A tract fixed to walls to the north of Alès in March 1944 in the Cévennes, where the small FTP camps were numerous, stated that the Resistance did not wish to suppress the black market, only to make it accessible to all. Appealing to the patriotism and goodwill of the peasants it requested them to keep to the prices which were listed on the tract and then added, 'Uncooperative sellers and buyers will be unmasked and severely punished. In the case of serious offenders, and all second offenders, we will not hesitate to destroy their entire livelihood.' The tract was signed 'La France Combattante' and in the list of goods and prices that followed, various stipulations were made, notably that all milk, at 8 fr. a litre, was to be strictly reserved for children and people who were ill and on no account was to be skimmed of its cream. This item alone testified to the intention of the local maquis

[72] Evidence from Henri Cordesse, 5 Apr. 1982.

[73] Abbé Étienne Chipier, *Souffrances et gloires du maquis chablaisien* (Reflets de Notre Temps: Thonon-les-Bains, 1946), 43–4.

to operate the controls on behalf of all the population and not just for its own benefit.[74]

According to Lucien Seince, a maquisard with the AS Maquis de Sérandon in the Haute-Corrèze, the maquis controls became legendary overnight. Like Guingouin's FTP they too used the term 'Préfecture du Maquis' on their posters announcing the controls. Immediate rumours abounded over their authorship, including assertions that at least nineteen heavily armed maquisards had put up the posters, whereas it was Seince, accompanied by two others, with one pistol between them, who were in fact responsible. He also claimed that the controls were always more effective than Vichy's own.[75]

The whole process of unofficial controls, which liberated peasants from Vichy prices but subjected them to those prescribed by the maquis, was at worst a fraught and embattled relationship but more normally a mutual acceptance of essential needs. The maquisards clearly needed food but they also needed to impose themselves and to assert their outlaw identity: peasants clearly needed to sell their produce but they also needed to demonstrate their obdurate self-determination. Pierre Laborie, historian of public opinion, notably in the Lot, has succinctly expressed this sense of obduracy: 'If ordinary peasants are attracted by order, they are at the same time, and contradictorily, fascinated by ways of bypassing the rules, their ideal being to obey only those laws with which they agree.'[76] The maquis broke the rules, undermined the order of Vichy, sabotaged the German war economy and communications, and in places redistributed the food and livestock they had liberated from German supply trains or Vichy depots. Their action in the countryside was in many cases a combative variant on the model of peasant autonomy, which Vichy doctrine had etherealized, but which the maquis recognized as an earthy assertiveness which could be mobilized in common practices of revolt. Historically speaking, the maquis discovered for themselves the practices which had last been widely deployed in the years of counter-revolutionary protest at the end of the eighteenth century, when bands of deserters from the Jacobin armies roamed much the same countryside in the south, and sought to establish an alternative power base and authority of their own. As Colin Lucas has concisely argued, 'We are . . . immediately brought to the question of whether this counter-jacobin youth was accomplishing traditional tasks of regulation in the local community.'[77] The same question can be asked of the maquis, and in both cases the answer is affirmative. Across 150 years the causes were profoundly different, but the

[74] AD Gard CA 328.

[75] Le Moigne and Barbanceys, *Sédentaires, réfractaires et maquisards*, 81.

[76] Pierre Laborie, 'Les Maquis dans la population', in *Colloque sur les maquis*, 44. This article is rich in original insights and ideas.

[77] Colin Lucas, 'Themes in Southern Violence after 9 Thermidor', in Gwynne Lewis and Colin Lucas (eds.), *Beyond the Terror* (CUP: Cambridge, 1983), 173.

mechanisms remarkably similar. The 'traditional tasks of regulation' assumed by the maquis were to grow substantially by the summer of 1944. Already in 1943–4 they signified a social as well as a military purpose to which rural communities were responsive.

In this assumption of regulatory powers, not all the relationships between the maquis and peasant producers were based on mutual needs. Maquis imposition outran the tolerance of the peasantry when sabotage of Vichy and German requisitions involved destruction of farm machinery, even though such destruction was rarely arbitrary. Binders and threshing-machines were widely used under Vichy supervision, and a high percentage of the hay bales or threshed corn immediately sequestrated by the Ravitaillement Général. Peasants were officially instructed to bring all their hay or corn to be controlled in this way, and in the Limousin Guingouin argued that the destruction of a common baler or threshing-machine would allow the peasant producers to conserve their produce. On 9 August 1943 in five different communes, close to Eymoutiers and Saint-Léonard-de-Noblat, five threshing-machines were destroyed by dynamite, and Guingouin concludes by claiming a dramatic decline in Vichy and German requisitions from the area.[78] The actions announced an unsentimental resolution to carry out any sabotage that could harm the enemy, with consideration of its effect on the rural population of secondary importance. In this case Guingouin believed he had peasant support, but evidence from postal censorship and oral *témoignage* throughout the southern zone suggests that this particular form of action, which disrupted the essential rhythms of harvesting and production, did little to promote the maquis as a protective presence in the countryside.

The Renseignements Généraux for the Languedoc region regularly emphasized that peasant sympathy for the maquis stopped abruptly at the point where destruction of harvests began, particularly where crops had been burned. Such acts were accredited more to 'malfaiteurs' than to the Resistance, but the image of the maquis invariably suffered by association.[79] Motions passed in meetings of food and wine producers called on the authorities to mount a guard on the harvests, under the law of 5 April 1884 empowering mayors with the right to appoint *gardes messiers* to protect rural communities from marauders. In the Lozère it was stipulated that such guards should come from peasants loyal to the regime, and the government-sponsored Propagande Paysanne expected them to be armed. A Vichy decree had made the retention of hunting guns illegal, except in regulated cases, but it was no secret that very few peasants had complied with the order, and it was now tacitly agreed that their own guns could be used by the *gardes messiers* or, if they had surrendered them, they should approach the

[78] Guingouin, *Quatre ans de lutte sur le sol limousin*, 90–1.

[79] AD Hérault 172W 4, Bulletins hebdomadaires de Renseignements, 11–17 Oct. and 25–31 Oct. 1943.

mayor and prefect for replacements.[80] The proposals remained largely at the notional stage. It was quickly learned by Vichy that any arms entrusted to such guards in country districts would merely provide easy prey for the maquis, who were already disarming railway and communication guards as well as the security officials who accompanied money transfers and the distribution of ration tickets.

The justification for sabotage of farm machinery was identical to justifications given for actions which disrupted the rhythms of industrial production or the railway system, all of which inevitably threatened as many livelihoods, in terms of lost work and wages, as the destruction of agricultural plant. Guingouin, who had been the *instituteur* of a small rural commune and knew his peasant environment, was knowingly stretching the limits of local support and tolerance. The dilemma of balancing hardship suffered by the French against damage inflicted on the Germans was present in all sabotage. It was because of the essentialism attached to agricultural production, as providing the most basic necessities of survival, that the dilemma seemed greater and the hardship less acceptable where the destruction of farm machinery was involved. The apparent ruthlessness of Guingouin's FTP in this respect was nevertheless conditioned by a different form of essentialism. Without the communal threshing-machines some peasants returned to the ancient practice of flailing the corn in their own farmyards, a return which many peasant producers had anticipated in the harvests of 1942 and which Guingouin advocated as a way of keeping the yield of the harvests away from the main itineraries of the Vichy inspectorate. The maquis latched on to these primitive forms of a rural economy, and in many places connived at illicit practices such as hidden distilleries, entering into a covert form of partnership to outwit the forces of control and occupation.

The authorities were very aware of the potential that these acts carried, creating, as the Prefect of the Tarn commented, 'a dangerous revolutionary climate which could have huge consequences'.[81] In the Languedoc area the weekly bulletins from the Renseignements Généraux in the rural areas show a swing of peasant support behind the maquis in January and February 1944, after disillusioned hopes of an Allied invasion, and hostility to maquis threats to the harvests, had brought a drop in sympathy in the last two months of 1943. Three factors were adduced to account for this change. First, there was widespread condemnation of the appointment of Darnand as Secrétaire-Général au Maintien de l'Ordre and growing resentment at the power of the Milice. It was the Milice which was increasingly accused of being the real terrorists, a sign that the maquis assertions that real justice lay outside the law was growing in acceptability. Secondly, young agricultural workers

[80] AD Lozère R 7244; 'Propagande Paysanne' (Summer 1943).
[81] AN F1C III. 1193, Tarn, report of 30 Sept. 1943.

of *classes* 1943–4 received a summons to STO medicals at the end of December, and thirdly, at the end of January, rural workers of *classes* 1940–1 were called on to serve for three months in Organisation Todt under revised STO legislation. These reports stop short of declaring that the peasantry was now an oppositional force, but at the very least they indicated a turbulence in the everyday life of rural society, which must be seen as the context as well as the effect of the maquis presence.[82]

The dependence of the maquis on peasant collusion was sharpened by the exposure of winter and the ravages of repression. Smoke could be seen more easily, tracks were left in the snow, and the more frequent descent of maquisards into the villages heightened the risks of chance encounter with the authorities. The lorries, which had become an integral part of maquis activity and were mostly powered by *gazogène*, were more prone to break down in the wintry conditions. All of these factors adversely affected the mobility of the maquis on which survival was based. They equally underlined the range of community resources which the maquis needed to enlist, including the skills of garage mechanics, mountain guides, experts to tap into telephone lines, and medical expertise. In the earliest maquis structures certain categories of resource were already prominent, especially the knowledge, leadership, and contacts of *instituteurs* and *institutrices*. Schoolteachers were, in fact, pivotal to many maquis organizations and activities. The men were frequently of officer status in the Reserve, and had the military knowledge which 20-year-old *réfractaires* lacked, and many were *adjoints* to the mayor, with access to official stamps and documentation: the women bore the brunt of the educational and often pastoral needs of the community during the Occupation, and many possessed medical skills. Both men and women teachers often knew the local countryside intimately, but also had knowledge of urban culture and practices. Many cycled long distances and were keen walkers or mountaineers. Above all, they had, only recently, taught most of the local men who were eligible for STO, and were often the first sympathetic authority to whom the men turned for advice and help when confronted with the dilemma of submission or *défaillance*. By August 1943 the *instituteur* Gustave Causse of Bédouès in the canton of Florac, at the Lozère end of the Corniche des Cévennes, had helped the local AS to place and recruit over thirty *réfractaires* or immigrant workers on the run. Of those who were French the vast majority were agricultural workers from nearby communes and all except four had been pupils at his own school of Bédouès, or at neighbouring schools in Cocurès, Ruas, and Florac. Initially he registered incoming recruits at the *mairie* as woodcutters attached to a lumber camp, and in the winter of 1943–4 he developed links with the FTP.

[82] AD Hérault 172W 4, weekly bulletins of the Renseignements Généraux. Compare AN F1C III. 1143, Bouches-du-Rhône, report of 3 Feb. 1944, which specifies the hostility of peasants to the OT requirements.

His daughter, who was at school in Mende, became a regular liaison between the Cévennes and the *chef-lieu*.[83] At the Gard end of the Corniche, Monsieur Lapierre, ex-schoolteacher at Tornac and retired at Saint-Jean-du-Gard, received requests from 'une quantité d'anciens élèves' for refuge and work in the months between STO and the tragedy at Aire-de-Côte on 1 July 1943. The deaths and deportations which occurred stunned the Cévennes, he reported, but strengthened the Resistance of the Vallée Borgne and the Vallée Française where his old pupils and recruits to the maquis were welcomed by the inhabitants of Saint-Etienne, Sainte-Croix, and Saint-Germain-de-Calberte. During the winter of 1943–4 some 300 *réfractaires* found refuge in this region. Each commune had its organizational leader and was subdivided into *quartiers*, each with its own head. A meeting was held every fortnight and liaisons were so well entrenched that within two hours all the isolated individuals, sheltered or working in different farms, could be brought together for action or dispersed into the woods. Monsieur Lafont, the Mayor of Saint-Etienne, placed a large disused farm, la Picharlerie, at his disposal, where the maquisards created their sleeping quarters and where a training camp was established. As for money, he said, it came from M. Régis, Directeur du contrôle économique at Nîmes who turned over the bulk of fines levied on black marketeers to a special maquis account.[84] The hunt for 'wanted' schoolteachers Joseph Huber and Louis Veylet obsessed the Lozère police in the summer and autumn of 1943. Huber, a teacher at Saint-Chély-d'Apcher, was accused of fabricating identities for *réfractaires*, while Veylet, a teacher from the Seine-et-Oise who had come to his parents' house at Marvejols, was listed by the police as an active communist, using sports organizations to recruit Resisters, and was believed to have been at Chambon-le-Château at the time of the escape of communists from the prison of Le Puy.[85]

At Marvejols further south Marcel Pierrel, a teacher of German at the Cours Complémentaire, and the *instituteur* Henri Cordesse worked closely with Huber and Veylet in all aspects of Resistance organization and the hiding of Jews throughout 1943. One of their early operations had been the installation of a camp at Bonnecombe on the Aubrac plateau, made up of anti-Nazi German workers.[86] None of these workers could speak French, so that the linguistic skills of Huber and Pierrel were critical. Pierrel was arrested by the Germans in the summer of 1943 and deported, but Veylet, closely pursued by the French, accompanied the German workers into the

[83] AD Lozère T 5880. 'La Résistance dans la commune de Bédouès', handwritten report by Gustave Causse, 4 Dec. 1947.
[84] AN 72. AJ 124, M. Lapierre. 'Rapport sur la formation des maquis des vallées Borgne et Française (Gard)'.
[85] AD Lozère R 7049, reports by Rispoli, 1 Oct., 3 Nov. 1943.
[86] See Ch. 2.

Cévennes where they formed a maquis under the leadership of François Rouan. Veylet was killed in the spring of 1944 during a German incursion into the area.[87] Other skills possessed by many primary teachers included a basic medical knowledge vital to the maquis. In the hills of the Margeride in the north of the Lozère, the maquis under the leadership of Ernest Peytavin relied heavily on the medical skills and ancillary care of *institutrices* Madame Chabanier at Chaulhac, Mlle St Leger at Fenestre, Madame Boyer at Chantejals, and the *instituteur* Monsieur Galvier and his wife at Albaret-Sainte-Marie.[88]

In the Aveyron, in the area of the small textile town of Saint-Affrique, the *instituteur* Raymond Fournier claimed that schoolteachers formed the most reliable network of support and involvement in the lives and actions of the maquis. It was possible to hide in one commune after another purely due to these professional connections. It was Mlle Salvignol, directrice of the Cours Complémentaire de jeunes filles in Saint-Affrique who first helped him to escape from STO and he was initially hidden by his sister, *institutrice* at Salelles. In what he called the 'terrain du maquis' west of Saint-Affrique where the FTP dominated the hills on the border with the Tarn, the *instituteur* or *institutrice* was at the centre of the maquis support structures in almost every village, notably at Montclar where the socialist influence of *instituteur* Ralland Caumes had carried the commune to the political Left just before the war, and at Plaisance and Saint-Sernin, where the animators of the Front National were both teachers, Monsieur Soudain and Monsieur Arnal.[89]

Schoolteachers proliferate in the maquis structures of the Aude, chronicled by Lucien Maury. He himself was a teacher at Lescale, and Françoise Maury, his wife, taught at Puivert. She said that 'the role of women was equal to that of men' and she herself concocted improvised codes for maquis liaisons, when the Maquis de Picaussel began to receive parachute drops and went into combative action.[90] The *institutrice* at Arcambal in the Lot, C. Brunet, left a report after the war, whose tribute to the propriétaire Marie Pouget we have already quoted, but unlike most other schoolteachers in the Lot who have commented on rural opinion, she was not inclined to represent it as favourable. With the exception of the Pouget farm she found 'the majority of the population indifferent or even hostile to the maquis'.[91] That was in the early stages of maquis formation, a time when the teacher Henri Cordesse in the AS at Marvejols in the Haute-Lozère encountered very

[87] Cordesse, *Histoire de la Résistance en Lozère*, 52–3; Joutard *et al.*, *Cévennes, terre de refuge*, 91–4; Éveline et Yvan Brès, *Un Maquis d'antifascistes allemands en France, 1942–1944* (Presses du Languedoc: Montpellier, 1987).

[88] AN 72. AJ 159, Colonel Peytavin (Ernest), 'Rapport de la Résistance active dans le département de la Lozère'.

[89] Fournier, *Terre de combat*, 218–25, and evidence from Raymond Fournier, 23 Mar. 1982.

[90] Evidence from Lucien and Françoise Maury, 24 June 1982.

[91] AN 72. AJ 157, C. Brunet, 'Vie des maquis dans la commune d'Arcambal', 6 Jan. 1950.

considerable hostility from the rural population of the area who were responsive to the Vichy notables and strongly influenced by the Bishop of Mende, Mgr. Auvity, who had thrown his episcopal weight behind obedience to STO. But even here there were knots of republicanism and secularism within the *petits paysans* and by the winter of 1943–4 they were winning over many of their neighbours. Realism had changed sides.[92]

The pressure of changing circumstances after STO also affected the village clergy and dramatized their position as confidants in the private world of their parishioners. Their ease of circulation made them prominent in public places; they had conventional freedom of access to homes in both towns and countryside, and they had greater immunity than other men from search or inspection either in the street or in their houses. The sanctity of the cloth, ideologically respectable in Vichy France, could be used as a cover by clergymen no less securely than the sanctity of motherhood by women. The Abbé Alvitre in the Corrèze, Abbé Souiry in the Lot, and Abbé Gauch in the Lot and the Tarn are three of several Resistance *curés* who have waxed lyrical about the *soutane* as a versatile piece of clandestine equipment, both literally and figuratively.[93]

In village after village STO forced the clergy's hand, making it impossible for their moral leadership to avoid entanglement with the barbed issues of submission or *défaillance*. Their shared family origins within the rural community made it highly likely that a younger brother, nephew, or cousin would be among those threatened with labour service in Germany, and their obligation to advise their parishioners or congregation could easily expand into active or tacit collusion with the *réfractaires*. Those who became involved did so in most areas partly because of this lateral identity with the local population. There were many Catholic *curés*, and in percentage terms even more Protestant *pasteurs*, who appeared to submerge their ecclesiastical identities in the secular discourse and exploits of the maquis, though in so doing they also justified their commitment as a religious duty. Pastor Gillier of Mandagout in the Cévennes, where Sabbatarianism and biblical fundamentalism combined with an intense individual sense of godly vocation, began his memoir of the Maquis des Corsaires with the words, 'It is Sunday . . .'. It was 28 July 1943 and the arrival of the first *réfractaires* at his presbytery. By the beginning of November the embryonic maquis had been contacted by Colonel Guillot of the ORA, who began to bring military training and financial help, but Gillier's own pastoral involvement was still important.

Christmas was approaching and my wife and I wanted to bring a little joy into the hearts of our men in the woods . . . Friends brought *saucisson*, cheese, biscuits and a

[92] Evidence from Henri Cordesse, 5 Apr. 1982, and Gilbert de Chambrun, 25 May 1982.

[93] Evidence from Abbé Alvitre, 21 Sept. 1972, in Kedward, *Resistance in Vichy France*, 253–4; evidence from Abbé Gauch, 15 Mar. 1991, and Abbé Souiry, 4 Apr. 1991.

good wine . . . allowing us to gather the men together one evening, round a small fir tree which they provided, for a frugal but joyous Christmas celebration. The day before, two Germans, driven out of their country in 1936 and hidden in a farm at Mandagout, came and spent the evening with us. It wasn't much, that evening; but nevertheless it meant a little joy in everyone's heart.

The familiar Christmas themes of frugality, gifts, and homeless refugees are brought together in this winter festivity, and the word 'joie' figures repeatedly in his whole account, tempered by 'mélancholie' at the eventual integration of the maquis into a conventional fighting unit at the Liberation.[94] The simple language and the unapologetic emotion could represent the attitudes of many of the Protestant community of this area, fulfilling in the acts of refuge and revolt a personal commitment to the religious and political memory of the eighteenth-century Camisards. A Cévenol did not need to be a *pasteur* to feel and react in this way.

The Catholic Abbé Chipier, who worked closely with the FTP in the Chablais region of the Haute-Savoie, explained his motivation in both horizontal and vertical terms: as the son of a small artisan, he shared the class origins of his parishioners, and at the same time 'my spiritual ministry pushed me into it'.[95] Abbé Ploton, who joined Libération (sud) in Albertville in the Savoie and became part of the AS organizing the maquis in the area, was happy to celebrate the *coups de main* of both AS and FTP units, one of which, at Cévins where the FTP stripped the gendarmes of their arms and clothes, he describes in dramatic detail.[96] Abbé Gauch became the 'curé du maquis' in the woods near Carmaux in the Tarn, and testifies to the important role of the Communist Party in shaping the Resistance mentalities of the industrial and agricultural workers in his extended parish. It was his pastoral oversight of scouts and young Catholic peasants which drew him into counselling those eligible for STO into becoming *réfractaires*, and he could not underline more emphatically the essential youthfulness of the maquis.[97] His sorties at night into the woods raised more than the occasional eyebrow among his parishioners, but whereas he used a camouflage of eccentricity to explain his behaviour, the Abbé Cambou further north in the mountainous woods of the Ségala, in the east of the Lot, was an overtly picaresque character, an unapologetic poacher and hunter elementally suited to maquis activity.[98] His good friend, the Abbé Souiry from the neighbouring Ségala parish of Terrou, followed him into the thick of maquis organization, liaison, and combat, and invariably found a gendarme or other figure of authority who would add to the protection afforded by his *soutane* by

[94] Gillier, *Les Corsaires*, 9.
[95] Abbé Étienne Chipier, *Souffrances et gloires du maquis chablaisien*, 17.
[96] Abbé Ploton, *Quatre années de Résistance à Albertville*, 54–5.
[97] Evidence from Abbé Gauch, 15 Mar. 1991.
[98] Evidence from Abbé Souiry, 4 Apr. 1991.

accompanying him respectfully, though often unwittingly, on his clandestine missions. Abbé Souiry's centrality to the life and operations of the Ségala maquis was largely responsible for bringing the village of Terrou to the attention of the Germans, who sacked it in frustration in 1944. He remembers a bottle of his favourite liqueur left inexplicably in his otherwise pillaged and ransacked *presbytère*, but he also recalls the pillaging by certain individuals loosely attached to the maquis and their attempt to hide the loot among his possessions. Vehemently critical of abuses within and by the maquis, whose personality conflicts he knew better than most, he still felt, in 1991, that his memoirs would be too controversial for publication.[99]

The role of a sizeable minority of village clergy underlines the way in which the maquis created an alternative world which stood outside Vichy society, underneath it in subversive imagery, above it in the dimension created by its claim to a higher morality and patriotism. Whether above or below, schoolteachers and parish clergy were well placed to exploit their role as both community conscience and practical resource. If nothing else, schools and churches were places of camouflage. Madame Prades, an *institutrice* in the Hérault, kept grenades in empty desks in her classroom; the Abbé Laire in the Corrèze kept a wireless transmitter in his belfry.[100] This comparability should not obscure the continuing division in certain areas, like the Haute-Lozère, between secular schoolteachers and Catholic clergy which was reanimated by Vichy's piecemeal support for clerical rehabilitation in the educational sector.[101] But wherever the maquis emerged organically from the local population and was constituted mainly of local agricultural and industrial workers, the period between STO and the Liberation saw a unified sense of purpose in which these traditional rivalries lost their force.

Neither in the educational nor the religious sectors did a constituted movement in support of the maquis arise. Teachers and clergy were structural to the maquis as informal networks of individuals. So too were members of the medical profession in the early stages, but, as the maquis evolved, the need for co-ordination of medical care produced two constituted movements. First, in 1943 the Service de Santé de la Résistance (SSR) emerged at national, regional, and departmental levels, with its doctors and surgeons more closely organized during the liberation struggles into the Comité Médical de la Résistance (CMR) attached to the Forces Françaises de l'Intérieur. Secondly, a looser organization known as the Service de Santé des Maquis came into existence, critical of senior doctors who were deemed

[99] Ibid.

[100] Evidence from Madame Prades, 4 Feb. 1982, and Abbé Alvitre, 21 Sept. 1972.

[101] See N. J. Atkin, 'Catholics and Schools in Vichy France, 1940–44' (University of London Ph.D. thesis, 1988).

to be too hesitant in adapting to the irregular life and needs of the maquis. This accusation appeared in a report on the organization after the war in the region of Montpellier by 'Jaubert' who further stated that it was medical students who abandoned their studies and gave themselves to the maquis, students who were rarely older than 25 and who took with them whatever medical supplies they could procure. Eventually, he added, they were well prepared for the battles of the maquis and formed the Service de Santé de l'Armée Française Populaire.[102] The truculent tone of the report was not merely the product of generational asperity. Its suggestion of inflexibility among certain doctors may have underestimated the difficulties of adapting sedentary medical practice to the mobility of guerrilla warfare, but there is some corroboration from the SSR that the maquis were initially thought to be too disorganized. On 18 January 1944 the National Directorate of the SSR complained tersely to the maquis leadership within the MUR of communication and organizational failures. Too often, the letter remonstrated, doctors were simply not given the necessary information: if medical supplies failed to reach the maquis it would be the fault of the *agents de liaison* within the maquis and not the doctors. One doctor per 100 to 150 men should be the norm, the doctors must be given the quickest routes to each maquis or to the maquis leader, and ideally the doctors should receive training from the maquis *écoles des cadres*. In return, the SSR undertook to investigate fully the dependability of all the doctors it recommended.[103]

As with so many documents prescribing national solutions to the problems raised by the maquis, this letter has all the ostensible signs of rational policy and sound practice, but gives little credit to the multitude of practical initiatives already taken on the ground. By early 1944 most maquis units had made their own medical arrangements through their community contacts, aided by the fact that many of the first organizers of the AS in particular were left-wing doctors who had individually rejected the social blandishments of Vichy. To these, the SSR later acknowledged, were added sizeable numbers of young, unqualified doctors within the student *réfractaires* from STO.[104] As yet the medical needs of the maquis were slight, and until the escalation of combat in June 1944 the incidence of serious wounds in most areas was too low to involve more than the occasional services of a surgeon or specialist. Hospitals, like most public institutions, had been intensively infiltrated (*noyautés*) by Resisters, as much for the provision of supplies as for treatment, and the hospitals of Cahors and Saint-Céré in the Lot became particularly famed for their Resistance activities, among which was the sheltering of persecuted Jews by a midwife, Mlle Lapeyre, in the

[102] *Le Volontaire*, hebdomadaire régional des FFI Montpellier no. 1, 8 Oct. 1944, 5.

[103] AN 72. AJ 80, letter from the Direction nationale du service de santé, 18 Jan. 1944.

[104] Ibid., report by Dr Maurice Meyer, Sept. 1943.

maternity wing at Cahors, and the dedicated service to the maquis of the Ségala by Mère Henry at Saint-Céré.[105] But hospitals were obvious targets for routine investigations by both the Germans and the Milice, so that most maquis groupings used makeshift locations in rural areas as their *infirmeries*. The Pouget family at the farm of le Poujoulat at Arcambal in the Lot looked after sick and injured maquisards, who were visited by Dr Jacques Garnal, a leading Resister from Cahors:[106] in the maquis of the Ain, Dr Jacques Guttières wrote in his diary, '10 May 1944. We are encamped in the village of Giriat. The peasants are very understanding and do their best for us. I have installed the infirmerie in one of their farms';[107] and in the valleys of the Cévennes, where almost all the country doctors were on call for maquis care, each doctor had located a barn, *bergerie*, or farm where treatment could be given, safely distanced from the main roads.[108] Such maquis centres of medical care proliferated in every kind of shelter, from caves to châteaux. They have not yet been adequately identified or researched, and are only occasionally focal points of maquis history, most notably in the case of the cave of la Luire near the hamlet of Chaberts in the Vercors, where twenty-four seriously wounded from the battles at the end of July 1944 were discovered and horrifically massacred by the German forces; two doctors and a chaplain were taken to Grenoble and shot and six nurses were deported to Ravensbrück.[109]

Where detailed accounts of medical presence in the maquis exist, as in the informative *Journal de Marche* by Guttières, it appears that no insoluble problems of recruitment of doctors arose, and that both the qualified and unqualified sectors of the medical world were substantially represented in servicing the maquis at the height of its confrontations with the Germans: for example a post-war report for the Gard is particularly fulsome in its praise for doctors in the mining area of Alès.[110] The period of intensive combat came at a point when the vast majority of the French population was sympathetic to the embattled Resistance, and Vichy was in a state of total disintegration, so that emergency medical services were only operating intermittently in full clandestinity or in seriously adverse conditions. In one insight into the earlier combats of May and June 1944, provided by the medical thesis of Jaqueline Retourné, presented shortly after the Liberation,

[105] Evidence from Pierre Combes, 27 Mar. 1991, and Abbé Souiry, 4 Apr. 1991.

[106] Evidence from André Pouget and Élise Jouclas, 5 Mar. 1991; and Cazard, *Capitaine Philippe*, 160–3.

[107] Jacques Guttières, *Le Chemin des maquis: journal de marche d'un médecin* (Piazza: Alfortville, 1972), 20.

[108] AN 72. AJ 80, Dr Cabouat, 'Rapport sur l'organisation et le fonctionnement du service de santé de la Résistance dans le Gard', 9 Dec. 1968.

[109] For the battle of the Vercors see Ch. 6. The first account of the massacre which gave figures and names appeared in Pierre Tanant, *Vercors, haut-lieu de France* (Arthaud, 1951), 166–71, 225.

[110] AN 72. AJ 80 (see 108 above for details).

the emphasis is on the experimental quality of much of the first medical activity in the maquis. Known by her *nom de guerre* as Médecin-Lieutenant Noëlle, the 23-year-old student doctor from Montpellier became an integral part of the maquis battalion of 500 men from the Haute-Lozère which fought in the battles of Mont Mouchet.[111] Most assertively she rejects the opinion of 'numerous psychiatrists' that the maquisards were recruited from those with a tendency to delinquence or disturbed behaviour. Nothing in her experience, she wrote, would confirm that opinion. 'Their motivations were more collective than individual', and she pointed to the *levée en masse* of 1792 as the historical comparison most relevant to the mobilization of 1944. A total of 100 men from her battalion were killed in the combats, thirty of whom, including a doctor and a nurse, had been wounded and had been finished off by the Germans with a bayonet or a bullet in the back of the neck. Very few of the seriously wounded who survived capture died of their wounds, indicating that emergency surgery was effective, but she points to numerous cases of delayed shock, due to the slow process of evacuating the wounded through a countryside seething with German soldiers. It was sometimes several days before they reached a maquis *infirmerie*, and it was in that period that the ingenuity of the medical carers was stretched well beyond their training and experience. Her own physical dedication was a byword among the maquisards, and it is with modest self-effacement that she describes the relief of arriving at the Hospice of Saint-Alban, fully equipped with X-ray, where a surgeon, Mlle Mendras from Marvejols, came to operate, and where the staff of nuns from the religious nursing orders willingly took over.[112] The juxtaposition of Catholic *sœurs*, many Jewish doctors, and Protestant or secular teachers with first-aid experience, was not uncommon in the medical structures underpinning the maquis. They made up a miscellany of cultures and beliefs, symptomatic of the plurality of elements within the Resistance.

It is apparent that medical personnel, like parish clergy and, to a lesser extent, schoolteachers, had good reasons for applying to the German authorities for circulation permits. So too did agricultural merchants, commercial travellers, hoteliers and restaurant owners who needed to forage for produce, and garage mechanics who were called on to service the lorries and vans throughout the countryside which were still permitted to operate. All these social occupations furnished significant numbers to the mobile structures of the maquis, supplementing the two most obvious categories of clandestine communicators, the *cheminots* and the postal workers who abound in maquis testimonies and accounts. A clear example, if somewhat specific, of the links between professional mobility and maquis organization comes from the

[111] See Ch. 6 for Mont Mouchet.

[112] Jacqueline Retourné (Médecin-Lieutenant Noëlle), *Quelques aspects du service de santé en campagne dans le maquis* (Imprimerie la Charité: Montpellier, 1945), 24.

cheese-making area of the Aveyron, where the director of the Société des Caves de Roquefort, Léon Freychet, and several members of the staff, including Jean Bosc, were at the origin of the maquis in the region of Saint-Affrique, the Maquis Paul Claie. Their freedom of movement to sheep-rearing farms throughout the area enabled them to hide, move, and feed *réfractaires* with comparative ease.[113] Far more typical and more anonymous was the activity of Yvonne Paulet, a war widow running a small *épicerie* in the working-class town of Bédarieux in the north-west of the Hérault, who used her grocery van, equipped with a *laissez-passer*, to make ostensible business sorties into the hills and convey food to the maquis near Avène and Ceilhes.[114] Her unpretentious, little-known history is a paradigm of the multitude of small-time connections between legal and outlaw enterprise which made up the structures of supply.

Restaurants, cafés, and small country hotels figure prominently in local maquis histories, as indeed they would in almost any history of French rural life. Pivotal points in the community, ideal for the apparent chance encounter, easily used for transmission of goods and information, they were also the most exposed to both social and inquisitorial visits from the Vichy police and the German forces. If cleverly used, German patronage could afford extra cover, which was not infrequently the case, but in the more isolated stretches of maquis terrain the visits by the forces of order were rarely of a relaxed social nature, and hotels are high among the list of sacked and pillaged buildings which litter the paths of reprisal. Café owners, like Aimé Pupin and Eugène Chavant, who were pioneers of the Isère and Vercors Resistance, or hotelier Odette Belot at Saint-Pons in the Hérault, are probably as well known both locally, and even nationally, for their clandestine activity as any Resisters from other occupations, such is the centrality of café life to French culture. The familiar claim that 'it all began with a game of *boules* or a drink at the café' is in no sense fanciful, nor do the numerous plaques on hotel walls, commemorating a Resistance event, exaggerate their importance. As with the Grotte de la Luire one particular hotel has taken on a symbolic status in the history of the maquis, the Hôtel de France at Entremont in the Haute-Savoie where the charismatic leader of the Glières maquis, Théodose Morel (Tom), was killed by a French officer of the GMR on 9 March 1944.[115] Less often remembered is the 40-year-old proprietor, Lucien Levet, who provided liaison, food, and shelter for the maquisards and who was deported to the concentration camps of Buchenwald and Dora, where he died at the end of December 1944. His activity

[113] Barthes, *Moïse ne savait pas nager . . . Histoire de l'Armée Secrète du Sud-Aveyron et le Maquis Paul Claie*, no pagination.

[114] Information supplied in June 1991 by her daughter, Dany Paulet, who knew little of her mother's activity until told by friends at her funeral.

[115] See Ch. 5.

was matched by scores of such hoteliers and restaurateurs throughout the rural, and urban, territory of Resistance.

Few of the structures outlined here were thought out in advance or implanted as part of a logistic plan of operations. Most developed from below in response to exigency, and the extent of their significance to maquis history still has the capacity to surprise and provoke, not least because the very exploration of these structures can be seen to overestimate and romanticize the rural entrenchment of the maquis. Overestimation would be a fault, and any rigorous search for the maquis will avoid romanticization by its revelation of the fear and hostility with which the maquis was undoubtedly received by many people. Fear and hostility are closely linked, but they are not inseparable. As the maquis extended the Resistance practice of threatening suspected collaborators, and carrying out acts of vengeance against infiltrators, Miliciens, and denunciators, those overtly sympathetic to the Milice, and those who broadly supported effective police sanctions against the maquis had good reason to express both fear and hostility. But a much greater proportion of the rural population, constituting in many areas a majority, felt fear and anxiety at the maquis presence, but without fundamental hostility. Acts of industrial sabotage and armed clashes between the maquis and the forces of order were often not seen by the population in terms of banditry, but any proximity of such events to their homes not unnaturally produced fears of reprisals. Such was the severity of German and Vichy repression from the winter onwards that public sympathy for the maquis frequently went hand in hand with very considerable, and justified, fear.

The Service du Contrôle Technique which organized the massive censorship of letters and telephone calls, both as a method of sampling public opinion and as an arm of police surveillance, reveals the fluctuations of support, fear, and hostility with less accuracy than the intelligence of the Renseignements Généraux, on which the prefectoral statements were based. Ostensibly the vast quantity of letters intercepted and read, amounting, for example, to over 255,000 in January 1944 within the five *départements* of the Montpellier region, should be an excellent guide to public attitudes.[116] But from early 1942 Vichy circulars stemming from the police secretariat within the Ministry of the Interior betray growing nervousness about the secrecy of the operation and the abuses to which the system was exposed. Local police and food inspectors were to be found confronting individuals with incriminating evidence from their intercepted letters, and this particular usage was firmly rejected by Vichy. Clearly it was leading to a growing public awareness of the existence of the interceptions, though the extent of the system remained largely unknown until many years after the

[116] AN F7. 14932, SCT 'rapport statistique', 4 Feb. 1944.

war.[117] Certainly Vichy moved to counter the breaks in secrecy by steadily centralizing control over the departmental commissions, whose job it was to carry out the interceptions and report to the prefects. In January 1943 the Vichy head of police, René Bousquet, suppressed the fortnightly syntheses of intercepted material and replaced them with monthly reports, limited to one copy only and sent straight to Vichy, and a year later Laval stopped all communication of the intercepted letters to the prefects. The commissions now had to report solely to the government.[118] The results of the interceptions have to be read in the light of this central suspicion of local security. By the winter of 1943–4 it is reasonable to assume, as oral evidence confirms, that the fact of postal censorship had been assimilated at some level into public consciousness, and was sufficient to deter most overt expressions of Resistance opinion and many other declarations which might be interpreted as subversive. Frequently the commissions found that specific individuals whose post they had been asked to monitor ceased to write letters, and Rispoli, head of police intelligence at Mende, found this quite predictable as early as August 1942 when he wrote to the Prefect of the Lozère saying that 'in terms of communist activity the postal control is unlikely to yield any results. The leaders of the party's central committee for the southern zone know full well that the control exists and have alerted their militants accordingly.'[119] Conversely, to judge by the hugely disproportionate number of letters attributed to sympathizers of Jacques Doriot's collaborationist Parti Populaire Français (PPF), it would seem that collaborators wrote more openly than any other political section of society.

With all these perspectives considered, it nevertheless remains that the excess of public condemnation of sabotage and *coups de main* over approval of such acts is overwhelming. In December 1943 in the Montpellier region, out of 4,352 letters mentioning acts which Vichy lists as 'terrorism', 3,976 were hostile and only 142 were sympathetic. For January the figures were 3,508 and 87 respectively, and in February and March the number of both reproving and approving comments increase but without any noticeable shift in the ratio of one to the other.[120] Very few of the reproving comments, however, contain within them a call for more vigorous police repression, only 47 arguing in this way in December, increasing sharply to 404 in January but still representing less than an eighth of the total. Examples of these were two letters from Mende and Sainte-Croix in the Lozère which included the statements, 'The maquis act in the name of patriotism, but

[117] The material gathered by the Contrôle Technique has been well used by Paul Abrahams to illuminate aspects of the Haute-Savoie during the Occupation. 'Haute-Savoie at War, 1939–1945' (University of Cambridge Ph.D. thesis, 1992). See also the article by Roger Austin detailed in Ch. 1. 5 above.

[118] AD Lozère VI. M2. 19, Bousquet to prefects, 6 Jan. 1943; Laval to prefects, 21 Feb. 1944.

[119] AD Lozère VI. M2. 21, Rispoli to Prefect, 19 Aug. 1942.

[120] AN F7. 14932, SCT 'rapports statistiques', 4 Feb. 1944.

fortunately the police are getting tough and I hope with all my heart that these youths are soon destroyed, for they commit all kinds of atrocities on poor innocent people,' and, from Sainte-Croix, 'For several days a large police deployment of *gardes mobiles* has been active in Saint-Germain, and have visited all the houses, destroying those that are deserted: the task is difficult in these mountainous regions, but we think that they will soon rid us of all these bandits.'[121] More typical of the reproving letters are two which were written from Barre-des-Cévennes in the early days of February 1944. One contained the words, 'The mountains are full of young men, and every day you hear of *coups de main*. These youths have to eat. But it won't lead to anything good. Terrible things are happening and none of the roads are safe.' The other makes the same admission: 'These youths from the mountains . . . come into the village and threaten the gendarmes, and whenever a gendarme is threatened he calls for several brigades to come from nearby. I assure you we're going to have trouble, and it gets worse all the time, all these youths are in hiding, and yet they do have to eat . . .'[122] These indications of ambivalence correspond more closely to the nuances reported by the Renseignements Généraux, and the overall tone is one of apprehension rather than outright hostility. At the height of the winter, with no detectable signs of an imminent Allied landing, fear of slipping into a state of unregulated violence was clearly widespread. In the Aude 880 letters in December 1943 considered 'terrorist' acts as a prelude to civil war, and only 90 as necessary for the 'libération'.[123]

Such figures, however self-selective, do convey something of the acute anxiety within the population. This was exacerbated in the Mediterranean areas by the German decision to evacuate coastal areas from mid-January 1944 to facilitate the construction of military defences, causing an increase of temporary population in the inland areas. The prefectoral reports abound with problems caused by this forced displacement, including a run on the banks and savings accounts by the evacuated families, and the growth of anti-German incidents in areas previously docile. Within the ensuing disruptions and rehousing, the maquis could count on a blurring of attitudes towards outsiders, as local particularisms were obliged to make concessions to the newcomers.[124] The severity of the German occupation of the coastal zones benefited maquis and Resistance recruitment inland, as resentment and anger followed the evacuees. Ordinances posted in the coastal towns in mid-February made forced labour the punishment for any insult to the German army, any failure to hand over tracts, newsreels, or information

[121] AD Lozère VI. M2. 21, intercepted letters, 17 Feb. 4 and 30 Mar. 1944.

[122] Ibid.

[123] AD Aude M2. 656, SCT synthèse, 25 Dec. 1943.

[124] AD Hérault 172W 4, weekly bulletins from the Renseignements Généraux, Jan.–June 1944, annotated by the Prefect of Hérault.

dropped from aircraft, any lighting of fires after dark, any photography near locked premises, and any failure to comply with requisitions. Death was the penalty for any subversion including failure of surveillance by any civilian entrusted with guard duties, yet another reason for fewer and fewer French people coming forward as security guards, and a contributing factor to the spiral of forced conscription, escape, pursuit, and, finally, recruitment into the maquis.[125] The problems on the coast were increased by the forced labour drafted into the area by OT. A report from police intelligence of the Toulouse region on 25 January 1944 numbered 4,750 youths from the Chantiers who had been put to work, building fortifications on the Mediterranean. It described their resentment, and noticed that many had escaped into the Massif Central. Whereas they used to try to get to Spain or North Africa, the report stated, now they were 'dirigés sur le maquis du centre de la France'.[126]

This localized turbulence in the Mediterranean south was one of many pointers to the growing involvement of all of France in some aspect of war-related disruption during the late winter and spring of 1944. It is far from surprising that opinions at this time should voice disquiet, fear, anxiety, and hostility, and that some of this should be directed against the maquisards, the target insistently specified by Henriot in his daily broadcasts. Yet even as popular anxiety was allowing some prefects in late February 1944 to discern a wider rural acceptance of rigorous repression, the maquis was showing confidence in its own growing control of large areas of the countryside, disputing the Vichy monopoly of rural identity and values. This was not the 'retour à la terre' that Vichy's Révolution Nationale had envisaged.

[125] AD Gard CA 367, German ordinance, 15 Feb. 1944.
[126] AD Haute-Garonne M 1526^1, Renseignements Généraux, 18 Jan. 1944.

5

Strategies and Localities, Winter–Spring 1944

THE spring of 1944 arrived slowly, as usual, in the high hills and mountains of southern France. In late March snow still lay on the plateaux above 1,100 metres, on the Margeride in the centre of the Massif Central, on the Montagne Noire at the south-west corner of the Massif, and on the Glières in the Haute-Savoie, all seen as natural bastions for the consolidation of maquis groups. The forests of meagre oaks on the expansive Causses in the Lot, and the woods of chestnut trees on the slopes of the Ségala bordering the Lot and the Cantal and in the steep valleys of the Cévennes and the Ardèche, were still without leaves in late April, allowing remote barns and shepherds' huts to be seen from many of the winding roads which linked the thinly populated hamlets to each other. The Milice, the GMR, and the Germans, aided by infiltrators, made frequent sorties along these minor roads, gauging the presence of maquis in the woods, and descending on the hamlets to extract information. They would even penetrate some way into the forests themselves. But when the leaves finally screened the woods, every bend in the road became a possible site for an ambush, with a comparative safety of withdrawal for the maquis, which gave them control over huge tracts of countryside. But that was not until May, June, and July. In the period between winter and summer the strategic evolution of the maquis groups into an effective combat force could not rely on the impenetrability of their terrain, while in the higher areas they were still facing the continued problems of basic survival.

And yet in these crucial months of February to April the internal power relations in rural areas were inverted. This inversion was by no means evenly spread across the southern zone, but it occurred in sufficient depth and breadth to allow the possibility of referring, in the spring of 1944, to Resistance France rather than Vichy France as the major determinant in the lives of much of the rural population. There was no equivalent inversion of occupiers and occupied. On the contrary, the very evolution of maquis areas into extensive power bases, dissolving and undermining Vichy authority, exposed rural people to the military power of the German Occupation. But the first signs of German desperation were there too. As maquis and occupiers met increasingly in a wide variety of conflicts, the Germans recognized their vulnerability in anything other than conventional, pitched encounters, and set out to terrorize the rural communities into inaction and submission through arrests, reprisals, and massacres. The strategies of the maquis had to take this German response into consideration, even though it was arbitrary and unpredictable, and reprisals undoubtedly problematized the widespread acceptance of some sort of direct action. But in most areas strategic decisions were made less in direct reaction to German repression than in consideration of the evolving maquis strengths at local level. Awareness of these strengths could not ensure military success for the maquisards, nor safety for their supportive communities. What it produced across the southern zone was a complex of organizations and initiatives which maximized local potential. Strategy and locality are inextricably entwined, to such an extent that it may well be impossible to write a single, adequate history of the maquis for the last six months of the Occupation which does justice to all the local developments. This study does not even attempt such exhaustive coverage, but approaches the crucial period of evolution through a selection of variants which pluralize the search for the maquis as it approached the months of combat.

Three norms appear to dominate the spring of 1944. The first is the growing consolidation of maquis groups; the second is the hardening of command within the two main, rival structures and conceptions of the maquis, the AS and the FTP; and the third is the elaboration of military action based primarily on mobility and disengagement. Had all three operated in all areas the possibility of a satisfactory history of the maquis would be less elusive, but many regions produced substantial variants on at least one of these supposed norms, and minor variations can be found in most places. This chapter sets out to detail the notable variants that existed in the Cévennes, the Lot, and the Haute-Savoie. It cannot hope to satisfy the justifiable claims of other areas for equal consideration, but at least something of the particularity of maquis evolution can be suggested.

The history of the maquis in the Cévennes from February to April queries any generalization about the steady consolidation of maquis groups. At the same time it is equally important to note how the area also exposed the divisions and uncertainties within the local Vichy administrations. A report from Rispoli, head of the Renseignements Généraux in the Lozère, to Montpellier was used by his superior to make out a strong case for seeing the situation in the Cévennes as militarily dangerous. On 13 January 1944 Rispoli reported the derisory figures of those attending for STO medicals: at Mende on 6 January 86 out of 250, at Marvejols on 9 January only 30 out of 203, and at the most industrialized of the three towns, Saint-Chély-d'Apcher on 11 January, only 11 out of 245. The *département* had been ordered to furnish 250 agricultural workers and 26 road-menders by 14 January: it had ended up with no more than 19 and 5 respectively. The results among foreign workers were the same. Of 118 from the Chanac TE camp summoned for STO only 11 appeared. Rispoli concluded that even when all the individual excuses had been examined, it would be obvious that a substantial number of young Frenchmen and foreigners had joined the forces of dissidence, and in the case of Spanish refugees he said it should be recognized that they had fought in Spain and 'had a certain experience of civil war'. It remained only for him to underline that STO was and remained exceedingly unpopular. His superior's conclusion was forthright. 'It seems that we are undoubtedly faced with a significant group of *réfractaires* in the mountains bordering the south of the Lozère and the north of the Gard. These mountains constitute a natural hide-out, very difficult to penetrate, which was previously used by the Camisards in the wars of religion. It appears urgent that we contact the region of Marseille with a view to a combined operation such as the one in the Montagne Noire in July 1943.' The date of this proposal was 17 January 1944.[1] Ten days later the number of maquisards in the part of the Cévennes which fell within the Lozère was estimated by the Prefect as over 400. He specified two 'infested' regions: the Col de Jalcreste, 18 km. south-east of Florac, and the border with the Gard at Saint-Andéol-de-Clerguemort. Units, each composed of ten men, were said to be 'beating the countryside', a phrase which acknowledged the signs that the hunted were indeed becoming the hunters in this particular rural area.[2]

There had been a maquis among the chestnut trees, oaks, and broom of the Jalcreste area since November 1943, composed of immigrant workers, structured by the pre-war, and now Resistance, organization, the Main d'Œuvre Immigrée (MOI). They had been among the first maquisards in the Lozère, located originally to the north-west of the *département*, but moved by the Lozère Resistance into the Cévennes.[3] There they were placed under the command of François Rouan (Montaigne), a tough, philosophical, outsider-figure, who had been tried twice for desertion as an officer from the French army, had fought as a Trotskyite in the Spanish Civil War, and had formed Spanish refugees into MOI units in the Ariège before taking to the maquis in the Cévennes. He was nominated maquis leader by the AS, his known Trotskyist leanings making him suspect to the FTP.[4] In November, when he took over command of the MOI group near to the Col de Jalcreste,

[1] AD Hérault 18. W 64, correspondence between Rispoli in Mende and the Renseignements Généraux in Montpellier, 13–17 Jan. 1944.

[2] AD Lozère R 5902, Prefect's note dated 28 Jan. 1944.

[3] See Ch. 2.

[4] For the activities of François Rouan (Montaigne) see Maruéjol and Vielzeuf, *Le Maquis Bir-Hakeim*; Éveline and Yvan Brès, *Un Maquis d'anti-fascistes allemands en France 1942–1944*; evidence from François Rouan, 25 Feb. 1982.

he was designated by André Pavelet, the organizer of AS maquis in the Montpellier region, as the man to unite the maquis groupings in the Cévennes.[5] A strategy for the unification of the AS maquis did therefore exist. The Cévennes, in the winter of 1943–4, might be seen to be heading for the norm that obtained in the spring of 1944, the coming together and consolidation of disparate maquis groups. And yet this did not happen until much later, partly, but not entirely, because the local FTP had established highly successful models of small-scale organization.

The area round Saint-Andéol-de-Clerguemort, specified by Dutruch, was in the centre of exclusively FTP country, up above the mining complex of Alès-la-Grand' Combe, from where many surface and face workers would go straight from their shift into the maquis for a night raid or sabotage, and return to work the next day. The mines were a major supply source of dynamite. At the heart of this 'chasse gardée' of the FTP was the battlefield of Champdomergue where the Camisards defeated the troops of Captain Poul, one of the most relentless opponents of the Protestant fighters in the early eighteenth century. An FTP camp was established in a deserted Cévenol farm or *jasse*, named after the battlefield, at an altitude of 900 metres, surveying the crests and valleys of the Cévennes, and Vielzeuf speaks of the 'atavistic' passion for freedom which made the local peasants into the protectors and suppliers of the FTP.[6]

The Col de Jalcreste was squarely in the Lozère, so the agitated reports of Rispoli and the Prefect Dutruch went to Montpellier, whereas the activities of maquisards only a few kilometres further south and south-east in the Cévennes of the Gard were the immediate concern of the Prefect Chiappe at Nîmes, who reported to Marseille. Despite Chiappe's arguments for making the Cévennes into a single administrative region, and the attempts by the Montpellier police chiefs to secure co-operation with Marseille, no effective, co-ordinated Vichy policy towards the maquis in the Cévennes emerged, Darnand being preoccupied in January and February 1944 with making a national example of the maquis in the Haute-Savoie. The local Vichy administrations fell back on their own police resources, but their ineffectiveness and the growing cover for the maquis provided by individual gendarmes in the small Cévenol towns, had three major results. First, each of the disparate maquis groups which were dispersed throughout the Cévenol woods and mountains, and were recruiting more and more *réfractaires* and foreign workers, felt secure in its independence. Secondly, the Germans decided that if any effective repression was to be launched in the Cévennes it would be by their own troops. Vichy's role to protect the German army under the terms of the armistice, reinforced by Bousquet's agreements with

[5] Éveline et Yvan Brès, *Un Maquis d'anti-fascistes allemands*, 111–20; Joutard *et al.*, *Cévennes, terre de refuge*, 91–7.

[6] Vielzeuf, *Épopée en Cévenne*, 123.

Oberg, was judged to be a failure. And thirdly, the local authorities who insisted on Vichy's role became steadily more fanatical in their determination to prove to the Germans that they were serious. In this zealous determination, the Milice were given the critical vanguard position, and in response the maquis began to pick off individual Miliciens and to threaten their families. The Milice infiltrated both uniformed and plain-clothes police structures and became well informed on maquis positions, the names of *réfractaires*, and the key figures within the maquis communities. The maquis made it a question of local honour to be equally well informed on the personnel and movements of the Milice.

At the end of January 1944 an imminent Milice raid from Nîmes on the Cévenol area of Lasalle under the Montagne de Liron was widely rumoured. The AS maquis in this area had been formed by a baker, Guy Arnault, and a local authority treasurer, Robert Francisque, and included the survivors from the Aire-de-Côte disaster of July 1943 under the leadership of René Rascalon. It had its own corps franc, numbering about twelve, which operated away from Lasalle on specific missions and incorporated two women *agents de liaison*, Cécile Villemenot and Rose Frankiel, who established communications with Resistance organizers in Toulouse and Montpellier and acted as a vital medical resource, Villemenot being a nurse and Frankiel a pharmacist. It was the corps franc which later assisted the maquisards of Bir-Hakeim in the profitable raid on the Paulhan clothing workshops, as a result of which the maquis of Lasalle became unusually well equipped.[7] On 31 January, in expectation of the Milice, the maquis blocked the approach roads to Lasalle, and when the Milice failed to take up the challenge the maquis decided on a triumphant display of its colours. On 1 February at seven in the evening it staged a march through Lasalle, placing wreaths on the *monument aux morts* to commemorate the dead of Aire-de-Côte. Reports to the Prefect in Nîmes estimated the maquis cohort at 80 to 120 men, mostly in uniform and led by their officers, and more than one report stressed that the reaction of the inhabitants of Lasalle suggested not only enthusiasm but active connivance in the preparation of the demonstration. The Prefect was indignant not to be told about it until the next day, confirming all his suspicions about the collusion of the Cévenol gendarmerie, but the attention of the prefecture was diverted by an audacious FTP attack on the Nîmes prison, the Maison Centrale, on the night of 4 February in which 23 prisoners were released. The two events were unrelated but as incidents grew in number and in bravura and the police reports enumerated every kind of theft, attack, and sabotage on a daily basis throughout February, the conclusions of the reports consistently pointed to the Cévennes as almost an autonomous region within the *département*, where perpetrators

[7] See Ch. 4.

of the actions, whether set in Nîmes, Alès, or the Cévenol villages themselves, could escape detection.[8]

Within the Lasalle Maquis, the pride in the demonstration led one maquisard to defy maquis discipline and send a lyrical account of the event to his parents near Marseille. Intercepted by the Contrôle postal, the letter taunted the Milice as cowards, and described the thoroughness with which the maquis had policed the roads in the area, turning Lasalle into 'une ville ouverte aux jeunes' in which 'un monde fou' from all the neighbouring villages shouted 'bravos frénetiques' as the maquisards marched singing, 'Vous n'aurez pas l'Alsace et la Lorraine'.[9] Two other intercepted letters from inhabitants of Lasalle, put into the same police dossier on the event, provided telling details of the festival atmosphere. All the lights were switched on—'la grande illumination', recalling the good old days of the 'fêtes nationales', while the maquisards are seen to be overjoyed at the sheer freedom of walking in the open.[10] Nîmes did not react by sending a punitive force, suggesting that the evidence of popular support dissuaded the Prefect from what would have been a confrontation with the whole population. But Marty in Montpellier did organize an attack on the Col de Jalcreste area in mid-February by a unit of GMR. They set fire to the largely deserted hamlet of la Fare, which had been used by Rouan's Maquis MOI, but failed to locate or confront the maquis itself.[11] Rispoli visited the area at the same time as the expedition, and his report told the prefecture in Mende that the 'banditry' of the maquis was widely seen in the area as patriotism, and that he favoured not a frontal assault but a policy of sealing off the access roads. The maquis, he argued, would be forced to try and break through the cordon once the peasantry in the area had exhausted their capacity to feed the maquisards at the worst point in their subsistence economy, February to March.[12]

This struggle to maintain control of specific localities within a traditionally defiant and refractory region reveals the divisions, inconsistencies, and frustrations within the local prefectures. They were effectively paralysed by the region's solidarity with the maquis, which displayed itself in a libertarianism of organization and action. Not for the first time the Cévennes had successfully outmanœuvred any attempt to impose an unpopular authoritarian control. This very success, symbolized by the maquisard 'fête' at Lasalle, encouraged the continued separation of small maquis units, the co-existence of alternative maquis strategies, and an ease of secession from one group to another. The ubiquitous community involvement of the Cévenol population allowed the maquis to remain fractured throughout the spring months of

[8] AD Gard CA 667, 'Attentats terroristes', Feb.–Mar. 1944.
[9] Ibid., letter intercepted 4 Feb. 1944. [10] Ibid., letter intercepted 4 Feb. 1944.
[11] AD Hérault 18W 25, report by Marty to Darnand, 21 Feb. 1944.
[12] AD Lozère R 5902, Rispoli to Prefect, 14 Feb. 1944.

1944, when maquis elsewhere were moving towards consolidation. Any splinter group could easily find its own supportive locality, and the region's particularities promoted a plurality of strategic decisions.

By January 1944 the Cévennes harboured not only the maquis groups already mentioned, but also Pastor Gillier's group of *réfractaires* at Mandagout in the Aigoual Massif, which was structured from January onwards by the Organisation de Résistance de l'Armée (ORA), a nearby AS maquis at Ardaillès organized by another Protestant minister, Pastor Laurent Olivès, and a maquis-école attached to the AS, created by M. Lapierre at la Picharlerie in the Vallée Française, while in the east of the Gard the motorized Maquis Bir-Hakeim was provisionally located at the Mas de Serret above the Gorges de l'Ardèche. Each valley within the series of wooded crests which stretched to the horizon appeared to service its own maquis, and there were fragmentations still to come. Not all the marchers who paraded through Lasalle had been equally enthused. A few days later eleven maquisards broke away to form the Maquis de Serre, otherwise known as the FTP 'camp No. 4' some six kilometres west of Lasalle in the Montagne de Liron. They followed one of the ancient Cévenol sheep tracks known as *drailles*, used in the annual transhumance and frequented by the Camisards in their tactical retreats from the dragoons of Villars. In the deep snow and icy winds the secessionary group set up camp in solid farm buildings, occupied by one old peasant and his dog, their food assured by the inhabitants of small hamlets in the vicinity, La Coste and Soudorgues. Aimé Vielzeuf, who has brilliantly pieced together their history, stressed the youth, idealism, and political fervour of their leader Jacques Baby, aged 19, born in Prague and educated in Paris and Nîmes, whose father was a teacher and a dedicated member of the Communist Party. Baby took to the maquis as an anti-fascist and Marxist, and it was his rejection of what he felt was the non-political atmosphere and inaction of the AS Maquis of Lasalle which determined his breakaway movement. With him from the start was a Cévenol *réfractaire*, Gérard Ménatory, whose poetic account of his experiences refers to the reanimation of the Camisard legends in the confident *mentalités* of the young group, as self-appointed francs-tireurs fighting for a local community as well as a national and ideological cause.[13]

The arrival of the SS division Hohenstaufen in Provence, technically for recuperation, gave the German authorities the opportunity to cut through the vacillations of the Vichy police and attack the diffused maquisards of the Cévennes in strength. From 26 February to 4 March 1944 they terrorized the maquis-held areas in the east of the Gard and within the Cévennes, criss-crossing the mountains in sudden flanking movements in an attempt to encircle the maquisards, and exacting terrible reprisals on the villages when

[13] I am yet again much indebted to the work of Aimé Vielzeuf, *Épopée en Cévenne*, 21–95.

the various maquis escaped further into the forests. At Ardaillès, where the AS maquis were attacked in the early morning of 29 February, the maquisards began to return the German fire before retreating into the mountains. The village was then burnt, a villager killed, and six others taken hostage, four of whom were hanged at Nîmes in public along with eleven others seized in the course of the repressive campaign. At the village of les Crottes close to the camp of Bir-Hakeim at Serret the Germans massacred sixteen villagers, including four boys aged 14 to 18 and four women between the ages of 35 and 75.

The police chief Marty in Montpellier claimed not to have been informed by the Germans of their attack. An infiltrator had told him of a planned meeting at top level between the maquis leaders of the region to be held at the Hôtel Nogaret at the Col de Jalcreste on 28 February, and he arrived there with a cohort of GMR only to find the hotel already occupied by thirty SS soldiers. The maquis leaders had been alerted by the German troop movements and Marty missed his anticipated coup, though he arrested one of the maquis organizers, M. Tourre, the postmaster at Florac, and narrowly missed the tax-collector of le Collet-de-Dèze, M. Huc, who was known to be another local organizer. Marty complained to the Regional Prefect that the German attack had effectively undermined any possibility of the co-ordinated campaign in the Cévennes that he had advised in January. The maquis were now unlikely to be taken by surprise.[14] At Nîmes the prefecture noted with little comment the escalating destruction of buildings and the mounting number of arrests and shootings perpetrated by the German forces: on 5 March twelve *réfractaires* taken prisoner and shot, on 6 March three women arrested at Bagnols-sur-Cèze, and forty inhabitants at Pont-Saint-Esprit.[15] The maquis of the Gard-Lozère region later claimed that Miliciens and GMR had accompanied the German attacks, but there was no official Vichy agreement to act as partners in the repression. Nevertheless what happened was anything but a chance series of raids on a subversive region in the hope of locating 'nests of terrorists'. It was a calculated attack on specific communities known by the Germans to be harbouring maquisards, knowledge which came partly from their own intelligence but mainly from the regular Vichy reports on *réfractaires* and *coups de main* within the area.

In one respect the German attacks revealed the substantial advantages of the dispersed and fractured nature of the Cévennes maquis. Almost all of the Cévenol maquisards as 'men in the woods' were able to escape this particular German onslaught. But on the other hand the reprisals on the villagers were all the more savage, and underline as forcibly as any other evidence the necessity of writing maquis history as a community

[14] AD Hérault 18W 25, Marty to Regional Prefect, 29 Feb. 1944.
[15] AD Gard CA 667, 'Attentats terroristes', Feb.–Mar. 1944.

phenomenon. It was the supportive communities that bore the brunt of these attacks, and in this sense the reprisals brutally affirmed the inseparability of maquisard fortunes from those of their carers and providers. The Occupiers treated them both alike. The Germans had the option of acknowledging the maquisards as belligerents but chose to treat them as terrorists beyond the protection of the rules of war. They had the option of arresting villagers suspected of active involvement with the maquis and investigating their case, but chose arbitrary terror, torture, and summary executions.

The severity of the massacre at les Crottes reflected the degree of German frustration at the escape of the Maquis Bir-Hakeim, the most talked-about maquis in the area. Stories circulated about its motorized journey across the Languedoc to the east of the Gard, its daring theft of weapons from the Intendance de Police at Montpellier, and the raid on the Paulhan clothing factory, and myths arose round the histrionic personalities and behaviour of its leaders Jean Capel (commandant Barot), Captain Paul Demarne, and Christian de Roquemaurel. Look-outs from the maquis had opened fire on a German convoy on 25 February near their camp at Serret, but a strong contingent of SS were unable to encircle them on the 26th and were contained by maquis machine-gun fire, suffering severe casualties. The savage killings in les Crottes were a direct act of German revenge.

The readiness of Bir-Hakeim to attack any German patrol and its ability to slip through cordons and disappear into the woods made it almost a model of a guerrilla force, but when it moved to the Cévennes and encamped at la Picharlerie in the Vallée Française in mid-March its activist policies and provocative style met an ambivalent reception from the local maquis leaders and the Cévenol population. Lapierre, who had initiated the maquis-école at la Picharlerie agreed that Captain Demarne, who had served with de Lattre de Tassigny, should act as instructor at the training camp, but only if Lapierre's own group, centred on Saint-Jean-du-Gard, remained separate from the 'Biraquins'. Rascalon and the maquis at Lasalle were even more determined to keep themselves at a distance, but the MOI group led by François Rouan, which had moved to a camp at Galbartès close to La Picharlerie was prepared for a closer relationship and became established as one of the federation of groups which made up Bir-Hakeim in this period of its rapid expansion into a force of over 120. The maquis had organizational and recruiting bases in Toulouse, Montpellier, Clermont-l'Hérault, and Pont-Saint-Esprit; Barot and Demarne were in contact with AS and MUR leaders throughout the area, and they lived dangerously, exploiting agents and double agents within the Vichy police and even the German entourage. Barot, who spoke good German, carried a false identity card declaring him to be an Intendant de Police, and as such received the salute of German and Vichy patrols when he drove assertively round the region, often on a self-appointed mission to eliminate a specific informer, or to recover a cache of arms. The Cévenol Resisters, for all their individualism, had little of his flamboyance, and the image of the Camisards before them was one of stern cautiousness and solid integrity, in contrast to which the reputation of the 'Biraquins' came to epitomize recklessness and a certain indifference to the effects of their action on the local community. When Barot attempted to unify all the Cévenol maquis under his leadership and openly recruited for Bir-Hakeim among other groups, he was met by the protective reflexes of Cévenol independence. After his appearance in Alès with a dubious German agent, and a further cycle of a Bir-Hakeim ambush and German reprisals in early April, an extraordinary meeting of leaders from all the local maquis told Barot that 'he must leave the region of the Cévennes and the Basse-Lozère'.[16]

This dramatic clash of style, leadership, and strategy was located firmly within regional considerations. A concept of acceptable local practice informed the decisions of the maquis leaders. Barot was judged to have endangered the community basis of the various Cévenol maquis. His urban insouciance put him outside the local *mentalités*, even though his manner and activism had exercised a formidable influence over young maquisards in the area. Bir-Hakeim moved out of the Vallée Française, but its turbulent history continued on the western fringes of the Cévennes.

The historians of Bir-Hakeim, Vielzeuf and Maruéjol, rightly point out that February to April 1944 was a time of rapid maquis growth and extended action, but also one of uncertainties and nervousness throughout the maquis, not just in the Cévennes.[17] The waves of German repression reached new levels of ferocity in this period, bringing the harsh realities of war to all parts of the *zone sud*: the Milice and the GMR mixed infiltration and victimization with direct conflict, and Henriot's radio propaganda, aimed at dividing the peasantry from the maquis, was at its peak of effectiveness. But generally, while maquis targets were diversifying, the tendency was towards a tighter and more co-ordinated strategy and structure. The Cévennes provides a variant to this, making it *sui generis* in this organizational aspect of its history, though not in others. Neither the intended leadership of François Rouan, nor the *de facto* dominance of Bir-Hakeim overcame the sense of autonomy in the region. Vichy was marked by it too, and the Germans were denied their decisive encounter. Consolidation did eventually come to the Cévennes, in the form of the Maquis Aigoual-Cévennes, but not until the summer.

The second assumed norm in the evolution of the maquis in the first four months of 1944 was the hardening of structure and strategies into two main tendencies or affiliations, namely MUR/AS on the one hand and FTP on the other. Maquis camps belonging to one or other of these two account

[16] Maruéjol and Vielzeuf, *Le Maquis Bir-Hakeim*, 89–90. [17] Ibid. 87.

for well over 90 per cent of maquis emplacements marked on the maps of the southern *départements*, prepared by correspondents of the Comité d'Histoire de la 2e Guerre Mondiale. Most histories of the AS and FTP have been written separately, perpetuating the divisions of the time and often sharpening the rivalries of winter to spring 1944, and there can be no doubt that resentments between the two were at their height in these months, when parachute drops of arms and ammunition were gathering pace and the repression by Vichy and German forces was intensifying. It was during this period that attitudes, based on certain real divisions of theory and practice, were inflated into generalities, so that the FTP were accused of widespread piracy of men, arms, and ammunition from AS camps, of indulging in forms of direct action which unnecessarily endangered the French population, and of political indoctrination in the interests of the Communist Party; whereas the AS maquis were no less roundly denounced by the FTP for wasting and hoarding resources which could have been used directly against the enemy, of keeping maquisards in a state of inactivity and frustration waiting for Jour-J, and of surrendering initiatives to British, Gaullist, and American agents, who were not necessarily accepted as working for the interests of the ordinary French people.

The search for the maquis at local level finds endless echoes and variants of these accusations and counter-accusations, but it also reveals a major variant in the Lot, which suggests the coexistence of other realities. The *département* of the Lot to the west of the Massif Central fell within the region of Toulouse, but its maquis terrain extended naturally eastwards into the Aveyron which was attached to Montpellier, and northwards into the Cantal, the Corrèze, and the Dordogne administered from Limoges. Through it ran the main road and rail links between Paris and the south-west, and it was an area which had been inundated with refugees during the *exode* of May–June 1940, to whom the Lotois people had shown great hospitality. The peasantry was engaged in subsistence farming and animal husbandry which effectively protected the population from the extremes of the *ravitaillement* problems experienced in the larger towns and monocultural areas. The forests on the plateaux in the centre of the *département* provided a wealth of hiding-places for *réfractaires* and maquisards, and the Ségala range to the east contained sharp escarpments, extensive slopes covered in chestnut trees, streams full of trout, and small villages isolated on the summits with extensive views, which constituted a natural area for mobilization, withdrawal, and retrenchment before further action in the vicinities of the main towns of Cahors, Figeac, Souillac, and Saint-Céré. It was in the rural areas close to these towns of the ancient region of Quercy that the community structures of the Lotois maquis were consolidated. There was no shortage of abandoned buildings on the Quercy plateaux (Causses) of Limogne and Gramat, areas of cumulative depopulation where the characteristics of peasant life were isolation and poverty on an arid, stony soil, covered with scraggy oak trees and valued only for truffles and delicate spring mushrooms, known as morilles. Robert Noireau (Colonel Georges) described the land as 'une terre à demi-sauvage' in which flocks of sheep eked out an existence on the sparse vegetation, but for the maquis, he wrote, it became 'une terre privilégiée'.[18] His account of the maquis in the Lot, which has been criticized locally for its unreliability, nevertheless accentuates a fact widely endorsed in the area, the unity of peasantry and maquisards. He introduces it with the evocative image of an unexpected and symbolic meeting between his group of maquis on a training march, and a single peasant who stood motionless on the road, in disbelief at the approach of the young maquisards. He was 'a typical old Quercy peasant with his jacket, black hat, velvet trousers, wrinkled face, small black eyes, and white moustache . . . This man represented the Lot, and the meeting between us was like an act of recognition.' His name was Paul Gouzou, and his farm became an annex to the maquis.[19]

On the edge of the Causse Limogne, not more than a few kilometres from the *chef-lieu* Cahors, the village of Arcambal had sheltered the first recruits to the AS Maquis France led by Jean-Jacques Chapou (Capitaine Philippe), and its growth and survival was a considerable community achievement involving many other villages in the neighbourhood, notably Belfort du Quercy, Cieurac, and Loubejac, as it moved ceaselessly to escape detection in the autumn and winter of 1943–4, occupying a vast variety of hiding-places: caves in the forest, round dry-stone shepherds' huts known as *gariottes* or *cazelles*, farm outbuildings, and empty châteaux. By early 1944 Chapou had been nominated by the AS as the leader of all maquis groups in the Lot whether on the Causse Limogne, on the Causse de Gramat centred on the village of Caniac-du-Causse, or in the hills of the Ségala notably in the localities of Latronquière, Prendeignes, and Saint-Perdoux, which was where Noireau was brought by the AS of Figeac to the group eventually known as the Maquis Bessières.[20] Chapou's leadership was welcomed collectively by maquis groups which included a substantial number of Spanish, and refugees from Paris, the north, and Alsace-Lorraine; he was acknowledged as a partner by the independent AS groupes francs known as the Groupes Vény, with their strength at Saint-Céré, and he was accepted individually by Noireau who became his second-in-command. Politically it was an unlikely partnership in that they occupied exactly the positions on the Left which were mutually hostile, Chapou a syndicalist in the Jouhaux tradition, suspicious of political intervention, and Noireau a communist, but neither was dogmatic, and both were responsive to the challenges and opportunities of the situation. Both had led their maquis groups in symbolic occupations of

[18] Robert Noireau (Colonel Georges), *Le Temps des partisans*, 90. [19] Ibid. 99–100.
[20] See Ch. 3.

Lotois villages on 11 November 1943, both had organized raids and *coups de main*, and both were strong authority figures. Had the norm of separate structures of development and command operated within the Lot, Noireau was well placed in the Ségala to establish an FTP *chasse-gardée* similar to the area north of Alès-la-Grand' Combe in the Cévennes. The Ségala with its small primitive mines at the village of Saint-Perdoux, buried in the woods, was an obvious place of hiding for workers from the industrial town of Decazeville to the south in the Aveyron, with its expansive open veins of coal (la Découverte) and its history, similar to that of Alès, of turbulent working-class subversion of Vichy authority. Chapou, by contrast, appeared anchored in the small-town syndicalist groups, teachers, and other professions which dominated the Resistance in Cahors, some 80 km. to the east. But throughout the winter of 1943–4 Chapou and Noireau consolidated the AS maquis of the Lot with no parallel FTP structures within the *département*. The local biographer of Chapou, Georges Cazard, is rhapsodic in his portrait; and indeed, admiration for Chapou's leadership was universal in the Lot. The authors of the history of the Groupes Vény wrote, 'Only Chapou was accepted by everyone ... He was the example to follow, the counsellor to listen to, the man of instinct. His policy was not to mount flamboyant operations, but to direct delicate actions, one by one ... By the end of 1943 he was the master and director of the maquis, chosen instinctively by all the maquisards of the Armée Secrète.'[21]

It is striking evidence of the unusual unity of purpose of maquis and groupes francs in the north of the Lot that so many different leaders should co-operate in the sabotage of the Usines Ratier at Figeac which was making propellers for the German air force. Those involved in planning the operation included the SOE agent Harry Peulevé, who was working with FTP units within the Corrèze; two recent SOE arrivals in the area of Saint-Céré, George Hiller and Cyril Watney; Jean and Marie Verlhac of the Groupes Vény whose kitchen in the village of Quatres-Routes, south of Brive, was used to make the explosives; Jean-Jacques Chapou, who had been contacted by both London and Algiers, it would appear, to explore the possibility of sabotage; the AS leader Henri Vaysettes at Figeac; Yves Ouvrieu of a Cahors *réseau*, known as Gallia, whom Pierre Laborie credits as the originator of the plan, and finally the Vény group of Saint-Céré who carried out the explosions on the night of 19 January 1944, successfully destroying three heavy presses within the factory.[22] At the same time both Noireau and Chapou were receiving a share of parachute drops organized by the British agents

[21] Picard and Chaussade, *Ombres et espérances en Quercy*, 74.

[22] Several histories contribute to different facets of the Ratier sabotage; see Cazard, *Capitaine Philippe*, 140–3; Picard and Chaussade, *Ombres et espérances en Quercy*, 123–50; M. R. D. Foot, *S.O.E. in France* (HMSO: London, 1966), 379; Pierre Laborie, *Résistants, Vichyssois et autres* (CNRS, 1980), 299, 303.

for the Groupes Vény,[23] and the effective co-ordination of the armed Resistance of the Lot under AS, Gaullist, and SOE leadership seemed well assured.

It was therefore nothing short of a *coup de foudre* in February 1944 when Chapou announced his personal adherence to the Communist Party, and a shift of maquis allegiance to the FTP. There had been no prior discussions with his AS colleagues in Cahors, and no intimation within the *département* of his changing ideas, though it was known that he had felt unhappy at several failures of communication in 1943. The news, wrote Cazard, 'had the effect of a bombshell within the Lotois Resistance. It was particularly unexpected from someone like Philippe who had shown such absolute independence of mind . . .'[24] It appeared later that he had been a listener to the Soviet radio and had followed the Russian successes, but it was the impression made by the FTP in the Corrèze to the north which had most affected him. They had procured sufficient arms for themselves to harass the Germans in a series of attacks, and a week's tour of the Corrèze had convinced him of the superiority of their strategy. He told Cazard shortly after his decision that the MUR/AS policy was temporization, based on an Allied landing which seemed never to come, and he had found his young maquisards 'avid for combat'. He had seen the communists at work in the Corrèze and 'despite the errors in their past' he felt they knew how to fight. They had promised him arms and he had accepted the rigours of their organization.[25] Robert Noireau, whose communist beliefs had played their part in Chapou's affiliation, though it is not known exactly when or how, judged that Chapou had made a functional choice, not an ideological one, and that he would probably have reverted to his independence after the war, had he not been killed shortly before the Liberation at a German road-block in the Corrèze on 16 July 1944.[26]

The circumstances of Chapou's change of allegiance, and those of his avoidable death, are still the focus of speculation and rumour in the Lot, but the reactions by maquisards to his dramatic move were no less significant than the decision itself. The vast majority of the different maquis groups under his command continued to accept him as leader, and their adaptation to FTP structures was unproblematic. Their new designation seemed uncontentious, and in most cases was not perceived as having a political connotation. It is accurate to say, as Pierre Laborie does, that within a month of Chapou's decision 'communist resistance appeared incontestably as the best organized and most powerful in the *département*',[27] but it is equally true to say that the consolidation of the Lotois maquis formed a single history from the period of AS dominance into the new phase of FTP affiliation. Chapou's

[23] Noireau, *Le Temps des partisans*, 157–8

[24] Cazard, *Capitaine Philippe*, 178.

[25] Ibid. 179.

[26] Noireau, *Le Temps des partisans*, 122. See also evidence from Maurice Darnault, 7 Mar. 1991.

[27] Laborie, *Résistants, Vichyssois et autres*, 291.

shift may seem an epic contribution to the rivalries between the AS and the FTP, but among the Lotois maquisards it is precisely the absence of a sense of strategic and ideological rivalry which calls for comment. The bombshell had its fall-out in the urban circles of Resistance. Little fell on the villages and woods of the Lot. Before March the AS maquis constituted the Maquis du Lot; after March it was the maquis FTP. But it was the same maquis and the same supportive communities, constantly enlarging their scope and involvement.

The substantial variant this provides to the widely accepted norm of parallel and competitive histories is given weight and colour by individual evidence. Jean Questa, a Spanish republican in the maquis at Caniac-du-Causse, emphasized the non-political attribution of the maquis; Pierre Couderq, an *instituteur* at Gramat recruited for the maquis by a local businessman Raymond Lacam, claimed that many maquisards only discovered at the Liberation that they were classified as FTP, and were astounded to find themselves described as communists; Joseph Rohr, a practising Catholic from Lorraine, who took to the maquis from Labastide-Murat and worked closely with Robert Noireau, was insistent that he was never once asked to become a communist; and Joseph Nodari, an *agent de liaison* within Chapou's Maquis France, and an agricultural worker from the area of Lalbenque, speaking the langue d'Oc and receiving hospitality and support from farms throughout the Causse Limogne, said there was no change in attitudes either within the maquis or within the orbit of support when Chapou took them into the FTP.[28]

What Chapou and the Lotois maquis gained from the move was an integration into a wider regional strategy involving the FTP of the Corrèze and the Dordogne, and Chapou himself was designated at the end of April as commander of these three *départements*, leaving the Lot and his *nom de guerre* 'Philippe', and becoming 'Kléber' in the Corrèze. Before that, the maquis of the Lot combined in a major diversionary action aimed at relieving the German pressure on the maquis of the Corrèze. On 11 April they occupied the large village of Cajarc on the left bank of the river Lot and rang up the Germans to say that terrorists had taken over the area. A running battle ensued between the maquis and a combined force of Germans, Miliciens, and GMR, and the maquis escaped with surprisingly few losses. It was a convincing display of the FTP's ability and resolution to fight, and its effect on the population was significant. Alongside it went the profound impression made by the execution of three Miliciens from Cajarc in the town square after a court martial under Chapou had convicted them of denunciations. The vigour of the FTP had already been turned against impostors in the area of Cajarc who were holding local peasants and

[28] Evidence from Joseph Nodari, 28 Mar. 1991.

traders to ransom in the name of the maquis, and Noireau had previously signed notices announcing the death penalty for four such 'faux-maquisards' in early January, when he was still within the structures of the AS.[29]

A report by the Renseignements Généraux of Cahors on the maquis of the Lot and the occupation of Cajarc estimated the combined strength of the maquis under Chapou at 400 men. The occupation, it said, demonstrated convincingly that several groups could be unified under a single command.[30] In Toulouse the Intendant de Police referred to the occupation as a major indication that the principal centre of Resistance in the Toulouse region during March–April was in the north and north-east of the Lot, but there is no specific attribution of the maquis to the FTP.[31] The Cahors report was completed in July and ran to 91 pages, full of places, names, numbers, and details of the maquis *attentats* and *coups de main*. It was well informed, due partly to the number of arrests made by the police, but also because of the obvious sympathy of the compilers for a phenomenon which they saw as representing the majority opinion of the *département*. It is this sense that Chapou's leadership and organization of the maquis within the FTP corresponded to evolving local attitudes, which marks almost all accounts of the Lotois maquis, both at the time and since. There is no hint that his strategic decision was schismatic or divisive at the local level, however unexpected and dramatic it was seen to be. A *département* in which communist candidates had stood in only two of the three constituencies in 1936 and had polled only 4,183 votes out of 30,293, appears to have accepted the FTP largely because they were seen not as doctrinaire communists but as effective maquisards. They were less political than the FTP in the Corrèze, and once the shock of Chapou's 'defection' had been assimilated, the relations of the Groupes Vény with the FTP were constructive. In many ways the sustaining of unity within the Lotois maquis across what many maquisards considered an unbridgeable strategic and political gulf made the Lot no less of a special case than the Cévennes.

[29] Laborie, *Résistants, Vichyssois et autres*, 314. A distinction between 'maquisards' and 'faux-maquisards' is made repeatedly and insistently in oral evidence, but it is far from easy to produce a definition of the 'faux-maquisard'. Villagers whom I interviewed in the Cévennes during 1981–2 and in the Lot in 1991 tended to suggest that the real maquis came first and the false maquis later. In many ways this confirms the picture given by maquisards themselves who state that common criminals, opportunists, and unscrupulous breakaways from the maquis all exploited the disintegration of Vichy authority in the spring of 1944. But it is clear that in many areas rural opinion preferred the 'harmless' *réfractaires* to the 'threatening' maquis, and that in certain places distinctions of real and false were made between maquis of different affiliations (AS and FTP). For one such inter-maquis confrontation, both at the time and in rival accounts later, see the thesis on the Haute-Savoie by Paul Abrahams, who gives the story of François Merlin, the mayor of Petit-Bornand and member of the AS who reported the FTP Groupe Lamouille to the police: 'Haute-Savoie at War, 1939–1945' (University of Cambridge Ph.D. thesis, 1992), 180–4. I am very grateful for his permission to allude to his research.

[30] AN 72. AJ 157, Renseignements Généraux, 22 July 1944.

[31] AD Haute-Garonne M 1526^4, Intendant de Police, Apr. 1944.

The third norm of maquis history between January and April 1944 would seem to be that of a mobile military strategy based on limited actions and the avoidance of pitched encounters. The paucity of arms and ammunition made available to the maquis was an obvious determinant in the elaboration of this strategy. Even more so was the overall nature of the maquis as it had developed in most places through refuge, revolt, the process of the hunt, and the plurality of its aims: foremost the liberation of France but also the local subversion of Vichy, the consolidation of rural resistance, and the occupation, protection, and policing of its own communities and terrain. But what exactly constituted the terrain of the maquis and what its occupation and protection should entail was far from generally agreed. This basic issue was disputed across and within the different regions of the south, and even though most maquis groups experienced their first combat in limited actions followed by disengagement, the variants to this had a certain logic of their own, not least in the Haute-Savoie.

In no area was the internal logic of maquis strategy during these months so apparent and yet so contested as in the narrow Alpine valleys east of Annecy. The reports, legitimated by the BBC, of large gatherings of *réfractaires* and Resisters in the mountains of the Haute-Savoie in March 1943, only a few weeks after the start of STO, had put the *département* into the foreground of Resistance 'mythology', using the word in the Sorelian sense of an energizing, motivating potential.[32] Anti-fascists on the run in the south, notably Spanish republicans, were drawn to the area, and no mention of the activities of the maquis in the clandestine press of 1943 was complete without a reference to the patriotic defiance of the Haute-Savoie. The effect of this early pedigree on the strategy of local maquisards as it evolved in early 1944 would be difficult to overestimate. It was no less influential on the expectations and reactions within Vichy; Darnand and Henriot becoming obsessed in January 1944 with the need to mount an exemplary police and propaganda offensive against the Haute-Savoie. In the reductionism of Vichy propaganda against the maquis throughout France, the explicit equation is of the maquis ('terroristes') and the Communist Party ('bolchevisme'), which are seen to be engaged in 'la bolchevisation de la France' through a Moscow-directed 'insurrection armée',[33] and both Darnand and the new Prefect of the Haute-Savoie were agreed that the elimination of 'terrorism' in the *département* should be an entirely Vichy affair. The Prefect's report

[32] See Ch. 2.

[33] A tract, entitled 'Pourquoi ces attentats?', widely distributed in the south by both the Milice and the German authorities in January 1944, accused both de Gaulle and the communists of conspiring to promote the Bolshevik take-over of France, and attempted to rally the Pétainist faithful to this conspiracy theory by carrying a photograph of Cardinal Lienart of Lille on the front page, accompanied by a quote from the archbishop promoting national unity and the virtues of patience, sacrifice, effort, and loyalty to the 'Chef qui . . . commandait à Verdun'; AD Hérault 172W 35.

during January 1944 gave eight pages of 'attentats', and he stated that since his recent arrival he had done his utmost to create a co-operative climate for police operations in the area by talking to mayors, teachers, and others of the 'tragic consequences which would ensue' if Vichy were to fail to restore order with its own resources.[34] Similar points were being made by prefects elsewhere, so that the Haute-Savoie was far from unusual in soliciting an increase in police activity under French control. What made the Haute-Savoie an index of Vichy's repressive determination, and its reductionist attitude to the maquis, was the fact that the area was not significantly dominated by the FTP but rather contained the full range of Resistance affiliations and political affinities.

The maquis assembling in mid-winter in the snow-covered valleys of Thônes and Glières were palpably not under the influence of the Communist Party, but on the contrary represented the culmination of long-term planning and organization by career officers from the 27e Bataillon de Chasseurs Alpins who made up the nucleus of the AS in the area. There was a centre of FTP activity, but that was further to the north, in the Chablais, where, according to the Renseignements Généraux, the protests from the peasantry at the FTP's *coups de main* for all kinds of provisions were more angry and insistent than in many comparable areas of FTP implantation.[35] The dominance of the AS further south and west brought contacts with the Ain, where Romans-Petit had created a network of camps and an officer-training school (*école des cadres*) at les Gorges, and had received the Anglo-French mission of Heslop and Rosenthal on 21 September 1943.[36] Romans-Petit's leadership and drive, together with his policy for the Ain maquis of long-term military training mixed with direct action, gave him stature well outside his immediate area of operations, and in December he was ordered to extend his command to the AS maquis of the Haute-Savoie. The visionary plans of Commandant Vallette d'Osia to create a secret Alpine army had been at the origin of the local AS organization, dating back to the occupation of the southern zone in 1942, and the first instruction camp at the Col des Saisies which he created in February 1943. His professional style and ideas succeeded in recruiting other officers from the 27e BCA, but had only ephemeral success in organizing the *réfractaires* available during 1943. The summer months were ones of slowly deepening roots and structures as elsewhere, but the hunt was mainly to the advantage of the pursuing forces. In September 1943 Vallette d'Osia himself was arrested, and although he escaped by jumping from a train, he felt his security in the Haute-Savoie was too precarious. He relinquished his command and crossed to England, leaving

[34] AN F1C III. 1187, Haute-Savoie, report of 6 Jan. 1944.

[35] Paul Abrahams, 'Haute-Savoie at War, 1939–1945', 185–200.

[36] The mission also included an American wireless operator, Denis Johnson, and an American courier, Elizabeth Reynolds. Foot, *SOE in France*, 93, 288.

his colleagues with a strongly imprinted *idée-fixe* of a fighting Alpine force to which he had devoted his Resistance activities. Romans-Petit brought the flexible thinking of his own experience in the Ain, and instituted a replica of his *école des cadres* at the small maquis camp of la Cola in the valley of Manigod, to which young recruits from Catholic youth organizations had been particularly drawn, giving it the local name of 'le Camp des Enfants du Bon Dieu'.[37] Lieutenant Pierre Bastian, the leader of maquis groups in the area of Thônes, had provided it with uniforms and equipment, and the success of the peasant population of Manigod in concealing its existence, when other camps in the area had been located by both Vichy and Italian forces, recommended it to Romans-Petit and subsequently to the Anglo-French mission of Heslop and Rosenthal. The *école des cadres* of Manigod was created in December 1943 in this high valley of fir trees and ancient chalets south of Thônes, a region which had been called the 'Vendée savoyarde' for its rebelliousness against Jacobin centralism at the time of the Revolution.

The training period for maquis leaders, who were intended for the whole *département* of the Haute-Savoie, was first eight and then fifteen days, and the first intake of forty-five trainees brought the number of maquisards at the camp to eighty-five. The military director, Lieutenant Louis Jourdan (Joubert) worked closely with the other officers from the 27e BCA, Lieutenants Pierre Bastian and Théodose Morel and Captain Maurice Anjot. He imparted what he called 'la science militaire et maquisarde', which entailed an acceptance of guerrilla attack and disengagement as a model, but not one which surrendered the essentials of a more conventional concept of military conflict. 'Pour bien faire la guérilla, il fallait donc être capable d'abord de faire la guerre.'[38] A fully operational training camp, and a military presence in the shape of young career officers and close to a hundred men, carried its own conviction to the authorities in London through the reports of Heslop and Rosenthal; but for a supply of arms and ammunition to be provided in sufficient quantity to turn these maquisards into fully-fledged soldiers, the drops had to be substantial. A secure 'terrain de parachutage', occupied and patrolled continuously, was thought to be essen-

[37] *La Vallée de Thônes et Glières pendant la 2e guerre mondiale (1939–45)*, 2 vols. (Amis du Val de Thônes: Thônes, 1984), i. 107. These slim volumes make up Nos. 9 and 10 of the *Revue annuelle proposée par les Amis du Val de Thônes*, and are a further example of the colourful local work carried out by ex-Resisters and sympathizers in collecting oral evidence. Although the valley was overwhelmingly affiliated to the AS the evidence of FTP presence and activity is duly credited.

[38] Louis Jourdan, Julien Helfgott, and Pierre Golliet, *Glières, Haute-Savoie, 31 janvier–26 mars 1944. Première bataille de la Résistance* (Association des rescapés des Glières: Annecy, 1946). Jourdan's account of the Glières events is closely followed in these pages, and much is owed both to his memoirs and to others in the book. They still remain the best *point de départ* for the history of the Glières.

tial. Numerous separate sorties to and from the villages to retrieve the containers not only ran a high risk of detection through the tracks in the snow, but also could result in the loss of valuable material buried in new-fallen snow before the transportation could be completed. The logic pointed to the occupation of a safe and defensible reception area, and the choice of the high, spacious plateau des Glières made good strategic sense.

Situated north-east of Annecy at a height of over 1,500 metres the plateau was flanked by the small villages and hamlets of Thorens to the west and Saint-Jean-de-Sixt, Entremont, and le Petit-Bornand to the east along the road from Thônes to Bonneville which wound between several smaller mountain ranges under the high and extensive Chaîne des Aravis. The climb from the villages was hard and rugged, but the access paths were narrow and plentiful, combining both ease of defence and opportunity of retreat, providing the plateau was not systematically encircled. A number of half-used chalets were grouped in small concentrations at various points on the plateau, giving the basis for an encampment, and fires could be lit to guide the British planes without being overlooked by any higher habitation in the area. A hundred-strong contingent of well-trained maquisards would provide constant look-outs and sufficient men to recover and stow the containers, and yet leave enough mobility for an engagement with the kinds of reconnaissance and punitive forces which had kept the Maquis de l'Ain on the move and disrupted the development of Vallette d'Osia's groups in the autumn of 1943. The historical account of the decision to occupy the Glières still needs to be told in hypothetical language, for only in such terms can the careful assessment of possibilities by the leaders at Manigod be reconstructed. The occupation of Glières, insists Jourdan, was conceived only as a solution to a particular problem of military supplies, and not as an end in itself. It was one part of an evolutionary process towards an eventual Alpine army: it was not envisaged as the moment of its actual creation.[39]

Nevertheless, within the thinking which led to the occupation were rational arguments based on the failures of the first maquis camps at Lanfon and la Clusaz in 1943 to survive attacks by relatively minor Vichy and Italian forces, and more immediately the destruction of the small FTP camp of le Cruet by German troops on 26 January 1944, accompanied by reprisals on the nearby village of Thuy. The officers at Manigod had no illusions about the intensity of the local war between maquisards and Germans, nor of the repercussions on the population. On 29 January, the day that three maquisards from le Cruet were to be buried at Thônes, the camp at Manigod carried out the execution of two German prisoners captured at Annecy-le-Vieux, after negotiations to exchange them for captured maquisards had been refused by the German authorities. The destruction of the camps and

[39] Ibid. 36.

the intensification of the violence in the valleys argued strongly for a more consolidated maquis force, capable of defending itself away from the immediacy of the villages.[40] Ironically, given the outcome of the events at Glières, the decision to leave the valleys and occupy the plateau was therefore partly based on the belief that the supportive villagers would be spared the escalating brutality of the confrontations between Germans and the maquis.

The access to the plateau at the end of January 1944 by the AS maquis from Manigod and Thônes was not led by Romans-Petit, who had been recalled to the Ain, but by Captain Théodose Morel (Tom), an ex-instructor at Saint-Cyr, aged only 28, whose optimistic, youthful charisma energized and moulded the men under his command into something very close to the image of the disciplined, pure, dedicated combatant which interchanged with the independent, outlaw figure within the maquis discourse. The trigger for the ascent was not just the imminence of the *parachutages*, but also the confirmed reports of the opening of Darnand's police offensive into the area. The call to move to the plateau was addressed not only to all AS maquis in the area, but was extended to two adjoining FTP camps, 'Maurice Coulomb' and 'Liberté Chérie', but within days other groups from the Haute-Savoie joined the planned contingent of roughly 200, swelling the numbers to 465 including a company of fifty-six Spanish maquisards, workers from Vichy's Travail Étranger in the mountains, who had been threatened with deportation. With a parachute drop of fifty-four containers on 14 February, the potential for an Alpine battalion now existed.

The afflux of volunteers to the plateau realized the latent ideas of a combative gathering of Resisters in the Haute-Savoie, nurtured in the locality since the 'risings' of March 1943, but at the same time their very number and the volume of arms and ammunition eventually parachuted on to the plateau radically changed the character of the occupation as envisaged in the first preparations. A second dynamic factor altering the planned scenario was the size of the Vichy force under Colonel Lelong, composed of the GMR 'Aquitaine' from the west of France, mobile forces of the Garde, and large numbers of Milice, which in total was sufficient to encircle the Glières and cut off the basic supply lines of the maquis, provisioned from the villages on the perimeter of the plateau. Encirclement was not conquest, and the Vichy losses were high in the clashes which occurred between mid-February and mid-March, but it did force the maquis into pitched encounters, theoretically incompatible with the mobile tactics of guerrilla action but corresponding to much of the conventional outlook and training of the officers at Manigod, which made such engagements more feasible and more acceptable to the Maquis des Glières than to most maquis elsewhere.

[40] *La Vallée de Thônes et Glières*, ii. 7.

On 9 March a further successful encounter with the GMR at Entremont turned to disaster when Tom was killed by the GMR commanding officer, Lefèvre, who had been taken prisoner but had been allowed to keep his pistol in respect for his rank. The anger and shock among the maquisards at Tom Morel's death coincided with a massive *parachutage* of 580 containers, and the two events propelled Tom's older successor Captain Maurice Anjot (Bayard) into a decision of entrenchment on the plateau. On 12 March came the first German bombardment from the air, and on 24 March the Wehrmacht took over the siege of the plateau from the Vichy troops who had been beaten back each time they had attempted to take it by storm. As a concession to Vichy the Germans gave the Milice a tactical role in the assault. The Maquis des Glières had become a fortress maquis, the maquisards the first *bataillon* of a Resistance army, and the uneven struggle against a vastly superior force of 20,000 men the pitched battle which most maquis elsewhere were determined, at this stage, to avoid.

Within two days the numbers, air power, and artillery of the Germans proved decisive, and Anjot ordered the dispersion of the maquis on the night of 26 March. They had fought from rock to rock and refused to surrender. It was estimated incorrectly by the maquis at the time that some 300 Germans and 100 Miliciens were killed, while the maquis losses in the battle and the retreat were 150, including Anjot, followed by 200 maquisards and villagers arrested, tortured, shot, or deported in the days that followed. The figures for German losses have subsequently been variously, and substantially, reduced, but there is agreement on the ferocity of the hunt in the area carried out by the Milice, the GMR, and the Germans. Twice the Germans descended to the barbarity of releasing captured maquisards only to shoot them like rabbits as they were forced to stumble away from their captors across open space.[41]

Those prisoners not killed immediately were either deported or shot after Vichy courts martial. The effect of German torture, alongside Henriot's broadcasts, achieved both physical and verbal dehumanization. The maquisards of Glières were represented by Henriot as crazed animals and criminals, and the battle presented as a victory by the Milice and the Vichy forces of order over a rabble deserted by their leaders.[42] The report of the local Prefect Marion to Vichy continued the process of distortion in a contemptuous rejection of the instant Resistance account of Glières, which he called a total romanticization: far from the death of over 300 Germans, he wrote, only '1 German was killed in the conflict, and that was an

[41] Jourdan *et al.*, *Glières*, 138.

[42] Henriot's broadcast was on 29 Mar. 1944. See J.-L. Crémieux-Brilhac, 'La Bataille des Glières et "la guerre psychologique" ', *Revue d'histoire de la deuxième guerre mondiale* (July, 1975), 45–72; also H. R. Kedward, 'The Vichy of the other Philippe', in G. Hirschfeld and P. Marsh (eds.), *Collaboration in France* (Berg: Oxford, 1989), 32–46.

accident'; far from defending themselves with heroism, the maquis 'hardly fired a single shot, but dispersed as soon as they saw the green uniforms'. As for the claim that 'some three or four hundred prisoners have been shot by the Germans . . . in reality I think one can estimate the losses sustained by the so-called maquis in the whole area of Glières to be between 80 and 120 men, among whom figure an appreciable number of Spaniards'. The Prefect's praise went out to Colonel Lelong, Darnand's appointment to the 'mission' in Glières, to whose devotion and efforts he rendered homage.[43]

This propaganda conflict over the Glières was not a mere postscript. Morel had vainly attempted to persuade Lelong to withdraw by appealing to his patriotism. Lelong had attempted to persuade Morel to denounce the FTP killings of Vichy police officers in the immediate vicinity of Glières, but Morel refused to act in any way which would divide the maquis. There had been a mooted exchange of prisoners, but Lelong went back on his word, and the maquis raid on Entremont, in which Morel was killed, was launched punitively against the GMR for this betrayal. The maquis took sixty-seven GMR prisoners and made them do much of the heavy work in transporting the containers. There is no hard evidence that they were brutalized by the maquis on the plateau, but after the battle they exercised their revenge and played a decisive role in the recognition and arrest of maquisards who had escaped.[44] This bitter confrontation in word and act forced Vichy and the Resistance still further apart, and was instrumental in Vichy's decision a month later to make no distinctions between 'Gaullist' maquis and the FTP,[45] and in the decision by the Resistance that Henriot should be assassinated. In this respect, as in so many others, the events of Glières were a forcing-house in the final polarizations of the Occupation, a fact which was clearly grasped in the Haute-Savoie at the time, but which has often been overlooked in the post-war disputes over the strategic validity of the 'montée au plateau'. The Prefect Marion, for all his repudiation of the maquis, acknowledged immediately that the population of his *département* had made its decision. Almost alone among the prefects of the southern zone he registered the public's disbelief and opposition to Henriot's broadcasts during late March and April, saying that the people of the Haute-Savoie rejected Henriot's account of events as a distortion of the truth. The vast majority of the population, he reported, was sympathetic not only to *réfractaires* but to all those in conflict with established authority including 'terroristes' and 'éléments de l'Armée Secrète'. He also signalled the escalating collapse of Vichy local authority through the numerous resignations from the municipalities.[46]

[43] AN F1C III. 1187, Haute-Savoie, report of 4 May 1944.
[44] Jourdan *et al.*, *Glières*, 99–104.
[45] AD Gard CA 367, R. Clemoz to prefects, 2 May 1944.
[46] AN F1C III. 1187, Haute-Savoie, report of 4 May 1944.

The occupation of the Glières was alone among military events in France between January and April to produce a major battle. As such it was as local and as individualized as many of the other variants on different aspects of maquis evolution during this period. It was also one particular resolution to the search for the maquis, one realization of the ideal of the combative maquisard. Many of the ingredients of the maquis discourse are there, not least the camaraderie of the men in the woods and the sense of being marked out for some special adventure: on 20 February the maquisards gathered on the plateau to swear to 'Vivre libre ou mourir'. Jourdan wrote in 1946 of 'quelque chose de très pur' and of 'un oasis d'idéal'.[47] Julien Helfgott and Jean-Isaac Tresca evoked the evening *veillées*:

> People would have been amazed to hear Austrian and Polish songs mixed with those from the French mountains, but there, round the fire—the living flame which embodied the determination of our struggle—we kept a place for all those who had rebelled against the tyranny of Nazism.[48]

Marc Bombiger, the doctor in charge of the *infirmerie* at the centre of the plateau, claimed that

> everyone was looked after and quickly cured of any sickness . . . The *infirmerie* became the family home, *par excellence*, even for those just passing through. The *veillées* there were delightful occasions and everything was seriously discussed.[49]

There is no reason to devalue these memoirs as a form of nostalgia; similar expressions occur too frequently and too widely in oral evidence throughout the southern zone to be a question of false consciousness. Idealism, mixed always with the memory of extreme physical hardship, jostled for primacy with the anger and resentment at infiltration, betrayal, and repression by the forces of collaboration. This depth of feeling was not a product of post-war imagination. For many anti-fascist veterans of the Spanish Civil War or struggles in Central Europe, it was their second or even third 'great cause'; for the young French maquisards it was their first. Naïvety and fantasies were there alongside pragmatism. Failure or pyrrhic victory were as regular in the maquis as success and exhilaration. Few memoirs, oral or written, disguise these lived experiences of the maquis, and few deny their emotional intensity.

How other maquisards saw the Glières events moves the issue away from the subjective realities of individual and community experience towards the disputed areas of public meaning. In 1946, when the Rescapés des Glières published their memorial book, another collective voice, that of the Haute-Savoie FTP, paid tribute to the patriotic heroism of Glières but vigorously denounced it as a 'monstrous error in strategic conception'. The concentration of forces in one position, the argument ran, made it all too easy for

[47] Jourdan *et al.*, *Glières*, 73, 50. [48] Ibid. 50. [49] Ibid. 98.

the enemy; the essential strategy should have been to retain the initiative in all operations, whereas the ascent to the plateau isolated the combatants from the mass of the people and gave the Germans the opportunity to crush them. Both the BCRA and the BBC are accused of promoting joint errors of *attentisme* and *rassemblement*.[50] This indictment was no more a product of post-war reasoning than the emotions of the survivors of Glières. It was a source of animosity at the time that the AS and the FTP in the *département* should view the *montée au plateau* so differently, and that the FTP's État-major should have refused to endorse the decision of the two FTP units who had been integrated into the *bataillon* on the plateau. Any expectation of an interlocked strategy by which the AS occupied the plateau while the FTP broke the encirclement from outside, foundered on the penury of arms and ammunition to which the FTP had access, a weakness compounded by their own acknowledged military inexperience: 'nos hommes manquent encore de savoir-faire'.[51] Had even a third of the massive drop of arms on 10 March been to maquis units beyond the plateau, the possibilities might have been altered, though this hypothetical proposition does little more than evoke a multitude of reasons why it was not even considered.

Glières was not fully planned as a military redoubt, either at Manigod, or by Heslop and Rosenthal, or in London. The weapons which were dropped in their hundreds, 'une abondante moisson d'armes',[52] did not include the heavier bazookas which might have made the artillery battles more equal, and no contingent plans were made for the plateau's reprieve. Tragically, the very abundance of the *parachutages* confined the maquis even more closely to the plateau, since the 580 containers needed to be located, emptied, and stored, and four men were required to transport each container in the deeper snow where sledges could not be used. The immobility enforced by the 'moisson d'armes' was not envisaged in sufficient detail at the start, and this must constitute the main area of miscalculation, both in France and in London. 'Rassemblement' without a clear function and back-up looks like a failure in strategic thinking. The accompanying judgement of 'attentisme' has, on the other hand, been vehemently refuted. It would seem that the most active sector of the maquis in the immediate area before the ascent to the plateau was at Thorens where over 100 AS maquisards were given authorization to sustain their morale by *coups de main* against Vichy and collaborationist targets. Morel himself in January 1944 received orders to attack any isolated German vehicle patrolling the roads, and once on the plateau he made his own decisions to launch sudden thrusts and punitive raids against the Vichy forces. The only section of the maquis to be fully equipped with skis was a groupe franc which patrolled the

[50] *R.1.3. Francs-Tireurs et Partisans de la Haute-Savoie* (France d'Abord, 1946), 89–102.
[51] Ibid. 94. [52] Jourdan *et al.*, *Glières*, 61.

extremities of the plateau, and they acquired their equipment by force of hand against the small groups of resolute winter holiday-makers in the area. These acts parallel those claimed as 'direct action' by FTP maquis throughout the *zone sud*, and the final running battle of the maquis against the Germans and Milice makes the suggestion of 'attentisme' still more difficult to sustain, even if the original intention of Glières was to receive the *parachutages* and continue the building of an Alpine army, itself a strategy of the long term.

The criticism of 'isolation' throws into relief the intense community involvement which preceded and accompanied the move to the plateau, and the readiness of the population to hide and care for those who escaped. The local postal services had been thoroughly infiltrated by the Resistance, so that ill-advised communications—not least by the maquisards—were stopped and their senders disciplined. The farms and chalets stored provisions, and at the *montée* the villagers put their carts, sledges, and mules at the disposal of the maquis organizer, Lieutenant Pierre Bastian.[53] For two weeks the food kept arriving, but Jourdan rightly admits that this close involvement was indeed broken by the encirclement effected by Vichy forces, so that the villagers were forced into helplessness. Here must surely lie the second area of miscalculation, though physical isolation did not bring with it any alienation of the maquis from the sympathies of the population.

Glières was not only a singular variant on the strategic evolution and conduct of the southern maquis in these early months of 1944, it was also a variant which warned against a merely partial integration of strategy between the maquis and the Allies, which appeared to promise so much but restricted and disabled at the same time. The FTP of the Chablais and elsewhere in the Haute-Savoie had their reasons for being critical of the AS and the Allies in the Glières, since their own guerrilla strategy was both under-equipped and undervalued, but some FTP maquisards have argued that at least their freedom of action was not circumscribed by the kind of incomplete co-ordination with London which they witnessed in the events of Glières.[54] But whatever the intensity of debate which still takes place in the Haute-Savoie on these issues, what cannot be disclaimed is the fact that the realization of an organized maquis army in the hills, and the reality of the battle of Glières reinforced the combative claims of the entire French Resistance, and it did so without disrupting the protean development of the maquis at local and regional level.

[53] Bastian himself might have survived had he stayed in the chalet which had hid him after the battle, but an injury to his head seemed to have affected his judgement, and he insisted on rejoining his men. 'Mes jeunes, dit-il, m'attendent là-bas: ils sont à bout; que feront-ils sans moi? C'est mon devoir de les rejoindre.' He was caught, tortured, and shot; *La Vallée de Thônes et Glières*, ii. 20.

[54] Evidence from Jean Vittoz, 19 May 1969.

These three studies of the Cévennes, the Lot, and the Glières reveal a number of key factors in the varying evolution and strategy of the maquis: the personality and charisma of the maquis *chef*, the uneven incidence of Vichy's military campaigns and German repression, and the variable distribution of arms and ammunition, which seemed to many maquisards both unjust and capricious. Of these three factors, the role of the leader has been underlined as probably the most significant in the development of the character and even the effectiveness of each maquis unit, and has received priority attention in the telling of the maquis story. The most contentious factor continues to be the access to arms and ammunition, and this too has featured at the forefront of memoirs and historical accounts, while the factor of repression, and particularly reprisals, is the one which has given the names of many otherwise unknown locations a prominent position in the bulky literature generated by anniversaries and memorial events.

What is everywhere apparent in the histories, but remains elusive as an explanatory factor, is the significance of locality itself, the most immediate context in which the maquis evolved. It seems uncontroversial, at one level, to say that the variants in evolution in the Cévennes, the Lot, and the Glières were consistent with strong local factors, but it becomes far more speculative to imply that local factors acted as cultural or historical determinants. There is good reason for the uprush of doubt at this point. Such an implication raises the spectre of regionalism, the ghosts of an ancient past, and the autochthonous power of folklore and local *mentalités* to shape the content and nature of a phenomenon which had a national aim, the liberation of France, and therefore a national history. Maquisards, from all areas, unite in the rejection of any idea that the maquis had regionalist aims, and in so doing they tend to be suspicious of any enquiry into local motivations or determinants which might appear to locate the maquis in the political history of regionalism and regionalist movements. The problem for the researcher is one of exploring the very real local and regional factors at work in shaping the maquis, without prompting the easily over-defensive reaction of maquisard patriotism. Region*al*, not regional*ist*, has to be the constant theme, and for obvious semantic reasons there is an advantage in using the words 'local' and 'locality' in order to avoid complications. But not all complications should be avoided, and a hint of regionalism can indeed be found in several maquis accounts, and occasionally in oral *témoignages*. It does at least appear possible to say that the local presence manifested by the maquis in January to April 1944 usurped Vichy's claims to represent the interests of rural and regional France, though this is not to suggest that the maquis came to embrace the regionalist concepts within Vichy's early propaganda.

A populist and cultural stress on regional *libertés*, in the plural, had been the Vichy response to the revolutionary concept of *liberté*, in the singular, which was pilloried by the French intellectual and political Right as abstract and therefore anarchic. Charles Maurras, prophet of Vichy's regionalism, defined *libertés* as factual and earth-bound, ensuring order and hierarchy. For forty years he had preached a return to ancient rural and regional rights, pre-revolutionary cultures, and communal pride, which he associated with his Provençal birthplace, Martigues, and which he claimed had been swept away by the centralizing tyranny of Jacobinism and the Republics. Vichy's regionalism, and its inseparable cult of the peasant, were proclaimed as non-political, but were rooted firmly in this highly politicized soil.

In 1941 the novel *Vent de Mars* by Henri Pourrat was awarded the Prix Goncourt. Embodying the spirit of the Auvergne, the novel was acclaimed as the model expression of Vichy's regionalist and rural ideology. With an earthy display of symbolism the prize was bestowed at Chamalières in the heart of the region. In Toulouse the notables who made up the Commission de Propagande Régionaliste headed by the Regional Prefect, adopted a report on 'Le Régionalisme' in which it was described less as an ideology than a 'method'. It was, they claimed, an analytical method leading from the particular to the general and vice versa: it was an experimental method based on the priority of experience; it was a social method applying collectively to all inhabitants of the region; and it was finally a regenerative method resulting in a growth in national strength through the regeneration of regions, provinces, and 'pays' 'which constitute the living and eternal reality of the patrie'.[55] At Nîmes, throughout 1941, the Prefect Angelo Chiappe hosted a succession of conferences, lectures, and working parties on the Cévennes, arguing to his Regional Prefect at Marseille that the Cévennes should be considered as an economic and political region in its own right and administered as such. He acknowledged its Protestantism and the historical importance of the Camisards to its folklore and traditions, and he clearly envisaged himself as the natural prefect for this projected new region.[56] In Alès, the industrial and commercial hub of the Cévennes, Gabriel Haon, president of the Literary and Scientific Society of the town, argued instead that the Cévennes should be attached to the Languedoc, though Monsieur Teissier, president of the wholesale wine producers of the Gard, thought this would not serve the interest of the Gardois *viticulteurs*, and preferred the existing Provençal connection.[57]

[55] AD Aude M 2585, report by M. Chauvet, 'Le Régionalisme', n.d.

[56] 'Région des Cévennes', written by Angelo Chiappe and sent to Vichy on 13 July 1942. The plan for such a region was still alive after the Liberation. On 11 Sept. 1944 the Syndicat d'Initiative de Nîmes et du Gard passed a motion in favour of a region Nîmes-Cévennes-Vivarais on the basis of economic interests linking the Ardèche, the Lozère, and the Gard, and with references to the role of Nîmes in 'héleno-celtique' civilization, and to the great 16th-c. fairs of Saint-Gilles and Beaucaire; AD Gard CA 1512.

[57] Ibid. Gabriel Haon's argument was set out in a booklet entitled *Régionalisme. Esquisse d'une organisation régionaliste et corporative* (Alès, 1941). His recommendation was adopted by the Société scientifique et littéraire d'Alès on 9 May 1941.

Such expressions of regional consciousness and concern were merely a small part of a huge body of literature, and of a large number of discussions and meetings, which gave an intellectual context to Vichy's Propagande Paysanne. Issued from Vichy by means of its regular *Bulletins d'Orientation*, this insistent propaganda extolled the *libertés*, the independence, and the strength of the countryside, while calling, with mounting desperation, for peasants to demonstrate more economic concern for those facing shortages (*la disette*) in the towns.[58] Whatever the initial declarations of Vichy, its rural policy was ultimately reduced to this: propaganda to secure the maximum level of agricultural products for the Ravitaillement Général. As the peasant producers proved more and more recalcitrant, the intellectual and administrative enthusiasms for regionalism and the countryside began to give way to accusations of peasant egoism and atavistic individualism. After STO and the entrenchment of *réfractaires* in the Cévennes, Chiappe's call for a single administrative unit lost its grand anthropological sweep and became a functional demand for a coherent police force. Vichy's 'retour à la terre' as a high-minded cultural concept was broken on the hard realities of peasant obduracy and subversion. Problems of prices, labour, and protection from STO and German requisitions, came to dominate peasant meetings with administrators. The cultural gatherings, the 'Soirées Occitanes', and the ceremonial occasions in the countryside, patronized by the urban bourgeoisie, disappeared. It was said that the collaborationist Chiappe was unable to attend a rural event in his 'own' Cévennes from mid-1943 onwards.[59]

A year later Vichy further alienated rural workers by the most universally hated of all its taxes, the 'impôt métal'. Announced in April 1944, the tax demanded two to three kilos of copper from every family, or the equivalent in money, calculated at 900 fr. per kilo. With monthly wages of workers averaging between 1,800 and 2,700 fr., this was an impossible imposition. The mayor of Chambéry declared that young families would be unable to meet it, the Prefect of the Lozère declared unanimous opposition within his rural *département*, the Prefect of the Ain said it was bitterly resented by the population and would result in wide refusals to pay, and in the Corrèze the message was the same.[60] In the area of Vialas in the Lozère tracts circulated saying that the *impôt métal* was for German ammunition, and if five million

[58] See *Bulletin d'orientation*, 9 (15 Nov. 1942), and 10 (30 Nov. 1942). Both of these numbers from the Propagande paysanne in Vichy highlighted the urgent problems of *ravitaillement* and the approaching difficulties of winter.

[59] Evidence from Henri Cordesse, 22 Mar. 1982, Jean-Pierre Chabrol, 2 Mar. 1982, and Max Allier, 26 Mar. 1982.

[60] AN F1C III. 1186, Savoie, report of 4 May 1944; 1165, Lozère, 5 May 1944; 1135, Ain, 5 May 1944; 1147, Corrèze, May 1944. There is an entertaining account of the origins and progress of the *impôt métal* in Pierre Arnoult, *Les Finances de la France et l'occupation allemande* (PUF, 1951), 395–9. Arnoult traces the tax to initial German insistence, but shows how farcical its implementation, or rather non-implementation, became. The Germans lost interest after the Allied Normandy landings.

families were to give three kilos each it would result in 15,000 tons or 600 million bullets to be used against their own children.[61] The tax was particularly resented by small proprietors in any wine-growing area, who had already traded in their copper for products used in the treatment of vines.[62] What began with the *Vent de Mars* and promises of regional and local priorities ended in a regime exerting centralized pressure through a network of tax and food inspectors desperate to maximize the proceeds of the countryside.

The relationship of the maquis to local issues evolved in the opposite way, beginning with the basic economic realities of food and survival and a series of informal, functional contracts which recognized, and indeed depended on, the input from rural communities. By the spring of 1944 deeper identities of interest had crystallized round the maquis as an expression of local pride and resilience, and as the overt manifestation of rural resistance against both the Germans and Vichy. The maquis occupations of Glières, Lasalle, or Cajarc, however temporary, affirmed the effective presence of the maquis not only in the national struggle but also in specific, named localities: André Malraux made this point in 1973 when he inaugurated the Glières monument on the plateau: 'Almost daily the broadcasts from London carried the message "Three countries are resisting in Europe: Greece, Yugoslavia, the Haute-Savoie" '.[63] Resistance tracts, in 1943–4, made eloquent appeals to the peasantry as a whole, referring less to regional identities than to French citizenship, but there were also direct evocations of regional assertiveness. A communist tract from the Vaucluse, distributed also in the Gard and further afield, aimed to rally peasant support for a national day of demonstrations on 14 July 1943. It began 'Paysan français . . . remember the long series of struggles waged by your ancestors to free you from serfdom' and it called on peasants to join 'comités populaires paysans' to outmanœuvre Vichy's corporation paysanne.[64] Such generalized references were made more specific by a tract fly-posted in the Perpignan area headed 'Catalans à l'action . . . pour un 11 novembre de combat au chant de la Marseillaise . . . Vive Le Roussillon. Vive la France', and still more by an FTP *papillon* in the Hérault in February 1944 calling on all French people to join FTP units, with the final appeal, 'To arms . . . Fight to make the Languedoc a worthy successor to Corsica!'[65]

A host of examples could be adduced to illustrate the recurrence of local exhortations in the Resistance press, just as maquisards themselves have constantly evoked the nature of the local terrain. Abbé Chipier's memoirs

61 AD Lozère R 7060, tracts found 24–5 Apr. 1944.
62 AN F1C III. 1156, Hérault, report of 4 May 1944.
63 *La Vallée de Thônes et Glières*, ii. 10.
64 AD Gard CA 328, tract 'Paysans', July 1943.
65 AD Hérault 172W 35, 'Tracts divers', 1943–4.

of the Chablais in the Haute-Savoie, written in 1945, specified the FTP of the area as workers from the towns, particularly Thonon, who had to balance concession and persuasion in their relations with the peasantry, but his language transforms the book into a celebration of the countryside:

The steep, stony paths of the local country regions . . . the 'route du Léman' . . . the goat tracks zig-zagging to the top . . . the mountains summon the *réfractaires* . . . suddenly, *there* is the mountain, its paths discreetly open. In the darkness or under the stars, the mountains welcome the flower of the nation's youth . . . led by Maurice Blanchard, the hero of the Chablais maquis. His prestigious name is on everyone's lips. He is the maquis outpost, its vanguard . . . he opens up the mountains, he makes them our friends.[66]

This literary convention of the hospitable, enveloping countryside is personalized in other accounts to indicate the traditional warm-hearted character of the local population. The tribute to the Savoyards in 1946 by Pierre Golliet in the first memorial book to the maquis of the plateau des Glières is of this nature:

Everything predestined this corner of France to become the theatre of the first armed insurrection; the lie of the land, the spirit of the population, the leadership qualities inherited by the Resistance from the *chasseurs alpins*. The maquis needed the mountains; the deeper the valleys the more the enemy feared to enter them and the easier it was for *réfractaires* to escape without trace and to mount their ambushes. The region of Savoy offered an ideal terrain for the strategy adopted from Corsica, which overnight had become a national institution. It also offered its traditions of hospitality: a Savoyard knows how to open the door and put people at ease by a simple 'entrez seulement', an idiomatic phrase which 'étrangers' might not fully grasp, but whose warmth they would immediately feel.[67]

When Julien Helfgott remembered with affection the regional songs which expressed so much emotion at the *veillées* of the Glières maquis, he stressed that they came not just from Savoyard areas, but from all the different provinces represented in the maquis, from Austria, Poland, and from the fifty-six Spaniards who fought on the plateau. In this way the maquis was shown to have regional sympathies but not restricted to any one region.[68] A report to the CFLN in Algiers on the state of the maquis had made the same point in early 1944, in its description of an 'average' maquis:

All classes and all regions are mixed together. Three students from Lille, building workers from Bordeaux, young peasants from the Languedoc, workers from Marseille, men from Lorraine, an officer in riding breeches, youths from the Chantiers de la Jeunesse. A bizarre collection: the image of France.[69]

66 Abbé Chipier, *Souffrances et gloires du maquis chablaisien*, 11–47.
67 Jourdan *et al.*, *Glières*, 11. 68 Ibid. 90–2.
69 AN 72. AJ 63. 'Dans un maquis', Service de documentation du commissariat à l'intérieur du CFLN (1944).

It only slowly became apparent after the war just how many maquis units were composed to a significant extent of men from the immediate rural vicinity and from small towns within the neighbouring areas. This localized feature of maquis history varies greatly from one maquis to another even within the same region, but the realization that there was a substantial number of *agriculteurs* in the maquis made it impossible to talk of maquisards generally as representative of the towns, as the first articles after the Liberation had tended to do.[70] With this realization came a greater awareness of the intricate rural and regional structures which made the maquis experience what it was, or at the very least provided its context. The local histories of the numerous maquis of the Cévennes by Aimé Vielzeuf are firmly set within the Cévenol culture and traditions. The Cévenol novelist, Jean-Pierre Chabrol, himself a maquisard with the FTP and whose grandparents had been peasants and shepherds, provided a preface to one of Vielzeuf's volumes in 1964. He notes that the peasants in what he calls 'ma montagne cévenole' handed over their old rifles from the First World War to the maquis, and he goes on to say, 'I was a child of the mining country, but it was only in the maquis that I got to know the miners; I thought of myself as a Cévenol of the purest blood, but it was only in the maquis that I came to know my Cévennes . . . tender and violent Cévennes.'[71] This approach to the maquis as a regional experience argues that the Cévennes comprised not just hospitable peasants and a terrain suitable for maquis operations, but also a culture of rebellion enshrined in the Camisard tradition of dissidence and guerrilla combat against unacceptable authority. The maquis novels by Jean-Pierre Chabrol, *Un homme de trop*, and by René Évrard and Aimé Vielzeuf, *Comme le scorpion sous la laùze*, have both explored the cultural relationship between the Cévennes and the maquis, using highly localized expressions and customs to give a documentary veracity to the barely fictional maquisards.[72]

[70] *Le Volontaire*, Hebdomadaire régional des FFI Montpellier, 4 (29 Oct. 1944) has an article entitled 'Paysans et maquisards' which interestingly argues that town and country grew closer during the period of the maquis, but the assumption is that most maquisards originated in the towns.

[71] Aimé Vielzeuf, . . . *et la Cévenne s'embrasa* (Éditions le Camariguo: Nîmes, 1981). Préface, Jean-Pierre Chabrol, 11–20.

[72] Jean-Pierre Chabrol, *Un homme de trop* (Gallimard, 1958); René Évrard et Aimé Vielzeuf, *Comme le scorpion sous la laùze* (Évrard et Vielzeuf: Nîmes, 1980). The novels consciously continue the tradition set by André Chamson, whose 'romans dans l'histoire' merged Cévenol fact and fiction. Chabrol's novel is loosely based on the FTP attack on the prison of the Maison Centrale at Nîmes on 4 Feb. 1944, when some twenty Resisters were liberated. Évrard and Vielzeuf fictionalize one of the many cases of infiltration into the maquis by agents of the Milice or the Germans. By making the central figure of the novel an infiltrator the authors set up a confrontation between his Henriot-like contempt for the maquis, which dominates his thinking at the outset, and the realities of maquis comradeship, discipline, and sacrifice which he gradually discovers.

As we have seen, almost all references to the Cévennes and the maquis, both at the time and since, have made references to the Camisards. After Louis XIV had repealed Henri IV's concessions to the Protestants of France, by the Revocation of the Edict of Nantes in 1685, the Cévennes became a terrain for lay preachers who kept the Protestant faith alive, resisting the destruction of chapels and the disruption of religious activities by force of arms where necessary. Referring to Christ's sojourn in the desert, they held meetings in the open air, and it was from this practice that the annual Protestant Assemblée du Désert eventually derived. In September 1935 the Cévenol novelist André Chamson celebrated the history and concept of resistance in the Cévennes with a speech to the Assemblée on the struggles of their ancestors which he entitled 'la Résistance d'un peuple'.[73] Within a few years it was to be revered as prophetic, as a link between the war which finally broke out between Louis XIV's armies and the Cévenol Protestants in 1702, known as 'la guerre des Camisards', and the war waged by their descendants, the maquisards, in 1943–4. Across the centuries, as Philippe Joutard has brilliantly shown, a resilient pattern of oral transmission kept the stories of the Camisards vibrant in the collective memory of the Cévenol peasantry, forming a legacy of popular resistance easily remobilized under the German Occupation.[74] Everything that the Camisards had done, their guerrilla tactics in small bands, their dependence on the support of small landholders and tradespeople, their elusive disappearance along mountain paths and into caves in the hillside, all was relevant. The life of the new outlaws had to be reinvented in many practical details, but even after 240 years the outlaw culture seemed familiar, and, above all, morally right.

Nor was the resistance tradition purely a Protestant one in the area. There had been Catholic brigandage and resistance against the centralizing force of Jacobinism along the borders of the Gard, the Hérault, and the Ardèche, from 1795 to the early years of the nineteenth century, and the Protestant Chamson was prepared to celebrate this too in one of his later novels written in 1977.[75] Gwynne Lewis, historian of this 'second Vendée', implies a number of possible comparisons with the Second World War when he refers to the 'Catholic, royalist *maquis*' of the counter-revolutionary period, and he writes, 'The massive resistance to conscription may legitimately be construed as the defence of the local community, in some cases of the local economy, against the rapid encroachments of the state.'[76] The words would barely need

[73] Joutard *et al.*, *Cévennes, terre de refuge*, 221. Chamson's speech was printed in *Revue du Christianisme social* (Oct.–Nov. 1935), 337–40.

[74] Philippe Joutard, *La Légende des Camisards; une sensibilité au passé* (Gallimard, 1977).

[75] I owe this reference to Gwynne Lewis, 'Political Brigandage and Popular Disaffection in the South-East of France, 1795–1804', in Gwynne Lewis and Colin Lucas (eds.), *Beyond the Terror: Essays in French Regional and Social History*, 1794–1815 (CUP: Cambridge, 1983), 195.

[76] Ibid. 230, 214. Compare the implications of the title of the book on the counter-revolution by François Lebrun and Roger Dupuy, *Les Résistances à la Révolution* (Imago, 1987). In the course

changing to do service for the refusal of STO and the rejection of Vichy authority in the Cévennes, as in many other areas where traditions of revolt still had the capacity of stirring the pride of local particularisms, such as the Thônes valley in the Haute-Savoie which had staged counter-revolutionary protests in 1793 in favour of refractory priests and had fought against the revolutionary armies. The struggle had scored the history of the valley. It was now the matrix of the Maquis des Glières, after hiding individual *réfractaires*. The SOE agent Francis Cammaerts found that the historical memory of the stand against Richelieu in the small town of Crest on the river Drôme still had the capacity to contribute to anti-authoritarian mentalities in the area where he established the first nuclear groups of his network 'Jockey'. 'What group', writes Paul Silvestre in his penetrating study of the Isère, 'did not seek to identify itself with some hero from the folklore of the Dauphiné or from the Pantheon of revolutionaries . . . potent images of hope', and he cites a group of maquisards who were peripatetic, moving from place to place with no more than a rucksack, who identified with the mythology of Louis Mandrin, the young brigand leader of the early eighteenth century, who entered popular legend as generous and open-hearted.[77]

West and south-west of the Massif Central, regional detail has also been used to deepen the cultural and historical roots of the maquis. The history of the Groupes Vény in the Lot appeared in 1980 under the title *Ombres et espérances en Quercy*, and presented a cultural iconography of peasant life and traditions in the region. The opening sequence of photographs shows the adding of wine to soup (*le chabrot*), the preparation of the *fête du cochon*, a pig and two peasants searching for truffles near Lalbenque, a flock of sheep leaving the *bergerie*, and a peasant woman preparing wool for a mattress. The preface starts with the statement that 'Tout ce qu'on va lire est le fait de gens du Quercy' and in the pages of background to the groupes francs, the old Quercy is presented as the 'ancien pays gaulois des Cadourques'. Other atmospheric photographs show the barns, farms, and châteaux frequented by the maquis, and there is an example of the numerous *gariottes* or *cazelles* which made excellent hiding-places both for men and for arms. The whole presentation might suggest a maquis which had more local than national significance, but these were the groups that received a high

of the book there are several allusions forwards to the comparable acts of local resistance during the Second World War. Jacques Godechot writes of the Toulouse area, 'Les "maquis" contre-révolutionnaires passent à l'action en mai 1799, ils coupent les arbres de la liberté, tirent des coups de feu sur les patriotes, les acheteurs de biens nationaux, les corps de garde' (p. 124). Alan Forrest, analysing those who refused to be conscripted into the Revolutionary Armies, concludes that their revolt carried certain local communities with them. 'Dans de telles conditions, les jeunes qui restaient dans leurs foyers ou qui vivaient dans la clandestinité au bord du village savaient que leur combat était celui de tous' (p. 189). I am indebted to my colleague Maurice Hutt for directing me towards this book.

[77] Silvestre, 'S.T.O., maquis et guérilla dans l'Isère', 16–17.

investment from the British Special Operations Executive (SOE) in arms, money, and agents. They were part of a wider movement of Groupes Vény run by a socialist officer Jean Vincent (Colonel Vény) with their origin in an intelligence network 'Froment', based on Marseille but integrated into the AS in 1943.[78] Two years before this publication, in 1978, Noireau's memoirs of the maquis of the Lot had developed strong local themes. Noireau specified the Quercy region as having a collective memory of

> various forms of armed resistance against foreign powers, against legal oppression and central authority . . . You could not find any Quercy child of school age without some knowledge of the proud history of the ancient tribe of the Cadourques. Every peasant believes he is in some way an heir to these ancient fighters, many of whom had their hands severed by the enemy leader, as a terrible price for their heroism. People in this part of the country are close to regarding all central administration as an intolerable burden. They are close cousins to the neighbouring Camisards of the Cévennes.[79]

Further south, the amalgam of regional identity and national purpose also marks the work of Lucien Maury for the *département* of the Aude. Maury is acutely conscious of the area's distant but still fertile links with the struggles of the Cathars against the Albigensian crusades. The Cathars were known as 'les purs', a phrase often used of the maquis.

> Whatever the social motivation of each individual, we were all the heirs of those who had forged our history in the ancient city of Carcassonne, in the austere châteaux of Lastours, Peyrepertuse, Quéribus, Puivert, and other citadels, where our ancestors had perished of thirst beside dried-up wells, behind impregnable walls, or died, burnt at the stake, the victims of intolerance and fanaticism.[80]

In an interview in 1982 Maury claimed that 'Le Catharisme est resté l'esprit de la Résistance', as strong in action against the Germans in the period of the Occupation as against Simon de Montfort in the early thirteenth century. He pointed out that his drawing for the cover of his local history merges medieval battlements into the monument for fallen Resisters to create a unified symbol of local history.[81] It is one of many suggestive pointers towards the cultural nature of the maquis, which varied at the time from the kind of intellectual dimension given to the Vercors maquis by the active presence of the writer Jean Prévost, to the functional value of local rootedness claimed by Joseph Nodari, an *agent de liaison* in the Lot chosen by Jean-Jacques Chapou for his familiarity with the economic world and the spoken patois of the peasantry.[82]

[78] Picard and Chaussade, *Ombres et espérances en Quercy, passim.*
[79] Noireau, *Le Temps des partisans*, 89.
[80] Maury, *La Résistance audoise*, i. 27–8.
[81] Evidence from Lucien Maury, 24 June 1982.
[82] Jean Prévost led a Company of 129 men, known as the Compagnie Goderville (Prévost's *nom de guerre*) in the battles of the Vercors. For Nodari, see Ch. 7, Oral memories.

And yet, despite all these rich and suggestive references to regional history and culture which might appear to announce a regionalist character to certain maquis, it has to be said that Lucien Maury repudiated any notion that the maquis in the south-west of France had Occitanist motivations or ideas, and so too did Jean-Pierre Chabrol for the Cévennes, while in the Lot, most maquisards who knew Robert Noireau regard his evocation of the Cadourques as either fanciful or irrelevant in explaining the Lotois maquis.[83] The photographs in the Vény book can be seen as providing context rather than explanation, and the multiplicity of local studies can be read as a tribute to local achievements rather than as a sub-text of regionalist particularism. In many ways it is more productive to invert the process of explanation and ask what the maquis contributed to regionalist consciousness rather than vice versa. It is certainly evident that the retrospective validation of the southern maquis as one source of inspiration for the revival of Occitanism in post-war Languedoc, and the dramatic swing of the movement away from the dominantly right-wing politics of Frédéric Mistral and the Félibrige, have given a new regionalist purpose to the search for the maquis in certain, mainly literary, writings.[84] But even in the recent publications of the Presses du Languedoc, affirmation of locality and region goes hand in hand with the recognition of the nationalism and internationalism of the maquis. What emerges from the recent Cévenol research is indeed a rediscovery of the maquis as a local phenomenon, but at the same time an equal rediscovery of its international character. If the Cévennes were 'eminently favourable to the implantation of the maquis' they were also 'favourable to a maquis made up of foreigners, notably German anti-fascists'. This sentence is the opening to a history of *Un Maquis d'antifascistes allemands en France*, which starts with a list of Cévenol geographical and cultural attributes which favoured the maquis and which have been mentioned many times in the course of this study. A base of regional particularities is thus established for the history of the German maquisards which follows, a history that reconstructs the life and actions of the maquis under François Rouan (Montaigne) in prolific detail.[85]

Such an unstinting recognition of fighters for the French Resistance, whose origins lay elsewhere, or whose religion was Jewish, is widely felt to be as overdue as any stress on local structures. A tribute to the revolt of Yugoslavs in Villefranche-de-Rouergue, against the Nazi army into which they had been forcibly enrolled, provides another example of this literature of acknowledgement, of which Florimond Bonte was a pioneer. The revolt of 17 September 1943 was put down by a horrific massacre of at least sixty of the

[83] Evidence from Lucien Maury, 24 June 1982, and Jean-Pierre Chabrol, 2 Mar. 1982. Doubts about Noireau's book were expressed in evidence from Abbé Souiry, 4 Apr. 1991, Pierre Labie, 11 Mar. 1991, and Joseph Nodari, 28 Mar. 1991.

[84] See evidence from Max Allier, Ch. 7, Oral Memories.

[85] Éveline and Yvan Brès, *Un Maquis d'antifascistes allemands en France*.

mutineers, the exact number hidden by elaborate German efforts to destroy the bodies. Those who escaped, notably Bozo Jelenek, found their way into various maquis units of the FTP and MOI in the Cantal, the Aveyron, and the Tarn.[86] It was one of the many routes by which anti-fascists arrived in the maquis, the most regular being the refusal of hundreds of Spanish republicans to submit to internment or deportation, and their individual integration into maquis units or their separate constitution of guerrilla bands such as Liberté in the Lot or the Ebre section who fought on the plateau des Glières. The Guérilleros Espagnols in the south-west and Pyrenean areas had experience of fighting behind the Nationalist lines in Spain, and had re-formed as embryonic brigades in France as early as 1942, structured by the movement Reconquista de España and specializing initially in groupe franc activity in the towns, allied to the urban FTP. By the spring of 1944 the 2e Brigade de Guérilleros Espagnols centred on Toulouse and led by Commandants Linares and Ramos counted some sixty men living as maquisards and fifty as groupes francs, with a hundred others in reserve.[87] Brigades of similar strength were nominally in existence in all the *départements* of the Toulouse and Montpellier regions, with a general leader in Jésus Rios, killed by the Milice in the winter of 1943–4 in the Ariège and succeeded by Luis Fernandez.[88] An independent and potentially formidable force, the Guérilleros featured constantly in Vichy's lists of activists under surveillance, and it was the regularity of Vichy arrests in the south-west that led many Spanish republicans to join maquis groups in the Massif Central, the Cévennes, and the Alps, strengthening their international composition to the point where Jean-Pierre Chabrol could describe the Cévenol maquis that he joined as something 'straight out of Henriot's propaganda', in which Spanish and other foreign languages seemed more prevalent than French. It was this international FTP maquis that taught him his solidarity with working people and his fervent anti-fascism, but also allowed him to relive the culture and history of the Cévennes.[89]

Chabrol came from the Génolhac area of the Cévennes, up above Alès, where the Communist Party had secured one of its rural footholds in the South of France, and even if regionalist causation has to be handled with care, can it not be argued more assertively that the politics of the locality were a major factor of causal significance? Political geography and the implantation of the maquis still has to be researched across the thousands of small communes that made up the basis of French political activity. It is

[86] Florimond Bonte, *Les Antifascistes allemands dans la Résistance française* (Éditions sociales, 1969); Louis Érignac, *La Révolte des Croates de Villefranche-de-Rouergue* (Érignac: Villefranche-de-Rouergue, 1988).

[87] Michel Goubet and Paul Debauges, *Histoire de la Résistance dans la Haute-Garonne* (Éditions Milan: Toulouse, 1986), 95–101.

[88] Maury, *La Résistance audoise*, ii. 166–83.

[89] Evidence from Jean-Pierre Chabrol, 2 Mar. 1982.

a mammoth task, whose ultimate value is open to question, given the heteroclite composition of most maquis groups, the chronological variables in maquis development, and the importance of patriotic sentiments and military skills which clearly cut across political categories. Certainly no study which emphasizes the local structures as integral to the history of the maquis can ignore the political issue, but at the same time it is the very emphasis on a plurality of local factors which discourages the use of political terms as a way of defining the nature of the maquis. A regular labelling of maquis groups as 'left-wing', 'right-wing', or more specifically 'communist' or 'socialist', has been deliberately rejected in this particular search for the maquis, in order to avoid such labels obscuring other equally important, but neglected, perspectives. It is not just that so many maquisards describe themselves as non-political at the time, but also that the combinations between maquisards and the community were often complex and unexpected. Communist maquisards in several areas were supported and protected by the obduracy of a conservative peasantry, while a left-wing rural area could promote the personal commitment to the life of the outlaw shown by a right-wing 'officier de carrière'. The youthfulness of the maquis, with an average age between 20 and 23, was itself a factor which it is surprisingly easy to take for granted. It often needs the jolt of an interview with someone like the Abbé Gauch, whose pastoral care was for young people, for the energy and also the receptivity of the young maquisard to be remembered. Far more maquisards became communist through maquis experience than were communist by motivation at the outset, but as the Abbé asserts they were no less open to other visions of a better post-war world. It was the idealism which made its impact more often than a set of pre-formed attitudes. And yet, in the same interview, the Abbé Gauch was under no illusion that when it came to explaining the local support for his FTP maquis there could be no doubt that left-wing sympathies in the Carmaux region of the Tarn were of causal importance.[90]

In terms of the political divide crystallized by the legislative elections of 1936, the last before war broke out, most areas where the maquis became established had voted overwhelmingly for the parties of the Popular Front. Of the thirty-six *départements* which formed the *zone sud*, fifteen elected only Popular Front candidates, and twelve elected a majority from the Popular Front. One *département* was equally split, leaving only eight in which the majority was against the Popular Front, and none at all in which the Right took all the seats. Even within the majority right-wing *départements* there were, in most cases, pockets of strong Popular Front support, and several of these became supportive areas of maquis growth and development: the area of Aubenas and Largentière in the Ardèche; Villefranche and Decazeville in

[90] Evidence from Abbé Gauch, 15 Mar. 1991.

the Aveyron; Bonneville and Cluses in the Haute-Savoie; Belley and Nantua-Gex in the Ain, which incorporated the town of Oyonnax, symbol of early maquis audacity; and Florac in the Lozère, the point where the conservative Haute-Lozère ended and the radical Cévennes began. When these areas are added to the *départements* where the Popular Front took all the seats, notably, for the scope of this study, Aude, Corrèze, Dordogne, Drôme, Gard, Haute-Garonne, Pyrénées-Orientales, Tarn-et-Garonne, Vaucluse and Haute-Vienne, there appears an obvious correlation between left-wing, or moderately left-wing, politics in 1936 and community sympathy for armed Resistance in 1943–4.[91]

Digging more deeply it is also possible to find political evidence at canton level which might explain the activism and determination of certain small networks of maquisards in areas surrounded by caution, incomprehension, or hostility. The FTP, for example in the Chablais area of the Haute-Savoie, had considerable difficulties with the peasantry and were insistently accused of resorting to provocative actions. Much of their energy and confrontational style would seem to relate to the existence of a vocal minority of communist supporters in the cantons of Thonon-les-Bains, Douvaine, and Évian-les-Bains where votes for the party candidate in 1936 ran at about 20 per cent of an otherwise hostile electorate. This active, but minority, situation of communist support contrasts sharply with the much stronger and even majority communist showing in certain rural areas, for example: Eymoutiers in the Haute-Vienne where Guingouin's maquis activities were centred; the Gardois Cévennes round Alès, repeatedly mentioned in this study; and several cantons of the Corrèze, where the FTP's activism had so impressed Jean-Jacques Chapou from the Lot.[92] In all these areas it makes complete sense to see the support structures of the FTP as prominent examples of the community culture of the outlaw. The support for the Chablais FTP, at least in the period of growth, could not be similarly described, despite the collective dedication of a small minority.[93]

The importance of left-wing, Popular Front, or what was often called solid 'republican' politics, for the history of the maquis and all other forms of Resistance, has never really been in doubt, and the few correlations noted here could be made more precise by further cantonal and communal details. But alongside evidence of this nature there is also the evidence of maquis which flourished in certain parts of the country where the Popular Front candidates had been defeated, in particular the Thônes valley in the Haute-Savoie, Saint-Affrique in the Aveyron, the Causse de Limogne in the Lot, and the small canton of Villard-de-Lans in the heart of the Vercors.[94]

[91] The electoral data comes from Georges Lachapelle, *Élections législatives, 26 avril et 3 mai 1936. Résultats officiels* (Le Temps, 1936).

[92] Ibid. [93] See Abrahams, 'Haute-Savoie at War, 1939–1945', 185–200.

[94] Lachapelle, *Elections Législatives.*

In all these places, community support for the local maquis was significant. With these areas in mind it seems possible to suggest a conclusion which accepts that the preponderance of left-wing localities in the *zone sud* must be credited as a factor in the growth and development of the maquis, but adds an important rider: the extensive support for the maquis in a variety of rural areas shows that the defence of *libertés* and of *liberté* came together in the armed Resistance. It was a complex but powerful combination. The politics of rural localities might best be seen to revolve round issues rather than parties. Support for the maquis and the struggle against Germany was just such an issue.

It is the absence of a clear map of hostile opinion against the maquis that vitiates talk of a civil war in France, which appeared to be gaining credibility in the spring of 1944. The ideas were counteracted not just by the primacy of the struggle against the occupying forces, but also by the very presence of so many anti-fascists from other countries in the ranks of the maquis. Jean Pujadas was one of the many Spanish political refugees in the *zone sud*, and he organized other Spanish arriving in the Ardèche, while training French maquisards in guerrilla tactics. He claimed forcibly that the Spanish contingent in the maquis reinforced the thrust of military action against the Germans. He himself tried to steer clear of any involvement in clashes between the French Resistance and Vichy, and the Spanish section on the plateau des Glières made the same point. Pujadas constantly pointed out to his fellow combatants that France was in no way divided in the way that Spain had been.[95] In theory most French maquisards also rejected the idea that the French people constituted two sides in warring confrontation. It was more a question of repeating the argument that France as a whole was increasingly resentful of an unrepresentative and tyrannical government which was in active collusion with the national enemy. But the involvement of even a very small minority of French people in the escalating brutality of German and Vichy repression undoubtedly provoked emotions and actions at local level which have been associated with the particular virulence of civil war.

The wave of German reprisals in the Cévennes, the Ain, and the Haute-Savoie spread to the Dordogne in early April to register scores of atrocities, deaths, and deportations. The signal given by this acceleration of German activity was that France was now a battle zone again and not just a country under occupation. It was the mark of maquis successes that the German authorities had decided to move on to the offensive and to carry out their punitive raids as military campaigns. At Vichy, Laval reaffirmed the duty of the French police to secure the safety of the German occupying forces, and stipulated that this obligation under the terms of the Armistice would

[95] Evidence from Jean Pujadas, 6 July 1982.

continue in the event of an Allied landing,[96] but it was obvious to any Intendant de Police that just as the maquis and the Resistance in the small towns were usurping Vichy's local authority, so the Germans had usurped Vichy's police functions *vis-à-vis* the maquis. Yet Darnand, a soldier by profession and a combatant by nature and experience, saw the situation as one requiring continuous military initiatives from Vichy if the regime was not to be entirely marginalized, and Lelong's mission to the Haute-Savoie had been deliberately designed to prove Vichy's capacity for this active combat. Even as the Germans were massing their troops for an assault on the plateau, Darnand was urging General Oberg to allow the formation of a new, heavily armed and mobile section within the Garde. 'In the coming weeks', he wrote on 22 March, 'I intend to carry out a certain number of raids on groups of Resistance and nests of terrorists. For these to succeed I need to mount flexible, well-armed units with their own transport, capable of acting with the greatest speed possible, and in absolute secrecy.'[97] Oberg refused the request, saying that the Garde had done little to inspire confidence, and on the same day as his reply the barracks of the Garde at Figeac in the Lot were raided by the FTP who seized 55,500 cartridges of different kinds, 210 grenades, a quantity of explosives, a machine-gun, sixteen rifles, and twelve automatics. The unit of the Garde was in Tulle at the time, and Bousquet expressed critical surprise that the Garde should have left so much behind. The response of General Perré of the Garde was to claim an insufficiency of transport.[98] Throughout April Darnand's instructions to local police chiefs emphasized the need for speed, mobility, and action not just in the location of the maquis but in their destruction, and he relieved Intendants de Police of their administrative responsibilities so that they could concentrate on the military deployment of their forces.[99] In most areas the Milice were given the lead in Darnand's campaign, in keeping with their recognition by the Germans in the assault on Glières. The commander of the franc-garde of the Milice, Jean de Vaugelas, who had led the Miliciens against the plateau, was put in charge of the Limousin region, where the FTP of the Corrèze and the Haute-Vienne were particularly effective. His appointment came shortly after the ferocity of the German campaign in the Dordogne, and to Resisters in the Limousin there appeared to be no discernible difference in methods or fanaticism.

The high military profile vested in the police by Darnand was an unwitting

[96] AD Hérault 18W 15. Laval's circular was dated 3 Mar. 1944.

[97] AN F7. 14894, Darnand to Oberg 22 Mar. 1944.

[98] General Perré's letter to Darnand is dated 3 Apr. 1944. Note that on 11 May 1944 Oberg told Darnand that he had decided to make available 3,195 men, previously involved in guarding German buildings and lodgings, to help Darnand's campaign against the 'terroristes'. The men, mostly from the gendarmerie, were employed in large towns throughout France, 1,930 of them in Paris; ibid.

[99] AD Hérault 18W 15. Circulars from Darnand dated 12 Apr., 19 Apr., and 21 Apr. 1944.

contribution to the chaos in day-to-day security operations caused by the Resistance *coups de main.* Sabotage, raids, thefts, and attacks on personnel increased in March 1944 to a point where the whole police structures of the *départements* were at breaking point. Regional prefects were besieged with urgent requests for police or security guards to protect mines, industries, roads, food depots, canals, railways, generators, power lines, even 'certains ouvrages d'art situés sur le canal du midi'.[100] In most cases the prefects counselled the mobilization of more 'requis civils', from those earmarked for STO but 'inapte Allemagne', though by this stage the resulting scenarios were all too familiar to Vichy administrators: either unarmed guards unable to deter armed attackers, or armed guards providing the Resistance with an easy source of weaponry and ammunition. The chaos intensified weekly, and Darnand's military ambitions did nothing to alleviate it, and everything to divide the police into explicit collaborators on the one hand and, on the other, those whose solution to the crisis was to look increasingly for a *modus vivendi* with the Resistance. The desperate requests for guards were accompanied by demands from companies, commercial enterprises, and individuals for compensation for goods lost through the attacks, but after instruction from the courts Vichy prefects met all such requests with a blanket refusal.[101] Since insurance companies would offer no protection either, the insecurity generated was a major economic factor in the dissolution of Vichy's credibility as a protector of property and guarantor of law and order. The state did continue what the Prefect of the Ain called 'a meagre compensation' for loss of work, but he pointed out that neither workers nor employers were coming forward to claim it, for fear that those identified as out of work would be taken for labour service in Germany.[102]

Fear is the main component of prefects' reports in the months when the German and Vichy repression intensified, and the Resistance attacks dramatically increased; fear of German reprisals above all, and widespread hatred for the Milice, but also fear of a more and more punitive maquis. There is no doubt that in March and April Henriot's broadcasts were widely effective, except in the Glières itself, in slowing down the growth of sympathy for the maquis, and it is clear that for many people the ideal solution was an Allied invasion which would force a rapid German retreat without internal conflict or escalating maquis violence. What the reports do not point out is that it was precisely the propaganda offensive by Henriot and the military campaigns orchestrated by Darnand that made this solution

[100] Ibid; request from the Prefect of the Aude, 6 Apr. 1944.

[101] An example of a company's loss is the theft on 24 Feb. 1944 of 116,250 fr. from M. Volpilière, 'entrepreneur pour le compte de la Compagnie des Mines de la Grand'Combe, au moment où il s'apprêtait à payer ses ouvriers'; AD Gard CA 667. The dossier on private claims for damages due to *attentats*, dealt with by the Prefect of the Hérault, Nov. 1943–Aug. 1944, is in AD Hérault 172W 49.

[102] AN F1C III. 1135, Ain, report of 3 Mar. 1944.

impossible, and that it was Vichy's descent into militarized and brutalizing repression that justified the punitive behaviour and *mentalités* within the maquis in the last months of the Occupation. The Resistance as a whole shared this hardening of attitudes, but maquisards were particularly prone to be highly judgemental, not just of collaborators but of any section of society unwilling to commit itself to the struggle.

Central to the discourse of the maquis, as we have seen, was the sense of purity and freedom from compromise which accompanied the move to the hills, experienced as a decisive break with hesitations. In the first period of embryonic formation this was qualified by uncertainties about role and survival, but with deepening social roots and community support these early anxieties declined, leaving problems of strategy but little questioning of the basic rightness of 'taking to the maquis'. There was a diversity of maquis attitudes towards the *coups de main* for food and other necessities, but when stigmatized as brigands, terrorists, and bandits they paraded their patriotism, developed collusive practices to gain peasant support, and organized maquis police to reassure the population that false, or renegade, maquisards would not be allowed to commit criminal acts under cover of the Resistance. Typical of this reassurance was the article on the Haute-Savoie in *Combat* in December 1943:

> Just recently the inhabitants of le Petit-Bornand and Entremont were subjected to a series of attacks on the roads by so-called *réfractaires* and maquisards.
>
> An enquiry carried out by the maquis revealed that it was really a band whose leader had been thrown out of one of our camps as a sympathizer of Doriot.
>
> This man was tracked down by one of our groupes francs and executed on 10 October at le Petit-Bornand. They had found Doriotist tracts and copies of *L'Emancipation Nationale* in his possession. The leader of the groupe franc informed the population that they need have nothing to fear, and that the maquis police would not tolerate any brigandage, and would take over the protective role of the Vichy police which is more concerned to hunt down patriots than look for bandits.[103]

The *Gazette de Lausanne* was quoted by *Défense de la France* as neutral confirmation of the maquis stand against common criminals:

> Young Frenchmen, enrolled by Resistance movements into a military organization, have recently undertaken a vast campaign of repression against ex-convicts and other undesirables who have attacked several Savoyard farms. There have been a number of armed encounters and the bandits have been made to pay for their crimes with their lives.[104]

The quote was preceded by an article entitled 'Terrorisme ou Résistance?' by a *réfractaire*, which epitomized the logic of the maquisard's position: 'Someone is bound to say "Do you deny that these young 'outlaws' too often

[103] *Combat*, 53 (Dec. 1943), 3. The article was entitled, even at this early date, 'La Haute-Savoie combat'.

[104] *Défense de la France*, 42 (15 Dec. 1943), 2.

have recourse to violence?" No, I don't deny it, but what I say is, "Whose fault is it?"' and he indicates the sacrifice of the nation's youth by the Vichy government. 'Illegality is the product of insecurity and need, and we are in a state of legitimate self-defence . . . No, it is not *we* who are the terrorists.'[105]

In numerous variations on this theme the maquis maintained the moral upper hand, but with increasing anger and bitterness at the acts of collaboration which made their outlaw existence precarious. The hard survivalism of the winter reinforced their self-image and exacerbated their intolerance of compromise. In many areas their *coups de main* objectified their judgements of French society: local people were informally or even formally assessed on sliding scales of 'culpability' before thefts and raids were perpetrated. Few such mechanisms were solely the product of maquis experience: most were informed by pre-existing judgements, most obviously social and political indictments of class exploitation, and more widely an indignation felt by those living on the edge of survival towards the injustice of conspicuous comfort and wealth. The strength of communist and socialist analyses of society offered much to the maquisard: they coincided too often with the realities of the situation to be brushed aside as ideological baggage. An individualist or anarchist suspicion of authority thrived equally on similar ground. To all these codes of judgement the propaganda of Henriot and the military offensive of Darnand brought a new degree of bitterness and a higher moral certitude. From the maquis standpoint, the activity of the Milice meant that there could now be no excuse whatsoever for mistaking the maquis for terrorists. Terrorism had been openly flaunted and embraced by Vichy. 'In the Haute-Savoie', reported *Languedoc ouvrier*, 'the police are attacking the maquis: these so-called forces of order are pitilessly engaged in combat against our young maquisards. They are led by the greatest bandit known to modern times; we mean Darnand!'[106]

It was not just the experience of the maquis in the Haute-Savoie which led the Resistance to turn the accusation of banditry on the accusers, and it is difficult to find the first occasion on which the inversion was made. FTP tracts in particular had regularly cast the Milice and the Vichy police in the role of terrorists, often naming individual officers: 'On Saturday 19 February, three bandits, Llauro, Frances and Julien Massie went to arrest two young Frenchmen who defended themselves. One of the bandits, Inspector Julien Massie, was shot . . .'[107] The Forces Unies de la Jeunesse

[105] Ibid.

[106] *Languedoc ouvrier*, Organe bi-régional de l'action ouvrière des MUR, 4 (15 Mar. 1944), 2. The report was headed 'Un champ de bataille', and its conclusion called on the 'masse ouvrière': 'Sauvez nos camarades de Savoie par le sabotage.'

[107] The tract was found in Montpellier in late February 1944. It ends with a rallying cry: 'Français aux armes! Par centaines rejoignez les détachements F.T.P. Formez partout ces puissants bataillons de milices patriotiques. Aux armes, et battons nous pour que le Languedoc soit une nouvelle Corse.' AD Hérault 18W 13.

Patriotique, formed during the autumn of 1943 as a Resistance organization of urban and rural youth, issued in February 1944 one of the most explicit inversionary pamphlets, called 'Miliciens assassins'. It began as if it were a broadcast by Henriot himself:

A wave of terrorism and banditry is sweeping across France. In the southern zone men of all ages, from all social classes and of all political persuasions, are found assassinated by the roadside far from their homes. Often the state in which the bodies are found shows that they have been cruelly tortured . . .

Who comes in the middle of the night to snatch these victims and assassinate them in this way? Who carries out cruel and bestial tortures? Who are the assassins? Who pillages the victims' homes and steals their money, jewels and valuables? . . .

These crimes are signed. They bear the infamous marks of the branch of the Gestapo in France, the Milice under the control of the sinister Darnand, the organizer of the St Bartholomew's massacre of French patriots . . . [108]

Later in the pamphlet there is a call to the gendarmerie and the GMR to assist the Resistance in identifying and punishing 'les fauteurs de guerre civile' and it is this indictment of the Milice for something much more than excessive police action, for nothing less than responsibility for civil war, which comes to mark a certain maquis response to the military encounters of February and March 1944. By extension the indictment covered anyone who still nurtured illusions about Vichy. If Henriot and Darnand signified Vichy, then any lingering Vichy supporter or willing administrator was technically aiding the war declared against the maquis. As Henri Cordesse said:

Among the maquis in this period there developed a mentality of all-out war [guerre à l'outrance]. Because they were given no quarter by the Germans and the Milice they would show no mercy to collaborators. This was 'une mentalité terrible'. I saw individual maquisards whose main aim was to avenge their comrades. It was very difficult to control, and this *mentalité* explains a certain number of 'mistakes' [*bavures*]. There was a level of passion that is very difficult to capture in words.[109]

Not all maquisards have endorsed, or would recognize, this 'mentalité terrible'. For many it appears too close to a civil war mentality, or still worse a vendetta mentality which they have struggled to eliminate from the history of the maquis, believing that it all too easily confirms the negative reputation of the 'hors-la-loi'. But most also agree that Darnand had effectively joined the internal war on Germany's side, that the Milice were widely using torture on prisoners and were intent on perfecting secret-service methods of warfare in search of the maquis. Darnand's circular of 21 April to all police chiefs placed primary importance on the role of information in the campaign against the maquis. He specified the importance of *agents de renseignements* who

[108] AD Hérault 172W 35, 'Miliciens assassins', Feb. 1944.
[109] Evidence from Henri Cordesse, 22 Mar. 1982.

had established '*and maintained* contact with the terrorists in question', and he underlined the need to sever the information links between the maquis and the surrounding community.[110] A fortnight later Raymond-Clemoz, Darnand's chief assistant in his ministry, issued his decisive circular saying that the police must make no distinction between different types of maquis, such as whether they were communist or not, but must in principle, hand over *all* information on *all* 'groups of dissidents' to the German authorities.[111]

The strategic response of the maquis in most areas was increasingly to eliminate the presence or influence of the Milice and their agents from areas of operation. It was an extension from the tactics employed in the temporary occupation of small towns and villages when the first step had been to neutralize the gendarmerie. That had rarely proved difficult. Throwing a wider 'cordon sanitaire' round huge areas of countryside involved well-founded trust in community involvement, but also the use of threats, murders, and exemplary punishment, as in the execution of Miliciens at Cajarc. In piecemeal fashion, from winter to spring, the maquis staked out areas for liberation, well before Jour-J. The bulk of the fighting against the Germans still lay ahead, but the process of internal liberation from the Vichy of Darnand and Henriot was already well advanced.

[110] AD Hérault 18W 15, Darnand to Intendants de Police, 21 Apr. 1944.

[111] AD Gard CA 367. Dated 2 May 1944, the circular from Clemoz was sent to all regional prefects. It started by saying that there was already an agreement between Bousquet and Oberg that the French police should inform the German authorities of all 'activités communistes et terroristes ainsi que les actes de sabotage qui pouvent en résulter'. The agreement was now extended to cover 'Les renseignements recueillis sur une organisation quelconque de dissidents'.

6

Insurrections and Liberations, Summer 1944

SECURING a local objective was always at the heart of maquis strategy, whether AS or FTP. For over a year the maquis had developed pragmatically, according to local strengths and possibilities, in close rapport with the Resistance groups, *sédentaires* or *statiques*, in the small and larger towns. The maquis had had no monopoly of sabotage, raids, or even attacks on enemy personnel. During this time, other branches of Resistance, notably the FTP of the towns, the groupes francs of the AS, the *cheminots* of Résistance Fer, and the factory, mine, and railway workers of Action Ouvrière, accounted for as many, if not more, acts of sabotage and subversion than the rural-based maquis. There were often interconnected structures of personnel, liaison, and supply which make a strict categorization of the various groups and actions difficult to achieve, and all groups had to face the same challenge of assessing the vulnerability of their targets, whether a French *bureau de tabac* or a German *traction avant*, and the risks that an attack would pose for the local population. In all these actions, which formed the combative history of the armed Resistance, there was a mix of bluff and calculation and of provocation and discretion, and in most cases constraints were imposed by a sober assessment of the local resources available.

In counterpoint to this local motif ran the insistent themes of national aims and strategies. From the start, both the FTP and the MUR had enthused maquisards with a national consciousness which carried with it the notion of a vanguard position in the re-emergence of internal France as a belligerent force in the war against Nazism. To this was added the progressively potent discourse of the Liberation. De Gaulle had popularized the idea that an 'insurrection nationale' would be a necessary component of liberation. He did so as early as April 1942 when he was establishing his mandate as 'head' of the Resistance, and although the term dropped away from his own speeches, it became central to Resistance propaganda of all kinds in 1943–4. Both FTP and AS groups rehearsed the revolutionary lines of the 'Marseillaise', 'Aux armes citoyens, Formez vos bataillons', and both saw the liberation of France and the overthrow of Vichy as coterminous. The maquis FTP, being so closely modelled on the FTP of the towns, undoubtedly inculcated a far more political and working-class image of a popular rising, but the community basis of so much of the AS maquis allowed it also to envisage the insurrection as a mobilization of the people. And beyond or alongside the projected risings there lay the expectations of Jour-J, and hopes of an Allied strategy which would maximize the maquis as a fighting unit, intensify the drops of arms and ammunition, and even buttress maquis activities with Allied reinforcements. The impact of this liberation discourse was polyvalent—but whatever element captured the imagination of the maquisard it reinforced the temptation to choose local objectives of greater and greater military or symbolic significance.

The theoretical unification of all the maquis within the Forces Françaises de l'Intérieur (FFI) appeared to underscore the national theme as the dominant one in the months of April, May, and early June 1944, but although, from 25 May, the BBC ceased all usage of the term 'maquis' in its broadcasts to France, there was no fundamental change in the nature of most maquis activity in the sense that local objectives, local organization, and still more, local constraints, remained paramount. Some historians have consequently exposed a disjuncture between the proposed national unity of the maquis and the persistence of disunity on the ground, and others have pointed to the local independence of maquis groups as a major military weakness of the emergent FFI. The hostility of maquisards to conventional military command, their obdurate preference for their own leaders and structures, and their impetuosity, are the facets of their history most often quoted as the underlying causes of this weakness, elevated by some commentators after the war into something akin to a fatal flaw in the national character, a symptom of the incurable individualism of the French.

This criticism derives mainly from a conceptual abstraction of how the maquis might, or should, have been a national military force. It does not address the real historical issue for the maquis, which was how to achieve a functional balance between national aims and local constraints. The issue became acute in the period just before and after the Allied landings of 6 June. The imminence and the actuality of Jour-J brought a major expansion in maquis activity, and with it a widespread assertion of national identity. Such was the accelerated pace of this assertiveness that problems of over-exposure were bound to occur. These problems stemmed rarely from any failures or shortcomings in national consciousness. On the contrary, they arose more often when the local nature and limitations of the maquis were subordinated to the realization of the maquis as a national force.

The mobilization at Mont Mouchet in May and June, the occupation of the town of Tulle on 8 June, and the combats of the Vercors in June and July can be analysed in this light, as over-extensions of limited local capacities. Each of the three events illustrates the pull of a different aspect in the ideas and discourse of liberation: the drive to mobilize the Resistance into a national army; the expectations of a popular, urban uprising; and the use of the maquis as part of the Allied strategy of the *débarquement*. All three occurred early in the summer when the Germans were still effectively in command of the southern zone. All three directly challenged that command, and in the temerity of that challenge revealed both the diversity and the cumulative power of the ideal of liberation.

The mobilization of both maquis and *sédentaires* in the Auvergne was decreed by Émile Coulaudon (Gaspard), the regional head of the AS, on 20 May. It appears that he was acting on his own authority, but also on the basis of a plan agreed by regional Resistance leaders to concentrate the disparate maquis in three zones: on Mont Mouchet in the Margeride; in the hills overlooking the Gorges de la Truyère; and in the volcanic region of the Plomb du Cantal. Coulaudon had been particularly influenced by a plan code-named 'Caïman' which gave the Auvergne a vanguard role in proving to the Allies that France was capable of liberating certain areas through its own internal forces in direct liaison with Allied strategy.[1] De Gaulle had stamped his authority on this plan on 16 May, although both he and Koenig repeatedly stressed that the maquis should concentrate essentially on sabotage. Nevertheless it was well known to Coulaudon that a *mémoire* of the CFLN dated 5 May had envisaged certain maquis actions which would be aimed at liberating carefully prescribed zones of French territory.

> These actions should aim at overpowering the enemy forces of occupation by a general rising unleashed at the opportune moment . . . At the very minimum these actions should tie down considerable numbers of the enemy, isolate them, and keep them surrounded until the intervention of Allied forces from outside.[2]

The 'plan Caïman' elaborated this general strategy, and specified the Auvergne as an ideal zone for early liberation. Coulaudon decided that Mont Mouchet was to be the main redoubt (*réduit*), and warning echoes from the experience of the Glières might seem to have been disregarded, but the size of the mobilization broke all maquis precedents, far exceeding that of Glières. It was aimed at a huge area overlapping the Puy-de-Dôme, the Cantal, the Haute-Loire, and the upper regions of the Lozère, and variations on Coulaudon's mobilization order were issued in all these areas, eventually attracting over 6,000 volunteers, who arrived in the Margeride, or attempted to do so, between 20 May and 9 June. Some 2,700 reached Mont Mouchet itself, while another sizeable grouping was assembled at Venteuges nearby; some 2,000 set up camp in the woods of la Truyère overlooking Chaudes-

[1] Gilles Lévy and Francis Cordet, *A nous Auvergne!* (Presses de la Cité, 1981), 195–7.
[2] Ibid. 195–6.

Aigues to the south of Saint-Flour, while a thousand or more remained unarmed well to the north of these mobilization points, in the woods of Saint-Genès-Champespe on the border of the Puy-de-Dôme or at Lioran in the volcanic hills of the Cantal.

It still remains uncertain whether Coulaudon's order for this massive popular mobilization was launched with or without Allied encouragement, though there is little doubt that his meetings with SOE agents, notably Maurice Southgate, had given him the confidence to envisage a military operation on a grand scale, while the parachute drops into the Margeride in March and April had indicated the summit of Mont Mouchet, at over 1,400 metres in altitude, as a potential *réduit*, easily located by French and British aircrews. The most rigorous historian and critic of Mont Mouchet, Eugène Martres, states that Coulaudon's order, issued well before Jour-J, was received with astonishment by the maquis and AS leaders at the level of local communes and cantons, even though there had been earlier discussions in the region to plan the ways in which the maquis would be assembled.[3] In these discussions the FTP had shown a willingness to co-operate, and it was presumably in the expectation of a unified response that Coulaudon issued his directive in the name of the FFI. But the unexpected timing and the sheer scale of the operation, together with its complete departure from previous strategies of mobility and disengagement, alarmed the local FTP leaders, and in the event no FTP unit tried to reach the Margeride. The volunteers who did so went from maquis groups in several *départements* and from villages, mining areas, and industrial towns as if responding to a conventional call-up, an astonishing displacement of young men which the Vichy and German authorities appear not to have registered as anything out of the ordinary, until the mobilization was well advanced. There were even sizeable groups of volunteers who travelled openly by train, asserting to surprised officials that they were consignments of a lumber force directed into the mountains. But for most it meant a long, final journey by foot. Paul Daigneau, interviewed by Gilles Lévy, vividly recalled the lack of boots suitable for such an arduous climb: 'The enthusiasm of the first few hours was followed by the pain of the long walk, our feet, wrapped in rags, bleeding in our clogs.'[4] They arrived to be sheltered in farms and villages *en route* to Mont Mouchet before being directed to the camp itself, whose headquarters was established at the Maison Forestière above the villages of Clavières and Paulhac-en-Margeride. The sheer extent and speed of this mobilization astonished its organizers and brought visible prestige to Coulaudon and his close military adviser, one of the few regular officers involved, Lieutenant-Colonel Jean Garcie. On 1 June the General Staff of the national

[3] Eugène Martres, 'Un exemple de concentration: le Mont Mouchet', in *Colloque sur les maquis*, 119.

[4] Lévy and Cordet, *A nous Auvergne!*, 201.

command of the AS maquis, led by Georges Rebattet, established itself at Mont Mouchet. The rising of the Auvergne appeared to have all the authority of both local and national direction.

Planned in March and April, and launched during May, the Auvergne operation preceded the Allied landings, but was conceived and executed in the expectation of imminent battles in France in which the internal maquis and Resistance would be called on to play their military part. The creation of the FFI and the preparation through coded messages for *plan vert*, *plan bleu*, and *plan violet*, which would unleash Resistance sabotage of railways, power lines, and telephone communications, once the landings had occurred, fired the imagination of many Resistance leaders besides Émile Coulaudon. But Coulaudon, argues Martres, projected not so much an escalation of sabotage and guerrilla tactics on to the local stage of the Auvergne, as a more confrontational military role involving the formation of a mobilized army. His directive proclaimed that 'L'Armée de la Libération est maintenant constituée en Auvergne', and this assumption of a national vanguard position exceeded local possibilities and took place in a vacuum of strategic planning. When Jour-J was finally announced, the assembled maquis were already in place in the Margeride, but what exactly should happen next was far from clear. Coulaudon and his colleagues, Martres continues, were 'embarrassés des 3,700 hommes qu'ils avaient rassemblés'. Unable to match the German artillery, they fought back courageously when the Germans took the initiative on 2 June, and inflicted a surprising number of casualties, but were forced to disperse once the Germans stepped up their military commitment, with considerable losses both to their own assembled maquis troops and to inhabitants of the villages in the area, on whom merciless reprisals were exacted. Mont Mouchet, unlike the Glières, was never encircled, but the secondary *réduit* above Chaudes-Aigues was almost completely cut off and it was there that the maquis losses were highest. The combats, Martres concludes, made little impact on the German war machine and did not objectively relieve the Allied front, hardly delaying the enemy units, and destroying none of them. According to Martres, Coulaudon would appear to have misread the potential of the mobilization: his enthusiastic anticipation of a national struggle outran the military realities on the ground.[5]

[5] Eugène Martres, 'Le Cantal de 1939 à 1945' (Unpublished thesis, Clermont-Ferrand, 1974), 686. I am grateful to John Sweets for pointing me towards this thesis, and I would wish to pay tribute to his own scholarly work: J. F. Sweets, *Choices in Vichy France: The French under Nazi Occupation* (OUP: Oxford, 1986). It is an excellent local study of Clermont-Ferrand, and all my own research and writings have always endorsed one of his conclusions about French Resistance: 'In order to successfully convey the atmosphere, or reconstitute the history of France under the German occupation, a reformulation of the definition of resistance is required. The notion of a small band of activist conspirators must be made to square with, or be incorporated into, a broader perspective that will account for the existence of an atmosphere in 1943–1944 in which resistance was nurtured by massive and widespread popular complicity . . .', p. 224.

Henri Cordesse, leader and historian of the Lozère Resistance, gives an experiential view of the mobilization. He visited Gaspard's headquarters on Mont Mouchet and was profoundly impressed by the simplicity and seriousness of the operation.

What was impressive was the obvious determination and fraternal warmth of these men surrounding their friend—and leader—Gaspard, facing up to the problems which confronted them: arms, equipment, food, transport, security . . . At over 1,300 metres the nights were still cold at the end of May. The discordance between the rapid enlistment of men—more than 3,000 by the beginning of June—and the poverty of materials was agonizing.[6]

Even the welcome increase in parachute drops brought unexpected problems: ammunition which did not match the armaments, and weapons including bazookas for which none of the raw recruits was trained. A raid on a clothing factory at la Canourgue in the Lozère, on the night of 22 May, organized by Alfred Coutarel, brought a rich yield of over 7,000 leather jerkins, giving the assembled maquis a uniform of their own,[7] and spirits were high when the Germans launched their first assault on 2 June, and higher still when the Germans withdrew after meeting greater fire power than they had expected. At five o'clock in the evening the maquisards from Mont Mouchet occupied the village of Paulhac and erected a banner proclaiming 'Ici commence la France libre'. Paulhac later paid heavily for this premature celebration, and already reprisals were wrecking the villages on the route back to Malzieu along which the Germans had withdrawn.

The second, and far more extensive, German assault was launched on 10 June, the day when General Koenig in London sent an urgent order to all FFI 'to put the maximum brake on guerrilla activity'. Initially encouraged by the enthusiastic response of the maquis to the *débarquement* of 6 June, Koenig realized that the Allies would not make it a priority to support maquis uprisings. His order was in direct contradiction to the green light given on the night of 5 June, and has been seen retrospectively as a wise piece of military rethinking. But at the time it appeared to make little sense to those maquis already actively engaged with the enemy, not least at Mont Mouchet, where the Germans arrived in force with mortars and other heavy artillery. By June 1944 the pattern of German repression had become established as multi-pronged attacks on the maquis, followed by reprisals on local villages. On 10 June, in the region of Mont Mouchet, this was reversed. The reprisals came first. At Ruynes twenty-six inhabitants were massacred at different points in this sprawling village on the edge of the

[6] Cordesse, *Histoire de la Résistance en Lozère*, 170.

[7] Ibid. The Prefect of the Lozère reported this raid on 23 May 1944 and specified that 350 armed men in 15 lorries had stolen 8,000 items valued at 15 million francs; AD Hérault 18W 14.

Margeride, including two women and a child of 8. They were pulled out of their houses and shot on their doorsteps, or, in the case of the *instituteur* Jean Chalvet and two neighbours, taken to a meadow and shot down after receiving the order to run. On the road from Ruynes towards Mont Mouchet the maquis had established barricades, and many maquisards died defending these road-blocks against fierce German mortar fire. Arriving at the village of Clavières the savagery of the reprisals continued, despite the attempt by François Broncy, the mayor, to parley with the advancing soldiers. He went out of the village to meet them, and his body has never been found. By the evening of 11 June the fighting had reached into the woods at the heart of Mont Mouchet, but when the German forces reached the Maison Forestière the withdrawal and dispersion of the maquis was complete.

The retreat from Mont Mouchet resembled the original mobilization in its surprising success. German efforts to surround the *réduit* had failed. The escape routes lay mainly to the south, and hundreds of the maquisards regrouped and joined the maquis already assembled above Chaudes-Aigues. It was there in the extensive woods and pastures of the Gorges de la Truyère that the battle ended, when a final German assault on 20 June succeeded to a far greater extent in encircling the maquisards. At Mont Mouchet the combatant and civilian dead were numbered at over 160, with an estimated 100 Germans killed in the fighting. At la Truyère the maquis losses were far higher, for comparatively fewer German casualties. The villages of Saint-Martial, the second headquarters of Coulaudon, and Anterrieux, were almost entirely destroyed in the combined land and air attacks which completed the encirclement.[8] The maquisards who escaped returned to more scattered guerrilla actions across the Cantal, the Puy-de-Dôme, and the Lozère. The *réduits* of the Auvergne had convincingly shown that internal French forces were prepared to engage in the independent liberation of their territory, but the means to achieve that end were far beyond the resources available or provided.

Even as hopes of a major success were disappointed, there was the conviction among the maquisards of Mont Mouchet that the Resistance had declared itself ready to fight and that the maquis had, on its own initiative, become the combative force that had always been envisaged. They had ceased to be the army of the shadows and had come into the open. They did so in the heartland of Vichy France, in a mobilization designed not least to demonstrate that the Auvergne, in which the spa of Vichy was situated, belonged not to Laval and Darnand, but to the Resistance. This reclamation

[8] The sense of defeat in the fields and woods of la Truyère is conveyed in the bare, sparse monument at Saint-Martial which is dedicated 'Aux morts de la Truyère, victimes du Nazisme, 20 juin 1944' but carries no numbers, names or reference to the nature of the combat. There is little collective memory of the events in the neighbourhood, and the contrast with the monuments and the recall of villagers in the Mont Mouchet area could not be more dramatic.

of their region from Vichy's 'usurpation', was high on the list of motivations given by those who volunteered. Interviewed at the Liberation, Émile Coulaudon had no second thoughts:

In May it was time to play the hand labelled '*débarquement* assured and successful'. You have to remember that we had survived the winter, and that 40 km. of forest allowed us an easy escape to the Lozère, in case of military difficulties . . . If we had hesitated to take the risk, it would have been the death of the Resistance: if we had played a waiting game we would have seen all our forces seriously discouraged . . .[9]

For many the mobilization was an act of self-realization; the size of the German force sent to deal with Mont Mouchet and Chaudes-Aigues was visible evidence that a genuine combat had been engaged. The relativity of success and failure is one of the recurrent discoveries in the search for the maquis. Oral interviews, given long after the events, substantiate reports at the time which suggest that the very act of engagement and the experience of combat carried their own justifications. The maquisards in the Auvergne were volunteers in an unequal military confrontation and it has seemed too dispassionate to apportion blame or pronounce a verdict of failure. The courage and the heroism against overwhelming odds is highly valued; the successful incident amidst heavy losses is not forgotten; the experience of commitment itself is remembered, and the overall success of the Liberation is seen to vindicate the partial set-backs. For these reasons the monument to the maquis of France now stands on Mont Mouchet.[10]

The events of the Auvergne have been intensively researched, and critically examined as military history. Implicit comparisons can be made with the resistance of Vercingétorix against the Romans in 52 BC from his citadel at Gergovie, and that of Sidoine Appollinaire, Bishop of Clermont, against the incursive Visigoths in AD 471. As military resistance these too involved either strategic mistakes or frustrated expectations, and their common local setting enabled A. G. Manry to call an article on these earlier combats, 'Auvergne premier haut-lieu de la Résistance nationale'.[11] It is the word

[9] Lévy and Cordet, *A nous Auvergne!*, 200. See also Coulaudon's testimony to the film by Marcel Ophuls, *Le Chagrin et la pitié* (1971).

[10] Alongside the monument there is now the Musée du Mont Mouchet which displays photographs and documents, maps, weapons and uniforms. The memory of local villagers on the route from Ruynes to Mont Mouchet is incorporated in a videotape of oral testimonies. They include the evidence of Madame Fontugne, the wife of the *gardien* of the *maison forestière*.

[11] *Revue historique de l'armée*, 3 (1968), 7–16. Vercingétorix initially refused to give direct battle to Caesar, conducting sporadic attacks from his citadel at Gergovie in the Auvergne against Roman stragglers and outposts. This guerrilla warfare was both humiliating and dangerous for Caesar, but Vercingétorix then made the fatal mistake of attacking Caesar in the autumn of 52 BC near Dijon and was defeated. Over four centuries later the Bishop of Clermont, Sidoine Appollinaire, held out against the Visigoths, confident that the Romans would come to his aid against 'the aryan heretics and barbarians'. The siege was terrible, but the Visigoths finally withdrew. The Roman Emperor, Julius Nepos, however, negotiated peace with the invaders and abandoned the Auvergne. Sidoine's final letter before leaving the Auvergne was a bitter

'nationale' that is important; it also corresponds exactly to the intentions of Coulaudon and the way in which Mont Mouchet has been memorialized. If the events were a miscalculation of local resources, it was in the pursuit of a national military role for the maquis.

Mobilization of all Resisters, both maquis and *sédentaires*, was one dramatic way in which the general idea of liberation was interpreted. It was an attempt to realize a national aim at local level. So too was the occupation of Tulle, no less exhaustively researched and analysed, and even more often criticized as over-impetuous and lacking strategic credibility. In this case the national image was one of popular urban uprisings facilitated by FTP action. A model was proposed in some detail in a circular on 'l'insurrection nationale' sent to all FTP leaders by the national command in May 1944, copies of which were seized by the Vichy police in several places, notably in a decimating coup against the Perpignan FTP on 25 May.[12] The document reminded FTP leaders that even as the inevitable Jour-J approached and events accelerated, the rule was still 'to avoid all set battles and only to engage in an offensive action when surprise could be assured'. Orders from the CFLN in Algiers were to be respected, but specific FTP notions of insurrection, in which the masses of the people would be led into combat as the culmination of an uprising, were to be sedulously cultivated and put into practice. In a town, the document stated, with a fairly strong German garrison still in place on Jour-J, the insurrection could be expected to start from a working-class quarter, or from a general strike in the factories, at which point the FTP should begin to organize the insurrectionaries into combat groups, eliminating any small pockets of police but not directly engaging with the major force of the enemy, who were expected to establish their position behind the fortified walls of well guarded buildings. The FTP would make sure that the uprising created its own barricades, ditches, and barbed-wire defences, and confronted the enemy with the reality of its isolation in the midst of a hostile, armed, and determined population. For such a plan to succeed it was vital that the enemy should be uninformed about what was happening. All communication lines to enemy positions were to be severed, and spies and traitors publicly executed. At this point the enemy might resort to aerial

indictment of his former allies, 'Was it for this that we endured hunger, fire and pestilence . . . is it for such devotion that we have been sacrificed?' The same issue contains an article by G. M. Levy, Chef de Bataillon, 'La Concentration des maquis d'Auvergne', 43–62. He gives his opinion that a greater supply of parachuted arms from the Allies would have enabled the maquis to destroy the German divisions pitted against Mont Mouchet, such was the 'high morale of the maquisards' at the outset (p. 61).

[12] Following an attack on 24 May 1944 on an employee of the Trésorerie générale de Perpignan, who was carrying 1,600,000 fr. to the Banque de France, one of the attackers, Pierre Stoll, was captured, and this led to the arrest of Pierre Auriol, Joseph Saury, two *gardiens de la paix*, and the discovery of a cache of arms and a huge number of FTP documents; AD Hérault 18W 15. For the FTP in the *département* see Georges Sentis, *Les Communistes et la Résistance dans les Pyrénées-Orientales*. The second volume has good information on the role of the *guérilleros espagnols*, 91–5.

bombardment, which would be of limited effect, or withdraw to muster reinforcements for a larger assault on the town, an eventuality which would take several days to organize, allowing the FTP to consolidate the uprising. While set encounters must at all times be avoided, the FTP should nevertheless show the maximum audacity in their offensives, and once a town was cleared of its enemy garrison it would become a *point d'appui* for further struggles in the surrounding area. It was finally noted that this model situation would not be found close to the fighting front where the density of German troop movements would create other conditions, but rather in towns surrounded by vast zones partially evacuated by the enemy and full of detachments of partisans. Both before and after Jour-J the authority of regional heads of the FTP would be crucial in determining the successful implementation of the national insurrection.[13]

An earlier document in May, issued by the Comité Central of the Communist Party, had already emphasized the essential FTP position that the national insurrection 'could in no way be conceived as belonging exclusively to the FFI' but must involve the participation of the masses, and in this involvement the role of milices patriotiques, established as armed Resistance groups within the towns and acting as the vanguard of the people, would be critical.[14] Both this document and the more detailed one from the FTP leadership kept the national image at the centre, with the implication that any local insurrection would be similar to any other. It was a theoretical position, no more and no less abstract than the idea of mobilizing the maquis and *sédentaires*, and utterly consistent with the way the FTP had evolved. When Jean-Jacques Chapou, once Capitaine Philippe in the Lot but now known as Kléber, regional head of the FTP in the Corrèze, took his maquisards into Tulle on 7 and 8 June, it was not in response to an urban uprising, but his occupation of the town occasioned popular support and delight at liberation, and in all respects aimed to establish Tulle as a microcosm of the national insurrection. It was two days after Jour-J, and Tulle was the *chef-lieu* of the Corrèze, with a sizeable armaments industry. A town of some 20,000 inhabitants, it had elected two Socialist deputies to the Popular Front elections of 1936, and was surrounded by hills and woods in which the activity of both FTP and AS maquis had been continuous since the summer of 1943. It also had a relatively small German garrison. Chapou, a socialist in origin but a convert to the effectiveness and audacity of the Corrèze FTP, as we have seen, had the positive experience of the temporary occupation of Cajarc in the Lot behind him, but on this occasion he intended the occupation and liberation of Tulle to be permanent, creating an urban *point d'appui* for escalating local action.

[13] AD Hérault 18W 19, 'Note pour les secteurs et les D.M.R. sur l'insurrection nationale'.

[14] AD Hérault 18W 13, 'Directives pour la préparation et la conduite de l'insurrection nationale'.

Eyewitness accounts of the seizure of Tulle vary widely according to the degree of support for the FTP action. The German garrison attempted a break-out from a temporary fortified position in the École Normale des Filles, as a result of which over fifty were killed in FTP fire and a further sixty surrendered, at least ten of whom were executed as members of the Gestapo responsible for tortures and atrocities. This execution of prisoners is still debated and is held by critics of the occupation as directly responsible for the reprisals that followed. It was the kind of public show of force which Chapou had initiated at Cajarc in the execution of Miliciens, and underlined the objective of a permanent occupation. The FTP set up their headquarters in the barracks of the Champ de Mars and the tricolor flag flew over the town. The remainder of the garrison held out at the station and in the armaments factories, but for fifteen hours the town was virtually liberated, its population no more apprehensive than the FTP themselves.

At dusk on 8 June a section of the heavily armoured SS Division Das Reich arrived at Tulle, heading for the Normandy front, but with instructions to deal with the maquis. The FTP in the town, following the general orders to avoid a set battle with vastly superior forces, withdrew. The SS did not pursue them. On the following day the Germans announced that 120 of the population would be executed for having staged the liberation of the town. After an arbitrary selection of victims, accompanied by appalling scenes of family distress and SS brutality, ninety-nine men were publicly hanged from the balconies of houses in the centre of the town.

Tanks and armoured cars from another section of the Das Reich Division arrived from the Quercy to be present at the selection of those to be executed. While the town was being occupied by the FTP on the 8th, this section had been engaged in the destruction of an assembly camp of maquisards some 85 km. to the south of Tulle at the farm of Gabaudet on the Causse de Gramat. Guided by a collaborationist gendarme, they had arrived by a little-used road to surprise over 200 recruits to the maquis, who had volunteered in response to the proclamation of de Gaulle on 6 June, 'Pour les fils de France, où qu'ils soient, quels qu'ils soient, le devoir simple et sacré est de combattre l'ennemi par tous les moyens dont ils disposent.' The camp at Gabaudet, organized by the FTP of the Lot, was in a state of relaxed euphoria at the announcement of Jour-J but in some confusion over the flood of volunteers which had exceeded all expectations. In the evening *corvées* within the large walled farmyard, straw was being prepared for beds, but no attention had been paid to security. The SS tanks were not observed until they had virtually reached the farm. The recruits could only run desperately in all directions, attempting to break out of the courtyard, trying to hide in the barns and the well, and crawling into the scrub of the Causse. They were shot like rabbits, or crushed under the advancing tanks. The farm buildings were fired, and eighty prisoners tied to the front of the tanks as hostages to deter maquis attacks when the unit moved on to Tulle. Among the thirty-five bodies left behind was the young daughter of the farm and several farm workers from the vicinity.[15]

The massacre at Gabaudet was followed by the hangings at Tulle, and Tulle was followed by the mass killings at Oradour-sur-Glane on 10 June, the most notorious and horrendous reprisal perpetrated by the Das Reich Division, or more specifically by the regiment Der Führer, who shot and burnt over 630 inhabitants of this Limousin village to the west of Limoges, asserting wrongly that it was a maquis centre and contained a depot of arms. Before and after these three days of intensive repression and reprisals, there were several other massacres in the Quercy, notably fifteen women and men of the small village of Frayssinet-le-Gélat on 21 May on the route from Fumel to Gourdon, and twenty-two men from Gourdon shot at Boissières on 30 June, the day on which the Groupes Vény under Commandant Druot engaged a German force far superior in number at the nearby village of Gigouzac, losing eleven men but inflicting many casualties, reported at the time to be as high as sixty.[16]

The embattled context in which the FTP seizure of Tulle was situated could be amplified still further by citing a multitude of maquis actions and German reprisals in the whole area surrounding the roads which led from Toulouse and Montauban towards Normandy and Paris. The scattered warfare between the Resistance and the occupying troops became concentrated round these vital arteries used for the movement of reinforcements and eventually retreat. Tulle was at a crossroads from the Massif Central to Limoges and from the south-west to Clermont-Ferrand, but General Hounau of the AS corps franc of Tulle would have nothing to do with the occupation, and later stated that the 'operation was pointless strategically since no appreciable military objective was secured'.[17] His criticism ignored the importance of the *insurrection nationale* to the FTP and it is this perspective which must be remembered if Tulle is to be understood. The miscalculation of the Corrèze FTP was less to do with the strategic position of Tulle, arguably of considerable military importance at that particular moment in time, than with its suitability as a vanguard of the national uprising favoured by the FTP. It was not a large working-class town, and although its northern

[15] Unpublished account of Gabaudet by Pierre Couderq, kindly made available by the author. Madame Berthe Couderq also generously entrusted me with original accounts of events in or near Gramat, written by schoolchildren at the time. These included several moving versions of the Gabaudet massacre.

[16] The citation on the monument at Gigouzac, signed by Vény, reads, 'Sous les ordres du Cdt. Druot, attaqué par des forces très supérieures en nombre et en matériel, a infligé à l'ennemi des pertes sanglantes, mettant hors de combat plus de 100 allemands S.S. alors que les effectifs du secteur IV ne se montaient qu'à 60 hommes. S'est replié ensuite en bon ordre conformément aux ordres impératifs reçus prescrivant de ne pas se laisser jamais accrocher, donnant ainsi un magnifique exemple de décision, de courage et d'abnégation.'

[17] AN 72. AJ 112, 'Souvenirs du Corps Franc de Tulle par le Général Hounau', Nov. 1980.

area resembled to some extent the 'quartiers populeux' which the FTP believed would be at the hub of the insurrection, the town as a whole was not sizeable or dense enough to erect the barricades anticipated in the model plan. Nor had the population taken the initiative. The FTP were the combatants, and all combat ceased when they withdrew. In these ways the Corrèze FTP, in their urge to show themselves as the vanguard of an insurgent people, had allowed a national goal to divert them from a sober appreciation of local potential.

The juxtaposition of the very different liberations attempted at Mont Mouchet and Tulle underlines the severity of the problem faced by both AS and FTP maquis in realizing their insurrectional self-image. The history of the Vercors between 9 June and the end of July has been more exhaustively examined than either of these two attempts and there is a corresponding wealth of interpretations and judgements, but where the details of the various memoirs and histories converge is in the portrait of maquisards and their supportive communities in the Vercors, excessively stretched by the imposition, and self-imposition, of a major liberational role. The battle of the massif du Vercors was not just another version of the events at Mont Mouchet, nor had the mobilization at Mont Mouchet been just another rerun of the Glières. All three had their own specific context and distinctive aims, even though all produced large concentrations of maquisards in more or less set battles with the occupying forces. Where the particularity of the Vercors lay was in the certainty which largely inspired the maquis that the Vercors had been accorded a planned and detailed role in the strategy of Allied invasion. It was firstly the 'plan montagnards' which was at issue. Developed by Dalloz and Alain le Ray in 1943, traded round the disparate authorities of the Free French and the Allied military command, apparently lost and abandoned, but refound and reappraised, the plan never became explicit French, British, or American policy, but nor was it ever explicitly countermanded in a way that would have been heard in the Vercors.[18] Secondly it was the constant recharging of energetic communications between the Vercors, Algiers, and London, which appeared to give the maquisards confirmation of their strategic importance, and kept alive their hopes of Allied reinforcements. A mass of telegrams and messages; meetings of leaders in France and Algiers; Allied finance carried by liaison agents; arms and supplies dropped by tricolor parachutes; and Allied missions landed in the midst of the massif with instructions to prepare a runway for what could only be the landing of heavy artillery or armed troops; all infused enthusiasm and high expectations in the maquis camps. In this case the

[18] Paul Dreyfus, *Vercors, citadelle de liberté* (Arthaud, 1969), 39–46, 335–43. See also evidence from Francis Cammaerts, Ch. 7, Oral Memories.

image of a vanguard role was not only created from within, but was given substance and credibility from without.

The coded messages sent to the whole of France from the Allied High Command on the night of 5/6 June were the long-awaited signals for the Resistance everywhere to step up all road, rail, power, and communications sabotage, and attempt the widescale disruption of German troop movements. Local regions received different coded messages to this effect, but it is not fully accepted by all historians that the Vercors received its own message, 'Le chamois des Alpes bondit', though all the other messages for the Rhône-Alpes region were clearly heard.[19] The Drôme, in which the lower half of the Vercors is situated, was mobilized by the phrase 'Dans la forêt verte est un grand arbre', and François Huet, leader of the Vercors maquis, Eugène Chavant, the AS leader in the Isère, and Marcel Descour, chief of staff of the FFI for the Rhône-Alpes region, had no second thoughts in calling on 9 June for all maquis and groupes francs in the area of the Vercors to mobilize in the massif. It is accepted that Descour had told Huet, when he appointed him commander of the Vercors at the end of May,

> The Vercors is the only maquis, in the whole of France, which has been given the mission to set up its own free territory [une terre de liberté]. It will receive the arms, ammunition, and troops which will allow it to be the advance guard of a landing in Provence. It is not impossible that de Gaulle himself will land here to make his first proclamation to the French people.[20]

This echoed the 'plan montagnards', though it is not known who Descour was using as authorization for his statement. His immediate superior, the regional head of the FFI, Albert Chambonnet, was certainly not in agreement. He was wary, in theory, of any concentration of the maquis, and after the events at Glières, where he had accepted the *montée au plateau* against his better judgement, he had declared himself 'firmly opposed' to the setting-up of a vast operation in the Vercors.[21] Like Descour and Huet he was a regular army officer, but he was more profoundly marked by the strategic imperative of guerrilla tactics, and his socialist politics encouraged him to talk of the FFI as 'une Armée Révolutionnaire'.[22] By contrast, Huet and Descour nurtured more conventional ideas of military formations, impelling them towards the kind of mobilization already in progress in the Auvergne, but strengthened by the conviction that Jour-J in Normandy would be followed in a matter of days by a second invasion in the south. Why else, it can still be asked, would the coded messages from the BBC and de Gaulle's own broadcast of 6 June have unleashed military action in

[19] Fernand Rude, 'Le Vercors', in Pierre Bolle (ed.), *Grenoble et le Vercors. De la Résistance à la Libération* (La Manufacture: Lyon, 1985), 154.

[20] Quoted in Paul Dreyfus, *Vercors, citadelle de liberté*, 130.

[21] Fernand Rude, 'Le Vercors', 151. [22] Ibid. 150.

the whole of France and not just in the old *zone occupée* in the north? In answer to this, Fernand Rude, in a recent critical account of the Vercors concentration, reaffirms that the universal messages were part of the Allied diversionary tactics to keep the Germans undecided about the exact location of the invasion, even after the first boats had reached the Normandy beaches, and he gives a more ambivalent meaning to de Gaulle's broadcast, stressing de Gaulle's insistence that Resistance action should be tied as closely as possible to the action of the French and Allied forces. If rigorously heeded, this might have deterred precipitate military action in the south while only the coast of Normandy was invaded.[23]

Expectations, in the charged and feverish excitement of Jour-J, needed only grains of sustenance to grow into certainties, and as volunteers came from Grenoble, Romans, Valence, Bourg-de-Péage, and Die, as well as from all the smaller towns and villages within or close to the massif itself, the motivating 'myth' of the Vercors as an integral part of the unfolding Allied strategy took root among the new recruits and flourished among the established maquisards, many of whom had expressed feelings of boredom in the long months of winter survival and the protracted monotony of unarmed training. Within days of 6 June the numbers had tripled, and by the middle of July close to 4,000 men were encamped in the massif, increasingly better armed as the parachute drops intensified at the end of June, though the weapons were overwhelmingly light. The heavy artillery was confidently awaited, along with the second landing and the Allied reinforcements. 'The weather', wrote Pierre Tanant, Huet's chief of staff, 'was magnificent in this month of June. The sky was a resplendent blue. It felt deliciously good at 1,000 metres in altitude. And above all, up there, on these verdant hills, one felt free.'[24] With a nod towards Revolutionary history, Paul Dreyfus, historian of the Vercors, calls the afflux of recruits 'les volontaires de l'an quatre de la guerre'.[25] Within a week of their arrival the 'Republic of the Vercors' had been created.

The inveterate republicanism of the whole Drôme area abutting and overlapping the Vercors, the hardened anti-Vichy sentiments of the Grenoble Resistance which had marked the town as permanently subversive in Vichy's eyes, and the socialism of the civilian leaders of the Vercors combined to make the Vercors more than a symbolic reassertion of the republic. Chavant for the Isère set up a civilian administration in Saint-Martin-en-Vercors, and Benjamin Malossane for the south of the Vercors and the Drôme established an assertive republican presence at la Chapelle-en-Vercors. Their combined writ ran across the massif, almost as if the Vercors were itself a *département* and Chavant and Malossane prefect and sub-prefect respectively.

[23] Ibid. 155. [24] Tanant, *Vercors*, 58.
[25] Dreyfus, *Vercors, citadelle de liberté*, 142.

Malossane allowed himself the power and freedom to revoke two mayors out of the five communes under his immediate influence, and on 3 July Yves Farge addressed a public celebration of the Republic at Saint-Martin in his capacity as clandestine Commissaire de la République for Lyon and area, appointed by the Provisional Government in Algiers. Contrary to rumours which circulated within France, the Vercors was not claiming anything like autonomy or secession by its self-styled republican status. It was a formal device for asserting the liberation of the massif from both Germans and Vichy. Central to its declaration was the expression of complete loyalty to de Gaulle and its acceptance of the Provisional Government. Nevertheless there was a scarcely hidden atmosphere of insurgency in the Vercors, a fact recognized by the greater support shown by the regional Front National than had been the case either at Glières or in the Auvergne.[26] Commandant Pons affirmed that 'Nous n'étions pas des militaires mais des insurgés',[27] and if there was friction anywhere in the Vercors it was between maquisards who identified passionately with this insurgent status and certain regular officers like Geyer who promoted a regimental air of military convention.

The fête of 14 July in the Vercors crystallized its political and military status as an outpost of liberation, saluted by an expression of admiration and support from Algiers, and a massive drop of arms and ammunition by seventy-two American Flying Fortresses, with clusters of red, white, and blue parachutes filling the daylight sky at nine o'clock in the morning. This gesture, more than the tricolor flag flown earlier in June at Saint-Nizier and visible from Grenoble, was as provocative as anything mounted by the internal French Resistance in the face of the enemy, and constituted the kind of positive proof to the maquisards that the Vercors was still special to 'imminent' Allied plans for the invasion of the South of France.

It was astonishing to most of those mobilized in the Vercors that the liberated massif had reached the national fête without either a second Allied invasion or a major German offensive. Francis Cammaerts of SOE, whose organizing and animating role in the Resistance of the Drôme and the south-east of France was one of the most effective and creative in the whole history of SOE in France, had repeatedly requested heavy artillery for the massif, and he had told London that the Vercors operation only made military sense in the light of a southern invasion within three weeks. When those three weeks had elapsed, he tried to persuade the Allied command at least to put the German airstrips out of operation in the immediate region of the Vercors, and he specified the aerodrome of Chabeuil near Valence. 'It could all so easily have been done,' he said. 'The German planes, earmarked for carrying troops, were an inviting target on the ground. But

[26] Cabane, chef départemental of the Front National, attended the Vercors celebrations of 14 July 1944. Rude, 'Le Vercors', 158–9.
[27] Ibid. 161.

no attempt to put them out of action was made.' Cammaerts was closely involved at all stages of the Vercors events: he had more empathy for the ideals and aspirations of the French maquis, both AS and FTP, than many other SOE agents, and he understood their structures of loyalty and command. At no point did he try to break their independence and assert control, but he rightly assessed their vulnerability, and did everything to instigate maquis action outside the Vercors to diffuse the German repression and keep Vichy preoccupied.[28]

The German forces in the sub-Alpine area were already dividing their energies between the maquis of the Ain and the Vercors. Within a few days after Jour-J the Ain maquis (FFI) under Romans-Petit had effectively blocked all local railways and roads in the area and isolated two-thirds of the Ain from the rest of France. They had created a free zone covering some 600 square kilometres and including the towns of Nantua, Oyonnax, and Bellegarde. On 10 June the Germans attacked the FFI in Bellegarde and forced them to withdraw, though with heavy German losses in the process. On 13 June they attacked the Vercors through the village of Saint-Nizier, the Achilles heel of the massif, which overlooked Grenoble. Repulsed by well-positioned maquis forces in the first assault, they returned to take and destroy the village, forcing the maquisards to retire further into the massif. The fighting at Saint-Nizier had been far heavier than the Germans had anticipated and they did not pursue the maquis fighters as they withdrew. The maquis of the Vercors had lost control of the entrance gate to the massif, but had marked a considerable triumph in the initial confrontation. There ensued a month with no German offensive, itself a testimony to the impact which the liberation of the massif had made on the military strategy of the occupying forces. The Germans had been forced to plan and prepare their response to the Vercors over more than four weeks. As Cammaerts observed, 'If the Allies wanted an operation in the South of France to keep major numbers of German troops away from the Normandy front for the critical first three weeks, the Vercors had succeeded beyond their expectations.'[29] Surely, argued the maquisards within the Vercors, the relative stability of their position must signify not just the success of local maquis groups in securing their local objective, but also open the way to the second Allied invasion and the sending of reinforcements. The arrival of an Anglo-American mission headed by Major Desmond Longe of SOE on 28 June, and still more that of French military construction experts under Captain Tournissa on 6 July seemed to confirm this prognosis: the landing strip at Vassieux began to take shape.

The carefully prepared German onslaught on the territory held by the maquis in the south-east began on 10 July with crushing attacks on the FFI

[28] Evidence from Francis Cammaerts, 18 Mar. 1991. [29] Ibid.

in the Ain, where the different groups of maquisards fought, dispersed, regrouped, and dispersed again in actions of a guerrilla nature, avoiding the conclusive set battle, but nevertheless unable to hold the territory they had liberated.[30] The German units moved through the countryside in dense military convoys which would have made comparatively easy aerial targets, but when requests to London for support from the air brought no response, there was resentment but no accusation of betrayal. Romans-Petit commented that they had always expected as much. 'We had never taken our wishes for realities: we relied only on ourselves.'[31] In the Vercors it was different. The airstrip at Vassieux awaited a landing force. The companies of the maquis had been given set defensive positions at the vulnerable points of access to the massif: they expected the Allies to bring in both men and heavy artillery. Confidence was high. Early on 21 July twenty planes towing enormous gliders were seen approaching Vassieux from the south. The construction workers on the ground, looking into the rain-filled skies, saw first the long-expected reinforcements. They then saw the German markings on the planes.

Four hundred experienced German troops disgorged from the gliders. The surprise was total. Counter-attacks failed to capture the German position. Bombardment from the air kept the maquis at a distance, and constant German reinforcements were dropped to Vassieux. Concentrated German offensives followed to the south and east of the massif, and through the open gate of Saint-Nizier to the north. The maquis fought from their given positions, but were overpowered in all respects by a force armed with the weapons necessary for medium and long-range artillery bombardment. Against this the machine-guns and the few bazookas of the maquis could do little. 'It might all have been different', said Cammaerts, 'if the maquis had possessed heavy mortars of their own.'[32] Desmond Longe sent a desperate telegram calling on the Allies to meet the demands for parachuted troops, though it is clear that he himself had been given no reason by SOE to expect such reinforcements when he arrived in the Vercors.[33] By contrast, the expectations of the vast majority of the Vercors leaders and maquisards had always been high, and their intimations of betrayal infused their last messages not only with desperation but with anger. Chavant's telegram on

[30] In early 1945 the Historical Section of the US Army formed a special unit to collect information on the activities of the FFI from 6 June 1944. Captain Lucien Galimand was appointed from the French side. The work was completed on 15 Nov. 1945 and runs to 1,581 pages followed by a conclusion. Its entries on the fighting in the Ain includes a comment on the FFI of the area by Colonel Grace, Commanding Officer of the 2nd Battalion, 179th Infantry Regiment, 'Never before have I seen a body of men with such an honest desire to kill.' Papiers Galimand p. 1016; AN 72. AJ 512–17.

[31] Romans-Petit, *Les Maquis de l'Ain*, 121.

[32] Evidence from Francis Cammaerts, 18 Mar. 1991.

[33] See Foot, *SOE in France*, 391–4.

the night of 21 July, with the German paratroopers in command of Vassieux but with hopes of relief still alive, was poignantly expressive:

> La Chapelle, Vassieux, Saint-Martin bombarded by German aircraft. Enemy troops parachuted into Vassieux. Demand immediate bombing. Had promised to hold out for three weeks; time elapsed since set up of our organization, six weeks. Demand supplies of men, food and equipment. Morale of population excellent, but will turn rapidly against you if you do not take immediate action, and we will agree with them in saying that London and Algiers have no understanding of our predicament and are to be considered criminals and cowards.[34]

No reinforcements arrived. On 23 July Huet ordered the maquisards to give up their position and disperse within the massif, to return to a nomadic maquis existence and to adopt the tactics of guerrilla action, both to survive and to harass the enemy. A recurrent criticism of the Vercors revolves round the timing of this tactic: should it not have been the strategy from the start, or at least several days earlier when the German attack began? Was there ever any hope of holding set positions? Were the expectations more self-induced than the maquisards could admit? Had the République du Vercors attempted too much, too early?

The atrocities committed by the Germans in the wake of the fighting, like the hangings at Tulle and the massacre at Oradour, were an index of the barbarity of Nazism and a sign of how disturbed and deranged the Germans had become by their inability to immobilize, capture, or kill every one of the armed Resistance who defied them. A military success by itself was not enough. Over 630 maquisards died in the Vercors fighting. A further 200 inhabitants of villages and farms were killed in reprisals. The wounded and their carers in the makeshift hospital of the Grotte de la Luire, close to Vassieux, were discovered and massacred. Destruction and inhumanity left their scars in every village, notably Vassieux, Villard-de-Lans, and la Chapelle-en-Vercors. Desmond Longe had warned his superiors on 21 July that 'if the troops of the Vercors are defeated, the reprisals will be terrible'.[35] Neither this nor any other message persuaded the powers outside France to advance or alter their plans. The history of the Vercors almost at once became a tragedy, a disaster, a mistake, a betrayal. Thirty years later, however, Alain le Ray, one of the proponents of the original 'plan montagnards' rejected the aura of disaster and strategic error. He suggested in a debate in 1975 that guerrilla tactics in the massif might have provoked even more reprisals, and that the battle of the Vercors tied down an important section of the German army and 'induced in the German war machine a kind of paralysis, both moral and material' in the very locality where the Allied forces would penetrate into France after the landings in Provence. It

[34] Dreyfus, *Vercors, citadelle de liberté*, 220; Rude, 'Le Vercors', 163–64.
[35] Dreyfus, *Vercors, citadelle de liberté*, 188.

is possible, he argued, to claim that the Vercors was not a disaster but a heroic achievement. 'The losses were too great, for sure, but the Vercors is a page of history of which France can be proud.'[36] Le Ray's judgement is one of many which protract and renew the controversy over the Vercors. Arguably not the least of its merits is the sideways glance at guerrilla tactics elsewhere which could not prevent, and might be seen to have exacerbated, the barbarity of German reprisals. And yet comparisons in that direction invariably become tendentious and inexact. There was no consistency in the German response to acts of armed Resistance which allows a meaningful correlation between different kinds of maquis action and the incidence of reprisals.[37]

The actions in the Auvergne and in the Vercors are remembered for their heroic achievements as well as their failures. The seizure of Tulle is remembered only for the town's subsequent martyrdom. As three distinct attempts to realize an insurrectional role they shared a common element in the over-extension of local capacities. Nodal points in the strands of liberation, they are nevertheless considered by maquisards as untypical of the mass of maquisard activity which put the Germans under pressure and dissolved the authority of Vichy between May and August. It was more typical to maximize and diversify limited, local actions which by their nature did not make the national headlines. These smaller actions have consequently featured only in local histories of the Resistance, with the result that controversies about the role, efficacy, and optimum form of maquis action in these four months constantly revolve round the bigger events. A shift of focus does not necessarily diminish the military controversies, since smaller actions in no way avoided tactical problems of how best to pursue the aims of liberation. Guerrilla warfare was elusive in more ways than one. What exactly it should or should not entail proved elusive to many who rigorously promoted its practice. It is rather that a shift of focus is also a shift of emphasis. The protracted search for the maquis into the abundant undergrowth of liberation actions reveals just how pluralistic and inversionary maquis history continued to be. There is no way in which all the disaggregated pieces which made up the mosaic of the maquis from early 1943 onwards can be discarded in the summer of 1944 and replaced by a single piece labelled 'combat', however complicated its detailed design. The myriad of smaller actions initiated by maquisards in the liberation period point to conclusions about the nature and aims of the maquis which must do justice to the whole of maquis history and not just its final stages. To start with, they point to an urgent need to pluralize the meaning of the term

[36] Rude, 'Le Vercors', 174–5.

[37] For reprisals in the Cévennes see Ch. 5 and for reprisals by the SS Division 'Das Reich' in the south-west see earlier in this chapter.

'mobilisation' which was such a key concept in the history of Mont Mouchet and the Vercors.

From March to May the steady acceleration in drops of arms and ammunition, and the increasing number of parachuted missions, bringing agents of the British SOE, the American OSS, and the French BCRA into southern France, allowed talk of a spring *débarquement* to assume a widespread confidence within existing maquis units. They understandably interpreted the upsurge in Allied provisions as a direct endorsement of their existing policy. *Terrains de parachutage* had been found and coded throughout the Massif Central, the Pyrenees, and the Alps, and the excitement and anticipation generated within quite small maquis groups by hearing their code announced on the BBC was a legitimating process of crucial importance, particularly for any group on the point of becoming critical of the long days of training for a Jour-J which seemed never to come. Most such groups were attached to the AS or the ORA and it was hardly surprising that certain units of the FTP, denied such external legitimation, should seek alternative means, and even descend to piracy of arms intended for other maquis, to register both their sense of injustice and their own activist identity.[38] It was from this inequality of arms distribution that the word 'mobilisation' derived its capacity to divide as well as motivate the maquis.

Assured of a supply of arms, it was feasible to mobilize, if not the thousands brought together in Mont Mouchet and the Vercors, at least more than the small companies of fifteen to forty who had survived the winter in varying states of discomfort and insecurity. Preparations for sites where over a hundred could be incorporated into something more akin to a regular army unit were invariably backed by London, where the SOE command was responsive to assurances from trusted agents that the military credentials of the operation were soundly based. Just such eminently respectable operations were mounted in the Toulouse region by, on the one hand, a three-man team, Georges Mompezat, Henri Sévenet, and an SOE wireless operator H. M. Despaigne known as Major Richardson, and on the other by the ubiquitous SOE agent George Starr and his *pianiste* Yvonne Cormeau whose record for regular and highly reliable wireless transmissions was astonishing. Starr and Cormeau armed and equipped numerous small groups to the south and west of Toulouse who remained on stand-by in their homes, whereas Despaigne was part of a more ambitious scheme to locate a significant fighting force in the Montagne Noire, south of Mazamet, with

[38] Jacques Bounin, Commissaire de la République for the Montpellier region, had been a non-communist member of the Front National, and had considerable sympathy with the predicament of the FTP. He regarded the Allied reluctance to supply the FTP with arms as an act of sheer stupidity, which left them no alternative but to procure arms from those who were more privileged; Jacques Bounin, *Beaucoup d'imprudences* (Stock, 1974), 127–40. Compare also evidence from Lucien Maury, 24 June 1982, and Raymond Fournier, 23 Mar. 1982.

strategic access to the two main roads leading from Toulouse to the Languedoc plain.[39] By early June a series of parachute drops in areas of the Tarn, the Aude, and the Ariège had enabled some four to five hundred men from as far afield as Castres, Toulouse, and Limoux to be alerted to the imminence of mobilization, knowing that arms and money were available in sufficient quantity.

The Pic de Nore in the Montagne Noire was chosen as the assembly point, a summit enclosed by extensive pine woods with gentler countryside to the south, accessible from Mazamet only by a steep climb, and commanding extensive views into the Hérault and the Aude within the Montpellier region, and northwards into the Tarn, administered from Toulouse. It was a perfect example of the 'frontier' rural locality which created maximum problems for the tenuous police network still available to Vichy, and it had none of the deceptive qualities of a fortress redoubt attributed to the Vercors at the same point in time. With the coded announcement of Jour-J the selective mobilization at the Pic de Nore was implemented, and the Corps Franc de la Montagne Noire (CFMN) came into existence, self-consciously refusing the term maquis and acknowledging no local superiors. The line of command was established directly between the authority of the SOE and General Koenig in London and the triumvirate in the Montagne Noire, to which was added the military expertise of Captain de Kervanoael, one of the very few regular officers who made themselves available, even to this remarkably organized and well-provisioned combat organization.

It took little more than a week for the controversies surrounding the CFMN to break into the open. Several hundred volunteers were turned away as being superfluous to the rationalized capacity of the Corps Franc, set initially at five hundred, and Despaigne acknowledged that this must have caused some local resentment.[40] At a subsequent date all those who declared themselves to be communists were permitted to withdraw after their request to leave without the normal retaliations attendant on 'changing camp' had been agreed in London. This political separation encouraged the judgement made in July by Serge Ravanel, the regional leader of the FFI, that the Corps Franc was 'a mercenary gang in the pay of international capitalism', a sweeping, ideological indictment which Ravanel, both as a communist sympathiser and as the bypassed local military authority, conveyed with some passion to a protesting Mompezat in a meeting in Toulouse.[41]

[39] Evidence from Yvonne Cormeau, 22 Jan. 1991, and from H. M. Despaigne, 18 Aug. 1979. Evidence from Maurice Buckmaster, 4 Nov. 1990, is particularly fulsome in its praise for Yvonne Cormeau's transmissions. He said that in her enormous number of reports, requests, and replies she never once made a coding error.

[40] Evidence from H. M. Despaigne, 18 Aug. 1979.

[41] Georges Mompezat, *Le Corps Franc de la Montagne Noire. Journal de marche* (Mompezat: Albi, 1963), 132.

The animosity towards the CFMN, of which this was a flamboyant example, was fuelled by the absence of any major military confrontation in the Montagne Noire until the Germans attacked in force on 20 July. It was as if the CFMN ought to have justified itself by acts of military bravura commensurate with its size and strength, even when criticisms of Mont Mouchet and the Vercors concentrated on the folly of pitched encounters. Local historians of Resistance in the Tarn point to several effective acts of harassment undertaken by the Corps Franc, and argue that the CFMN did not over-extend local capacities, that they lost very few men and provoked only minimal reprisals.[42] Their demonstration in full uniform at the town of Revel on 14 July, where they arrived in over thirty lorries, impressed the population by its dignity and discipline, and Mompezat wrote that the Germans believed the CFMN was much stronger than it really was, and mistakenly imagined that it possessed a range of heavy artillery. Illusions of power had always been carefully cultivated within the maquis, and here was a body of several hundred men who kept thousands of German troops in the south-west, on the illusory basis that the CFMN had the means to meet a substantial German offensive. The *Journal de Marche* of the CFMN argued that

> the results exceeded all expectations. The Germans ceased all convoy operations on the roads close to the Montagne Noire. The power of the Corps Franc seemed so great to them that they took more than a month to mount their attack of 20 July. In so doing, they kept a significant number of their troops inactive at Carcassonne, Alzonne, Castelnaudary, Castres, Mazamet, and Revel, which they might well have used elsewhere.[43]

This internal account of the CFMN, edited by Mompezat, is less dismissive of the word 'maquis' than Despaigne in his oral testimony, but the two memoirs converge to give a picture of an organization with a strong sense of its own authoritative identity. It swept aside the local residue of Vichy's rural presence by evicting the Chantiers de la Jeunesse in the forest of Ramondens, and taking over their relatively comfortable facilities: it insisted on the hierarchical separation of officers and men at meal times; it methodically solved its *ravitaillement* problems by sending a specialist group under lieutenant Cormouls to buy food well away from the local area, or to raid stocks hoarded by profiteers; it created its own medical structures; it restrained, trained, and disciplined the more intemperate recruits, and it kept the tightest of security controls. It was neither surprised by a sudden attack nor betrayed from within. It comprised almost 1,000 men by mid-July, made up of local French, mainly from the Tarn and the Aude, and from all occupations including the middle-class professions, numerous Alsace-Lorrai-

[42] Fernand Chaynes and Émile Saulière, *Le Tarn et les tarnais dans la deuxième guerre mondiale* (Éditions de la Revue du Tarn: Albi, n.d.), 13–20.
[43] Mompezat, *Le Corps Franc de la Montagne Noire*, 231.

ners who had deserted from the German army, a few Russian deserters, several Spanish and Polish anti-fascists, a few Italians, a few Belgians, one Dutchman, one Croat, one American, parachuted in, and one Englishman, Despaigne.[44] It was divided into three camps, but the *esprit de corps* of the whole CFMN was sedulously cultivated. When it was faced with the heavy German air and land onslaught of 20 July, it resisted effectively for two days, during which one of the leaders, Henri Sévenet, was killed. An accurate calculation of the superiority of the German forces, based on excellent intelligence, then led quickly to a decision to disperse. Separate units re-formed in the range of hills from the Monts de Lacaune in the Aveyron to Mont Caroux above the mining complex of the Hérault, retaining their Corps Franc identity and participating fully in the final combats of the Liberation in mid-August.

Here was a maquis whose life-style contrasted vividly with the rough, egalitarian, opportunistic nature of most smaller groups, and yet despite its conventional army structure and routines it was not the product of the ORA, nor did it gamble on its capacity to survive a conventional pitched battle. It avoided the fate of the maquisards in the Vercors and at la Truyère, and from the start of the operation through to the final dispersal, all the leaders believed in the flexibility of guerrilla combat. Yet the CFMN incurred not just the ideological hostility of Ravanel and local communist and FTP leaders, but also the contempt of Lieutenant-Colonel Redon, the head of the FFI in the Tarn. Redon admitted to a certain grudge against the Corps Franc for their refusal to liaise with the FFI at both departmental and regional level, but in his post-war report on the Tarn, which amiably acknowledges the huge disparity in methods and attitudes among the various maquis, he can find nothing but a caustic form of words to describe the CFMN.[45] Redon, along with many others in the vicinity of the Montagne Noire, regarded the mobilization to the Pic de Nore more as an *im*mobilization. It was a harsh judgement which stemmed less from a strict military assessment of the CFMN's actions than from local discontent with its combination of material ease, its plentiful supply of arms, and its arrogant independence.

At more than one locality in the South of France the very advisability of mobilization on 6 June was questioned, and Koenig's abrupt reversal of policy on 10 June, while confusing and demoralizing to many, made sense not only to the leaders of the CFMN who carried it out to the letter, but to several Resisters who criticized the hasty over-exposure of untrained volunteers to veteran German forces who were still in effective control of the south. It was clearly the lack of sufficient arms training and military

[44] Ibid. 80.

[45] Lt.-Col. Redon, 'Souvenirs de la Résistance dans le département du Tarn, 1944', 20; AN 72. AJ 198.

leadership which provoked a cautious attitude of many Resistance leaders to a *levée en masse*, and this caution was reinforced by the arbitrariness of German reactions and an awareness of the role that sheer misfortune could play if a mobilization proceeded in an over-optimistic, improvized manner. In the Montpellier region the shock of events at a turn in the road between Puisserguier and Saint-Chinian on Route Nationale 112 severely affected local attitudes towards the ideals of insurrection and mobilization. On the night of 6 June a group of young volunteers from Capestang and Montady in the heart of the Languedoc *vignoble* west of Béziers responded enthusiastically to the news circulating in the area that a maquis was forming in the *garrigue* above Saint-Chinian. A police report states that those from Capestang went openly to a *boulangerie* and elsewhere in the small town to load up a lorry with bread and other supplies, requisitioned another lorry at Puisserguier and took the main road towards Saint-Chinian. At Fontjun at the Col de Cébazan they fortuitously encountered a lorry of German soldiers. Five of the would-be maquisards were killed instantly, and eighteen others were arrested, including Juliette Cauquil who had accompanied her husband Roger Cauquil, the driver of one of the lorries. All those arrested were shot on the following afternoon in the Champ de Mars at Béziers.[46] At this late stage in the Occupation they died, unarmed, in search of the maquis, and questions throughout the area were asked about the tactics of promise and incitement which had led to such a carefree mobilization. The maquis which they might have found was to become the Maquis Latourette under Jean Benes and Jean Girves, supplied by the AS in Saint-Pons led by Émile Fontès, but severely marked by the initial trauma of the mobilization. Morale was low among some twenty-five maquisards until parachute drops in the mountains of the Saumail brought them a renewed sense of purpose. In the interim, wrote one of the maquisards, Jean Viste, there were ten days of inaction, and 'seeing that no *débarquement* had occurred on the Mediterranean coast, Benes advised those who could easily return to their homes to do so'.[47]

Redon, in the Tarn, was also turning away volunteers. A more junior officer, Bertrand, commented that Redon was forced to do this for lack of arms, but that those turned away found it incomprehensible after all the

[46] The police report on the incident claimed that Roger and Juliette Cauquil were only reluctantly part of the volunteer group, and that Juliette Cauquil only accompanied her husband because she feared his life was in danger from the 'terrorists'; AD Hérault 18W 15. Local Resistance histories maintain that all were volunteers, cf. Jean Sagnes in collaboration with Jules Maurin, *L'Hérault dans la guerre* (Éditions Horvath: Saint-Étienne, 1986), 132. The executions in Béziers, reported the Renseignements Généraux, had deepened the sympathy of the local population for the maquis: 'Une sourde colère se propage un peu plus chaque jour' (5–11 June 1944); AD Hérault 172W 4.

[47] Unpublished memoir of the Maquis de Latourette written by Jean Viste (June 1990), 3. Kindly communicated by Armand Calas of Saint-Pons.

promises and assurances emanating from London and Algiers.[48] Both logically and paradoxically Redon accepted the GMR unit 'l'Albigeois', which deserted Vichy and took to the maquis on 7 June, as did the GMR group 'Mistral' shortly after. It was logical because they were armed; it was paradoxical because they had been the enemies of the maquis throughout the winter months. The majority of the urban police from Albi also came under Redon's command from the middle of June, and he initially encamped these police recruits at Mont-Roc. Here they adapted so badly to rural life that Redon sent most of them back to their homes and their jobs in Albi, adding in his report that 'as a result we had their complicit support when we came to assert ourselves in the *chef-lieu*'.[49]

Further west, on the other side of Toulouse the Renseignements Généraux reported that over 900 had volunteered for the maquis from the cantons of Rieumes and Saint-Lys and commented,

> They are people from all social classes who had been sent into a frenzy by the Allied landings. They left their villages and towns and headed for the woods. No communist influence can be traced. But these new maquisards were so unused to such a life that they were disbanded on the night of 22/3 June, and most of those who had 'gone astray' returned home. Several leaders, however, remained behind to restructure the group.[50]

At the very least, these examples of disagreement and hesitations about mobilization show how ambiguous or even deceptive it could be at a military level. Nor were military criteria the only grounds on which mobilization was disputed and assessed. It had also to be seen as the climactic finale of four years of civilian Resistance against Germany and Vichy, in which thousands of unarmed and militarily inexperienced people, both men and women, felt themselves to be mobilized. Large numbers of these had already been involved in structures of Resistance, and many in the community and collective structures of the maquis. Others, who had not been involved in Resistance, now wanted to be so, and these included not just those who were changing sides at the last moment, but also 17- to 20-year-olds whose youth had kept them in the margins of active commitment and who had not been exposed to motivating factors such as STO. For these especially, the excitement of mobilization was strong, following on the months of intensive propaganda, by word and action, organized by the Forces Unies de la Jeunesse Patriotique (FUJP) which in many areas provided a rigorous apprenticeship to the activity of groupes francs and the maquis.[51]

[48] AN 72. AJ 198, M. Bertrand, 'La Mobilisation au maquis', n.d.

[49] AN 72. AJ 198, Redon, 'Souvenirs de la Résistance dans le département du Tarn, 1944', 30.

[50] AD Haute-Garonne M 1526², 'Situation du maquis', 28 June 1944.

[51] An example of Resistance action by the FUJP is provided by Pierre Combes in his unpublished 'Récit d'un coup de main: destruction par les F.U.J.P. des archives du S.T.O. à Cahors le 3 février 1944', which he kindly made available to me. The commando raid which

Resistance literature promoting this 'civilian' mobilization invariably aimed at strengthening the links between the population and the maquisards. Throughout May and June tracts incessantly urged women towards a 'mobilisation générale et active' structured into comités féminins and comités des Femmes de France which led on to the Union des Femmes Françaises (UFF). High on the list of actions specified in such tracts was a renewed system of *marrainage*, practised widely in the First World War when women set themselves up as *marraines* to soldiers at the front, sending letters and parcels of food and clothes. They were now called on to set up support committees for the 'vaillants jeunes gens qui composent l'Armée de la Libération, les maquisards' and to impose themselves on the Prefectures by sheer weight of numbers.[52] These were insurrectional calls, utilizing legitimized methods of familial pressure, and turning Vichy's glorification of the family against itself. To *marrainage* were added calls for women to mount demonstrations and general strikes, frequently advanced as the necessary complement to effective maquisard action. The FUJP argued a similar line in tracts aimed at young people. Inciting them to form units of milices patriotiques in the towns, the tracts presented these milices as the youth-equivalent of the maquis and the FTP.[53] A special number of the communist *Travailleur du Languedoc*, published on 9 June in the Hérault, started with the quote from de Gaulle, 'L'insurrection nationale est inséparable de la libération nationale', and went on to define the milices patriotiques as wider than a youth organization: they were 'la levée en masse organisée de tout le peuple français'.[54] With such definitions the lines between military and civilian mobilization became ever more blurred. In May the upper echelons of non-communist Resistance had also promoted a blurring of distinctions by declaring that all the paramilitary branches of the MUR were now united into the Corps Francs de la Libération (CFL). This umbrella label was intended to bring Action Ouvrière, groupes francs, Résistance-Fer, the

he describes was a total success. The documents stolen related to every aspect of STO, including labour within France, and contained all the names and addresses of those marked as *défaillants*. The young Resisters carried away hundreds of kilos of papers and scattered them on the wheel of the Saint-James water mill in the river Lot. Their only regret was that the pay of employees in the STO building happened to be among the documents, and that made the headlines next day in Cahors, though the publicity given to the whole raid was exactly what they had intended. The STO organization in Cahors was effectively sabotaged, and both the FUJP and the maquis of the Lot gained considerably in status. The raiders also took a typewriter which they gave to the maquis, and Pierre Combes adds, 'Jacques Chapou me donna, quelques jours plus tard, en échange, une mitraillette sten, et ma visite ayant correspondu à l'abattage d'un bœuf, je repartis lesté également d'un joli morceau de viande . . . Nous conservâmes précieusement les cartes de travail en blanc et les tampons officiels' (récit dated 20 Nov. 1989).

[52] AD Hérault 18W 13, tract found at Rodez, Aveyron, headed 'Femmes, mamans de Rodez', June–July 1944.

[53] Tracts found in Montpellier on 13 June 1944; AD Hérault 172W 35.

[54] *Le Travailleur du Languedoc*, numéro spécial (9 June 1944). The article was headed, 'Préparons l'insurrection nationale!'

Armée Secrète, and the maquis together, and was interpreted by many as the long-awaited commitment of the Gaullists to unrestrained *action immédiate*, both in rural and urban areas. It was welcomed by the FTP for that reason, and it seemed possible that the CFL and the FTP within the Forces Françaises de l'Intérieur would now have less cause to differ on either tactics or targets. As a structural development the CFL also appeared to be a recognition that the closely interlocked structures of the town-based FTP and the maquis FTP were a model to be copied. This could only boost the notion that arming the maquis must also mean arming the activists in the towns, and that separate categories of military and civilian mobilization would be increasingly unrealistic as the struggles for liberation intensified.

Finally there was the factor of mobilization as a circumstantial response to the savage spiral of German arrests, round-ups, and reprisals. Vichy increasingly failed in its attempts to implement STO in the first few months of 1944, Boyez admitting on 5 April that since 1 January only 13,000 had gone to Germany instead of the 273,000 Vichy had planned.[55] The register of those born in 1924 had not been completed in many areas, but in May Vichy announced that the *classe* of 1945 would now be registered as well by the end of the month. This remained a dead letter. In June, following the Normandy landings, the Germans decided that the pressure of the Allied bombings made further requisitions of labour through STO impractical, and Laval circulated the prefects on 23 June to say that the departures to Germany had been suspended. He added that a public announcement to that effect would be unwise.[56] STO was finally acknowledged to be at an end, but it had already been bypassed throughout the spring and early summer by alternative methods of conscription, mounted arbitrarily by the Germans through massive *rafles* of men found in the streets. Twelve hundred men were seized in Montpellier as they came out of the cinemas on 19 April, and over 80 were dispatched the next day to Germany.[57] On 12 May a section of the Das Reich division entered Figeac in the Lot, plundered and brutalized the population, and piled 600 men into lorries, took them to Montauban and deported them to labour and concentration camps in Germany.[58] The Prefect at the time numbered those arrested as 1,200, of whom, he reported, only 100 had been freed, and although this was an overestimate, his general point about the sociological width of the round-up, if not the exact details, was accurate: people taken from Figeac, he wrote, included almost all the *fonctionnaires* and those in *professions libérales*, most

[55] AD Hérault 17W 3, Boyez to prefects, 5 Apr. 1944.
[56] AD Hérault 13W. AC 183, Laval to prefects, 23 June 1944.
[57] AN F1C III. 1156, Hérault, report of 4 May 1944. This report gives the figure of over 1,000 seized and 85 deported, while the Regional Prefect had reported on 26 April that 1,200 had been seized and 82 deported; AD Hérault 18W 64.
[58] Aimé Noël, *Figeac d'hier et d'aujourd'hui* (Noël: Figeac, 1984), 51–2.

artisans, members of the magistracy, almost all teachers at the boys' schools and all pupils from the Collège de garçons over the age of 16.[59]

Over 1,100 men were arrested in Perpignan in the Pyrénées-Orientales in mid-June, and 34 immediately deported, and 500 were seized in Béziers between 28 May and 3 June and 30 sent to Germany.[60] All these round-ups were unexpected, and unexplained to the Vichy authorities. The pattern was followed throughout the *zone sud*, and many prefects made little secret of the fact that they were sympathetic both to the plight of those seized and to those who took evasive action and went to the hills. Not that the more collaborationist elements within Vichy regarded the issue of STO as closed: on 7 August a circular from the assistant director of the Police Nationale told prefects that although Laval had announced the suspension of departures to Germany this did not apply to those under arrest or surveillance. These could still be sent to Germany with his permission.[61]

When the acts of reprisal are added to the indiscriminate round-ups and the residue of Vichy collaborationism, the pressure on the population in a multitude of localities to look to the maquis as a place of refuge, or as a receptive and mobilizing organization, was high. One example can stand for hundreds of similar situations. Close to the small industrial town of Ugine in the Savoie a German convoy was ambushed by the maquis on 5 June. Eleven German soldiers were killed. The Germans at once arrested all men in sight and shot twenty-nine of them, some of whom, said the Prefect, had only just arrived on the bus from the Haute-Savoie. About 1,500 male workers from the town immediately took to the mountains, at the same time as the mobilizing messages which heralded Jour-J. Some 75 per cent of the workers, according to the Prefect, returned to the town after German assurances that the reprisals at Ugine had been terminated. Abbé Ploton, an organizer of the maquis in the Albertville area, wrote that the AS felt they could only keep 50 of those 300 who considered themselves mobilized in the mountains above the village of Héry, adding that 'it would have been foolish to keep them all in the maquis without arms'.[62]

Mobilization, therefore, was anything but a simple drafting of fit and suitable volunteers into a military machine with allotted military tasks. It was largely a question of improvisation, and it was shot through with non-military considerations. Yet it was precisely this multi-layered process of mobilization which allowed the disparate nature of the maquis to bear fruit, and most of its diverse objectives to be secured. What is often forgotten

[59] AN F1C III. 1163, Lot, report of May 1944.

[60] AD Hérault 18W 64, reports from Prefect of the Pyrénées-Orientales to Minister of Interior, 22 June 1944, and from Regional Prefect to Minister of Labour, 12 June 1944.

[61] AD Haute-Garonne 1769/5, Mino to Prefects, 7 Aug. 1944.

[62] Abbé Ploton, *Quatre années de Résistance à Albertville*, 89–90; the Prefect's report was dated 5 July 1944, AN F1C III. 1186, Savoie.

is that the maquis differed from a conventional army not just by virtue of its guerrilla tactics and its outlaw, terrorist status in the eyes of Vichy and the Germans, but also because of the interchangeability of home and fighting front. We have already suggested that women and older men left at home in a village and faced with a German repressive force might well be considered to be closer to the battle front at that particular moment than the maquisards safely concealed in the woods, but the inversion worked the other way round as well. Maquisards in all regions had direct access to the life and politics of the home front. Uniforms, armbands, a weapon in the hand, and a sudden confrontation with what they variously described as the terror and exhilaration of being under fire, brought maquisards close to the traditional soldier's mentality, with its highly ambivalent attitude to the home front, at once dismissive of the politics of civilian life and yet also insistent that combat and sacrifice gave soldiers a moral right to a say in the running of their country. But whereas conventional soldiers, well away from home, normally only experience impotence in making this right prevail, the maquisards were physically in a position to play a formative role on the home front. The decision whether or not to exercise this role varied widely from maquis to maquis, but the very presence of the maquisards, imposing themselves suddenly on a village or small town, and indissolubly linked with the population by the structures of support and recruitment, and the shared experience of repression and reprisals, made the maquis a dynamic factor in the final collapse of Vichy power and the pursuit of liberation politics. If the battle front was wherever the French were confronted by German repression, the home front was wherever Vichy was confronted by internal dissidence, whether by the Resistance in the towns or by the maquis in the hills.

A local profile of the home front in the Aveyron, presented in the official reports of spring and summer 1944, conveys just how intense the confrontation between Vichy and the maquis continued to be, even as combat with the German forces began to dominate the maquisard scene. With a sideways look at the Lozère it is possible to glimpse something of the desperation, and the ultimate failure, of Vichy to curb the subversive power of the maquis within the Montpellier region, a desperation identified initially with Marty, the regional Intendant de Police. Whereas the Cévenol regions of the Lozère had preoccupied Marty in the winter months,[63] it was the Aveyron which absorbed most of his energies from March until his departure from the region in late April, when much of his personalized campaign was taken up by Hornus, his successor, and Dutruch the Prefect of the Lozère.

The Aveyron, locked into the Massif Central by the high plateaux of the Causses Sauveterre, Méjean, and Larzac to the east, the wooded Ségala to

[63] See Ch. 5.

the north-west, the Monts de Lacaune to the south-west, and the rugged heights of the Mont Caroux to the south, was a politically right-wing *département*, its dominantly agricultural population electing four anti-Popular Front deputies out of five in 1936. Rodez, the *chef-lieu*, was a bastion of conservative Catholicism, symbolized by its fortress cathedral, but the industrial area of Decazeville and Aubin in the north-west, with its vast open-cast mines, La Découverte, accounted for the one left-wing deputy, and in Aubin the communist candidate had led the field in the first round of voting. The FTP in the area was built solidly on this working-class support. Other mining areas, providing FTP volunteers and explosives, lay just across the frontiers of the *département*, at Carmaux in the Tarn and at Bousquet-d'Orb and Graissessac in the Hérault. In the sheep-rearing areas of the Causses a significant lead to Resistance had been given by Alfred Merle, an industrialist in Millau and by Léon Freychet, one of the directors of the Roquefort cheese company. Freychet's religious links with the minority Protestant circles in the market town of Saint-Affrique, and the social influence of the two men throughout the local world of agriculture and commerce, created a wide network of AS initiative and support in the hiding of *réfractaires* and the creation of maquis groups, well located in scattered farms and ready for instant mobilization at Jour-J.[64] The FTP also had a *point d'appui* in Saint-Affrique through the schoolteacher Raymond Fournier, and in the Causses the FTP formed a company known as the Maquis Alfred Merle, named after the AS leader, who was arrested on 6 February 1944 and died in the hands of the Gestapo in Rodez five days later. Fournier comments that the very use of his name by the FTP bore witness to the fraternity of the Resistance in the Aveyron, and the schoolteacher Renée Salvignol in Saint-Affrique was one of several women whose liaison work was vital both to the AS and to the FTP. In March 1944 she was arrested and tortured by the special anti-maquis police known to Resisters as the infamous Marty Brigade, but she not only survived but did so without providing Marty with any of the information he was seeking.[65] He was already well informed, through the same process of infiltration that he had practised in the Cévennes, and among his first comments on the Aveyron was a comparison with the Cévenol area, in which he stated that the Aveyron maquis were considerably more disciplined than those in the Lozère.[66]

Marty did not usually deal in such generalizations. His reports had the precision of in-depth investigation, listing the names of small villages, isolated farms, and individuals suspected of harbouring maquisards. In his initial report on the Aveyron in March he wrote that 'from lists found in the

64 Barthes, *Moïse ne savait pas nager . . . Histoire de l'Armée Secrète du Sud-Aveyron et le Maquis Paul Claie*, no pagination.

65 Pen portrait of Renée Salvignol in ibid.; Fournier, *Terre de combat*, 157.

66 AD Hérault 18W 15, report from Marty, Mar. 1944.

maquis of Sucaillou and Poulguières, it would seem that every maquisard has an automatic pistol and that a third at least are armed with light machine-guns'. He credited this degree of weaponry to the effects of parachute drops and the efficient organization by agents from London, and in the first of a stridently worded series of demands to the Regional Prefect and to Vichy he called for a detachment of GMR to be stationed at Rodez.[67] For the whole Montpellier region of five *départements* he claimed that a single GMR force, the 'Roussillon', comprising 131 men, was totally inadequate. When those from this force defending various Chantiers de la Jeunesse in the Aveyron and the Lozère were discounted, and the regulations governing hours of service and leave were considered, he argued that only a handful of men remained for the active pursuit of maquisards. Meanwhile a serious sabotage of electrical power had put 2,500 workers in Decazeville out of work and the *département* as a whole, he believed, was subjected to the escalating menace of the maquis.[68] On 3 April he turned his sights on to the local police, as he had done in his diatribes against the Cévenol gendarmerie. Using a metaphor tapered both to the locality and to the underground nature of Resistance, he told the Commissaire des Renseignements Généraux in Rodez that 'camps of *réfractaires* are literally growing like truffles in your territory' and accused the Aveyron police intelligence of transmitting more words of complaint against the GMR than information about the maquis. He ridiculed a local inspector's report which stated that the population of Decazeville was not only peacefully calm but had shown no signs of involvement 'one way or the other', and savaged another inspector who had earlier described the twelve maquisards, whom Marty had found armed and in uniform at the farm of Sucaillou, as '*réfractaires* peacefully involved in wood cutting'. Marty saw both reports as negligent in the extreme, and concluded his letter with another withering critique of the attitudes prevalent among the local police.

> I cannot let the opportunity pass without seriously rebuking the reports, now classified in the archives of the Central Administration of the Police, which will give future generations the impression that my repressive measures in the Aveyron have been, not law and order operations, but raids carried out by gangsters.[69]

If Marty had any sense of the ironic it was no longer on display in his final report on 14 April to Darnand, just before he left the region, when he sketched a summary of his findings on the maquis in all five *départements* and concluded with a paragraph on his own activity, which more than justifies the archival 'calumnies' in Rodez.

[67] AD Hérault 18W 14, Marty to Regional Prefect, 20 Mar. 1944.
[68] Ibid.
[69] AD Hérault 18W 25, Marty to Chef du service départemental des Renseignements Généraux, 3 Apr. 1944.

Up till now, for good or ill, I have maintained a semblance of order in the Region by methods of intimidation (rapid raids on sentry posts, destruction of maquis territory with dynamite, the dynamiting of houses used by 'maquisards'; reprisals by means of dynamite against Resistance sympathizers; a reputation, somewhat exaggerated, for the brutality of my Personal Brigades, etc.). But such methods will not be successful in the long term unless they are buttressed by a real force.[70]

The methods were inherited by Hornus, who reported to the Regional Prefect on an operation into the Mont Aigoual aimed at capturing the Bir-Hakeim maquisards in the Château de Fons on 11 May 1944. He arrived with 50 GMR to find the château only recently vacated, with sleeping-bags and the remains of a meal left behind. 'Following the prescribed procedure,' he wrote, 'we set fire to the château.'[71]

Marty and Hornus were unusually zealous in their untiring pursuit of maquisards into their rural strongholds; theirs was a fanaticism which outran the norms of police behaviour in this period and continued into the period after Jour-J. They carried with them the authority dispensed by a major secret document issued by Darnand on 25 April, which detailed the behaviour expected of the French police in the event of a coastal *débarquement* or an airborne invasion. The invading troops could only be presumed to be the Allied forces, but this was not made specific. There was no doubt, however, about the instructions, which bound the police to continue their duty under the Armistice as detailed in the key paragraph of general principles: 'In specific terms, the forces of order must assure internal order, and thereby contribute to the security of those elements of the army of occupation *which are not actively engaged in combat* . . .' A footnote clarified the meaning of the italicized phrase by saying that it meant the part of the army which 'found itself outside the battle zone in the literal sense of the word'. This would mean eventually all those German troops not fighting in Normandy but still present in the South of France. A more particularized section headed 'Outside the Battle Zone' labelled all invaders whether by sea or air as dangers to public order and enjoined the police to inform the German military authority immediately. As for 'groupes illégaux de résistance', the document foresaw that such groups would seek to mobilize at certain points and should be considered as 'threats to public order and insurgents against the French government' and dealt with accordingly.[72] No instruction was given to inform the Germans of such groups, but just such an instruction was communicated several days later on 2 May to all prefects, with the crucial phrase at the centre of the circular stating:

[70] AD Hérault 18W 14, Marty to Darnand, 14 Apr. 1944.

[71] AD Hérault 18W 25, Hornus to Regional Prefect, 13 May 1944.

[72] The secret document was entitled 'Instructions particulières précisant les conditions d'application des mesures énumérées dans l'instruction générale aux forces françaises du maintien de l'ordre, dans l'éventualité d'un débarquement ou d'opérations militaires se déroulant sur le territoire français'; AD Hérault 18W 14.

Because of the impossibility in practice of making precise distinctions between the different organizations of the maquis, which in the majority have been infiltrated by the Communist Party, it is specified that, within the meaning of instructions already in force, any information obtained on any dissident organization whatever must, in principle, be conveyed to the German authorities.[73]

In the Montpellier region the German Commander of the SD, Colonel Tanzman, demanded that the Intendant de Police should inform him on the whereabouts and movements of all 'groupes de réfractaires', and anticipated that German forces would act wherever the French police were unable to be effective.[74] It was the circular of 2 May that technically covered the Prefect of the Lozère, Dutruch, when he sent on to the German authorities the coded message received from the gendarmerie at Florac indicating that the Maquis Bir-Hakeim was at the Château Lapeyre at la Borie, a commune of la Parade on the Causse Méjean. On 28 May, the morning of the *fête de Pentecôte*, German forces, acting on the Prefect's information, surrounded the château and surprised the maquisards, who were able to offer only desperate and unavailing resistance. The maquis fought well, according to a German report, and were 'clearly trained by professionals'.[75] Thirty-two maquisards were killed in the fighting, and a further twenty-seven taken prisoner to Mende. On the following day, in the commune of Badaroux just outside the *chef-lieu*, all the prisoners were shot and the local inhabitants were forced to bury the bodies on the spot. The Maquis Bir-Hakeim had been decimated, but those few who escaped and those who had not been at la Parade, regrouped under François Rouan in the rocks of Mourèze near Clermont-l'Hérault, and the name, reputation, and almost mythic status of the maverick maquis survived into the liberation combats and beyond. The German report made it clear just how crucial the information supplied by Vichy officials had been.[76] It was for their part in communicating this information that Dutruch and two gendarmes were executed after the Liberation.

Mobilization at Jour-J in the Causses was undoubtedly overshadowed, but not undermined, by the horror of events at la Parade and Badaroux. At the top of Vichy's regional administration the concurrent shock had been the arrest and deportation of the Regional Prefect and the Prefect of the

[73] AD Gard CA 367, circular from R. Clemoz, 2 May 1944.

[74] Tanzman's demand was conveyed to Darnand by the Regional Prefect in a letter dated 6 May 1944; AD Hérault 18W 14.

[75] The Germans admitted that, in order to achieve maximum surprise, they had deliberately broken the custom of not mounting attacks on days of religious festivals. The report was dated 29 May 1944 and arrived in the Lozère archives after the Liberation on 2 Dec. 1944, presented by the Comité du mouvement Allemagne-Libre. It was translated and published in a special edition of *La Lozère libre* (21 Jan. 1945), which pointed out that Allemagne-Libre was a movement of anti-fascist Germans who fought with the Resistance; AN 72. AJ 159.

[76] Ibid.

Aveyron. The Germans were convinced that the two Vichy authorities had failed to protect their interests and their security. It was a symptom of the brutal shift of gear in the German running of the Occupation that French officials, from mayor to prefect, were increasingly arrested, shot, or deported for failing to prevent outbreaks of Resistance action in their area. Within this context, the acting Prefect of the Aveyron was quick to cover himself by a statement of powerlessness within his *département*. On 12 June he reported that 'the growth of the maquis had reduced prefectoral authority to impotence'. The number of maquis was such, he declared, that the forces of order taken together could no longer match them. 'In addition', he added, 'the population has almost unanimously turned towards the maquis and is entirely on their side. In these conditions, with the forces available, it seems impossible to mount any kind of police action whatsoever.' He suggested restricting Vichy authority purely to the tasks of *ravitaillement*, and even this would not be easy since a certain number of gendarmes had joined the maquis, and the commissions empowered to buy and collect food from the peasantry no longer dared to venture into their prescribed areas of authority.[77] By early July the mining area of Decazeville was declared, not by the Resistance but by the prefecture, to be almost a self-governing entity. After fifteen days and nights of incessant maquis attacks, wrote the Prefect, the 90 GMR and the 85 gendarmes in Decazeville had to withdraw to Rodez. 'From that moment, the town of Decazeville has been entirely occupied by the maquis, coming from communes on the border of the *département* and from Bagnac and Montredon in the Lot.' The mayor and municipal council had resigned and the Prefect had accepted their resignation. He had decided to try to restrain the maquis by appointing a municipal head who had the support of the workers and the trade unions and he had designated M. Froment, bursar of the hospital at Decazeville, whose sympathies lay with the socialist majority of the population. He also acknowledged that the mining area had only been supplied with adequate provisions thanks to trade-unionists who had accompanied food convoys and ensured that the prices set by the maquis were respected.[78] Four years after wresting a municipality from its left-wing authority, Vichy was now handing it back, acknowledging that the maquis, which was largely FTP, was the dominant force on this particular home front.

The 'autonomy' of Decazeville, conceded by the Prefect in early July, was celebrated on 14 July with demonstrations and festivities in the town and surrounding area which the regional Renseignements Généraux described in vivid detail. Several hundreds of maquisards were reported as arriving in a flood of requisitioned vehicles under the emblem of the FFI to head a series of parades to war memorials in all the local communes. The parade

[77] AD Hérault 18W 25, acting Prefect to Regional Prefect, 12 June 1944.
[78] AD Hérault 18W 13, acting Prefect to Minister of Interior, 12 July 1944.

in Aubin numbered over 3,000 people, in which 'all dissident groups, including the Young Communists were represented', and in the evening public dancing was organized which went on well into the night.[79]

Managers and directors of the Commentry-Fourchambault mines and factories of Decazeville provided their own regular accounts of the situation, sending lengthening lists of thefts, stoppages, sabotage, and requisitions to the relevant Vichy authorities. In the face of the Prefect's withdrawal of all police from the area, they too declined to accept any responsibility for any consequences that might ensue, reserving the right to prosecute the public authorities for their failures at a later date.[80] They had not followed an injunction by Marty in April to form their own protective police, and the authorities in Toulouse noted on 30 June that the mining companies had made no attempt to sack workers who had staged a strike to celebrate the Normandy landings on the afternoon of 6 June. In fact, the chief mining engineer in Toulouse stated that 'no disagreement had been reported between employers and workers over the incident and he saw no reason for anyone to interfere'.[81] Vichy had lost control of Decazeville. It had also lost the sympathy and confidence of the industrialists in the area.

This profile of the Aveyron suggests that the whole *département* had become a 'pays du maquis' at least two months before the landings in Provence on 15 August and the final overthrow of Vichy. The phrase 'pays' or 'terrain du maquis' was loosely used throughout the south to indicate tracts of countryside through which Germans were unwilling, and Vichy officials often unable, to pass. These maquis territories were far from homogeneous: some were fairly remote configurations of woods and hills, and others were the immediate vicinities of small and larger towns, as in the case of Decazeville. It is yet another cumulative effect of maquis history that the FTP tended to establish their liberation territories within easy reach of towns whereas the AS and ORA often chose to dominate more distant stretches of the rural hinterland. It was the logical result of differing structures and tactics, and, above all, of the contrasting relationships to sources of arms and explosives. A *terrain de parachutage* was the main supply line for the AS and ORA: an explosives depot in a mining area or a police arsenal in the *chef-lieu* of a canton were frequent FTP sources of armaments. The FTP not only needed to procure their arms from such sources, but were also repeatedly drawn back to the towns by the exceptional number of communists and other FTP members under police arrest or in the hands of the Milice and Gestapo. Liberating comrades involved as much military acumen as most

[79] AD Hérault 18W 13, report from the Commissaire divisionnaire du service régional des Renseignements Généraux, 15 July 1944.

[80] AD Hérault 18W 13, Directeur des mines et usines to Regional Prefect, 27 June 1944.

[81] Ibid., report from M. Barbier, ingénieur des mines, for the arrondissement minéralogique de Toulouse, 30 June 1944.

other guerrilla actions. It was a liberation goal which kept the locality at the centre of operations. In many *départements* the FTP circled threateningly round the towns waiting for a decisive moment to pounce. This was the case in the Gard, the towns in question being the *chef-lieu* Nîmes, and the centre of the mining area of the Cévennes, Alès. Between March and July 1944 the police in these towns, as elsewhere, were called on to construct 'îlots de défense', later ironically called 'îlots de résistance' in the Vichy documents. They consisted of buildings surrounded by sandbags, in which automatic weapons were sited, and which were listed in the plan for the towns as a 'blockaus' or 'abri de tir'. The plan for Alès showed twenty *blockaus* designed to defend five groups of important buildings. A circular from Darnand's ministry in mid-March had been at the origin of these *îlots*, and a later one at the end of May specified that on no account should stocks of weapons or petrol and oil be allowed to fall into the hands of assailants. Rather, they should be destroyed. A week later Darnand stipulated that the *îlots* must be constructed in complete agreement with the German authorities, who must be given access to all the relevant plans.[82] Like so many of Darnand's preparations and decisions for military action against the Resistance, these elaborate plans, for which architects were still being hired in late July, ran into local problems of resources and widespread incidents of non-co-operation. The regional Intendant de Police in Marseille noted the escalating difficulties in effecting the plans for Alès, and only skeletal defences were eventually erected.[83] The projected *îlots* were nevertheless a telling example of the extent to which Vichy was prepared for the closest co-operation with the Germans in the military defence of the status quo. They were also a fitting symbol of the final inversion of the hunt. Behind the theory of the *îlots*, behind the architectural drawings and the sandbags, Vichy was trapped, ensnared, and at bay.

An analysis of most of the prefectoral reports to the Minister of the Interior sent from the *zone sud* in the summer of 1944 reveals critical differences of emphasis from one prefect to another, but gives an overwhelming impression of the success of the multi-pronged mobilization of the maquis in June, in terms of its impact on Vichy authority and power. The Aveyron was not *sui generis*. The Lot is also described as practically in the hands of the maquis, with the exception of Cahors; government power in the Corrèze is portrayed as lacking all reality since it 'cannot carry out any of its functions'; in the Haute-Savoie the maquis FTP are reported to be in total control of the arrondissements of Thonon and Bonneville where they 'make their own laws', and in the Ain the Prefect's lines of authority to the region of Nantua were severed, he was encircled in Bourg by large maquis forces, and he had

[82] AD Gard CA 764, circulars from Darnand, 13 Mar., 31 May, and 5 June 1944.

[83] Letters from Commissaire central de Nîmes to the Intendant de Police (July 1944); AD Gard CA 764.

lost contact with the north of the region of Belley.[84] In the Savoie whole cantons are graphically pictured as subject to 'the terrorism of village revolutionaries who know no other law but their own caprice'.[85] All these reports are for June 1944, to which the situations in the Vercors, the Auvergne, and the Montagne Noire have to be added, as well as the barely disguised despair of the prefects of the Gard and the Lozère at the ungovernable character of the Cévennes, which had marked their reports from March or even February onwards.

The German offensives of late June and July severely curtailed the geographical extent of maquis dominance, but this was not translated into a major restoration of Vichy power, due to the multitude of resignations by mayors and other authorities, and the secession of large portions of the gendarmerie directly to the maquis. Not all the resignations signify a clear upsurge of sympathy for the maquis. Already in late March and early April the Germans had ravaged certain municipal authorities, particularly in the Corrèze, where the mayors of Venarsal, Lonzac, and Noailles were executed after a German convoy, *en route* for Eymoutiers, had been captured by the maquis. The Prefect listed 3,000 arrests and 55 executions and vividly described the horror and terror of the population who, he said, had previously backed the maquis without any thought for the future. Now mayors were resigning in all directions, 'creating a real crisis for the administration'.[86] As similar acts of German terror multiplied and extended across the south, and became not only a retaliation *after* encounters with the maquis, but often, as at Ruynes-en-Margeride, the *first* offensive act, the pressure of understandable fear accounted for much of the internal dissolution of municipal authorities. In early June the Prefect of the Lot tried to protect the gendarmerie from the escalating German arrests within their ranks, by suggesting that Vichy should demobilize them as keepers of the peace and use them merely as 'agents de renseignements'.[87] In the Var mayors were resigning in all areas in late May, and this was attributed to pressure from 'co-citoyens' rather than the Germans, while in the Ain mayors in all parts were refusing to fulfil their responsibilities partly in protest against the activity and power of the local Milice under Agostini.[88]

The collapse of municipal *cadres* throughout the south, which accompanied the period of mobilization and insurrection, was a crucial sign of Vichy's overall loss of power. It was also the main index of local inversion. In the

[84] Renseignements Généraux of the Lot to the Minister of the Interior (22 July 1944), AN 72. AJ 157; AN F1C III. 1147, Corrèze, report of July 1944; AN F1C III. 1187, Haute-Savoie, report of 4 July 1944; AN F1C III. 1135, Ain, report of 3 July 1944.

[85] AN F1C III. 1186, Savoie, report of 5 July 1944.

[86] AN F1C III. 1147, Corrèze, report of 15 Apr. 1944.

[87] AN F1C III. 1163, Lot, report of 3 June 1944.

[88] AN F1C III. 1194, Var, report of 1 June 1944; AN F1C III. 1135, Ain, report of 3 July 1944.

four years of Vichy government it was the issue of *ravitaillement* which predominated at municipal level, even at the high points of conscription for STO. With the resignations of May, June, and July, the function of provisioning the whole community as well as the maquis itself was increasingly assumed by the forces of Resistance, wherever a *pays* or *terrain du maquis* could be said to exist. The acting Prefect of the Aveyron had acknowledged this to be the case at Decazeville. In the Cévennes the Prefect of the Lozère reported at the end of July that 'the FFI are intervening more and more in the domain of *ravitaillement*, requisitioning livestock from the farmers, forcing butchers to sell meat without ration tickets, fixing retail prices . . .'[89] Romans-Petit and Georges Guingouin in the Ain and Haute-Vienne respectively, representing between them the AS and FTP strands of the maquis, both came into their own in June and July as alternative authorities on the home front, organizing and authorizing the supply of provisions to the population within their territory. Their self-proclaimed authority, followed by their published memoirs after the war, tended to over-individualize the process of inversion.[90] More commonly it was the collectivity of a maquis unit working with *sédentaires* who took over the crucial aspects of food control and marketing. Denise Guillaume recollected the process in a commune in the Aveyron, and her *témoignage* gives a laconic view of how it led on to a total inversion of power:

We were a bourgeois family from Montpellier and as usual in the summer we went to the commune of Prades-d'Aubrac in the Aveyron. My parents were in regular touch with the local maquis, and the village was involved in supporting its activities. The maquis never terrorized the peasantry. They acted together, and the raids on places like a *bureau de tabac* were a kind of partnership. The population played an agreed role in these raids. The FTP maquis asked my mother and myself to help control food prices, by finding out what the Vichy market prices were and the level of those charged independently by individuals. We then drew up a list between the two, typed it out and posted it on the *mairie*. The peasants willingly agreed to accept these prices. That was in June 1944. We also rerouted milk which we knew was bound for the black market, and distributed it to the poorer families, some of whom were immigrant workers whose children badly needed it.

In July we received instructions that the Comité local de Libération (CLL) was to be formed of all parties represented in the Resistance. There had only been Radical-Socialists in the commune before the war. So we did a bit of sociological investigation and decided who would look right to represent the Communist Party, the Socialist Party, and the Catholics (the future MRP). My mother really hand-picked them all, and my father was unanimously elected as president. Although only 16, I was seen as educated and so became effectively the municipal secretary. At a suitable moment we knocked at the *mairie* and told them they had been replaced. There was no problem. The maquisards came into the village with red scarves and

[89] AN F1C III. 1165, Lozère, report of 25 July 1944.
[90] Romans-Petit, *Les Maquis de l'Ain*; Guingouin, *Quatre ans de lutte sur le sol limousin.*

sang the Internationale and the Marseillaise, and the new CLL, with its fictive party members, was duly installed.[91]

The undertones of *Clochemerle* in this *témoignage* by no means represent the norm of story-telling about this period, but the lighter touch recurs frequently enough in other memoirs and recollections to remind us of the sense of irony, the triumph, and the pleasures of vengeance which marked the local overthrow of four years of Vichy authority. The celebratory aspect of inversion was not just an event on the day and evening of liberation whenever that occurred, it was a motivating factor throughout the whole summer from late May into August. It represented the festive side of that 'mentalité terrible' which Cordesse perceived in the maquisard's quest for revenge against the traitor and the Milicien. There was a jubilant note of poetic justice in the declaration of the Republic on 6 June at Annonay, the paper-making town in the north of the Ardèche. From the balcony of the Hôtel-de-Ville, the president of the clandestine Comité local de Libération, Jacques de Sugny, called on Pétain to submit himself to the will of the people. The ritualized triumph was all the sweeter since de Sugny, a notable of Annonay, had joined the communist-run Front National, and it was the FTP maquis which in large measure had encircled and occupied the town, although the AS maquis were also represented and the operation was a display of FFI co-ordination. Annonay, on the edge of the Vivarais, was the home of the Montgolfier brothers, inventors of the hot-air balloon, and the Resistance festivities accompanying the town's occupation are remembered for the *éclat* and the calculated risks of a pioneering event. It pre-dated by a month the similar Republican festivities in the Vercors and occurred a day before the FTP occupation of Tulle, but unlike the outcome of the Vercors and Tulle, the memory of the event, though darkened by the battles that followed, has retained an aura of inversionary success. Vichy police, arriving on 9 June, were met by de Sugny and something akin to a mock battle was agreed by both sides. Ten days later the strategic importance of Annonay, close to the Rhône valley, brought a large combined Vichy and German force to the town, and some two hundred maquis denied them access for several hours before withdrawing into the mountains. The GMR took over the town but the Gestapo and the Milice, despite their failure to locate the perpetrators of Annonay's Republic, did not resort to the savagery of Das Reich in Tulle.[92]

During June and July there were very few maquis units who did not enjoy turning the tables on some aspect of Vichy authority well before the final liberation of their area. The neutralizing of the gendarmerie and other municipal officers on 14 July, during a parade to the *monument aux morts*, was so widespread across the south that it was reported by the Renseignements

[91] Evidence from Denise Guillaume, 7 Dec. 1984.

[92] René Maisonnas, *La Résistance en Ardèche* (Éditions le Regard du Monde: Aubenas, 1984), 59.

Généraux in a way that resembled any newspaper's account of a local fête in times of peace, not least because the events confirmed what the police had confidently predicted.[93] Vichy received so much information to substantiate the popularity of these inversionary episodes that it seems nothing short of an absurd delusion when certain prefects continued to think and write as if Philippe Henriot had been proved correct. The height of Henriot's influence had either been in the late autumn of 1943 when disappointment over the expected *débarquement* undermined the public's readiness to invest hopes and resources in the maquis, or in March and April 1944 when the failure of the Maquis des Glières, and the first batch of savage reprisals in the Limousin, undoubtedly affected not only the public at large but also the morale of would-be maquisards. His manipulative skills were seen to decline in May, and the nature of the Normandy landings swept away the corner-stone of his propaganda, which relied on the equation of a *débarquement* with a communist take-over of France.[94] His assassination on 28 June 1944 silenced a voice that could no longer claim to control the public's sense of reality, but the very real power that he had exercised over people's attitudes towards the maquis did not evaporate overnight. It was indeed a delusion for any prefect to imagine that the maquis could only stage their celebratory irruptions on the municipal scene by terrorizing the population, but it was less absurd to report that many of the actions of the maquis were still seen as transgressive. Henriot had popularized a typology of the maquisard as bandit, which lost much of its influence in the summer of liberation, but never entirely disappeared.

It seemed to some maquisards cruelly paradoxical that suspicion of the nonconformity and irregularity of their position should continue into the period when their role in delaying, harassing, and diverting the Germans by irregular, guerrilla tactics received full recognition by the Allied powers. This suspicion, which, at its extreme, amounted to a hostile denunciation of the maquis as social deviants, angered maquisards increasingly as their power and legitimacy were consolidated, but there was, at the same time, a considerable diversity of opinion among maquisards on the issue of their irregular position and practice. Within the maquis discourse of 1943 and the survivalist tactics of the winter, there had been a certain provocative acceptance of the transgressive nature of outlaw status, and a readiness to flaunt convention in *coups de main* which established the maquis as a determined but uncomfortable force in the growth of rural Resistance. Some maquisards look back on the early and middle periods as the authentic maquis epoch, when the irregularity of being an outlaw was accepted as a challenge and adopted as an identity. In the summer of 1944, as the military confrontations with the Germans grew daily in number, and the maquis

93 e.g. 'Incidents survenus au cours de la journée du 14 juillet 1944', report of Renseignements Généraux of Montpellier region (15 July 1944); AD Hérault 18W 13.

94 Henriot, *Et s'ils débarquaient?*, *passim.*

became better armed, better uniformed, and conspicuously organized into brigades, battalions, and companies, a claim by maquisards to a more conventional military status clashed with a strong residual pride in their outlaw origin and irregular military history. It was during the combats of the summer that many maquisards established an inner certainty that the maquis were not political, were not social revolutionaries, were motivated only by the purity of patriotism, and were indignantly neither outlaws nor bandits. Such a conviction sealed the process of legitimation by which many in the maquis came to see themselves as comprising the established and official internal army of France, as regular as it could be in the circumstances. Alongside these were just as many others who demanded military recognition but as the irregular armed forces of the Resistance with a positive outlaw history and a role to play in deciding the social and political changes at the Liberation. Deviance and transgression, from the illegal defiance of STO onwards, had been a powerful dissolvent of Vichy rule and had created new incentives to confrontation with the Germans. Until both Vichy and Nazism were completely overthrown there seemed to be a justification in continuing the irregularity of organization and action, not least because even a recognized guerrilla status and practice still involved a marginalization in society and a continuing, even escalating, problem of securing provisions, transport, and other daily requirements.

Given the wealth of oral, written, and archival evidence, it is clear that maquisards of almost all tendencies implemented some form of inversionary requisitions during the summer of 1944, inversionary because they were advanced as official and legitimate against the official legitimacy of Vichy. Warnings about requisitions distributed by the maquis in most areas emphasized that they were not an end in themselves but a necessary adjunct to the struggle against the occupier. A typical poster displayed at Peyriac-Minervois in the Aude on 24 July began:

> In order to wage the national struggle and fulfil the missions entrusted to them by General Koenig, the forces of the maquis are compelled to carry out requisitions of various kinds (food, arms, vehicles, etc). These requisitions are official and will be settled by money payments when an individual is only of modest means, and by 'bons de réquisition' when people more comfortably placed are affected. The 'bons' exchanged by the FFI will carry the stamp of the French Republic and an official signature. They will be reimbursed after the Liberation.

The poster went on to tell the population to notify the maquis police when bogus requisitions were made by provocateurs or common criminals, and suggested that the maquis would always be open to appeals against suspected injustice.[95] The requisitions, in the name of the FFI, or with the declared authority of a local committee of liberation, or sometimes personalized in

[95] AD Hérault 18W 13, poster 'Avertissements' signed 'le comité d'action immédiate, C.F.L. et F.T.P.', July 1944.

the name of de Gaulle, General Koenig, or a local FFI officer, still seemed to some maquis leaders to be an unnecessary descent into illegality. The British wireless operator in the Corps Franc de la Montagne Noire, Major Despaigne, called requisitions a glorified form of stealing. It was consistent with his wish to be dissociated from the label of maquisard and its aura of irregularity.[96] Others have left memoirs or interviews which insist on the scrupulous nature of their transactions, to a point where 'requisition' is used more as an alternative word for payment, so insistent are they that all debts were regularized after the Liberation.[97]

And yet it is not just the endless lists of armed thefts, raids, and attacks, which the Vichy police continued to file in spiralling numbers from April through to August, which suggest a more complex story. There is also a widespread inclination among maquisards to make exceptions which legitimize raids against collaborators, exploiters, and illicit marketeers, and there are accusations and counter-accusations about which maquis units indulged in thefts and victimizations. All point to 'faux maquisards' or 'voyous' as the main perpetrators of individual thefts and arbitrary terrorization, and there seems no doubt that the dislocations during the summer, together with the very considerable level of hunger in most of the southern towns, the collapse of effective Vichy policing and the ease of masquerading as maquisards, must account for a substantial number of the incidents filed as 'vols' and 'attentats' in the archives. Nevertheless, in the period of mobilization and insurrection that followed Jour-J, certain thefts are readily admitted as necessary Resistance acts. These include most of the thefts of cars, lorries, petrol, tools, spare parts, medical equipment, and of wholesale quantities of food, clothes, and tobacco, which abound in the police records. If there was a general maquis policy, common to both AS and FTP, it was to use 'bons de réquisition' to avoid the appearance of unplanned and haphazard actions, and there was still the contract element with the population which had been so structural in 1943. Where a scenario of mock violence would have been enacted there was now a requisition order from a Resistance authority. To take two examples from hundreds recorded by the police, a 'bon de réquisition des F.F.I.' was given for 4,842 francs worth of cigarettes and tobacco in a raid on a tobacconist at Saint-Pons in the Hérault on 31 July. The raiders were described as 'dressed in khaki uniform, embossed with the insignia of the Resistance'.[98] Earlier, at a slightly indeterminate date in May or June, a lorry with 2.5 tons of potatoes and two casks of *choucroute* was requisitioned on the road from Meyrueis to Lasalle in the Cévennes. The note of requisition mentioned 'the needs of the Resistance' and was signed 'J.L.'.[99]

[96] Evidence from H. M. Despaigne, 18 Aug. 1979.
[97] Evidence from Lucien Maury, 24 June 1982, and Francis Cammaerts, 18 Mar. 1991.
[98] AD Hérault 18W 13, 'Attentats terroristes', July 1944.
[99] AD Hérault 15W 237, 'Réquisitions F.F.I', June 1944.

Critics of the maquis ridiculed the requisition orders as the easiest of false promises, but they were vital protective guarantees for those who received them, and had the maquis made the system universal there would probably have been little reason for controversy. But it was never likely that they would do so. Their raids and attacks on Vichy establishments, on collaborators and on hoarders and exploiters were in quite a different category. They were felt to be self-justifying, even by a maquis so consciously 'conventional' as the Corps Franc de la Montagne Noire.[100] Though police often surmised that an individual was burgled or murdered because he or she was a member of the Milice or 'worked for the Occupation authorities', the maquis saw no need on such occasions to leave explanations behind, or to suggest that goods taken from such sources might eventually be restored.

It was this relativity in the process of requisitioning which was ultimately more transgressive than the thefts themselves. It was an assumption of the right to decide who should be treated in one way and who in another. It embodied an inversionary code of justice, on which most maquisards were generally agreed, but whose application varied from one maquis to the next. Mistakes and injustices within the alternative code could and did occur; maquisards do not deny this, though most argue that the injustices were surprisingly few, given the volatility of the situation. It was implicit in the Resistance challenge to Vichy that those who aided, or prospered from, the German Occupation would have action taken against them. This process of evaluation and retribution was there from the start of the AS groupes francs and the FTP in 1941. The maquis were not pioneers in constructing the idea of selective and retributive justice. It was their armed power, the ubiquity and elusiveness of their presence, and the local disparities in the choice and frequency of their requisitions which kept the typology of bandit alive, even in the period of growing public acclaim.

In some areas, but by no means all, the FTP made no secret of their greater political involvement in requisitions and retribution. Where they were composed, in a majority, of locally active members of the Communist Party it was part of their fundamental ideology to carry the struggle on the home front to the very doors of those who had led an easy life under Vichy and the Germans. They were more open in their political motivation because they saw all Resistance in more political terms. The legacy of communist and trade-union struggles between the wars, and the hopes of social revolution which had been generated in the Popular Front period, surfaced in the ways in which their targets were chosen, and in their broader concept of collaboration. French people who passively supported Vichy were far

[100] Evidence from H. M. Despaigne, 18 Aug. 1979. In the weekly summaries of maquis activities made by the police in the *département* of the Aude there is an entry for the week ending 8 July 1944 which reads, 'Réquisition de 544 œufs par le Corps Franc de la Montagne Noire à Lacombe'; AD Aude M 2641.

more numerous than those who were the regime's active supporters, and these in their turn numbered far more than those who collaborated with the Germans. When it came to the need for requisitions, the more fervent political members of the FTP saw no reason why the first category should be spared, and when it came to retribution they tended to emphasize the points that the latter two categories had in common rather than those that distinguished them from each other. Nevertheless, some of the 60 per cent of all FTP maquisards who had not been, or did not become, members of the Communist Party, claimed to have shared the general hopes for social and political change without encountering any party indoctrination, and some have stated that they only became aware that the FTP were linked with the Communist Party when they were suddenly treated differently by other maquisards at the Liberation.[101] Raymond Fournier, the departmental head of the FTP in the Aveyron, argued that ten out of the twelve FTP units in his area were led by non-communists, a marked contrast, for example, to the depth of committed communism within the FTP in the Chablais area of the Haute-Savoie.[102] Abbé Gauch was introduced to the maquis in the Lot and the Tarn by an officer in the ORA, but in his rural parish near to the mining community of Carmaux he gravitated into the FTP. He said politics were insignificant: it was rather that the FTP more naturally represented the ideas and aspirations of the workers in the area.[103] Michel Bancilhon in Aubenas was adamantly non-political, and as an architect in the Ponts et Chaussées found himself recruited into the AS by other professional friends, but in 1944 after disagreements with certain AS officers he moved to the FTP.[104] Gilbert de Chambrun, aristocratic head of the FFI in the Lozère, worked far more closely with the maquis FTP than with the AS.[105] These examples could be supplemented by hundreds of others to break down the simplistic notion that the FTP was always a coherent and doctrinaire political organization. Perhaps it makes some historical sense to argue that the town-based FTP were more political than the FTP maquis, though in the summer of 1944 it becomes increasingly difficult to keep their histories apart. Since many units were an amalgamation of the two it is often meaningless to try to do so.

The political issue, merely touched on here as a sub-text of requisitions and transgression, needs to be discussed at a level where the very definition of 'political' is seen in all its complex relativity. Serge Ravanel was far from alone, either among communists or among many others, in describing the

[101] Evidence from Joseph Nodari, 28 Mar. 1991, Pierre Couderq, 12 Mar. 1991, Pierre Boyer, 24 June 1991, and Pierre Labie, 11 Mar. 1991.
[102] Evidence from Raymond Fournier, 23 Mar. 1982, and Romain Baz, 10 May 1969.
[103] Evidence from Abbé Gauch, 15 Mar. 1991.
[104] Evidence from Michel Bancilhon, 5 July 1982.
[105] Evidence from Gilbert de Chambrun, 25 May 1982.

well-endowed and conventional Corps Franc de la Montagne Noire as political, and several AS groups or leaders, and officers in the ORA were described in the same way. But the sense in which the word is used in these cases needs careful distinction from the sense of 'party politics' which is the more normative usage when the term is employed by maquisards in their memoirs and interviews. The wider, more social and ideological meaning, by which the AS could be seen as no less political than the FTP, can only be fairly presented in a larger study of the politics of the Resistance, but the genuine currency of such a usage was guaranteed by the enormously wide connotations of such words as 'libération', 'insurrection', and eventually 'épuration'. Under the subject of requisitions the clearly transgressive act of raiding a bank raised all these wider political issues. Eight out of the twelve bank raids recorded in the Gard between 4 July and 22 August were acknowledged to be the work of the FTP. Signed receipts in the name of the FFI but giving also the name of an FTP company or the code-name of an FTP leader, or both, were exchanged in all eight cases. Of the remaining four raids, two were anonymous and no receipt was given, and the other two were acknowledged by vague notes in the name of 'the maquis' and 'the FFI' respectively. The sums taken varied between 10,000 and 74,000 francs, and neither the sums nor the raids were exceptional within the history of the FTP.[106] Many maquisards categorically repudiated bank raids as openly inciting the reproach of banditry, and attributed the FTP's predilection for such raids as clearly political. In reply, those who carried out the raids have questioned whether they were qualitatively different from requisitions of vehicles, tobacco, or food, and suggest that the wish to exclude banks must be seen as a political position in the wider meaning of the term. There can be no empirical resolution to this debate.

Few of the culminations of maquis history in the summer of 1944 were without elements of paradox or ambiguity. The problems of adjusting local capacities to national aims, the different meanings and realities of mobilization, and the ambivalences involved in inverting power on the home front, all register a high level of complexity in what might otherwise seem a simple escalation of action leading to the triumphs of liberation. Even the final combats, to which most maquisards attach a primacy of importance, were full of ironic twists and uncertainties. The instructions received before and on Jour-J appeared to indicate a clear role of harassment and sabotage to delay the German reinforcements heading for the north, and this was carried out with particularly dramatic successes and losses on the roads from the south-west through the Quercy and the Limousin. The cycle of ambushes followed by German reprisals and atrocities both lionized the different maquis of the area and scarred the villages and towns through which the

[106] AD Gard CA 1294, 'Prélèvements forcés effectués dans les caisses', 14 Oct. 1944.

increasingly harried SS troops chose to pass. But the Germans did not leave the south-west, or anywhere in the south, *en bloc* during June, July, or even August. Elements of the Das Reich Division continued to circulate in the very regions through which it appeared they had staged a concerted withdrawal; heavily armed troops were left in the large towns, and the major German assaults on the Vercors and the Montagne Noire were not until long after the flurry of activity after Jour-J had subsided. By early August the maquis appeared to dominate in most areas and Vichy was in the last stages of internal dissolution, and yet it was not clear whether the maquis should content themselves with the *terrains du maquis* they had established or seek to extend their power into the central towns of each canton where the Germans were few in number or non-existent. A sudden German arrival or return was a permanent threat and a frequent reality. So many local accounts of this period chronicle a surge of liberation leading to an unexpected reversal when the Germans re-entered the liberated territory. A combat which promised to be the last in the area often turned out to be no more than the third, fourth, or penultimate encounter. It would be easy to judge this uncertainty as the symptom of poor strategic planning at the top, but it was paradoxically more a sign of the effectiveness of the maquis than of any obvious failures. The fact that the Germans stayed in their garrisons until the last minute, and then altered, improvised, and retraced their routes of retreat across the South of France testifies to the very significant impact of maquis mobility and the ubiquity of their reputation and power. The cost for the maquis and their supportive communities, however, was the presence of the unexpected right up to the final Liberation, as a few examples can be used to show.

In the Tarn, as elsewhere, the news of the Allied landing in Provence on 15 August was received as the final signal for an all-out maquis offensive. On the following day well-armed FFI units converged on the mining town of Carmaux from all directions and forced the garrison to surrender. A number of successful battles were fought in the vicinity, and a German relief force failed to retake the town. The maquisards moved on to the *chef-lieu* Albi where the garrison was largely composed of Mongol troops, pressed into the German army after the invasion of Russia. On 19 August the garrison fled south towards Castres, subjected *en route* to maquis attacks and Allied aerial bombardment, and within twenty-four hours the German commander at Castres had surrendered. Four thousand German soldiers became prisoners of war. The local success seemed total, and the occupation of the Tarn at an end, but fears of another Tulle or Oradour-sur-Glane surfaced almost immediately as heavy columns of German troops approached the *département* from Toulouse. All the liberated areas were at risk, for it was far from obvious whether the Germans would press towards the centre of the Tarn and try to pass through Albi, or keep south through Mazamet into the Hérault. In the event they did both, and the maquis of the Tarn found themselves on 22 August engaged in harsh fighting in Albi, the town they had just liberated, while to the south there was a series of costly battles between Mazamet and Saint-Pons on the road skirting the Monts du Saumail. At Saint-Pons, where maquisards from the Corps Franc de la Montagne Noire, the FTP Maquis Valentin, and the AS Maquis Latourette severely delayed the German retreat, the town was explicitly threatened with total destruction. It had been a supportive community for the burgeoning maquis of the area: Odette Belot, the *patronne* of a small hotel, was an imaginative *agent de liaison*; and Armand Calas, one of a group organized by Émile Fontès, made endless supply runs into the mountains on his motor-cycle; and it was from Saint-Pons that General de Lattre de Tassigny had staged his abortive attempt to take to the mountains before escaping to the Free French.[107] Fortunately for the town, the hospital consultant Dr Joseph Bec had not only the humanity to tend both French and German wounded during the battle itself, but also the foresight to put the Germans into the hospital beds and the French wounded on to mattresses on the floor. His gesture was enough to deter the German commander from his stated intention of killing all the town's inhabitants.[108]

The paradox of liberating Albi *before* the major battle in the town, and of holding thousands of German prisoners only a few miles from the route of a powerful German convoy, was typical of the ironies of maquisard experience throughout the south. It was said, by way of understanding the surrender of the French armies in June 1940, that no soldier wants to die at the *end* of a war. The proximity of the end of the German Occupation in August 1944 accounts for the readiness of several German commanders to surrender to the maquis rather than risk their lives in a final combat, but the same argument might have been used by the maquis to justify passivity in the face of the departing Germans. This was not the case. The 11th German Panzer Division did cross the Languedoc on 13 August without any attack being mounted, but after the Provençal landings when the war seemed even closer to being over, the southern maquis intensified their active combat and no other German column crossed the south unscathed. As a result many maquisards in all areas were killed only a day or a few hours before their locality was free, and this gives an added poignancy to the monuments on

[107] Evidence from Armand Calas, 18 June 1991.

[108] Evidence from Dr Joseph Bec, 18 June 1991. A similar history was enacted in the town of Ussel in the Haute-Corrèze when the Germans took the town on 17 Aug. 1944 after heavy fighting in the maquis-controlled countryside. At the hospital there were both German and maquisard wounded, cared for without discrimination by the surgeon Jean Boisselet and the nurses of the hospital, many of them volunteers. On arrival the German commander ordered the execution of 50 hostages as reprisals for maquis action, but the German wounded spoke up for the surgeon and the medical staff, and the order was withdrawn; Le Moigne and Barbanceys, *Sédentaires, réfractaires et maquisards*, 405–9.

the roadside, marking the site of the final local ambush and the names of those who died. At Colombières-sur-Orb in the Hérault the same column that had been attacked and delayed at Saint-Pons was ambushed again by other maquisards. The monument, typical of hundreds throughout the rural heartland of the maquis, reads:

> Here on 22 August a hundred volunteers, supported by the peasantry of the valley, attacked 4,000 Germans. Five patriots were killed: Lyon Caen C. born 1910, a commercial traveller from Bousquet-d'Orb, Courtes A. born 1907 a warrant officer from Estréchoux, Gordillo P. born 1925, Lahuerta A. born 1922 and Lebrau J.M. born 1922, all mineworkers from Estréchoux.

When the column had passed through, the valley was free. No one reading such monuments can prevent the thought occurring that it would have been all too understandable had the maquisards shouldered their light arms and conserved their lives as the German retreat rolled past their locality: all five of those killed had come as volunteers from the mining communities across the hills. It is the record of the commitment of those five, as symbols of the entire armed Resistance, which reminds us that combat by the maquis at all times remained a choice.

On the same day similar choices were made in the south of the Aveyron. On 21 August the town of Saint-Affrique was surrendered willingly by the German commander Colonel Muntzer, who had defied his superiors at Rodez by turning a blind eye to the local maquisards and even making 2 million francs available to them after a pact with the maquis leaders.[109] A section of the Maquis Paul Claie triumphantly took over the town, and it was this maquis which responded to the call by Gilbert de Chambrun to sabotage the road through the Causses from Millau to Lodève at the long incline known as the Pas de l'Escalette. On 22 August when the sabotage had been effected, the special section responsible could have returned to the various maquis camps away from the road, but chose to head in the direction of the approaching Germans. At la Pezade they met two vanguard German lorries, and gave battle. The Germans brought up mortars, and all twenty-two maquisards were killed either in the battle, or afterwards when the Germans shot and mutilated the wounded. The event was partly witnessed by a shepherd, and the details confirmed by German prisoners taken in the following days.[110]

Closer to the Rhône valley in the Ardèche, Privas, the *chef-lieu*, was an example of a town completely encircled by maquisards from the end of July, waiting for an opportune moment to move in. The garrison refused to surrender so that when, on 11 August, the FFI increased their pressure they

[109] Barthes, *Moïse ne savait pas nager... Histoire de l'Armée Secrète du sud-Aveyron et le Maquis Paul Claie*, no pagination; also, evidence from Pierre Boyer, 24 June 1991.
[110] Ibid. no pagination.

risked provoking reprisals on the scale of Tulle. Instead the Germans evacuated the town the next day and Privas was therefore liberated by the maquisards three days in advance of the Allied arrival in Provence. A German return remained a possibility but was never mounted, whereas on the Rhône itself, in concert with Allied bombing, the FFI of the Ardèche and the Drôme forced the Germans to retreat from Tournon to Tain-l'Hermitage on 24 August, only to see the Germans return to occupy the town three days later and shoot eleven members of the population chosen at random.[111]

It is clearly invidious for these very few examples of local combats to be mentioned when hundreds of other skirmishes and battles have an equal claim on the process of public memory and historical reconstruction. Written memoirs and local studies of the maquis usually reach the months of June to August 1944 within very few pages. At a rough estimate, about 80 per cent of all such writings concentrate on the period after Jour-J. In statistical terms this is commensurate with the numerical size of the maquis which quadrupled with the mobilization that followed 6 June. Georges Guingouin, who became regional leader of the FFI in the Limousin and has come to personify the outlaw Préfet du Maquis, declared that his rank would have been that of General if the 8,750 men of the FTP, the 4,100 men of the AS, the 1,050 men of the ORA, the 21 squadrons of gardes, GMR, and gendarmes, and the milices patriotiques under his command in the Haute-Vienne in August had been fully acknowledged.[112] The numbers in the Limousin were unusually high, but the expansion of the maquis everywhere into thousands of FFI fighters, and the impressive number of combative encounters with the Germans can only be conveyed by reference to the collective wealth of local studies of the Liberation which have proliferated in recent years.

The search for the maquis in the last three months of the German Occupation will find a maquis that has largely been discovered in the excellence of these local studies and one that is subsumed in the wider history of the Allies and the Resistance from June to August, in an abundance of political and military accounts. This study does not presume to summarize the enormous range of histories of the Liberation that now exists: the amount of local detail would be overwhelming. Rather, this particular search has its own culmination in a number of images and oral recollections which attempt to evoke the life and identity of the maquis from post-Liberation perspectives. It was a common experience for maquisards to march proudly and triumphantly into the large town of the region, and share in the popular euphoria of the liberation, only to find that their lives

[111] Maisonnas, *La Résistance en Ardèche*, 74.
[112] Guingouin, *Quatre ans de lutte sur le sol limousin*, 215.

and actions in the maquis were inevitably unknown to most of the liberated population. Describing, identifying, and explaining themselves has been an ongoing process ever since.

7
Images and Memories, 1944 and After

IRONICALLY the first visual image that most French people had of the maquis was an urban one. As the German troops surrendered or departed, the liberated towns welcomed marching columns of FFI who staged a number of triumphal parades to the *préfectures*, the *mairies*, and the *monuments aux morts*, bearing their arms, displaying their company emblems, and led by their local leaders. Many columns included a number of women in uniform or wearing armbands, who had been *agents de liaison*, medical staff, or organizers of the maquis social services, and indeed a few women carrying weapons who had been combative members of certain groupes francs or town-based FTP. The cross of Lorraine inside a Victory V was painted on many of the lorries which accompanied the FFI and the clenched-fist salute was the dominant gesture. The ecstatic admiration of the welcoming crowds expressed itself spontaneously when maquis leaders were lifted high in the main squares, and the maquisards and people embraced and sang the 'Marseillaise', before the columns regained their order and returned in formation to their improvised barracks within the towns. The image was essentially one of military discipline, an impression which the maquis had consistently given in the short occupations of scattered towns throughout the *zone sud* from 11 November 1943 through to 1 May and 14 July 1944.

The urban element was accentuated as the first newspapers of the post-Liberation period marked the progress and success of the FFI by a series of bulletins on the liberation of towns throughout France. In the Montpellier region two densely printed pages emerged on 23 August called *L'Information du Languedoc* whose headline proclaimed, 'Carcassonne, après Toulouse, est libérée par un assaut des F.F.I.'. The news articles carried the latest communiqués from General Koenig announcing, firstly, that in the south-west and the Massif Central:

The FFI have liberated the following *départements*: Indre, Haute-Vienne, Dordogne, Corrèze, Cantal, Lot-et-Garonne, Lot, Aveyron, Tarn-et-Garonne, Gers, Basses-

Pyrénées, Haute-Garonne, Haute-Loire; which includes the towns of Châteauroux, Limoges, Périgueux, Tulle, Aurillac, Agen, Montauban, Rodez, Pau, Toulouse, Albi, and le Puy.

A second communiqué specified that in the south-east the whole of the Haute-Savoie had been liberated by the maquis. The local leader of the FFI had sent a telegram to General Koenig stating: 'I promised you a month ago that we would liberate the Haute-Savoie by our own means. This has now happened. The colonel commanding the German garrison of Annecy surrendered unconditionally half an hour ago.'[1]

The next edition of the bulletin enlarged its headlines to announce the liberation of Paris, and the fourth and last number on 26 August celebrated the entry of the reconstituted Maquis Bir-Hakeim into Montpellier. The day before, 25 August, a number of maquis units and milices patriotiques had waged a last battle against a retreating German convoy outside the town at the village of Montferrier, which to some seemed an unnecessary and costly gesture, but to most appeared to incarnate the sacrificial commitment of the volunteer army of liberation. It was in just such phrases that *L'Information du Languedoc* proclaimed the epic quality of the maquis:

> . . . tough, strapping youths from the Midi, from Clermont-l'Hérault, Lodève, Frontignan, Sète, Mèze etc. . . . and among these heroic soldiers of the secret army who have been absent for three years from our lives and homes we find a few Poles . . . two English officers . . . the chaplain Level who took to the woods three years ago, and Captain Montaigne simply dressed as an ordinary maquisard . . . These 'maquisards' arrive in our town as regular, organized, and militarized soldiers. And with them comes the final liberation of our town . . . Vibrant, sincere, incomparable homage is paid to the troops of the maquis, our compatriots, our liberators . . . Those whom the vile Vichy radio treated as terrorists are acclaimed, and carried shoulder high . . . an unforgettable moment when women and men cried and embraced the maquis, when people, united in a unanimous feeling of patriotism, rediscovered the immortal soul of France . . . one of those historic moments which will have pride of place in the annals of our local history . . .[2]

The scene, the report, and the language were common to moments of liberation throughout France. Whether American, British, French, or FFI, the first troops to enter the town were the liberators. It was only later that arguments developed and intensified over who were the 'real' liberators, and whether some towns were not liberated at all, but just abandoned by their German occupiers. In 1973, for example, Pierre Bertaux, the liberation Commissaire de la République in Toulouse, wrote that Toulouse was not liberated by the FFI nor by the FTP, but by the fact that

[1] *L'Information du Languedoc*, 1 (23 Aug. 1944), Bulletin publié par le Comité régional de Libération.

[2] Ibid. 4 (26 Aug. 1944).

the Germans decided to leave, and this judgement was in response to three different accounts which claimed liberation of the town by Resistance units. By contrast, Bertaux added, Cahors and the Lot were 'genuinely' liberated by the FFI.[3] In 1984, in a personal memoir of the liberation of Mâcon, to the north of Lyon, Marcel Vitte described the last retreat of German troops along the *quais* bordering the river Saône, and then added,

> This, then, was the moment to enter Mâcon, On Monday, 4 September, therefore, in bright sunshine, Mâcon was liberated without a battle and without loss. Certain people regretted the apparent ease of the event, and spoke of a day without glory.

Had he stopped his commentary at that point, he would have left the emphasis purely on the town, but he continued to say,

> Certainly Mâcon did not experience the victimization and the battles which marked the history of Villefranche, Tournus, Sennecey-le-Grand, Montceau, and Autun, but the liberation was there, and as for actions and casualties, we had known both in the area, in the ambushes which had demoralized the Germans and had successfully cleared the roads.[4]

It is this wider geographical span, this recognition of the multitude of rural skirmishes and outlying battles, which needs reinforcement in the often tendentious and sterile arguments over who liberated the main towns. In these arguments, fuelled by words such as those used by Pierre Bertaux, it becomes part of the longstanding town-centred historiography of modern France to imagine that the ultimate validity, or invalidity, of the maquis is exposed in the number of large towns which saw a 'genuine' battle of liberation between the FFI and the Germans. The penultimate phase of maquis activity, in dominating 'pays' or 'terrains' within large stretches of rural France, and the role of villages and small towns in helping to consolidate that dominance is all too easily subordinated to the way in which the *chef-lieu* of the *département* finally fell to the Resistance. A number of misleading dichotomies were created, not just at local level but within national histories of the Liberation: it was *either* the FFI *or* the Allies; the Germans were *either* defeated *or* they retreated of their own accord. A more nuanced summary of liberation would encompass all four explanations. No account which plays down the decisive military role of the Allied *débarquements*, and no account which minimizes the guerrilla successes of the FFI can stand as a valid history of the Liberation. In a résumé of Allied and French military events in August in the south-east, General Alain le Ray, leader of the FFI in the Isère, declared in 1975:

[3] Pierre Bertaux, *Libération de Toulouse et de sa région* (Hachette, 1973), 24–30.

[4] Marcel Vitte, 'Un été 44 à Mâcon. Occupation et libération', *Annales de l'Académie de Mâcon*, 3e série, 60 (1984), 122. Kindly communicated to me by William Fortescue.

The American force responsible for fighting its way up the Durance valley planned to reach Grenoble in ninety days, three months after landing on the Mediterranean coast. They covered the distance in seven days, almost without incident.

How was such an amazing trajectory achieved in such time? Why did the Germans retreat?

No one, starting with the Germans themselves, disputes the fact that this retreat was caused by the pressure of the maquis of Dévoluy, of Lus-la-Croix-Haute, of the Vercors, of Trièves, and of the Oisans.

The headlong flight of the Germans in the Dauphiné had begun. It accelerated in a series of capitulations. It was our reward for the long, cruel years of struggle.

No one has the right to forget.[5]

Similarly, the colourful details of liberation which give credit only to local French volunteers and ignore the contribution of many other nationalities to the French Resistance, cannot survive critical analysis. Dr Akhmet Bektaev, a member of the armed Resistance in the Tarn, left a memoir declaring that the difficulty of remembering foreign names has often been used by historians as a reason for omitting them. He therefore wrote that at Carmaux he met two miners, Pietr Grigorevitch Diadchouk from the Ukraine and a Pole named Ankitovich who were already involved in the Resistance. With their help, the release of forty prisoners held in Carmaux was organized, all of whom joined the maquis in the mountains. They were joined by twenty Yugoslavs and Croats who had fought in the Spanish Civil War, and a detachment of maquisards was created under the command of Djamankoulov and Ivitch with Bektaev in charge of medical care. They were, he claimed, the first battalion of Soviet partisans in the south, working alongside the FTP. Diadchouk led a party back into the German camps to incite further escapes by Soviet soldiers who had been conscripted against their will, and eventually 98 Georgians formed another maquis detachment under Ichiknieli Otar. All fought in the liberation battles of the Tarn.[6] As for the Spanish *guérilleros*, such was the military confidence gained in the liberation battles across the Languedoc that their militant organization, the Union Nationale Espagnole, seemed ready to take the war directly to Franco. The Liberation Prefect in the Pyrénées-Orientales spoke of impatient bands of Spanish maquisards mustering at the frontier, and threatening the Spanish Consulate in Perpignan.[7] The impatience was seen as intemperate by other Spanish Resisters who had formed the Junte Espagnole de Libération, and who met at Carcassonne on 26 November 1944 in a meeting attended by 1,500 Spanish republicans to criticize the belligerent tactics. Despite the

[5] Bolle (ed.), *Grenoble et le Vercors. De la résistance à la libération*, 135. Compare evidence from Francis Cammaerts, 18 Mar. 1991, who is equally insistent on the magnitude of the Resistance achievement in clearing the whole Route Napoléon and thereby saving countless numbers of lives.

[6] AN 72. AJ 198, post-war report by Akhmet Bektaev, n.d.

[7] AD Hérault 136W 1, Liberation Prefect's report, 28 Aug. 1944.

successes in the maquis, they argued, arms were insufficient for a confrontation with the Spanish state.[8]

What was called the 'excitability' of the Spanish in Perpignan was far from uncommon among maquisards generally at the local prospect of liberation, and it is therefore all the more remarkable that some areas and towns were liberated by agreements and German surrender rather than by pitched or running battles. In the Limousin the number of maquis actions of all kinds, the barbarity of German reprisals, and the intensity of repression by the Milice, pointed towards a possible final conflagration in the area, and yet the surrender of Limoges and Brive was engineered through negotiations which spared incalculable quantities of lives. In both cases, agents representing the Allies were crucially involved, allowing the Germans to convince themselves that they were dealing with regular and not irregular officers, but when Brive surrendered its garrison of 500 soldiers on 15 August and Tulle a further 300 on the following day, and Limoges was left open to the FFI on the evening of 21 August, the maquis could parade its diplomacy as well as its force of arms. The decisive shows of maquis strength which had forced the agreements had taken place away from the towns, and the maquis had shown strength of a different but equal kind in settling for a negotiated withdrawal of the Germans. The inhabitants of all three towns found themselves celebrating the entry of the maquisards as liberators without fear of a punitive German backlash.

The surprise registered by many town dwellers at the orderly military image of the maquis was compounded by the air of mystery which continued to surround the maquisards once the first scenes of celebration had passed. Who exactly were they? Unlike the smaller country towns which tended to greet the maquis as 'nos gars' returning to their families and homes, there was a far more attenuated sense of identity between the inhabitants of the larger towns and the armed individuals and groups who began to patrol their streets. The newspapers of the Liberation tried hard to personalize the various maquis units, but as *La Voix de la Patrie* in Montpellier declared on 30 August, 'We have little knowledge of who these victorious soldiers really are. The Vichy press called them terrorists and bandits . . . and for our part we lose them in a welter of initials. Who are the FTP, the CFL, the FFI and the ORA?'[9] The paper, which represented the Resistance record and aims of the Front National, went on to give a quick sketch of the main maquis units, but detailed identification was made no easier by the understandable desire of maquisards and their leaders to perpetuate the *noms de guerre* under which they had forged their maquis identity.

[8] AD Hérault 136W 1, Liberation Prefect of the Aude to the Commissaire de la République, Nov. 1944.

[9] *La Voix de la Patrie*, 2 (30 Aug. 1944), le journal du Front National pour le Languedoc et le Roussillon.

With the war far from over within France and Europe, Gérald Suberville, who had organized the highly effective sabotage work of Action Ouvrière in the Montpellier region, spoke on the regional wireless as 'Janvier', head of the Hérault FFI, and gave the continuing presence of the maquis a renewed local purpose. The role of the FFI, he announced, was not yet finished: the enemy had been driven out of the region, but 'la patrie est encore en danger'. The Milicien and the traitor were still there.[10] Within the last weeks of September a series of orders from the Provisional Government began to lay down ways in which the FFI would be incorporated into the regular army, but in the early days after the liberation of each *chef-lieu*, the forceful image of the FFI as avengers, which Janvier evoked in Montpellier, emerged to dominate the period between the jubilation of the parades and the departure of the regularized maquis for the front. The threads of *libération* and *épuration*, already entangled by the spring of 1944, were now inextricably enmeshed. There would be many who came to believe that *épuration* threatened the very essence of *libération*, but they were not preponderant nor did they have a monopoly of moral integrity: there was an equal moral resonance to the arguments of those who claimed that *libération* would be meaningless without *épuration*. The crux lay in deciding who should decide.

Prolonging the case-study of the Montpellier region, it emerged from the very first reports of liberation administrators to Jacques Bounin, the Commissaire de la République, that the maquis did not arrive from the hills with the intention of establishing a military rule over the towns. There had been Commissaires de la République at the time of the French Revolution and in 1848, and a main purpose of the seventeen regional Commissaires, clandestinely appointed by the CFLN in Algiers as early as the winter of 1943, was to pre-empt the installation in France of the Allied Military Government of Occupied Territory (AMGOT), known familiarly to anglophone Resisters as 'Ancient Military Gentlemen on Tour'. Bounin heard of his appointment in May 1944, and as a non-communist member of the Front National was well placed to deal with most political strands of the Resistance. His first task was to preside over the selection of the various Liberation Committees, regional, departmental, and local, and to appoint the prefects in the six *départements* within his region, now extended to include the Gard. The aim was to have all these levels of civil administration in place by the time of the Liberation so that a smooth transfer of power from Vichy to the Resistance would be assured. The unknown quantities were the political aspirations of the Communist Party and the military intentions of the FFI, but within days it was clear that the communists had no wish to break the all-party alignment within the Provisional Government, nor to realize a radical social revolution however much it was desired by certain Resisters,

[10] Ibid.

both communist and non-communist, at the grass roots. As for the FFI, Bounin wrote,

> They came down from the mountains amid rumours (but only rumours) that they intended to pursue the national insurrection to the very end, i.e. to seize the reins of civil power. In fact there was no such problem. I went to meet them after the battle of Montpellier and invited Chambrun and his entourage into the council room in the prefecture. I took the chair and he sat on my right: there could be no mistaking the fact that I was in charge.[11]

The meeting established that the FFI would be a welcome presence in Montpellier for several administrative reasons, notably the control of food supplies and the suppression of indiscriminate requisitions and pillaging. Bounin did, however, remonstrate that certain individuals, in possession of arms captured from German prisoners, were playing at soldiers and terrifying the civilian population. The result was a public inability to distinguish 'the glorious fighters that you are from petty trouble-makers'.[12]

This initial period of public apprehension amid scenes of armed force lasted for a few weeks at most. There were expressions of fear and anxiety in Toulouse and Limoges, in Béziers, Cahors, Marseille, and Toulon, in Lyon, Annecy, and Clermont-Ferrand, and most major towns presented some examples of arbitrary intimidation and abuse of military power. In oral testimony maquisards have consistently stressed that the organized units of the FFI were, if anything, the main force of order in the Liberation period and that abusive use of force stemmed from the number of last-minute volunteers within the towns who found themselves with a gun in their hands but no history of maquis life or combat on which to depend for their combative identity. The temptation to prove their Resistance credentials in demonstrations of force was, for many such individuals, irresistible. Inevitably the tendency of civilians at the time was to generalize from such actions, just as the tendency of maquisards looking back is to minimize them. Two reports on the area of Villefranche and Decazeville in the Aveyron can, however, serve to reassert the volatile nature of the situation, and the importance in all accounts of varying angles of opinion.

Cut off from all telephone contact with Montpellier, the Aveyron lived in its own world for many days at and after the liberation by the FFI, while the *arrondissement* of Villefranche, incorporating the mining towns of Decazeville and Aubin, continued its assertive independence which had nullified the last few months of the Vichy administration. The Liberation Prefect in his first written report to Jacques Bounin at Montpellier seemed barely less despairing than his Vichy predecessors, claiming that the 'entire population of the *arrondissement*, including the workers . . . is truly terrorized, and the

[11] Bounin, *Beaucoup d'imprudences*, 155. [12] Ibid.

word is not too strong, by heavily armed groups of FTP'. He firmly believed that the leaders of these groups fully intended to seize power in the interests of the Communist Party, even though their actions were not entirely endorsed by their military superiors within the FTP. In short, he feared a possible clash between the local FTP and other FFI from the rest of the *département* or with the regular French troops when they arrived from the south-east. The date of the report was 24 August.[13] A month later the Sub-Prefect at Villefranche summarized his first few days of office as ones which saw a conflict of authority between himself and the FFI, but announced very considerable improvements in that respect ever since. Rather than separating the FTP from the FFI in order to accentuate their political motivation, as the Prefect had done, the Sub-Prefect refers throughout his report to the generic category of the FFI and admits that they had good reason to criticize the lack of firmness and direction given by certain branches of the new liberation authority. 'The relationships between the FFI and the population', he wrote, 'are not as strained as certain interested persons would like us to believe. What *is* true is that segments of the population, out of sheer self-interest, would like to be rid of the soldiers of the maquis as quickly as possible, and to return to the tranquillity of peacetime. They would like to blot out the war and its constraints.' He was not, he said, one of those who was prepared to forget that France had been liberated thanks to these 'impatient and turbulent youths', and he advised a continuous programme of public education to remind self-regarding citizens that France was still at war, and that French blood was still being spilt for their freedom and well-being.[14]

The high moral tone of this report is far from untypical of much of Resistance opinion at the Liberation, but with the widespread sympathy for the achievements and sufferings of the FFI went an increasing certainty that force of arms was not force of law. In the immediate aftermath of the Liberation, military courts set up by the FFI tried well-known, or suspected, Miliciens and other collaborators with a speed and determination which shocked many. Within a fortnight they were replaced by special courts of justice, and the complaints received by the authorities from that point onwards mostly concerned the slow and ponderous process of the *épuration* which appeared to many Resisters to be missing its mark. A debate on the new courts was staged in the Comité Départemental de Liberation (CDL) in the Gard on 16 September. Captain Lucien, representing the FFI, argued that all the Miliciens arrested by the FFI should still be judged by military justice since they had taken up arms against the Resistance. Sixty such Miliciens were still awaiting trial in the *département*, said Lucien, at which

[13] AD Hérault 136W 1, Liberation Prefect's report, 28 Aug. 1944.
[14] Ibid. Sub-Prefect's report, 2 Oct. 1944.

point he was rebuked by Dr Arène for the degrading treatment they had received. The doctor declared that 'We degrade ourselves by such treatment. In the last 48 hours there has been a reversal of opinion and in one hour we have lost the benefit of all we have done over four years.' Lucien replied with a defence of rough justice: 'I'll simply say that the majority of the FFI have been outlaws. They are lads from the mining areas of the Gard; they have been hunted; they have been imprisoned; they have been tortured by Miliciens whom they now recognize. It is understandable that they should want to beat them up.' The president of the CDL, Dr Benedittini, tried to mediate between them. He himself came from the mining area, and from 1940 had sheltered first Belgian refugees and then Jews, before becoming a doctor for the Maquis de Lasalle and a leading member of the Front National in the Gard. He drew attention to ten recent executions carried out by the FFI after an attack by Miliciens on a railway carriage containing local Resisters, and while he acknowledged that the attackers would have been condemned by a court martial he added that someone had said to him, 'When I read the communiqué on the executions, I felt the signature at the bottom should read, Feldkommandantur.' Benedittini then asked Lucien to ensure there would be no more summary reprisals, nor any recurrence of the shaving of women's heads 'which had done us so much harm'. The debate continued, and Lucien's protests that the FFI were doing no more than pursuing self-evident collaborators were not without echo among other members of the committee. In the end the new courts were accepted on the basis that six officers from the FFI would be among the 50 jurors who would serve on each of the two courts in Nîmes and Alès; but the divisions of opinion on the initiatives taken by the FFI continued throughout October.[15]

The sessions of the CDL in the Gard afford an excellent glimpse of the ideological debates among Resisters which followed the Liberation, even if the degree of open-speaking and the level of passion varied hugely from one CDL to another. The CDLs of the Hérault and the Aude, by way of local comparison, contented themselves with a far more administrative agenda, though on 5 September members of the Hérault committee registered considerable indignation, not at the existence of the military tribunals, but at their slowness in arresting and trying the major local collaborators. The implication, borne out by events in a number of large towns, was that the small-time collaborators had been the all too easy target of those with the new-found power to arrest, prosecute, and judge, and a week later Pastor Cadier protested at the severity of the sentences. His protest prompted a unanimous vote in the CDL saying that human rights,

[15] AD Hérault 136W 9, 'Séances du C.D.L. du Gard'.

in particular the rights of defence, must be respected, and the President concluded the discussion by announcing the imminent replacement of the courts martial.[16]

The context within which the arguments for and against military justice were propounded was one in which daily revelations of Nazi and collaborationist atrocities kept the necessity and morality of the *épuration* in sharp focus. In Montpellier the Caserne de Lauwe had been the centre of tortures carried out by the Milice and it was there that a leading local Resister, Marcel Guizonnier, had been tortured to death on 11 August. 'On 6 September', wrote Jacques Bounin, 'his body was found, disfigured with beatings, his limbs scarred with burns, his genitals smashed . . .'[17] In all regions there were similar discoveries, and in such ways the public was confronted with the indescribable cruelty of the Milice which had continued right up to the last days of the Occupation. The revelations enflamed emotions and underlined the strong moral case for a thorough *épuration*. Although the majority of the FFI distanced themselves from retributive acts after the Liberation, those who willingly adopted the image of avengers felt themselves more than vindicated by the details of collaboration that emerged. It can only be in the interests of civil freedoms that Captain Lucien's case for continuing military courts was rejected by other Resisters and by fellow members of the FFI, but it would be unhistorical to minimize the amount of public support for tough measures against leading collaborators or to imagine that the avengers were in all cases perpetrators of injustice.

Generalizations about the role of the maquis in all the celebrations and turbulence of the Liberation are difficult to substantiate. But it would not seem unreasonable to suggest that, whatever the precise actions of the maquisards, the Liberation as a whole, with its utopian ideals, its upsurge of popular power, and even its abuses, presents a powerful image of a world turned upside-down, which suitably crowns the inversionary history of the maquis. It seemed to many that a revolutionary situation existed in France in August and September 1944, but this is no longer seriously maintained. The solidarity of all political parties behind the continuation of the war, and in support of the Provisional Government, was an overwhelming factor neutralizing any hope of a political revolution and mitigating major programmes of social reform promoted by certain Resistance authorities. There is no room here for a study of the hopes and frustrations of many French people who took the notion of a revolutionary opportunity seriously. But confrontation, violence, and an atmosphere of radical change certainly accompanied the celebrations in many southern areas, and although the

[16] AD Hérault 138W 17, 'Séances du C.D.L. de l'Hérault'; AD Hérault 136W 9, 'Séances du C.D.L. de l'Aude'.

[17] Bounin, *Beaucoup d'imprudences*, 151.

period of popular power was short, it appeared promising and exciting to many maquisards, though disturbing and dangerous to others. Henri Cordesse was made Liberation Prefect in the Lozère, and his elevation from *instituteur* to the highest administrative post in the *département* was itself inversionary, and was seen as such by the population of the Lozère. One of his first acts of authority was to place several highly Pétainist members of the local aristocracy under house arrest to protect them from possible victimization. He was well aware of the great potential, and popular demand, for change, and compared the Liberation to crossing the equator: it was a time of great festivity but also of destabilization. The context of the Liberation was 'a psychological and economic context bearing no relationship to the normal course of events'.[18] It was a time when people were self-consciously aware of the immensity of the moment, and yet it was, in many ways, happening in a vacuum, out of time.

The Liberation was a particularly local event for many areas like the Lozère and the Aveyron, cut off as they were from national directives at the crucial point in the change-over of power.[19] The most fundamental problem was intensely physical, the provision and distribution of food, and on this one element alone many people judged the efficacy of the FFI and the new Liberation authorities. The everyday meaning of freedom and liberation was uncomfortably tested by the availability of goods which Resistance newspapers had said were being kept from the population by Vichy and individual exploiters. The goods now had to be found, and the hoarders and profiteers exposed and punished. The onus on those with a uniform and a gun, with a lorry or a sidecar, was to make the Liberation work at this most basic level, without arbitrary harassment of individuals and without evidence of corruption or self-aggrandisement. It propelled maquisards and the milices patriotiques into authoritative actions and decisions which in other times would have been taken by the police and specialized *fonctionnaires*. Many were very young: many came from outside the towns in which they now found themselves assuming administrative responsibilities; many were of other nationalities.

The power exercised by these forces 'from below' prompted many, though not all, of the new authorities to retreat from possible agendas of social change and display a highly conventional concept of power. For example, on 19 September the new Prefect of the Var filed a critical report on the local situation to Raymond Aubrac, the Commissaire de la République in Marseille who was one of the most radical of the regional authorities. In it he complained that 'there are too many foreigners in the FFI. It is humiliating for a French person to be stopped and verified by a Spaniard or Italian

[18] Henri Cordesse, *La Libération en Lozère* (Cordesse: n.p., 1977), 51.

[19] See Bounin, *Beaucoup d'imprudences*, 140, where he says that he had no contact with either *département* at the time.

who hardly speaks French.' The most serious problem, he wrote, was the continuation of FFI groups who have no regular training and who claim to live autonomously championing the people's rights. He specified the groupes francs known as 'La Coquette', whose record against the Gestapo, he admitted, had been brilliant and who had played a spectacular role in the battle of Toulon; but they could not be allowed, he declared, to do what they liked, arresting people and confiscating their goods.[20]

Here was a Liberation Prefect, like the new appointment in the Aveyron, who knew the milieu of professional groups in the Resistance from within, and had nothing but praise for someone like Monsieur Picoche on the Var CDL whom he described as 'an excellent Republican, the soul of the town of Hyères, a man of legendary courage and leader of the maquis for two years who has sacrificed everything for the Resistance. He is married with three children and is head of an important company of public transport.' In contrast, his adverse comments on the presence of foreigners in civil policing, his description of the milices patriotiques as 'dangerous', and his warning that the youth of the FFI should be placed firmly under police control,[21] all typify the widespread suspicion within the new Liberation authority towards forces emanating from the Resistance who had previously been marginal or subordinate to the traditional structures of power. Such forces, from both the maquis and their supportive communities, included agricultural and industrial workers, women, immigrants, and youth, none of whom had featured in the echelons of established administrative power before or during the war, but all of whom had experienced the responsibilities of comprehensive decision-making in the alternative power structures of the Resistance. The unease found in many official post-Liberation reports can be traced not just to the methods employed by these forces, but to their very presence within the makeshift administration.

It became almost a ritualized reaction of the Liberation authorities to stress the transience of these forces and to plan for their relocation in the margins of power. The Provisional Government moved even further than its local authorities in that direction when on 28 October it decreed the dissolution of the milices patriotiques, and although the Conseil National de la Résistance countered with a compromise suggestion that the milices should be transformed into Republican Guards, there were extensive protests from those Resistance groups and local newspapers for whom the milices had embodied the 'esprit populaire' of the Liberation.[22] From the battle of Bouvines in 1214 through to the eighteenth century the milice had represented a citizens' army, recruited to supplement the regular troops, and the appropriation of the term by Darnand's Milice under Vichy was seen as an

[20] AN F1C III. 1194, Var, report of 19 Sept. 1944 [21] Ibid.

[22] e.g. protests were recorded in the session of 2 Nov. 1944 of the CDL of the Hérault, AD Hérault 138W 17, and expressed strongly in *La Voix de la patrie* (2 Nov. 1944).

obscene distortion, which the milices patriotiques had set out to rectify. Their dissolution was not opposed by all members of the FFI. The disagreement on the issue was a major element reinforcing the growing differences between those who believed the FFI had the right to civil power at the Liberation and those who claimed only a military identity. But even with this considerable disunity, the dissolution was widely criticized as the first demotion of the armed Resistance. It was followed shortly by the largely insensitive assimilation of the FFI into the regular army, with a loss of most of their special characteristics, and lower ranks for the leaders around whom the maquis had first achieved a status of their own. It was at this point that the image of the disinherited maquis began to take shape.

This image is still a potent one, even if the collective anger it once provoked has been dissipated over the years. Its appearance in an otherwise harmonious discussion can cause discord and the discovery of unsuspected differences of memory and opinion.[23] It emerges whenever it is suggested that the culture of the maquis might have constituted a threat to conventional structures of society. Some maquisards warm to the notion of a liberation period when major fissures in the embedded strata of society suddenly appeared. Some had no expectations of structural change. Many wanted changes, but not on the scale of an inversion in cultural dominance. Others looked and worked for the perpetuation of an ideal of equality which they believed had been realized in the Resistance. It would be difficult to adjudge the relative prominence of these different points of view, but there is little doubt that the ensuing image of the maquis as disinherited by decisions from above was one to which a wide range of maquisards came to subscribe. In many respects the disillusion which the image conveys was common to much of French society in the year that followed the Liberation. The new Prefect of the Aude spoke for a considerable majority of French people in early September:

> They all hope that the new Government of France will move towards a wide programme of social reform: improvements in peasant life, social welfare, a progressive economic policy tackling the monopolistic companies and the need for revised wages and salaries, the democratization of the army, education, the financial world, etc. This would assure the nation a vitality and power which would earn the world's respect. There is a great feeling of hope among the people which the new Republic must not betray.[24]

It was exactly such a wide reforming aspiration which did, eventually, feel itself betrayed. Within it, the specific hope of a new egalitarian army was

[23] Some collective interviews I conducted with several maquisards led to disagreements and a request for the recording to be destroyed. I therefore have even more respect for the work of Jacques Canaud who conducted many collective sessions in the Morvan. See his excellent *Les Maquis du Morvan* (Académie du Morvan: Château-Chinon, 1981). It is an exceptional work.

[24] AD Hérault 13W 1, Liberation Prefect of the Aude, 7 Sept. 1944.

especially close to the expectations of maquisards. Most maquis leaders had broken with officer rituals and conventions, except in the area of command. Orders were rarely disputed, but it was felt that the style of life in the maquis made a reality of ideals which envisaged an army of the people. It is true that this was neither universally attempted nor achieved, but in retrospect this feeling of equality forms a dominant public and private memory of the maquis.

The celebrations of the Liberation were for everyone. The celebration of the 152nd anniversary of the battle of Valmy on 20 September 1944 was a particular fête for the FFI. In the historical recreation of the almost mythical popular victory over the Prussians, the twin concepts of revolutionary patriotism and a popular army were reverentially paraded in most of the Liberation newspapers. In Montpellier, three weeks earlier, a rousing speech by Emmanuel d'Astier, the provisional Minister of the Interior, had set the local FFI on the path of Valmy:

> The worker, the employee, the intellectual, and the peasant created the Resistance. See with what meagre weapons and slender means they formed this powerful army of the people, the Forces Françaises de l'Intérieur, which single-handed has liberated more than half of France.[25]

When it came to the anniversary itself, the regional edition of the socialist paper *Le Populaire*, in its first post-Liberation issue, carried a large front-page photograph of the FFI celebration in the place de la Comédie in the centre of Montpellier, with the words: 'More than a century and a half after the battle of Valmy, the people have once again risen up victoriously and have re-established the Republic.'[26] From the rostrum, Gilbert de Chambrun, as regional head of the FFI, went further than the celebration of a victory, whether 1792 or 1944, and declared that the goal of the FFI had first and foremost been the liberation of the country, but closely following that they aimed at 'the creation of a democratic army, which will never again be the army of capitulation'.[27] In this phrase alone lay a whole history of FFI hostility towards the regular army leaders who were seen to have capitulated in 1940 and to have done nothing, or worse, during the whole of the Occupation. In defiant rejection of what was constantly labelled the shameful record and antiquated structures of the traditional army, eloquent sections of the FFI offered visions of an 'armée nouvelle'. In *Le Volontaire*, the regional weekly of the FFI in the Languedoc, the visionary language of military pioneers proclaimed that the French army had been reborn through the tactics of guerrilla warfare, discovered by the French people themselves: 'It can truly be said that the maquis saved France by giving the defeated, humiliated, crushed nation a new power, a new hope . . . Today, no French

[25] *La Voix de la patrie*, 3 (29 Aug. 1944).

[26] *Le Populaire du Bas-Languedoc, Rouergue et Roussillon*, 1 (24 Sept. 1944).

[27] Ibid.

person can doubt the achievements of the maquis. The maquis has been the *avant-garde* of the *nouvelle armée populaire française*.' The first number of the paper went on to analyse the weaknesses of the old army, and specified the internal divisions between the troops and the officers. A further article gave a high profile to maquis discipline, and to the maquis police which had hunted down *faux maquisards* and the pillagers who had dishonoured the name of the maquis. Now discipline was even more necessary among the FFI. 'We have won the war, now we must win the peace.' The FFI was being watched by both the population and by de Lattre de Tassigny's army from Africa. 'We must show ourselves worthy of constituting the Armée Nouvelle.'[28]

This first local proclamation of the new army was accompanied by constant affirmation of confidence in de Gaulle and the Provisional Government, but by the third issue on 22 October the editorial is full of discontent. There are complaints of being forced out of positions of responsibility, downgraded, and subordinated to regular officers who are lampooned as 'the mothball army (des naphtalinards)'; there are accusations that the battles and the sacrifices of the maquis are already being contested or forgotten, and that the contributions of women and peasant communities remain unknown or ignored. The paper aimed at historical reassertion, reconstruction, and re-education as well as the future re-formation of the army, and carried insights into the work of women liaison agents as well as the range of personalities among maquis leaders.[29] By the end of October its embattled tone was overlaid with anger. It discerned a campaign against the FFI similar to the infamous attacks of Philippe Henriot and with a similar aim of divorcing the FFI from the people. A note of despair had crept into the idealism; 'God protect us from our friends. We'll look after our enemies', ran one of the headlines, and a searing contempt for sections of society which had grown fat while the maquis were starving permeated most of the articles.[30] The disinherited maquis is almost a fully formed image in these numbers of *Le Volontaire*. It had taken less than two months to gain substance, and within the meetings of the Gard CDL there was equal anger at the signs of disinheritance. On 30 September a long report from the officer commanding men from the FFI of the Gard in the pursuit of the Germans into eastern France, stated that the FFI were being used by the regular army as untrained shock troops, without support, proper arms, or services. He claimed he had lost 40 members out of 120 in battles in the Jura due to 'deplorable lack of concern by the regular officers'.[31]

In this single but pivotal issue of whether or not the FFI should be the embryo of a new democratic army, two rival interpretations of the Resistance

[28] *Le Volontaire*, 1 (8 Oct. 1944), hebdomadaire régional des FFI.
[29] Ibid. 3 (22 Oct. 1944). [30] Ibid. 4 (29 Oct. 1944).
[31] AD Hérault 136W 9, 'Séances du C.D.L. du Gard'.

and the maquis can already be discerned. They dominated the historiography of the Occupation for at least two decades after the war. Whereas Resisters from all branches of the internal Resistance talked loosely of the people, France, and the nation, and filled their speeches at the Liberation with phrases evoking the unity and victory of the French people over the Germans, in reality most had a realistic view of the Resistance as a minority movement in occupied France, based on their own lived experience as clandestine or outlaw activists. In the weeks of sobering hardship and adjustments which followed the Liberation, this selective view of the Resistance as belonging not to the nation as a whole but to those who had worked, fought, and died in its various movements, networks, and volunteer armies, ran into conflict with the position upheld and propagated by de Gaulle, for whom the national insurrection meant the renaissance of the whole nation, and who declared that the new France must be made and composed of all the French. As these two radically different views took shape, the words 'people' and 'populaire' were yet again contested as they had been since the French Revolution. In the selective interpretation of Resistance activity, the words stood for the people who had actively made and supported the Resistance. Still more selectively, for many in the FTP and the Front National they indicated the working class of urban and rural France. On the other hand, 'le peuple français' was used by de Gaulle as an organic concept to reunite the nation. Orders and decrees by the Provisional Government in the name of the people moved consistently in that direction, backed by many Resisters who accepted the Gaullist priority of the nation. It was soon apparent that the 'selective' view was increasingly seen by de Gaulle as divisive, troublesome, and even subversive, while the 'nationalist' view was challenged by a crescendo of Resistance voices as a travesty of history, which diminished their minority struggle and made unacceptable concessions to those who had chosen passive or active acceptance of Vichy.

No attempt should be made to allocate all Resisters to one or other of these two views: there have been many overlaps, variants, and combinations. But as two sharply divergent interpretations, they were present in the immediate post-Liberation arguments over the *épuration* and the role of the FFI. The new Sub-Prefect at Alès, who championed the miners and FTP of the area, spoke for the selective view in his report of 22 October 1944 by criticizing those who refused the hard lessons of the Occupation:

> Unfortunately certain sections of the upper classes are demonstrating by their calculated indifference that they have learnt nothing from the four years which we have just survived. France needs a good crack of the whip. The people who have given everything and who sacrificed themselves continue to work and struggle on alone . . .

Public opinion unanimously demands the punishment of all traitors. It is false to say that the people are thirsty for blood: they are thirsty for justice.[32]

Some of the discontent from Alès was integrated into the Liberation Prefect's report of 2 November, but the sting was drawn, and the Prefect concluded with the contrary observation that it was certain undisciplined sections of the FFI who were threatening the post-Liberation efforts of reconstruction, and he added that it was vital that every individual should meditate on de Gaulle's affirmation that 'La France doit être faite de tous les Français'.[33] Eventually the Prefect's moral homily was one among many which constituted a dominant critique of the *épuration*, carried in the influential novel by Jean-Louis Curtis, *Les Forêts de la nuit*, in the strictures against a judgemental Resistance by Jean Paulhan, and in the inflated statistics of the *épuration*, given credibility in the histories by Robert Aron.[34] In the face of this critique it is easy to forget the multitude of complaints at the slowness and ineffectiveness of the *épuration*, which were communicated to the prefects and the CDLs throughout the autumn and winter of 1944. To many Resisters it seemed as if the France of all the French was tantamount to the reinstatement of the culpable and the compromised. In a questionnaire to ex-Resisters in the Aveyron in 1990, sent out by history teachers at the Lycée of Saint-Affrique, there was a question on attitudes to the *épuration*. Out of the 96 replies received, the breakdown of views was as follows: the *épuration* was, Sufficient 18, Excessive 4, Very hard indeed 2, Insufficient 56, No comment 16. In written evidence many of the respondents claimed that their return to jobs had been made difficult by the fact of their Resistance, particularly for the working class. They had the feeling of not being given the consideration they felt they deserved.[35] Few such questionnaires have been carried out, so the figures cannot claim representative status, but they chime with the views expressed in a sizeable proportion of the oral memories which follow this series of images. Georges Guingouin's conclusion in his memoirs has become a classic of the genre: 'Guilty of having scaled the highest peaks, the Limousin Resisters were the most vilified and the most persecuted.'[36] It was not just a cry from the political Left. Major Despaigne

[32] AD Gard CA 314, Sub-Prefect of Alès to Prefect, 22 Oct. 1944.

[33] Ibid., Liberation Prefect's report to the Commissaire de la République, 2 Nov. 1944.

[34] Jean-Louis Curtis, *Les Forêts de la nuit* (Julliard, 1947); Jean Paulhan, *Lettre aux directeurs de la Résistance* (Éditions de Minuit, 1952); Robert Aron, *Histoire de l'épuration*, 4 vols. (Fayard, 1967–75). In contrast to the 30,000–40,000 deaths estimated by Robert Aron, Jean-Pierre Rioux points out that the most careful inquiry conducted by the Comité d'Histoire de la Deuxième Guerre Mondiale 'makes it possible to accept as free of serious errors the figure of 9,000 summary executions, to which can be added the 767 executions after trial'. Jean-Pierre Rioux, *The Fourth Republic*, trans. Godfrey Rogers (CUP: Cambridge, 1987), 32.

[35] 'A propos du questionnaire: sauvegardons la mémoire', *Résistance en Rouergue*, 84 (1990). The teachers were Ch. Font and H. Moizet. The questionnaire was kindly communicated to me by Pierre Boyer.

[36] Guingouin, *Quatre ans de lutte sur le sol limousin*, 232.

of the Corps Franc de la Montagne Noire stated firmly that 'after the war it was a black mark against you if you had been in the maquis or in a unit like the CFMN'.[37]

The issue of disinheritance and the fluctuating successes and failures of maquisards in their struggle against it is clearly a subject ready tailored for the history of collective memory pioneered by Henry Rousso.[38] Ceremonies, anniversaries, monuments, associations, pamphlets, and books all testify to the resilience of the maquisard presence in the remembered history of the Occupation. It could even be said that the history of the maquis has been prioritized at the expense of other groups and movements of armed Resistance and sabotage. But what is noticeable is the extent to which the maquis in retrospect has been assigned to a largely inferior canon of history, transmitted by methods seen as lightweight, or even dubious, such as stories, anecdotes, and polemic. The maquis, ostensibly due to its association with requisitions and retributive justice, was allotted this lower historical status almost immediately after the Liberation. Within a few years the high–low, serious–popular antinomies within Resistance historiography were firmly established. These were cultural antitheses as well. In the 'low' culture of the maquis, *noms de guerre* were seen to play the role of masks, social marginals came to the centre of the stage, and guignolesque figures abounded. They could easily be found in the accounts and the memoirs of the maquisards themselves. Colonel Redon, FFI leader in the Tarn, spoke of his co-organizer, called Armagnac, who ran units of groupes francs with terrifying names like 'Gueules d'Acier':

> Armagnac passed for a communist sympathizer, but to this penchant for 'extremism' he added a scowling harshness in a fairly young but severe face, and affected a contempt for everyday politeness. I felt I was up against a real tough guy, who wouldn't think twice about beating up his bourgeois colleague every evening as a training exercise.

In fact Redon discovered that he already knew Armagnac by his real name, Galinier, when they were in the army together at Nîmes in 1928–9, at which time Galinier was nicknamed 'le séminariste'. He thus came to realize, in his own words, that the 'terrible Armagnac was only terrible on the outside. In any case he was an excellent guerrilla leader.'[39] Similar images of other such personalities throughout the local histories of the maquis are etched by a number of writers with a fine sense of realistic detail. They can now be seen to comprise one of the richest miscellanies of popular characterization in modern French history.

[37] Evidence from H. M. Despaigne, 18 Aug. 1979.

[38] Henry Rousso, *Le Syndrome de Vichy* (Seuil, 1987); also Henry Rousso, 'Pour une histoire de la mémoire collective: l'après-Vichy' in Denis Peschanski, Michael Pollak, and Henry Rousso (eds.), *Histoire politique et sciences sociales* (Éditions Complexe, 1991), 243–64.

[39] AN 72. AJ 198, Redon, 'Souvenirs de la Résistance dans le département du Tarn'.

The relegation of the maquis in the historical canon was also due to the fact that its local, rural, and highly diffuse nature broke the parameters of both Marxist and liberal historiography, which continued to be dominantly town-centred for many years after the Liberation. Shifts in cultural emphasis can be achieved by removing the masks and giving names to the anonymous; by giving the centre of the stage in 'serious' history to those normally marginalized; and by setting the guignolesque figures within the community culture of the outlaw. In just such ways the search for the maquis in this particular book has been one of relocation and reassessment. To the same extent it has re-emphasized the most insistent images which have emerged during the process of searching and finding. Many of these are images of rural presence, redrawn and reanimated in the retrospection of oral testimonies. As final images they are visual, tangible, and evocative.

Smoke from cooking had to be avoided, especially in winter. There were beds of bracken, or perhaps of hay. There was the pungent, bitter smell of broom in full flower; there were wild daffodils in the meadows of the green, soft slopes at the centre of the Massif Central, and clumps of primroses on the banks of the fast-flowing rivers that ran past the Glières and cut through the Vercors. Further south the ground under foot was more rebarbative: sharp needles of fallen chestnuts and paths of shaling rock that slipped at every step. The sheer beauty of views across vast stretches of hills is vividly remembered, the calm and quiet, except for birds, cigales, and the distant barking of dogs and the crowing of cocks in the farms. There was contrast with the machinery of war, the training with grenades and sten guns, the unrelieved burden of duties. There was fear of the dark, of the noises made by a hedgehog like someone hiding in the dead leaves. There was a possible German road block at every turn into the village: the enormous distances covered on foot, the precious lorry running on *gazogène* which took an hour to start, the *gariottes* in the Quercy, and the *burons* in the Auvergne for shelter and hiding; the interminable chestnut soup and chestnut stew, the thin coffee made out of barley, the festive killing of a sheep or a pig.

Increasingly arms and uniforms were important for impressing the villagers. Isolated from the war, cut off in their rural fastnesses, there was all the more need to bring the war to the locality. There was a heady mixture of outdoor life, extremes of heat and cold, and ideological commitment. The driving force of hunger was controlled by the need and willingness to share. There was the charisma of the leader who appeared to know, who received orders from up there, out there; the excitement of parachute drops which recognized their existence and affirmed their intentions. Language was relatively insignificant when skills were so practical. Physical gestures, from the smallest to the most heroic, were binding, creating trust and interdependence. Deep friendships were established by shared knowledge of the terrain, of armaments, of the sense of danger, of behaviour in a tight corner, readiness to lead, but also to obey. There was a solidarity of situation and cause, across nationality, class, and gender.

Different food brought diarrhoea, there was homesickness, boredom, and a sense of uselessness when no activity was in sight. Any adventure was better than none. There was fishing with grenades; there were outings to join the illicit dancing in the villages, sexual exploits, which made deprivation less common than might be expected. Voices were carried on the wind, or in the stillness: the sense of distance was complex. Careful plans were put out by the unexpected presence of a local person, a postal worker, a road-mender, someone looking for the mushrooms of the woods. There were periods of nervous waiting. War took place in a kind of vacuum: little pockets of action existed in a huge expanse of ordinary, everyday life. At the end it was the reverse, the conflicts expanded and accelerated, the everyday life diminished. It was difficult to say which was more unreal. Peasant maquisards were better than the town workers at adapting to the irregular rhythms. The emphasis on the practical and the military tended to distance even political activists from the world of politics. Being non-political was not so much a deliberate stance as a by-product of survivalism at a basic level. Visions were of the immediate future: a successful raid, a safe return, a large meal, a long sleep.

Questions of money were collectivized. There were no regular individual payments: occasional ones only. After the Liberation huge withdrawals from the Banque de France brought some sort of wages. The stress on purity of motive was accentuated by the nature of the opposition: because of German barbarity there was an extra need to show humanity. This curbed excesses, kept a moral purpose alive. Alongside lay a righteous indignation and an urge to recreate justice. Resentment was easy to cultivate: the outlaw mentality was chosen but also imposed. Feelings of being abandoned and marginalized spurred on the drive to return, to re-enter the towns, to take centre stage. Precipitate re-entries were a constant temptation. Guerrilla action bred an inexactness of events. Details were lost, exaggerated, underestimated. They never quite knew what they had done. An ambush, sabotage, derailment had to be left at a crucial point. They saw a German soldier fall but could not stay to verify the damage. It was ontologically vital to have results. From maquis to maquis there was an intrading of achievement.

Liaisons meant long and lonely treks on foot or by bicycle which confirm the realism of the fictitious Juliette in Elsa Triolet's *Les Amants d'Avignon*; providing food and supplies took women into the mountains after work and after dark. There were emergency operations in barns, bodies needed burial, casualties were smuggled in and out of hospitals. In villages and farms, home-made brandy and *vin ordinaire* were drunk by an assembled group from a single glass in case of a sudden knock at the door, and the need to escape. The use of patois confused and diverted the pursuers, children and shepherds led the hunted to caves by sheep tracks known often by hearsay alone. There was always one inhabitant, one village, one area that refused. Conflicts of loyalties, conflicts of fears made for uncertain receptions. Foreigners were not always made welcome.

The searcher of the present or of the future may well be critical of all forms of war. Many maquisards started as pacifists; many remained anti-militaristic. There is a temptation to imagine the ancient peace of villages and countryside where nothing had changed over centuries. Then came the incursive maquis. But there was already a profound disaccord between this rural peace and the poverty and depopulation. Things had changed, buildings had become empty, communities had died. From a taciturn peasantry there comes an image of the maquis as at least a shudder of life.

Finally, there is a revealing absence. The images of rebellion and cynicism within the ranks of the fighters, so common in most recollections of war, are missing. Even the jokes, the laughter, and the misunderstandings are played down so that the committed seriousness of the volunteer cause is never in doubt. There is a relentlessness of intention, action, and the telling of combat. It stretches the belief of listeners and readers: it hovers close to romance, and it has to face up to critical dissent. Its claims are constantly rejected, contextualized, minimized, or simply queried. It has earned a healthy, and unhealthy, disrespect. But there is understatement too, there is modesty and perspective, and a readiness to demythologize. Not all the voices are one.

Oral Memories

Jean-Pierre Chabrol (Génolhac, Gard, 2 March 1982)

I first made contact with Resistance groups in the Sorbonne. I was a *lycéen* in Paris, aged 15 in 1940. My professor of philosophy was in touch with Combat. The Gestapo came looking for me. I went back to my family home in the Cévennes. In the spring of 1944 I decided to join a maquis. I was a Gaullist with expectations of finding a kind of regular army. By mistake I found myself in a maquis FTP formed of miners, peasants, and old members of the International Brigades, Spanish, Italians, and Poles. I wanted to leave at once. It was the kind of maquis Henriot talked about. They said, 'Do you want to change camp?' I said 'Yes'. I only later found out that meant you'd be killed. They were very tough. They did away with any suspicious characters. Luckily for me a communist official recognized me and said, 'He's alright. He's the son of the *instituteur*: he's a bit of an idiot, but OK.' I stayed. It became my re-education, a new life.

Peasants gave us food. And we carried out raids; for example, when we knew the Germans were about to take a flock of sheep we raided the *bergerie*, tied up the shepherd, beat him up a bit to make it look genuine, and took the animals. Every day there was some sort of action, a raid, or a sabotage. Miners would come from the day shifts to help us at night. Then they would go back to work. We would walk 10–12 km. for some sort of action, then back again the same night. And there were always duties—fetching wood, food, water. And night guard duty, some way from the camp.

We weren't really afraid of the dark, but it was easy to get lost. But there were strange noises. A hedgehog in the dead leaves—it farts, it breathes, it snores just like a man. At dusk or at dawn I saw smoke coming up from Alès. I felt as if I were on another planet, isolated. I imagined life down there, people going to the cinema, making love, eating, listening to the radio. Surely they had forgotten us. The war seemed to go on and on. I thought it would never end. And here we were; we didn't really exist. We didn't really count.

But when we went down to the villages we were welcomed with tears and kisses. We went down to Bessèges one night. We occupied the station, the gendarmerie, everything. When people woke up they thought it was the Liberation and started singing the 'Internationale' and the 'Marseillaise'. They begged us not to go back, but they knew we had to. There was no question of peasant hostility. Miners were all from peasant families. And even foreigners down the mine are part of a fraternity. The peasants I knew all seemed to be cousins: there were enormous extended families. They all knew each other. The period of the maquis was 'le temps des jeunes'.

In my first maquis up in the Bougès mountain we went on an operation along exactly the same paths as the Camisards had used. I only found this out fifteen years later. At the time I knew little about the Camisards, nor about Karl Marx. For the Protestants, the outlaw and the exile were sacred. Later on they hid Ben Bella and other FLN members during the Algerian war. But there was no question of Occitanism in the maquis. No one mentioned it. The language was a joke: we derided it if anything. We spoke more Spanish than Occitan. But above all it was important to see yourself as French.

I'm not sure if I enjoyed being an outlaw. There were moments of happiness; but I also suffered a lot. The maquis meant everything to me. It gave me a sense of the importance of ordinary things: every bullet was precious. There were no individual weapons: they were shared out according to the job in hand, and you had to account for every bullet fired. Your most important possession was your pocket knife. There was no democracy. You obeyed orders. Equality, yes. All had the same rights. The leader of the camp had not one grain of tobacco more than the others. There was a sort of savagery, being young. You killed with a kind of joy. Death meant nothing. I remember going to the cinema in Mulhouse in the war that followed the Liberation and being terrified by a thriller on the screen. But in the real war I had no such fear.

The Liberation meant going home. Everyone mobbed us in the villages. It was the same in Alès. Not a single girl had slept with a German: we didn't shave anyone. Women had been vital as *agents de liaison.* A girl called Gilberte, aged 16, sent us information about German troop movements, all written by hand. It was very useful. She was deported to Ravensbrück, but survived. I met a young woman after the war and talked to her about the maquis and the important note we received, and she said 'Gilberte, that's me'. The women didn't fight alongside the men, but they fought in the Camisard period: they were important as fighters then. In the Resistance they transported arms.

Max and Madame Allier (Montpellier, Hérault, 26 March 1982)

MONSIEUR. I was originally from Montpellier, but I grew up and studied in Paris. I was taken prisoner of war in Alsace in 1940 but escaped and went back to my grandmother's family in Montpellier. I knew nobody outside the family and it took me two years to become part of the Resistance. I refused to continue to be a journalist on a Vichy paper, so I took a job supplying wine-growers with copper sulphate. By September 1943 I was in the AS in Montpellier, but was forced to leave because two close friends in the AS were arrested by the Gestapo. We went to the village of l'Espérou in the Cévennes, in the heart of the massif de l'Aigoual. I had been there for holidays when I was a small child. We stayed with a peasant family who ran a small hotel and already had two sons in the Resistance.

In l'Espérou we spoke entirely in Occitan. I heard no French for several weeks after arriving. The hotel family were all in the Resistance, not for political reasons but out of sheer instinct. It was curious that l'Espérou was a Catholic enclave in a dominantly Protestant region. But they were just as pro-Resistance as those in the Protestant village of Valleraugue nearby. Don't forget that Catholics in the Gard had launched their own resistance, *la terreur blanche,* against the imposition of the Revolution. When it came to Resistance the religious differences took second place. For example, the other hotel in the village was run by a Protestant and there had been rivalry before the war. That ceased altogether under the Occupation.

People spoke Occitan, but they never talked about Occitanie or Occitanism. I had learnt it in childhood, but it took me three weeks to understand the local accent. They spoke it particularly in their leisure activities, like playing boules. But at school the children were forced to speak French, even though the *instituteur* came from the locality.

All the youths in the village were *réfractaires*. They would live in the village but leave for the woods the moment a German convoy was announced. We had regular evening *veillées* at the hotel, when the maquisards came together round bottles of wine. Much of the talk was about hunting: they all had their hunting guns. Eventually they all became part of the Maquis Aigoual-Cévennes.

The peasants were very poor. They made wine out of corn which was very bitter, they cut wood, made goat's cheese, and cooked with chestnuts. Our small child was two and a half in 1944, and for two months before the Liberation we ate chestnuts in varying ways for every meal. I myself cut wood and made charcoal. I was part of the village support system for the maquis, but I never joined them. I felt I was much older than they were.

MADAME. We called the maquisards 'les jeunes'; they were all related to the villagers. On one occasion when the Germans arrived and all the men had left for the woods, only the women were left in the little hotel. A German officer came in and said 'Aren't there any men in this village?' They decided to wait for them to return, and installed themselves in the hotel, drinking champagne and singing round the piano. They tried to get us to join in. But suddenly the order was given to leave. As they did so they said, 'Next time we come we'll burn the whole village.'

MONSIEUR. I saw the Germans arrive and jumped into the woods from the hotel. I was very anxious leaving the women like that. There were so many stories circulating about Germans killing women.

MADAME. On one earlier occasion when the Germans arrived I was knitting, alone with my little daughter and I was faced with a single German soldier who spoke French. He said he was looking for terrorists. I said, 'Who do you mean by terrorists?' He stayed a long time in a threatening way. When he left he said 'Filthy prostitute'.

MONSIEUR. After the war I wrote Occitan poems about the Resistance. The old Félibrige was completely bypassed by the Resistance. The new generation of Occitanists looked to the Institut d'Études Occitanes set up at the Liberation. It was a revolt against the older tradition. Resistance was the history of the ordinary people, of peasants, miners, and workers. Cathars, Camisards, Protestants, Resisters—they were all in revolt against central authority.

Henri Cordesse (Montpellier, Hérault, 22 March and 5 April 1982)

The difference between rural communities in the Haute-Lozère and those in the Cévennes was fundamental. In the Haute-Lozère they were mainly sympathetic to Vichy and very influenced by the big landowners and the

Bishop of Mende. I met widespread incomprehension in these areas.[40] I couldn't persuade them initially of the justice of our position. We had only one positive value in their eyes: *réfractaires* could provide useful labour. But things slowly began to change in June and July 1943 when *agriculteurs* were affected by STO. There were small pockets of republican anti-clerical peasants among the rest, who helped us enormously and by the end of 1943 their voice began to be heard by their neighbours, and Vichy was increasingly criticized. But it was a slow change. In the Cévennes, on the other hand, the maquisards were like fish in water. The Cévenol peasants had a strong commitment to freedom.

The first maquis in the Haute-Lozère was made up of committed anti-fascists and men from the International Brigades. There were several Austrians and Germans among them. Life was incredibly hard for them. The winter of 1942–3 was slow to clear in the Causses. To keep them we had to indulge in more and more illegal actions and in August 1943 I became clandestine, leaving my job as a schoolteacher. At the start of 1944 we took many of these anti-fascist maquisards into the Cévennes, where they were welcomed. The peasants there accepted everything except the overt provocations of the Maquis Bir-Hakeim, which exposed the communities to more risk than was necessary. The peasants there still refer to the Biraquins as 'voyous'. After 6 June 1944 the maquis in the Haute-Lozère finally became established. We were involved in operations at Mont Mouchet, and then grouped together many new maquis after the dispersal.

In the last months in the Haute-Lozère several individual maquisards took to dubious adventures, for their own benefit. Slang words like 'Do over' (e.g. 'Faire un bureau de tabac') and 'Pinch' ('piquer') became all the rage. It was difficult for those of us responsible to distinguish exactly when a peasant had been wrongly treated. The facts were not easy to establish. Towards the end we had to develop an alternative system of food distribution, when Vichy rule crumbled, and at that point you could say we started 'protecting' the peasants in that area, but not really before that, except in the Aubrac where we did seize animals which had been earmarked for the Germans and redistributed them to the maquis and the local population. But that was more a question of diverting goods than of 'protecting' the peasants.

It was vital for the maquis to establish an aura of force and power. Many people who never took part in an attack or a raid nevertheless welcomed the news that the maquis were doing something active. The maquisards had to create a climate of mystery and effectiveness. They were on the run and had made a political commitment. They had to make an impact. The use

[40] Henri Cordesse was born in 1910, was an *instituteur* at Marvejols in the Haute-Lozère, was leader of the AS and an organizer of the maquis in the *département*, and became Prefect of the Lozère at the Liberation. His background, early Resistance, and motivations are given in Kedward, *Resistance in Vichy France*, 278–80.

of any explosives was crucial for this. Some just enjoyed the sensation of having a pistol in their hands. We couldn't always pick these types out in advance. Our selection process wasn't sophisticated enough. But they were a minority. For most maquisards, however, it was still necessary to feel part of a fighting tradition, to live up to the 'images d'Épinal' of hard, tough warriors. And there was a mentality of 'war to the bitter end'. They were given no quarter by the Germans or the Milice, so they would show no mercy to collaborators. It was 'une mentalité terrible'. We saw maquisards whose sole aim was to revenge their comrades. This was difficult to keep under control, and it explains the blemishes in our history. There was a level of enthusiasm which it is impossible to represent in words. At the Liberation there was a spontaneous demand for justice. How does one account for the same scenes enacted everywhere, without any knowledge of what others were doing? Perhaps there is an element of truth in the notion that a victorious army always acts in the same way. The sexual retribution, in the shaving of heads and so on, was occasionally directed against pretty girls who had merely enjoyed going out to the cinema a lot. We touched rock bottom there. It demonstrated how merciless we could be. But such acts were exceptional, *not* the norm.

In the Haute-Lozère there was little consciousness of regionalist traditions. It's true that people took their history into their own hands, but it was not knowingly an Occitanist position. Gilbert de Chambrun, the regional FFI leader, made the connection between Occitanie and the maquis in a post-war fête at Marvejols, but no connection was made at the time. In fact in the Haute-Lozère the traces of the Huguenots in Marvejols, for example, had been lost over the years. But in the Cévennes it was quite the reverse. As schoolteachers we were, of course, the adversaries of Occitan language and culture. Recently that has changed considerably, but it was certainly the case in the 1930s and 1940s. I was born in 1910 and inherited Occitan as my mother tongue, but the post-1914 generation in the Haute-Lozère rarely grew up speaking Occitan. The older peasantry had to speak French for practical reasons, but between themselves they spoke Occitan and they trusted those who could understand it much more than those, like the workers from Clermont-Ferrand, who couldn't. That had its significance in the level of sympathy shown to different maquisards. After the war Occitanism was seen as having been associated with victory over the Germans, but that was a retrospective judgement. Again, in the Cévennes it was different, where the FTP round la Grand'Combe were mostly Cévenols, but even there you couldn't say Occitanism was a motivating force.

In sociological terms no one job or profession had a special relationship with the maquis. *Instituteurs* were prominent in the leadership because most of them had done their military service. But in the Haute-Lozère the *instituteurs* were not notable recruits for active Resistance. In the rural communes most *instituteurs* enjoyed being 'Le Maître' and were all for a quiet life. There were workers from Saint-Chély and from the metallurgical factories of Fouga at Béziers; there was eventually a good number of *agriculteurs*, and the miners from Alès and la Grand'Combe were heavily involved. In terms of sabotage, the SNCF workers were exceptional. There were no collaborators in any station on the line from Béziers through Sévérac, Marvejols, and Saint-Flour to Clermont-Ferrand. Not a single train got through from Sévérac to Saint-Flour between 7 June and the Liberation. The *cheminots* worked closely with the maquis; they were able to blame the maquis for all derailments, so they suffered very few arrests or reprisals. The commitment of the *cheminots* went back to the 1930s. Their union had been very hostile to Munich. Postal workers were also important. In the Haute-Lozère we couldn't have managed without the wives of the republican peasants I've already mentioned. Being a 'mère de famille' carried far more responsibility than being a 'père de famille': their involvement counted for more in that sense. Their risks and sacrifices were greater.

In the end some of the heroic legends of the maquis are an over-selective choice of the facts. They suppress the fear that maquisards experienced, and they underplay just how hard and difficult it all was.

Maurice and Berthe Pouget (Montpellier, Hérault, 24 May 1982)

MONSIEUR. I was born in 1914. I was *instituteur* in a small hamlet in the Haute-Lozère 8 km. from Marvejols and 8 from Saint-Chély. It was very isolated. The population was about 30. There were 16 children at the school, falling to 10. I'd been a trade-unionist before the war and had joined the Communist Party.

MADAME. I was mother of two children, the first born in 1940, the second in 1942.

MONSIEUR. The village was very Pétainist: made up of peasants who had small pieces of land, rearing animals, doing a bit of subsistence farming. Everyone had a small garden for vegetables. We had no problem with food.

MADAME. People came up on the train from Béziers and the south and got off at Saint-Sauveur station, and came and traded soap and oil for eggs, butter, and potatoes. There was no systematic *marché noir*. All very small stuff. Life wasn't difficult, though the bread was of very poor quality. People talked very little about the political situation, and told us nothing. They knew we were communists.

MONSIEUR. No, nobody knew that in the village, at the time. It's true that anyone with Gaullist sympathies in the commune had to keep very quiet.

MADAME. We had to watch what we said.

MONSIEUR. The first sign of any movement in opinion was over STO. The peasants thought the prisoners of war would return. When they didn't, the attitudes to STO changed. There were no *réfractaires* from the village. Another teacher called Pouget lived in the village where I was born, further south in the Lozère, the village of Massegros. He encouraged youths to go on STO.

MADAME. He was a real Pétainist. He became a Milicien. But his propaganda didn't work. The young went into the maquis.

MONSIEUR. I think he was a unique phenomenon among teachers in the *département*. Some *curés* were Pétainist. Others kept quiet and helped *réfractaires*. Teachers on the whole were ideologically opposed to Vichy.

MADAME. There was still a rivalry between church and school. Catholics were still in favour of private schools.

MONSIEUR. My brother-in-law from near Paris was designated for STO. He refused to go and came to Massegros and stayed with my mother, who delivered the post in the village. The gendarmes said, 'Who is this young man who doesn't speak patois, and who has a Paris accent?'

MADAME. Your mother told them to clear off—in patois!

MONSIEUR. He wasn't arrested. He stayed until the Liberation. He was a *réfractaire*, not a maquisard. One day a group of thirty maquisards came to our village and demanded food and drink. They weren't made particularly welcome, but they got what they needed. It was just after Mont Mouchet.

MADAME. They were just on their way through. There were also *voyous* who came to demand food. It was they who convinced the peasants that Henriot's broadcasts were right. The maquis *were* seen as terrorists.

MONSIEUR. Yes, they were seen in the Haute-Lozère as foreigners, *voyous*, and extortioners. After 6 June 1944 attitudes changed, but even then people were still suspicious. They couldn't accept that Henri Cordesse, a local *instituteur*, should become Prefect. A prefect ought to be someone important from above.

I was never involved in acts of Resistance—being lame since birth meant I couldn't walk without limping. I was very conspicuous. And the village was very isolated from maquis action.

MADAME. The village became very frightened after the reprisals at Paulhac in Mont Mouchet.

MONSIEUR. We kept our belief in the Resistance. In the school I had no truck with Pétainist activities, no singing of 'Maréchal, nous voilà'. The inspectors delayed my promotion.

The peasants would never have betrayed anyone to the authorities. Eventually two sides developed in the commune, pro- and anti-Pétain. But there was no betrayal. At the Liberation everyone danced in the village. They even unearthed their hunting guns and fired off a few shots.

MADAME. When it came to the elections the peasants realized they had been misled by Vichy.

MONSIEUR. The collaborationist mayor was defeated. He was a big landowner in the commune, but he left the area. People talk of thousands of people shot at the Liberation. It's not true.

MADAME. They ought to have shot a few more while they had the chance.

MONSIEUR. The other Pouget went off to fight in Russia. He never reappeared. His son also went into the Milice, and was killed fighting the maquis towards le Puy.

Maquisards returned to their anonymity. In the Haute-Lozère they have never been seen as heroes like the *poilus* in the First World War. They caused too much fear and were seen to undermine public order. But they probably have some respect now, finally. Books and histories have done them more justice.

François Rouan (Montpellier, Hérault, 25 February 1982)

I came from the mountainous region of Ariège, and went to the *lycée* at Foix. In 1934, aged 20, I took my engineering diploma at Aix-en-Provence at a college where 80 per cent of the students were influenced by Marxism. Called up for two years military service in October 1934, I was put in a closely supervised unit because of my political views. I went to Tunisia and Corsica, building fortifications and laying telecommunications, alongside young men on probation and from reform schools. I felt at home in their company, marginalized by the army. I reached the rank of sub-lieutenant, but when the Spanish Civil War broke out I deserted and went to fight against fascism. I think I was the only French officer to desert and arrive in Spain still in officer's uniform. My politics were Trotskyist, and for that reason I had been expelled from the Communist Party in 1934. I fought with the International Brigades and was wounded. On my return in 1938 I was put on trial for desertion and given two years, but was amnestied because my lawyer was a friend of Daladier. He had me sent to the Côte d'Ivoire to get me out of the way.

When war broke out I came back to France as part of the Bataillon de Tirailleurs from the Côte d'Ivoire. I was awarded the first Croix de Guerre in my area of the war and reintegrated into officer rank as captain. We fought all the way back to the Dordogne until the armistice was declared. I was given the job of taking the remainder of the Tirailleurs back to Africa, and once there I tried to escape to join the Free French sympathizers, but was arrested, sent back to Marseille and tried a second time for desertion. I was put in the Fort Saint-Jean which was occupied by the Légion Étrangère. The atmosphere was sympathetic to France Libre and I easily escaped, to return to my home region, the Ariège.

I spoke Catalan and Spanish and had numerous friends from Andorra and Spain who had been at the *lycée*. I was soon involved in a *groupe de passage*, which was well organized with excellent contacts with British Intelligence. We smuggled Poles, Czechs, and men from the RAF across the border, for which I later received the DSO. It became a movement of anti-fascist Resistance, grouping together immigrant miners, construction and forestry workers—all very ordinary men. We were, in our terms, the *real* MOI—that is, 'mouvement ouvrier internationaliste', which the PCF took over in 1941 and called 'Main d'Œuvre Immigrée', getting rid of 'internationaliste' with its Trotskyist associations. We were outlaws already and I was completely clandestine, living in miserable circumstances from hand to mouth. But then I had saved a little money. For the others life was very hard, and it remained hard in the maquis right through to the Liberation.

I was married in June 1942. My wife was in a Resistance group in Perpignan.[41] Her job as a cashier in the Grand Hôtel was excellent cover. But I was forced to go on the run and we left for Montpellier with false identity cards. It was easy to get them; everyone knew someone in a *mairie* who could arrange it. In Montpellier I was introduced to the groupe franc run by Combat, and in May 1943 I took to the maquis and was nominated leader of the AS maquis in the Lozère.

Our job was to run two kinds of maquis: maquis de planque where we hid, fed, and trained young recruits who had no military experience, and maquis de combat. We had high hopes of an Allied *débarquement* in the autumn of 1943. Our arms were a few carbines and mausers, and we made molotov cocktails. We spent much of the time walking to get food, covering some 40–50 km. a day. I was leader of a maquis of German anti-fascists, but became part of the Maquis Bir-Hakeim when it arrived in the Cévennes. As a well-known Trotskyist I was suspect to the FTP in the area.

Many in the maquis and in the groupes francs had been difficult, rebellious youths. They had come to prefer the risks and the beauty of revolt to the comforts of the home. It was a sort of *gauchisme*, 'avant le mot'. My wife was no less involved in risks: she undertook extremely dangerous liaison tasks for the maquis, travelling to and from Toulouse. She travelled in compartments full of German soldiers, as the best form of cover. They often carried her suitcases for her. She had a real nerve.

[41] Madame Rouan was initially present at the interview but did not stay. She wanted to say that she and her small child had been arrested by the Germans and she had suffered terribly at their hands and could no longer talk about it. François Rouan said she had been badly tortured for her Resistance activities.

In the Maquis Bir-Hakeim we never allowed requisitions or thefts. People gave us things, or we paid for them. We had two forgers in the maquis and had a supply of excellent forged money. We also received money through parachute drops, and we came to know people who were well placed to help us. We refused to be seen as bandits, or pillagers. We found out where the Germans were about to requisition potatoes, lentils, and butter and took the goods in advance, redistributing them to other maquis and the population. We supplied families with milk for their children, and often, for this reason, received gifts of food from people who were basically suspicious of the maquis. They knew we had a maquis police which dealt harshly with false maquisards and robbers.

German reprisals were atrocious. I'm still affected by the memory of les Crottes where all the population was massacred, including the very young. We had confronted a German force nearby, but were able to withdraw after inflicting considerable losses. They then turned on the village. It was the SS and the Milice combined. We couldn't have allowed for this; it was war, and ambushes had to be carried out suddenly when the information announcing a convoy arrived. We had no time to weigh up the possible consequences.

In the maquis, and in the support for the maquis, the role of *instituteurs* was important: they were the 'curés de la République', they came from the people, they had a high status in the villages, and they were consulted about everything. The sense of regional solidarity was important too. Right across from the Cévennes to the Ariège, the Languedoc was a unifying element. The Cévenols welcomed young men from the Ariège—they had the same thriftiness and capacity for hard, tiring work. There was certainly an Occitanist sentiment among them: Occitanie was 'la petite patrie': my parents spoke Occitan to us in the evenings, and it was usual for anecdotes and dirty jokes to be told in patois. It had more flavour. But we spoke French in the maquis—it was an international community.

In the Cévennes the Camisard tradition was vital. People were proud of its heritage. The youths from the area knew all the old Camisard hide-outs. The one near us at Calbertette, close to Saint-Germain-de-Calberte, was a veritable fortress. Only four men were needed to mount a full guard. And the Cévennes were a haven for refugees and foreigners. The Cévenols had their own individual faith: it wasn't always exactly what the *pasteur* wanted, but even though I was from a humanist, atheist background, I shared the same acute sense of conscience. We knew right from wrong.

At the Liberation, de Gaulle acknowledged the social demands by making certain reforms and nationalizations. But many maquisards left the maquis with a feeling that they had accomplished only half their task. We were proud, and we had been gratified when de Gaulle appointed Koenig as head of the FFI. He was famed for his victory at Bir-Hakeim, but he was also Jewish. Many maquisards became Gaullist supporters due to his appointment. The Jews in the maquis were formidable fighters, and very intelligent. They were some of the very best in the Resistance.

Henri and Madame Prades (Lattes, Hérault, 4 February 1982)

MONSIEUR. The maquis was hard, very hard, but at the same time it was exhilarating. We committed crimes in the maquis: it is still not easy to talk about them. But we were only 20 at the time. We did stupid things, like shaving women's heads at the Liberation. But there was also a lot of bravery. I was 22 in 1942, just married and we were living at Saint-Saturnin not far from Clermont-l'Hérault.[42] I'd finished at the École Normale in 1940 and was therefore an *instituteur*, but because my father was a foreigner Vichy law prevented me from teaching, although I was born and bred in the locality. I wasn't at all political. I was in the Chantiers de la Jeunesse in 1941–2, and organized Resistance acts, like sabotaging the deliveries of wood that were meant for the Germans. I was refused the normal good conduct reference when I left. I then kept my head down at home. In March 1943 I was called up for STO but managed to get a postponement until July. They kept coming for me. Finally I had to leave. My wife packed me a suitcase and I made as if to get the STO train from Montpellier and picked up my 1,000 fr. but went to Ganges instead.

MADAME: I was from Ganges and knew the mayor. All the *mairie* were in the Resistance, all Protestants, making false identity cards for the *réfractaires*. I was there too, and on 19 July I went into labour with our first child.

MONSIEUR: I had to leave. I'd been told to go to Ardaillès in the massif de l'Aigoual where Pasteur Olivès had organized a group. But it was just after the German attack on Aire-de-Côte, and we had to disperse.

Two of us went down towards le Vigan. Not all the peasants were hospitable. They were frightened, some of them. An old woman refused me a piece of cheese. We got to Aulas, where the *institutrice* directed us to a nearby farm. We knocked at the door. Imagine the scene: they were all seated round the large table, the patriarch, an old woman, and five or six children from very young to aged 20. The peasant was a veteran of 1914–18 and very patriotic. They sat us at the table for a meal, then lodged us in fresh hay in the barn. We slept for twenty-four hours. Eventually we made contact with the others in the Aigoual; we cut wood and made charcoal. In

[42] Monsieur Prades did most of the talking in this interview, but Madame Prades continuously reminded him of names and facts, and provided him with corrections to his story. They frequently spoke together.

1944 I was sent to make contact with Bir-Hakeim which was then near Clermont-l'Hérault at Mourèze. I stayed with the maquis there. It was near the village where my wife was *institutrice.*

In Bir-Hakeim most were young *agriculteurs* from the region, but there were also those who had fought in the International Brigades; some came from Paris, others from the Aveyron, Lozère, and everywhere. There were teachers and doctors in the group too. Demarne and Rouan were the leaders: Demarne was anti-communist, Rouan was a Trotskyist. Demarne was very outward-going, imprudent, and went around with a revolver in his hand. Rouan was very cautious—the epitome of cunning and calculation.

We were hardly ever refused food at this time—spring and summer 1944—but we had to requisition from wholesalers. We promised reimbursement at the Liberation. We also requisitioned a bank once, but we never burgled houses. What we did was to go to well-known Vichy or pro-German families and demand things directly from them.

Life in the maquis? Never a dull moment. We were always training or carrying out *coups de main.* We used to mix with the local villagers, so the men had no sexual hang-ups. We weren't an isolated maquis up in the woods away from everything: in fact not many were in this region. The local peasants were mostly left wing and very sympathetic. Being an outlaw was just right for me. It was an extraordinary feeling.

MADAME: It was the optimism and hope that were extraordinary.

MONSIEUR: I got to the point where the possibility of being killed just wasn't important.

MADAME: And there were such deep friendships.

MONSIEUR: I've never known such friendship—right across the political spectrum. They were all like brothers.

Our achievement was to create a climate of insecurity and panic for the Germans. When Demarne was killed the Germans celebrated. We were that important. The women were the *agents de liaison.* They did a terrific job. They looked after the wounded and provided food and clothes.

MADAME: What the women did was just as dangerous as the actions undertaken by men. Women were often taken as hostages. I myself hid grenades in the empty desks in my classroom. But no search was ever made.

Robert Bonnafous (Saint-Geniès-des-Mourgues, Hérault, 26 February 1982)

I was only 17 when I was forced to leave for the maquis. A friend and I had discovered Gestapo codes in the PTT at Montpellier, but we had left tracks and fingerprints. My friend was arrested so I left. The contact point was a small hotel in Montpellier where I was told what to do: to take a train into the country and get off at a small station where I would be met by a man holding a newspaper. It was 6 June 1944. I did exactly this and we walked a further 5 km. into Clermont-l'Hérault. I spent a night there and was then collected by a maquisard who was procuring food. We walked through the *garrigue* to a farm amidst the rocks. Everyone was huddling under the bit of roof that was left. It was pouring with rain. I had arrived at the Maquis Bir-Hakeim which had been regrouped after the massacre at la Parade. My father had been in the police but had died in 1938. I was still at school, but all the police of Montpellier knew me. There was an *ex-chef de la gendarmerie* in the thirty or so maquisards I had joined.

I was immediately given a *nom de guerre*. It was forbidden to reveal your real name. I'd spent two months in the Compagnons de France, but my generation more and more resented the imposition of Pétainism, all the flag-saluting and praise for the Maréchal. In Montpellier we had been really hungry. We had wine but nothing else. We resented the peasants who had plenty to eat. I was still very suspicious of them when I got to the maquis, but although I was a town dweller I loved the country. We certainly didn't terrorize the locals. We protected them. It was important to come from the region—you got on much better with them if you did. Anyway the maquis had 'specialists' in making good relationships with the peasants. The rest of us stayed in the maquis.

At my age I thoroughly enjoyed being an outlaw. It was very like Robin Hood. I used to go barefoot. Every time we killed a German I would be offered his shoes. And the camaraderie was marvellous—risking your life for your friends. To begin with I was too young for military action. I'd had no training at all. When I arrived we had very few weapons. But there was a series of parachute drops and eventually we were well stocked—even with anti-tank guns.

The combats of the Liberation were my first taste of war. We were about 300 by then. I can say that Bir-Hakeim genuinely liberated Montpellier, but the Combat de Montferrier just afterwards wasn't really a great battle. If anything it was a military error, a rather ridiculous confrontation, just a few guns against a whole German column. I'm speaking now as an army officer—I stayed in the army after the war. I believe the maquis were necessary, but we could have done with more military leadership. The army officers of the time joined too late and did too little. After the Liberation the regular officers were scornful of the maquisards, they treated them like the Armée d'Afrique. We were split up and not allowed to fight as maquis units: but militarily that was better.

No one ever mentioned politics in Bir-Hakeim. Rouan, the leader, was a revolutionary but he was also very circumspect. At the Liberation it was the civilians and the milices patriotiques who went berserk and shot a whole lot of people who were merely petty criminals, or who had done nothing. And some of the so-called Miliciens who were shot were only kids, 16 or 18 years old. Those who shot them were the real bastards. They had been frightened during the Occupation and now they took it out on others. When we saw what was happening we retired outside Montpellier. After we had left, the milices patriotiques strutted round the town with their weapons, taking all the glory.

I spent nine years in Germany after the war, twinned with a German unit. I love the Germans, with their courage and organization. The great tragedy was that we had to go to war with them at all. What is Nazism? There were Nazis and Nazis. Some came from old traditional families who realized Hitler could restore the country. And he did. When we crossed into Germany we found the workers' flats really well furnished. There was nothing like that in France.

Michel Bancilhon (Aubenas, Ardèche, 5 July 1982)

I was born in 1917. In 1939 I was mobilized into the air force. After the defeat I returned to my profession as an architect, working at Aubenas for the Ponts et Chaussées. I was contacted by General Cochet's network and formed the first Cochet group in the area, distributing tracts in 1941–2, and demonstrating hostility to the Légion des Combattants by graffiti and fly-posting. Very few members of the professional middle classes were involved in Resistance at this time. At the end of 1942 I was contacted by Pierre Limagne on behalf of Combat and asked to form the Armée Secrète in the south of the Ardèche. The maquis only started after STO. Our job was to hide, feed, and equip the *réfractaires*. It was a sort of *Intendance*. There were already numerous Jews in hiding in the area, and we had to burgle the *mairies* and steal materials to make false identity and ration cards for them. I myself sheltered Jews in my house. There were about 30 or 40 of us in Aubenas involved in these acts of refuge—seeking out farms in the mountains, contacting peasant farmers. It was slowly built up, bit by bit, gradually. At the same time we formed groups of six within the AS and began to look for possible *terrains de parachutages*.

There was no opposition from the peasants. One or two mistrusted us, but provided the *réfractaires* behaved themselves they were very sympathetic. The problem came later with *faux maquisards*. Whereas we would burgle a *mairie* in the locality making sure we had the agreement of the mayor and the staff, with them it was different. It's true we were involved in illegal actions, such as making off with a whole truck of tobacco at Largentière, and this enabled *voyous* to rob and steal as if they were maquisards. But peasants were really very helpful. When we wanted a van or lorry to transport potatoes or new recruits into the maquis a peasant would always lend us one. By the end of 1943 we had set up quite an organization.

The Ardèche had always been a republican area—fairly to the Left. My sector of the AS was socialist-inclined, with several communists. But there were all sorts—bridging the main divide in the region which had always been between Protestants and Catholics. I myself was a Protestant, but I got plenty of support from Catholics and *curés*. Aubenas was really a market town, not a big town like Valence or Lyon. There was no hostility with the surrounding countryside. Peasants would send food to relatives in the town. Of course everyone used the black market, especially for meat. The peasants were mostly very poor: they had to earn their living. Naturally they put up the prices, but on the whole there was very little extortion. No, the peasants were very amenable to *all* our approaches. I'll tell you an anecdote. At the end of 1943 a maquis was formed at an altitude of 1,200 metres on the edge of the mountains of Gerbier-de-Jonc and the rumour spread among the maquisards that local peasants were about to denounce them. So we dressed up one of our group as a Milicien and he went from farm to farm asking for any information about the outlaws. He was turned away by everyone; peasants in this area don't talk. And the *curé* in the area spoke up for us from the pulpit.

In the winter of 1943–4 life was very tough for the maquisards. I'd got married in 1943, but had to leave my wife somewhere safe, while I moved from place to place. There was little we could do at that stage to harm the Germans, and anyway the German garrison at Aubenas was harmless enough, just territorials. They showed no interest in us. But early in 1944 we began to sabotage railways and disrupt German transport in the Rhône valley. But we had no arms until the first parachute drop in February 1944. It was my job to recover all the containers. My team picked up all drops in the area until 6 June. We were all activists in the local Resistance. Another anecdote: I knew one *attentiste*, who had been left-wing before the war and took it on himself to distribute tracts saying 'Don't attack the Germans'. He had a large beard. I took him to the barber's and had his beard shaved off. Then I took him home. That was it: no more trouble. But when we took Privas a number of men turned up in army uniforms who had done nothing in the Resistance. It disgusted us. I took my 300 men and said 'Let's go'—so we just left.

The Resistance was very strong in the public services—railways, postal services, and Ponts et Chaussées. It was particularly effective in the PTT. We knew everything about German movements direct from the post office in Valence. One official in the PTT at Largentière put a telephone line completely at our disposal, cutting out all risk of being overheard. The PTT was incredibly important to us.

By June 1944 we had 2,400 men in the southern Ardèche structured into companies, equipped with arms, but still mostly living at home. After 6 June they all took to the maquis. The whole organization owed an incredible amount to a Spanish anarchist who had fought in the Spanish Civil War and had become a communist. He gave us all the know-how and ideas about forming the companies—about sixty to seventy men in each. I had nothing to do with the politics of the Resistance—I kept to the military side. In the end I was attached to the FTP. I had some disagreements with certain career officers in the AS but that's another story. Yves Farge approached me to be a *sous-préfet*. I refused. Why? What would my men have thought if I had taken it? I was a military man: I'd led them into action. I wasn't looking for a political reward. Far from it. Quite the opposite.

We hadn't wanted a civil war. It was forced on us. We made several punitive attacks on Miliciens before 6 June 1944. Most Milice came from outside the locality. We had to kill them: it was war. They were enemies. As for the *épuration* I don't know how many people were shot, perhaps forty in the whole *département*. I can't say; certainly not hundreds. Some maquisards said we were disinherited at the Liberation, but on the whole I don't think we were. Of course we thought we were the best: after all, we had done the fighting, but you couldn't base a new society just on that. We didn't liberate France by ourselves. We needed the Allies.

Édouard Montcouquiol and Jean Pujadas
(La Chapelle-sous-Aubenas, Ardèche, 6 July 1982)

MONTCOUQUIOL. The first maquis were not set up by young men. They came out of the Resistance networks run by older people from all sorts of jobs. We all had the same love of freedom. We were, if you like, 'la classe républicaine'. No party politics, though. I was an *agriculteur*, and had fought in 1940.

PUJADAS. My Resistance started in 1936 in the Spanish war. I fought the whole war against the fascism of Franco. I came to France as a republican refugee, and in 1940 I was sent to work in a factory in the Doubs. As the Germans advanced we evacuated the factory to Aubenas. By profession I was a cinema mechanic.

MONTCOUQUIOL. From late 1942 onwards my job in the Resistance was to find places to hide *réfractaires* and refugees, and set them up with some sort of work. They came from Spain, the north, Paris. Most just wanted food and shelter.

PUJADAS. They were simple *réfractaires*, but then that took some courage, since there could be reprisals against the parents. And then, there were those of us who organized false identity cards, and started to create structured companies. But we had very few arms, just a few hunting guns.

MONTCOUQUIOL. Ninety per cent of the peasants were on our side. We couldn't have managed without them. At first it was easy to hide individuals, but once we tried to create groups it was much more difficult. We seriously lacked experienced leaders. Youths of 18 not surprisingly made lots of mistakes. I had some military training from the war, and an ideological training too, from trade-union activity before the war. We had been anti-militarist at the time: we fought in 1940 almost against our will.

PUJADAS. The maquis wasn't the regular army. You hid, emerged for an ambush, harassed the enemy, then withdrew. I had to go round all the groups showing them how to use the weapons dropped by parachute. The instructions were all in English, and nobody understood English. It was not easy, with so many different nationalities to explain to—Germans, Yugoslavs, Poles, and so on. Our *agents de liaison* were mostly women, but there were no women in the maquis, not even as nurses. We had access to the hospital at Aubenas due to a sympathetic surgeon and most of the nursing staff.

The Maquis Bir-Hakeim came into our area briefly. They were crazy. You couldn't take on the Germans like that: they left the villages open to reprisals. It couldn't be an open war. It was guerrilla war. We had learnt it the hard way in the wars against Napoleon.

We got very little help from the regular army officers and those who were running the Chantiers de la Jeunesse. The Chantiers were never a training ground for Resistance. If the leaders joined us it was only when they knew the Germans had lost.

MONTCOUQUIOL. We were all outlaws. We're still seen that way.

PUJADAS. No, no I don't think so.

MONTCOUQUIOL. Yes. The regular army officers still treat us as outlaws. Because we were once against the law we'll always be seen as 'terrorists'.

PUJADAS. No. I was a 'terrorist' once. Not now. Even then I was not against the law, but against Nazi and fascist law.

MONTCOUQUIOL. Once a terrorist, always a terrorist in their eyes. Take the gendarmes who joined us. Their careers were ruined. They've been denied promotion.

PUJADAS. I don't think we were disinherited.

MONTCOUQUIOL. Not us personally. But in the administration if you had been in the maquis it wasn't easy to become a *fonctionnaire*. Those who were used to being in command found it very difficult to accept that maquisards were in control. We did want social change, and there were big deceptions in that area.

PUJADAS. But the Liberation was made by everyone, not just idealists. There were politicians too. Idealists like to believe that what they think is true. Politicians have to deal with reality. We had beaten fascism. France was a free country. Normal administration took over. We were a democracy. You have to let the people decide. De Gaulle's government had communists and socialists, all sorts. It represented the whole country. And there were elections to find out what people wanted.

It hadn't been a civil war. Not French against French, but France against the German occupiers and the collaborators. Most of France was on the side of Resistance.

MONTCOUQUIOL. But Pétain was our enemy. We were sold out in 1940. Vichy was against the Popular Front. I know. I was seen as a dangerous 'red'. I wasn't a communist at all, but I'd been involved in trade unions and I'd been anti-militarist. I was seen as a public danger.

PUJADAS. No. We were fighting the Germans and fascism. We never mounted a single operation against the police force of Vichy. It was nothing like two armies against each other, as in Spain.

Raymond Fournier (Rodès, Pyrénées-Orientales,[43] *23 March 1982)*

I was a Resister from the moment we were literally handed over to the Germans at Angoulême in 1940. I knew we had been betrayed. I was 20 at the time, a native of the Aveyron and a recently qualified teacher in the *cours complémentaire* at Saint-Affrique. I was lucky to get back there and not become a prisoner of war. I'd been associated with the Jeunesses Communistes since Munich but I was first contacted in Saint-Affrique by Combat. In the winter of 1942–3 I was given the job of finding hiding-places for *réfractaires*. I was soon completely clandestine, living under a false name, but was giving lessons in Spanish. In 1943 the police came looking for me. I would certainly have been arrested and deported had it not been for the quick thinking of an *institutrice*, Mlle Salvignol, who put out her bicycle, warning me to escape. It was 4 May 1943 and I went from one schoolteacher to another, including my sister who taught at Salelles. Whenever I was in trouble I could depend on colleagues to cover me. Schoolteachers were prominent in the Resistance: their *laïc* tradition and hostility to Vichy made them ready to defend democracy.

I was still attached to the AS and took to the mountains. I was in good physical shape and could walk very long distances. I carried a revolver with

[43] This was Monsieur Fournier's home at the time of the interview, but his maquis activity had been in the Aveyron. Rodès, his home, should not be confused with Rodez, the *chef-lieu* of the Aveyron.

me that I'd been given by another teacher. I went from place to place encouraging groups to set up small maquis camps, but I felt I was kept at arm's length by the AS because of my communist sympathies. They seemed to set up endless committees but they didn't trust me with crucial information or give me any important job to do. I was living dangerously, moving around such a lot, but I eventually came into contact with the Front National and was appointed to regional responsibility for the FUJP, young people who were ready to help the maquis and join it whenever possible. From that job I became responsible for the FTP in the Aveyron.

A maquis needed to be a good size to protect itself and secure food. If you'd been on guard all night you needed to rest in the day. We could have established maquis with 200 men as early as January 1944 but it wasn't advisable. Such a large grouping only made sense when we were in control of the terrain, not until July and August 1944. Our maquisards came mostly from the locality, but there were miners from the north who had come to the mines at Carmaux, and Spanish and Poles in good number. The French maquisards were *réfractaires* on the whole. Becoming a *réfractaire* was an act of Resistance. Every *réfractaire* was a Resister, but not yet a combatant, not yet a maquisard. Those who joined the maquis were mostly workers to begin with, because peasants were protected from STO but you have to think dynamically. The situation changed and we had young *agriculteurs, fonctionnaires*, salaried employees, a bit of everything, eventually. The same with politics: all shades of opinion were represented.

A maquis tended to form round a leader. Leaders weren't imposed on a group from outside. To be a leader you had to have a certain dynamism and yet be careful and prudent. Everyone in the *département* knew who I was, but I didn't get to know the real names of the FTP leaders until after the Liberation.

For food and tobacco we tended to pay with *bons de réquisition*. We didn't steal. If we took things without promising payment it was *une prise de guerre*, for example a raid on a Milicien for clothes, weapons, and food. We did demand money from post offices and banks, but again these were official requisitions on behalf of the Resistance. An anecdote: I was in Saint-Affrique, and a tobacconist whom I knew fairly well told me to come and take his stock of tobacco. So I readily agreed. Only later did I realize that he had sold half of his quota on the black market, far above the controlled prices, and to avoid suspicion and probable imprisonment he arranged for us to take the rest. He then told the authorities that the maquis had taken the whole stock. The peasants also sold above market prices, but they were poor, and only made a bit extra. It was the big stockists who kept goods away from the market and then released them gradually at hugely inflated prices: they were the real *marché noir*. Not the peasantry.

There were no discernible regional traditions in the Aveyron which helped the maquis, not really. It wasn't a revolutionary *département*. No one in our circles of the FTP thought in regional terms, and no one spoke Occitan. In fact Occitan had been killed by the very *instituteurs* who were in the Resistance: we were the agents of centralization. Some *curés* continued to speak it, and even preach in Occitan. I don't think the destruction of Catalan in the Pyrénées-Orientales was nearly so complete. It was more used there.

The shortage of arms in the FTP was a major blunder by the British, the Americans, and the Gaullists. It was idiotic to think the FTP was totally communist. Out of twelve FTP maquis in the Aveyron, ten were led by non-communists. The Allies and the BBC encouraged us to resist and take to the maquis, and then they refused to arm us. It was a crime. So many young maquisards died because they hadn't the necessary weapons. By contrast the maquis ORA had plenty, but didn't use them until the end. And they were often made up of officers who had been Pétainist until late in the war. The Allies and de Gaulle were basically afraid of popular maquis, those that had grown at the grass roots. They were afraid of action by ordinary people. But if we hadn't acted, the soul of France would have been crushed.

At the Liberation we were received with joy in Rodez. There were a few stains on the maquis record, but they were not typical. We caught and shot those who pillaged or terrorized the population. In no sense was it a civil war: the vast majority of French people backed the Resistance. How can people call it a civil war when there was only a handful of collaborators? The maquis, however, certainly felt disinherited. Nobody wanted us. We were undesirables. Although I went on to command a battalion in the last months of the war, I was refused a teaching job in the Aveyron when I returned. They would only offer me one in Calvados. And I was nominated for the Légion d'Honneur, but never received it. I'm glad really: I have the honour of not having it! Even the Communist Party was suspicious of the maquis. They had to demolish the prestige of Guingouin and Charles Tillon. I'm still a nominal member, but not very active.

My wife-to-be was also in the Resistance. She was 17 at the time in the Lozère, a proud descendant of the Camisards. The local farms were full of maquisards, and she and her younger sister guided new recruits to these farms. She became, in effect, both a recruiting agent and an *agent de liaison*. The role of women was *so* important. Take Madame Lacan at Rodez: she was a saint. She ran a small restaurant and she created *partisans* and *partisanes* around her. She was sensational.

Pierre Boyer (Saint-Affrique, Aveyron, 24 June 1991)

I did my eight months in the Chantiers de la Jeunesse in 1941–2. I had no choice. I was just 20 in 1940 and had tried to volunteer for the army, but they sent me home, and soon after it was the Armistice. What had made me really angry was the Italian declaration of war, a real stab in the back. So I did the Chantiers, but I've often wondered why at least 99 per cent of those called up to do so went along without protest. Why weren't there more *réfractaires* from the Chantiers? Our camp was at Bousquet-d'Orb in the Hérault: we did a bit of road-mending, made charcoal, cut trees. But it wasn't a deliberate training for the Resistance or maquis. We were all in line behind Pétain at the time.

When I got back to Saint-Affrique, helping in my father's wholesale grain business, I got involved in a few gestures of Resistance, like breaking the windows of collaborators, but for me the turning point was STO. I was one of the first called up in March 1943. There were forty of us, and thirty-six went off to Germany. My parents were friendly with Monsieur Freychet, the directeur général of Roquefort cheese: he was the pioneer of Resistance in the area, and he piloted me away from STO into an outlying farm. I was also helped by the Protestant *pasteur* in Saint-Affrique who was a Belgian and an early Resister. My family was one of about a hundred Protestants in the town. Many of the thirty-six who went would like to have escaped but didn't know how to do so, or where to go. I was lucky to have this family contact with the Resistance, and the gendarmes didn't want to know. They asked a few questions then turned a blind eye.

As the year went on the number of us in the farms grew considerably, all placed there by the AS. Occasionally we would rendezvous for an operation of some kind, and then go back to our different farms. The peasants were pleased to have the extra labour. They fed us and gave us somewhere to sleep, but we did *them* a favour as well. None of the *réfractaires* was paid. It wasn't my ideal situation, working in the fields and looking after sheep. I wanted to handle a machine-gun and dreamed of being a combatant. The special brigade set up by the police chief Marty came looking for me at one point; I don't know why me. I must have been denounced I suppose. Luckily I was away from the farm at the time. But I was then sent to a more isolated place in the hills near Saint-Sernin-sur-Rance. I was a *réfractaire*, living like that for over a year—until the end of April 1944. It was Freychet's plan to keep us all in the farms until the time was right to create a maquis. Some of the earlier maquis lived miserably throughout the winter, sleeping in caves, with water dripping down on them, unable to light fires in case they were seen.

On 4 May 1944 I was called to become group leader of about ten to twelve maquisards. We moved continuously, about twelve to fifteen times, in a radius of about 30 km. round Saint-Affrique. We became part of the Maquis Paul Claie, named after Freychet's *agent de liaison* who was caught in Rodez. The Germans believed at first he was the leader, but when they thought he might be covering for someone they increased the torture. He swallowed his cyanide pill to make sure he never betrayed Freychet. The tactics of the maquis were Freychet's own: we remained in small groups, which grew from ten to thirty to fifty, living in separate camps and always on the move. The Germans never attacked us directly in the hills. Our losses were all on the roads when we confronted them or were caught in an ambush. Our orders were to wait until Jour-J, but the actions we staged after the Normandy landings didn't increase dramatically. It was more the run-up to the landings in Provence which brought us the most active combat. In organizational terms we lacked good, trained, military leaders. Far too few of the regular army officers joined us. We never talked politics—even though we had plenty of opportunity. Mounting guard all night gave you ample time for discussing things. But politics, never. There were Germans, Poles, Austrians, all sorts in the maquis as a whole.

An anecdote: I was chosen to meet de Gaulle's special envoy to the area. I was very proud. We were near Montlaur at the time. I put on a smart civilian suit and went down into the village of Lapeyre for the rendezvous. I went into the local café: everyone looked at me. I asked the patron if he had seen anyone. He said no. After a while an odd-looking character trundled up on a bicycle, wearing a traditional Breton beret. I thought this can't possibly be the special envoy. But it was. We exchanged pass words and went off, he on the bicycle, me on foot back to the maquis. He slept on a hay mattress just like the rest of us. We were amazed: to us de Gaulle was a kind of god.

The liberation of Saint-Affrique occurred shortly before we went on to the liberation of Montpellier. The German garrison in Saint-Affrique was mostly made up of Russians. They were only too happy to surrender. Not a shot was fired. Earlier, our maquis had made a pact with the German garrison commander, Colonel Muntzer, that if he didn't attack the maquis we would not attack him. He kept his word, and when we caught him by coincidence in an ambush, we kept ours. He was allowed to go free, and take the German wounded back to the hospital in Saint-Affrique. As a gesture of gratitude he gave us 2 million francs which had been hidden in one of the German cars. Before that, four or five German officers had turned up to a Protestant bazaar in the town. They sat down with everyone else and produced a large box of cigarettes which they said was to be sold in aid of the maquis.

At the liberation of Montpellier I was in a special maquis unit—a sort of maquis police. So I was in the town for several days. I was shocked to see the Tribunal Militaire try young collaborators in groups of ten, and sentence them all to death. And it wasn't the Resistance or the maquis who shaved women's heads and paraded them around naked in a cart. It was people who had done nothing in the Resistance. Most of my comrades from the maquis joined up in the army, and I noticed that the regular troops who had landed in Provence seemed to be prejudiced against the FTP. They said we were OK if we were FFI but not if we were FTP. I myself didn't join up. My father's grain business had collapsed during the war: he had probably been too generous. He was at his wits' end, so I had to go back and help him out.

Looking back I have to say that it wasn't the maquis who liberated France. The Germans in the Aveyron were frightened of us. They thought we were far bigger than we really were. At the end they were psychologically scared and exhausted. We found them collapsed over their motorbikes, all in. We achieved that. That was something. But when I see the rows and rows of American graves in Normandy; Canadian graves, British graves. That's an entirely different level. We kept our heads high; we participated in the Liberation, but we owe everything to them. We didn't have the means to do more. And then the French people in their forties and fifties did very little. Apart from a few older leaders, it was left to the young to do something.

Joseph Nodari (Cahors, Lot, 28 March 1991)

I was there right at the start of the Maquis France in the spring of 1943, started by Jean-Jacques Chapou. I knew his family—he was worth his weight in gold. I came from Lalbenque and was basically a peasant. I did a bit of everything: I knew everyone, I knew the whole area. I was young, only 21, and they made me an *agent de liaison*. I spoke patois and was a real local. The maquis was always on the move, from one stone building to another. People were very helpful—especially in the village of Belfort-du-Quercy: they were terrific. Lalbenque wasn't bad, Aujols quite good; at Cremps there was a sympathetic *curé*. Most of our food was given to us. Chapou was very strict: there was no requisitioning without payment. We never stole anything. If Chapou heard that a maquisard had committed a robbery he punished him. He never accepted a maquisard without checking him first.

I was there on 11 November 1943 when he occupied Marcilhac and laid a wreath at the *monument aux morts*. Most of the population were overjoyed, but some were hostile. We had no arms at the time, just a couple of revolvers from the First World War and a hunting gun. The winter was very hard. We lived in barns and it was very cold. Then we moved into the empty château of Loubejac. That was much better. But we were betrayed from within, by Hercule who came from up north, and the Germans burned down the château. Hercule had been an infiltrator for six months: I'd slept alongside him all over the place. He was eventually caught in the north after the Liberation: a maquisard recognized him in a cinema. He was brought to Cahors and shot.

My *nom de guerre* was 'Favoris' because I had long sideburns. I had to travel huge distances. I did Caylus to Cahors and back in one night: about 80 km. On foot. I sometimes had a bike. The gendarmerie had to be watched. They were OK in Belfort and in Castelnau, but not in Lalbenque. You had to suspect everyone. The safest towns were Cahors and Figeac. There were gangs of *faux maquisards* who robbed people. There's no way I could have done that. I was too well known by everyone. I was punished once by Chapou for going on leave without permission. But on the whole I was left to my own devices to find ways of doing the job. I supplied food, I took messages, I collected arms from parachute drops. I was never in one place for long. Only Chapou knew where I was.

I loved dancing. I used to go to local dances, which were forbidden at the time. We danced to a gramophone. We also played a football match between two maquis units, France and Jean Bart. It was near Belfort. Some Germans passed us in the train and cheered. They had no idea it was the maquis. Then another time I went to my brother's at the village of Saint-Hilaire. His boss was there with his son who was a *réfractaire* but hadn't joined the maquis. He was courting in Vaylats and asked if he could wear my clothes to impress his fiancée. I agreed. I gave him my clothes but not my revolver. I put it on the table. He went to Vaylats, and we played cards. One of the players banged his cards down on the table; the revolver fell to the ground and went off, shooting his brother in the thigh. We had to get the bullet out on the kitchen table. Whenever he sees me now he says, 'you're the one who shot me in the arse'.

At the Liberation we were ignored. Those who had done nothing got the medals. We were left empty-handed. But we'd often gone two to three days without eating. We came from all parts of France; there were sailors from the south coast; the first three members of Maquis France came from Cahors, the fourth and fifth from Paris. I was never caught, but I was fired at. The bullet broke a branch between my legs. I was lucky. I always carried a grenade. I wouldn't have been taken alive. I could tell a lot of stories: I got on well with people, though I didn't like Colonel Georges. I was never a communist—and no one in the FTP was ever asked if they were communists or not. At the Liberation they executed twelve people in Cahors: one execution of a mere kid was a total injustice. Chapou would never have allowed it to happen if he had been alive.

Maurice Darnault (Pradines, Cahors, Lot, 7 March 1991)

I returned to Cahors in October 1942, on leave from the North African army which I had joined in 1940. I was 22 in 1943 and had turned clandestine, pursued by the Renseignements Généraux. I had been a member of the young communists since 1937, and was also wanted for STO. In May 1943 I joined the Maquis France, created by Jean-Jacques Chapou. There were twelve of us, and I contacted other groups to see if we could unite together. I didn't meet Colonel Georges until much later. Colonel Collignon was one of the local leaders, but Chapou was mainly responsible. The different maquis groups were called France, Jean Bart, République, Liberté, Imbert, and Gabriel Péri. In February 1944 they all passed into the FTP because the FTP in the Corrèze and the Haute-Vienne were seen as more active than the AS. Some stayed or went into the Groupes Vény and the ORA, but the vast majority followed Chapou.

We were involved in very few actions before we became FTP. Most of the villagers and rural workers helped us—and no one really worried about whether maquisards were communists or not. Some 80–90 per cent of the maquisards were non-political. Chapou became a communist but he would probably have reverted to trade-unionism and socialism after the war. At first we were mainly looking for places to hide, close to villages. There were very few Germans around initially, but when we occupied Cajarc in April 1944 it was to divert Germans, the GMR, and the Milice from repressive campaigns in the Corrèze. Before that, we were constantly on the move from one building to another. Life was very hard and we had little to eat, often only a few onions. We wanted to do something useful, more than just *coups de main* for ration cards. We wanted to fight. The gendarmes turned a blind eye for the most part. But the Milice were far more dangerous, infiltrating in plain clothes. We attacked the Chantiers de la Jeunesse and dressed in their uniforms. Uniforms were an important proof that we were soldiers. Discipline was tight, and the structure of command was well organized. Chapou refused to countenance any thefts. We found people who would give us things, and supply us regularly with food.

To begin with we were called by our Christian names, Pierre or Maurice—but soon there were Pierre I, Pierre II, and Pierre III, so we gave each other *noms de guerre*. We didn't choose our own. I was called Bayard, after the sixteenth-century Chevalier Bayard who was known as the 'Chevalier sans peur et sans reproche'. Winter was very tough. Our cuisine was very basic and we had to avoid all smoke. We went from shepherds' huts to isolated barns, often using the local *gariottes, bories*, or *cazelles*. We moved almost every week, our numbers sometimes fragmenting to a mere three or four. But in the late spring of 1944 we formed military companies according to the order of original formation, Maquis France as Company No. 1, Jean Bart Company No. 2, and so on. Jean Bart had been named after the famous seventeenth-century sailor, when a contingent of young naval servicemen from Toulon landed up in Cahors, and I was made *commissaire des effectifs* in the company. Up until 6 June 1944 we were the army of the woods, but the volunteers came thick and fast after that and we were unprepared and inadequately armed to incorporate them all.

In all the months of hiding and moving there were no problems about our sexual life. We were relatively well known in the villages, and took part in occasional dances. People met up and relationships were made. For example, I met my future wife at Loubejac where we occupied the château for over three weeks. The whole village was involved in helping us. My fiancée's parents, Alexandre and Marie Lafon, did marvels for us, procuring flour to make bread, killing sheep and calves for us. Ernest Fournier was equally supportive, and Élizabeth Roques, widow of a First World War veteran, made us jam and was a mother to us all. The neighbouring village of Souques also provided us generously with food. The maquisards were originally from Cahors and towns in the north of France, but later there were many young rural workers. Very few used local patois—perhaps two or three out of the thirty in Jean Bart. Regionalism was unimportant. People came from all parts. There were anarchists from Spain, many of whom were troublesome in other areas, but Chapou knew how to discipline them.

We liberated Cahors, but that is quite an impressive-sounding word. In fact the Germans left first, but we had certainly played an important role in harassing the German retreat. In the ambushes we confronted the Germans head on, especially in the area bordering on the Corrèze where our relationships with the Corrèze FTP were vital in co-ordinating action. After the Liberation the Lot saw very little *épuration.* If there was any settling of scores it was done by people who had done little of the fighting. The Lot was really quite united. It is very small in numbers—more like one large village—everyone knew everyone else. It meant that relationships between *statiques* in the towns and the *tactiques* in the field (i.e. the maquis) were always good. The *statiques* were not necessarily communist, though most were in the Front National.

Pierre and Reine Labie (Lalbenque, Lot, 11 March 1991)

MONSIEUR. My parents had come down from Paris to Lalbenque in 1940. I was the last of five children and was 15 at the time. I was undernourished and very weak, but they fattened me up in the country and in 1941 I went to work for Monsieur Leiris, the local agricultural and grain merchant. He was commissioned to pick up goods requisitioned by Vichy from the peasants and take them to the station. The peasants had to put out maize, beans, corn, and so on on the side of the road and we would pick it all up in a lorry. It was difficult for the peasants to get out of this: you never knew who was in league with the authorities. Vichy had inspectors who went from farm to farm checking on produce and livestock. Normally with animals it was possible to put some of them out in the woods or with a neighbour until the inspector had gone. That was normal practice in the countryside. All prices paid were imposed, and they were far too low.

I worked like this, carrying sacks, loading, occasionally driving the lorry, until early 1944 when I was summoned for a medical for STO. I was really too young but they had designated thirty or so from every large business, and I was one of those. I already knew about the maquis through various villagers in Lalbenque, notably Paul and Lili Rey at the baker's, Maurice Cloud also a baker, André Courtès a mechanic, and Joseph Nodari an agricultural worker. I contacted Nodari and he came and picked me up and took me to a camp near Figeac. It was a training camp in the middle of the woods where we learnt to handle weapons. It was all very military, run by an officer and a sergeant. We knew we were in the FTP but we had no idea that the movement was seen as communist until after the liberation of Toulouse. No one was political. We were just simple country people.

Before joining, the image I had of the maquis was of hardened fighters, taking on the Germans—nothing else. My parents had talked a lot about the First World War so I was very patriotic. I'd also met the maquis a couple of times during the winter when working for Monsieur Leiris. They had hijacked my lorry full of potatoes and beans. I was loading up in the country and M. Leiris was there with his money for paying the peasants: the driver was my brother-in-law. It was almost night and out came a car with armed men. They made us drive for 10 km. then put M. Leiris and my brother-in-law into a stone outbuilding and drove me and the lorry for about three more hours to a place where I unloaded. They then drove back again, picked up M. Leiris, who was pretty cross by then, and returned the lorry. They left his money intact. It was in February 1944, and the boss went to the gendarmerie and said that bandits had stolen the goods. But he gave no further details. The second time we were guarding the railway line. They were always recruiting local men to inspect the tracks. We didn't have any arms—it was a laugh really. We called the duty 'a picnic party'. The maquis arrived, the same men who had taken the lorry, and told us to look the other way while they mined the rails. But they deliberately stopped the train from Toulouse before it hit the broken track and exploded. It was just as well that they did, because it was full of German tanks. If that lot had gone up, Lalbenque would have been destroyed.

The maquis I joined was made up of all sorts, rural workers, Jews, foreigners, and so on. When the *débarquement* took place we were on our way to Gabaudet, but were sent off, Nodari and myself, on a liaison mission, because we both knew the area so well. We missed the massacre at Gabaudet by half a day. It was a terrible set-back for the maquis. We had been ordered to hold up the Das Reich Division by all possible means, but there was a limit to the damage we could inflict on such a heavily armoured unit. But we made some impact, and there was a great moment on 14 July when the parade in Figeac took place—the maquis, American and British parachutists, flags everywhere, and a massive drop of arms in red white and blue parachutes. It had all been a very military experience for me. I didn't encounter any kind of Robin Hood nostalgia. It shouldn't be romanticized: Noireau's book goes too far in that direction. There was certainly a spirit of vengeance, we knew who the traitors and Miliciens were, *and* the *faux maquisards*. Families had been badly tortured. You wanted to deal with those who had done it. It was a war like all wars, as in all countries. The traitors were shot at Cahors at the Liberation. But in the villages there were no personal vendettas, certainly not here.

MADAME. There were large numbers of farms where the men were absent as prisoners of war. Women did as much for the Resistance as anyone else, and a great deal more than most army officers. The country markets had been suspended: people bought everything with ration tickets, but women were the ones who travelled everywhere. They were in all the country buses. Lili Rey, for example, was an *agent de liaison*, travelling round from Lalbenque. People here didn't really believe Henriot's broadcasts, although they had been pro-Pétain at the beginning. You all knew somebody who knew somebody who was hiding out in the woods.

MONSIEUR. By May 1944 we had all our food and provisions well organized. We had stopped raiding local tobacconists, but took it straight from the big factory in Figeac, distributing a good deal to the population as we went back through the town. We also distributed food from lorries and railway trucks earmarked for the Germans. But right to the end the *statiques* remained crucial to our survival: there was never any attitude of superiority towards them just because we were the fighters. On the contrary, we were enormously respectful of their losses and sacrifices. André Courtès, for example, was caught. He used to meet the young recruits at the station and take them to the maquis. At the very end, of course, everyone took to the maquis, all ages too. Our cook was well over 50. The ordinary maquisards all felt pretty disinherited. The big guys got the perks—as in all politics. It was de Gaulle's men who took over civil power. The odd thing was that Miliciens then became the outlaws in the woods. Some of them hid out until Christmas.

Abbé Gauch (Cahors, Lot, 15 March 1991)

The little village of Arcambal is just to the east of Cahors and I was the *curé* there, aged 32 in 1943. I was also chaplain to the Scouts and to the Jeunesse agricole catholique. In 1943 I was asked by a German Jesuit to help prevent French youth being sent to Germany on STO, so I began to find farms on the Causse Limogne where they could hide. It was easy for me to counsel young men because of my job, and I was soon in liaison with the embryonic maquis, through an air force officer, Marcel Mathieu from Castres, whose wife came from Arcambal. He was already associated with the ORA. I also worked alongside Jean-Jacques Chapou (Capitaine Philippe) finding places for the *réfractaires*. We even hid them in an old Roman aqueduct near Laroque-des-Arcs, a few kilometres outside Cahors. The villagers of Arcambal were sympathetic, and the baker made extra bread for the maquis.

Before the maquis really developed in the Arcambal area I was denounced and had to escape from the Gestapo. I went to the Tarn where Mgr. Moussaron, the Bishop of Albi, made me *curé* of the parish of Laparrouquial and gave me the pastoral care of the young maquisards, mostly grouped in the Carmaux area where there was the important FTP Maquis Stalingrad. The villagers had no idea that I was the *curé des maquis*, though I had to tell the Marty family, who were essential for securing the provisions I needed. My parishioners were rather surprised that I went out so often at night, but they weren't used to having a young *curé* and when I went off on my bicycle they just thought I was a bit crazy.

The maquis FTP that I worked with lived in the woods and in farms, and I promised them all the food they needed providing they didn't pillage. They agreed. They were young agricultural workers for the most part, in an area which was more or less sympathetic to the Communist Party. Local opinion was pretty unanimously in favour of Resistance—even the middle-class industrialists in Carmaux were in favour. The *curé* of Carmaux was a Resister and was very influential.

We were lucky in the area because there were no German reprisals. But the FTP were starved of arms, deliberately so. They were not trusted. But in fact my FTP maquisards asked me to give them lectures on religious doctrine, which I did, and at the Liberation they all volunteered for the regular army, whereas other FTP in the south-west often kept their arms and stayed in Toulouse. They thought about revolution, but not really seriously. It was amusing for me, because eventually I had a Spanish republican to drive my lorry with provisions to the maquis, and one day he said, 'I can't believe it. Here I am driving a *curé* around, when a few years ago I was killing *curés* in Spain.'

There wasn't enough co-operation between the different maquis. Each group wanted to be the first to act, the first to do something. Had there been co-operation between the ORA and the FTP there would have been fewer losses. As for local 'mentalités' I have never been interested in history and folklore. It is the present and the future that interest me. It was this that made sense of the maquis: it was a commitment to life. The maquis were essentially youthful, not utopian really: they were passionately committed to creating the future. Take Chapou for example: he had the image and status of Robin Hood, but he also had a very open mind. He wanted to settle the age-old conflict between state education and the church schools. He frequently told me that it no longer had any *raison d'être*.

Simone Conquet (Cahors, Lot, 22 March 1991)

My own village was just over the river Lot from Saint-Cirq-Lapopie, called Tour-de-Faure. My mother and sister died of Spanish flu just before the end of the First World War. When my father came back from the war I was only 4 and I remember what an emotional meeting it was at the station. There were Russian prisoners of war in the area, taken after the Russian Revolution, and they were very kind to me. So too were all my father's fellow workers at the brick works. I think that kindness was very important to me, because when I became a schoolteacher it seemed natural to help Jewish refugees after the defeat. I was at the Collège of Montcuq and I sheltered the young son of the Jewish editor at Gallimard. I didn't do much but he was grateful.

I knew about the *réfractaires* and tried to encourage one of my colleagues not to leave for STO. I was very surprised when he said he would go. He didn't have much courage. And then there was one *réfractaire* who was hidden in a cave in my village. The others fed him. He went off to a maquis but didn't like it much and came back into hiding.

In 1943 I was given a job teaching English in the College at Cahors. It was then that I started taking messages to villages outside Cahors. Not all the peasants were in favour of the maquis. At the Liberation, letters of denunciation were found at the Préfecture. There was one I remember which said, 'I am a farmer in the Ségala. I fought in the First World War and am a loyal French citizen. There is a maquis unit in the woods opposite my farm.' It was signed with a full address. It was difficult to believe. When I went round I was often surprised at the absence of security. It often seemed to be fairly chaotic. I cycled everywhere and was never arrested. I had to bluff my way through police blocks going out of Cahors and coming back. Sometimes I went by train, arriving back after the curfew, but I always got a pass from the authorities at the station. I suppose technically I was an *agent de liaison* for the CDL in Cahors, and was one of two or three women on the committee at the Liberation, alongside Madame Lurçat. I was also involved in social care for the families of Resisters and deportees, giving out money to those who needed it. When the deportees returned from the camps, I was one of those whose job it was to help them resettle. I can never forget the distress—it was terrible. The things they had suffered. When I was offered a Resistance medal I said, 'Give it to those who have suffered so much.' I wasn't a religious person but I was deeply affected by it all. I wasn't a feminist really: it just seemed human decency to do something. And I did nothing compared with someone like the officer at Cahors gendarmerie, Commandant Vessières, who sheltered Jews and Resisters and did so much for Cahors Resistance; or Madame Lurçat whose courage as an *agent de liaison* was enormous; or, of course, Jean-Jacques Chapou: he was such a great leader.

Joseph Rohr (Labastide-Murat, Lot, 3 April 1991)

To begin with, local people were cautious about having *réfractaires* in their farms, but this quickly changed. I was taken on as a *bûcheron* in the woods known as La Braunhie near Caniac-du-Causse, where I helped set up the Maquis de Caniac. I was originally from Lorraine where I was born in 1915. Together with three of my brothers I escaped from there when the Germans started forcing us into the German army. Technically I was a deserter, refusing to become one of the 'malgré nous'. We came to the Lot because we knew there were other Lorrainers in Gourdon, Figeac, and Boissières. I met Jean-Jacques Chapou who came out to Caniac from Cahors looking for places to hide *réfractaires*. The village of Caniac became totally involved in the life and structures of the maquis, with Monsieur Delmas the *instituteur* animating all the services and support. He was terrific, and all the villagers were incredibly generous. Just to the north, in Labastide, Monsieur and Madame Mespoulet at the ironmongery and Charles Maury, a builder turned grocer, were at the hub of the *statiques*. Maury looked after the question of *ravitaillement* for the maquis in the whole area, and Madame Mespoulet was the local *agent de liaison*. There was also a marvellous young doctor, unqualified at the time, called Dr Baron, while in the mountains of the Ségala the *curé* Cambou was a natural maquisard. He was in his element: a fisherman, hunter, and poacher, he brought us constant supplies of fish and game. His view was that poaching was justified if it fed people in need.

We moved into the Ségala after the Germans raided Caniac. Our headquarters were at le Bourg near Lacapelle-Marival. The winter of 1943–4 was not particularly hard for us: we were young and fit and had straw, hay, and blankets provided by the local peasants. We paid them by distributing food that we took from the Chantiers de la Jeunesse and from a goods wagon that we detached from a train in a *coup de main*. It was in the Ségala that I met Yvonne Monteil, my wife to be—she was an *institutrice* at Saint-Médard-Nicourby and she and another *institutrice* at Labathude became *agents de liaison* for the FTP in the area. The most celebrated *agent de liaison* was Simone Selves, who became the wife of Jean Lurçat, the tapestry designer and artist from Aubusson. He was a Jewish refugee in the area and was closely involved in all Resistance activities, and she was famed for her missions and knowledge of the whole maquis scene.

Because I'd been an army instructor in the Maginot Line, I was given military responsibilities in the maquis. Most of the parachute drops were intended for the Groupes Vény, not for us, so we organized a few expeditions to recuperate some of the arms for ourselves—but not a lot. Colonel Georges, our leader, was a fairly strong communist at the time, and a brilliant organizer, but he never put political pressure on us to become communists. Colonel Collignon in the Groupes Vény was also a great leader. We were not really an alternative society in the sense of being an illegal organization like the black marketeers. They were not in favour of us at all. We set up a maquis tribunal at Latronquière to judge *faux maquisards* and exploiters. Ordinary people helped us because we were needy and hungry: it was a human impulse. People in the Lot are very open and friendly: although I came from Lorraine, I was a musician and I quickly picked up the local accent. People invited us into their houses for a meal, or an evening of story-telling and amusement. There was a Spaniard who was very funny and was widely invited to entertain people, and there was Richard Dudon, a Gascon, who organized evenings of charades. Someone would play Hitler, and someone Mussolini. It was a good laugh. We didn't attend dances—it was too dangerous. Our policy was not to endanger the local people. I suppose we were all rather disinherited at the Liberation. We didn't get the army ranks we deserved. And our losses were high, especially when we were sent to dislodge the Germans at la Pointe-de-Grave in the Gironde. It was fierce fighting. I must confess combat made me very frightened, and I would never claim to be a hero.

Abbé Souiry (Prendeignes, Lot, 4 April 1991)

I was the *curé* at the village of Terrou in the Ségala, and had been associated with Resistance since 1941. In 1943 I was asked to find farms and jobs for *réfractaires*, especially young men from the Chantiers de la Jeunesse. I myself organized food for them, and worked closely with Jean-Jacques Chapou and the Abbé Gauch from the Cahors area. The first maquis in the Ségala was the Maquis Timo, and there were also the Groupes Vény. Later Robert Noireau (Colonel Georges) and the FTP were the dominant force in the area. There was endless haggling over arms; those who had any, like the Groupes Vény, had pressure put on them to share. Rivalry among leaders was commonplace—and there's still a lot of mystery about the skulduggery of the time.

At the start, the *coups de main* were mainly for food, but the maquis also burgled and stole from collaborators. One bloke brought a whole lot of stolen treasures from a château to hide in my house at Terrou: he said he'd killed seven of the occupants. The Spanish maquis groups, Liberté and République, were particularly involved in these *coups de main*. Some individuals broke away from the maquis and formed isolated groups, living on their own. I'd call them racketeers. Their action flaunted the ideals of the Resistance. My friend the Abbé Cambou was very different. He first put me in touch with the maquis. He had a great sense of humour and a strong personality, and was highly respected. He loved fishing and shooting—he was a real poacher. When he was asked after the liberation of Toulouse to go with the maquis of the Lot to the Pointe-de-Grave, he was delighted—there were lots of woodcock in that region.

The *soutane* was a marvellous cover. I was often sent to other maquis as an *agent de liaison*. I cycled everywhere in my *soutane*, crossing the whole *département*. Gendarmes would often accompany me; they were very deferential. Women, like priests, were also less suspect. Édith Mir in Figeac was a great Resister, travelling as far as Lyon, and Simone Selves, daughter of a Figeac chemist, was a crucial link. She married Jean Lurçat from Aubusson who combined Resistance activity with his art. He set up his tapestry workshop in a château, and worked in glass as well.

I know far too much about the maquis to write my memoirs. I couldn't hide some of the unsavoury facts. We had a special group in the FTP for liquidating collaborators. One Lorrainer was said to have killed 98. And there were internal betrayals due to failures of security. The maquis lacked experience, training, and good middle-ranking officers. Most of the first maquisards were workers from the mining area of Decazeville, or from the Ratier factory at Figeac; later there were agricultural workers. There was no conflict between those from the towns and the peasantry—that came later, after the war, but it's always easier to win a war than to establish peace. There were also many Spanish republicans, whom I knew well. I spoke Spanish as well as the langue d'Oc, though knowing the patois was not particularly important in the maquis. We were all fighting for France, for freedom, not for the region. The maquis was made up of men from all parts of France.

In all villages there were people both for and against the maquis: I wouldn't say I knew of any village that was 100 per cent in favour, even my village of Terrou. The Germans thought there was a huge Resistance network in the village and raided it twice, finally burning it down on 2 June 1944. All the villagers had left for the woods. The hospitals at Cahors and Saint-Céré were very important to us. In Cahors there was Dr Garnal and in Saint-Céré Mère Henry who did everything for those wounded in the maquis.

There were too many abuses at the Liberation, too many excesses. But when they sent us to the Pointe-de-Grave it was a way of getting rid of the maquis. I went as chaplain. We were disinherited because de Gaulle was basically afraid of a concentration of communists from Limoges through to the Lot. But who were we? The true Resisters were just ordinary people, *les inconnus.*

Pierre and Berthe Couderq (Gramat, Lot, 12 and 27 March 1991)

Also present was Mlle Micheline Bismes from Aujols, Lot.

MONSIEUR. I returned to being an *instituteur* in Gramat after being demobilized. It wasn't until 1942 that we realized what Resistance had to involve. It was not just a military operation which we could leave to those with arms and training. It affected every aspect of life. We had to create the maximum difficulty for the Germans in every possible way. I was part of the Gramat AS run by the industrialist Monsieur Raymond Lacam. By 1943 we had pigeon-holed the whole of Gramat: we knew exactly who was for us and those whom we had to distrust. There were Pétainists everywhere whom you had to be careful about, and some outright collaborators. For example, our first parachute drop went to the wrong place, and dropped inside the grounds of a château. The châtelain immediately informed the Germans in Cahors, and they came to pick it up. And the adjudant at the gendarmerie in Gramat and his wife from Alsace were completely pro-German. It was they who betrayed the maquis at Gabaudet, for which they were eventually caught. Both were shot.

In the AS we set up groups of six, each with a leader and we totalled about 150. We did everything to undermine STO and find farms for the *réfractaires.* The men on the run didn't really offer much in the way of steady labour to the peasants, because they moved on from place to place. But they were useful to a certain extent. My old pupils came to ask me how to avoid STO and I gave them contacts in the country. My fellow *instituteurs* were not all of a similar mind. I was really only one out of five in Gramat to see it this way, until 1944 opened their eyes. And my own activity was largely due to my friendship with Monsieur Lacam.

Gramat was a law-abiding community, with no traditions of revolt. Just a quiet town of old, rural France. As Resisters we knew we were a minority. We had to watch out all the time. But in the countryside, although the peasants were always worried about pillagers and robbers, and we had to convince them we were genuine, I never knew of any collaborators in the small villages—and no informers either. The little village of Lauzou just outside Gramat was entirely on our side. In the early days of the maquis the *réfractaires* used caves for shelter: the peasants knew exactly where they were located.

Gradually more and more of us took to the woods, sometimes for only a few days at a time. Our main job was to pick up the parachute drops organized by an English agent, and hide and distribute the weapons and explosives. It's true we were *attentistes* in the sense that we didn't waste our efforts on attacking just anything: we wanted to remain elusive and inconspicuous until Jour-J. Then when the *débarquement* happened we all became maquisards with constant action from June to August, all-out sabotage and confrontations to wreck the German line of reinforcements to Normandy. We had an excellent telephone system into the woods outside Gramat, connected up to the railway telephones through a small workers' hut. We had a line through to Figeac in the south and Brive in the north. It was easy to plan railway sabotage and monitor the movement of German troops. The men recruited as *gardes-voies* were no problem, and we made sure we didn't let them stray on to any part of the track wired up to explosives.

MLLE BISMES. My father, a farmer in Aujols, was frequently called up for guard duty on the railway—and when the maquis came to organize a major derailment inside the tunnel at Cieurac on the main line to Toulouse, they went through a whole pantomime, tying up the guards and shutting them in a shed to make it look as if they had been taken by surprise. It was commonplace. In ways like that the peasantry in the whole area were really Resisters without knowing it: their co-operation was vital to the daily life and activity of the maquis.

MONSIEUR. Many landed notables were sympathetic too. We used several châteaux. For example we had a medical centre at the Château de Roumegouse, staffed by volunteers, working in co-operation with the hospital at Saint-Céré, which fully deserved to be given the Médaille de la Résistance after the Liberation. Cahors hospital too.

We never saw any GMR, and the Milice were not a problem at Gramat. It was purely the treason of the adjudant of the gendarmerie which caused the major tragedy of the area at Gabaudet. But the FTP leaders were culpable for neglecting security there. Recruits had massed there after the *débarquement*; morale was high, victory seemed imminent. Fortunately many had been dispatched to various maquis units. But there were not enough arms for everyone, so a large number were preparing to bed down in the farm. It was 8 June, and the Germans got within a hundred metres or so before they were seen. Then it was sheer hell. The scene that met the Red Cross from Gramat next day was horrific. And peasants working in the fields in the neighbourhood were shot down as they worked. Earlier, before the *débarquement*, on 11 May, the Germans had threatened a massacre at Gramat. They had rounded up all the men early in the morning, and kept them all day in a field. They picked out the Jews and made them carry rocks from one side to the other until they dropped. The Germans laughed, made them get up, beat them, and forced them to carry on. It was inhuman. But the army unit suddenly left, and the men were released, except for the poor Jews who were taken off. They had been sheltered as refugees in the town.

MADAME. That was a traumatic day in Gramat—coming ten days after an exciting day when the maquis occupied Gramat on 1 May. I was a schoolteacher teaching at the college, and at the time I was very much occupied with the birth of our daughter. Nevertheless, we kept things for the Resistance, and hid one Jewish child in the cellars of the college. After the massacre at Gabaudet, and before the end of the school term, I got the children to describe the day of the maquis, the day of the German round-up and the terrible story of Gabaudet. I still have their essays. They were written when their memory was still very fresh.

The essays kept by Madame Couderq were written by 13–15-year-olds, and, given the rarity of this kind of evidence, two are translated here in full, documenting two children's experiences of the FTP in Gramat:

1 May 1944. The First Occupation of Gramat by the Maquis,
by J. Rivière, age 14, whose father was a gendarme

On 1 May 1944 about 7 o'clock in the morning I was just finishing washing before going to school when suddenly a man of small stature, dressed in a leather jerkin, khaki trousers and wearing a cap burst into our flat in rue Saint-Roch.

'Hand over your weapons and no funny business,' he said to Papa who was having breakfast. He pointed his gun at Papa's throat. Without moving Papa said, 'You can put up your gun, I won't give you any problem. I am doing my bit for the maquis, and we are both on the same side.'

Immediately, the maquisard put down his gun and readily accepted a glass of wine.

While the man was drinking, my father took his rifle and revolver and all the ammunition he possessed and gave them to him. The man frightened me: he looked unwell and had not shaved for several days. After about 10 minutes the young man said to my father, 'You go ahead. I have to take you to my commander who is at your brigade headquarters. Don't do anything silly.' My father dressed and went out.

Since I wanted to see what was happening I followed a few seconds later. Imagine my surprise to see armed men in all the streets, on the look-out and checking the comings and goings of people in the town. On arriving at the courtyard of the gendarmerie I saw ten of these men with guns pointed, ready to fire on anyone who resisted their demands. It was very risky at the time: there were Germans on the prowl in the area who could have arrived at any moment.

They stayed in the town from 7 o'clock until two in the afternoon then, quietly they left, taking all the weaponry from the gendarmerie with them. Seeing that my father was no longer in any danger I went back home to reassure Maman.

1 May 1944. At Gramat, by Simone Desplat, age 13

It was early morning on 1 May (1944). My sister had gone to fetch milk. My brother and I were at home with my parents. Suddenly we heard machine-gun fire coming from the gendarmerie. Thinking that it was the Germans, Papa went off to bring Jeanine back. But a short time afterwards he came in laughing and said to Maman 'It's the maquis.' I quickly said to Maman, 'Can I go and see?' 'Yes, all in good time, you can go with Papa.' We went off and met a man in the market-place who said, 'They're occupying the *mairie* and the post office.' Then we went down a bit further and we saw bread in all shapes and sizes spread out on the benches in the square. It had just been requisitioned. A few maquisards got some flowers from a lady. Someone said that they were going to parade to the war memorial. Others had guns slung across their shoulders and were walking about. One little maquisard asked a man to lend him his bicycle so that he could join his mates who had gone to the station. One of the leaders showed us his arm in a sling and said, 'Look! They did this.' I should think he was one of the most courageous ones. Further on, one poor fellow, badly dressed, was sitting on the back of a bench, drinking from a wine bottle that someone had given him. Then at midday the commander gave a whistle. The men lined up and paraded to the war memorial, saluting and singing the 'Marseillaise'.

Then they got into their lorries and went off, shouting, 'We'll be back!' After they had gone my father said, 'Come on, let's go home.'

Lucien and Françoise Maury (Quillan, Aude, 24 June 1982)

MONSIEUR. A large proportion of the *département* of the Aude is covered in forests, but a maquis needed water as well. Picaussel was almost a model maquis area, and excellent for parachute drops, being well above the local German headquarters. The population was favourable for three reasons. The leaders were known to them: both I and my adjoint were local *instituteurs*. Our contacts with London carried status. And thirdly the ancient Cathar mentality was still alive—an old tradition of liberty and resistance just as strong as in the struggles against Simon de Montfort. There was a kind of Languedoc inheritance which was important. Catharism for some conjures up a country of troubadors, courtly love, and an easy life in the sun. But it was a tough and difficult religion resisting the abuses of Catholicism. Catharism was a rejection of the temporal side of the Church. I have no doubt that Catharism was still the spirit of Resistance. But, the struggle against the Germans was different from the struggle of the Cathars against the north of France. Resistance was based on the unity of the French. The origins of the maquis cannot therefore be sought in the regionalism of the Cathars. I come from the Ariège but I've never felt any less French than the Parisians.

Both my wife and I spoke Occitan from time to time. It was useful for making good relationships with the peasantry. Schoolteachers were very close to the population. We were both teachers. It was only a modest profession but it carried status. I also had done my two years military service from 1935 to 1937 and was recalled at the Munich crisis of 1938 as an officer in the Reserve. This military training equipped me, at age 28, to be a leader of the maquis, but I had wanted to be a *lycée* teacher of literature. My studies were cut short by the war. I don't think the *laïc* attitudes of the *instituteurs* were particularly important in the maquis. Several teachers had had a religious upbringing. I felt I was in a minority among my generation of teachers, most of whom were for peace at any price. But you have to stand up and fight at some point. Eventually many pacifists were converted to war by Hitler, and there was a discernible shift among teachers during the Spanish Civil War. I must also point out my temperament as a keen rugby player. We had a combative nature. There were many rugby players in the maquis.

It would be quite wrong to say that Resistance and the spirit of Carnival had anything in common. Carnival is not an expression of refusal but an acceptance that 'anything goes'. It was a popular festival, but ideologically it is a bluff. It's an intellectual craze to exalt the spirit of Carnival. Take this statement, for example, from a recent picture postcard: 'Carnival is the struggle of nature against modernity, of people against power. It has survived centuries of censorship and is an incarnation of cultural resistance.' That's an entirely intellectual interpretation, *not* a popular one.

The Aude is a monocultural region, but in the farms higher up there was a little bit of everything. When peasants were on our side we arrived *as if* they were hostile. A little bit of theatre was staged to make it look as if they had no choice. But if peasants were really against us then we cut out the play-acting, making our raids at night. On the whole these were a rarity. It was barbaric really, the darkest point of the Resistance. They were grave mistakes. It allowed all abuse to be imputed to the Resistance. Of course there was abuse. We were not saints. But the vast majority of crimes of the period were not committed by the maquis. We were *not* bandits.

MADAME. I was an *institutrice.* When my husband was hunted by the Gestapo he left his job as a teacher and signed up in the Beaux Arts in Toulouse as cover. While he was away there was a parachute drop. I made up a code on the spur of the moment and sent him the message. The role of women was equal to that of men. There were nurses too, parachuted in sometimes. Everywhere there was an absence of men, due to the number of prisoners of war. In the film *Lacombe Lucien* far too much importance was given to accident; not enough to choice. And I found *Le Chagrin et la pitié* unsatisfactory: it concentrated too much on the unusual aspects. The schoolmaster in *Lacombe Lucien* refused to accept Lucien into the maquis. We never refused anyone, though we studied them carefully: some of the very young ones could have been set up by the Milice.

MONSIEUR. We blindfolded new arrivals when we took them to Picaussel. One problem was our poor relationship with the FTP due to the fact that we, the maquis AS, received parachuted arms, whereas they were denied them. In fact they fully deserved to have drops of arms. They fought well. They stole half of my parachuted arms at the beginning, but I have to say they used the weapons to good effect. It was a decision made at the top. Of course they called us 'attentistes' but we were constantly involved in sabotage. Everything depended on the locality, the size of maquis as well as everything else. At Picaussel we could mobilize a large number, alternating those on active duty. In fact the local villagers could choose which maquis to join. We also recruited further afield, going as far as Limoux. Any stranger arriving unexpectedly was immediately signalled to us by the villagers. They kept us fully informed.

Yvonne Cormeau (Kegworth, Leicestershire, 22 January 1991)

On 22 August 1943 I was dropped into France to join George Starr (Hilaire) as his radio operator in the Wheelwright circuit. SOE never gave women jobs higher than wireless operators. They thought no French person would obey instructions from a woman, but I found that I had no problems at all in that respect. George Starr never interfered in what I sent. He told me what he wanted and which dropping zones, and I did the rest. We covered ten *départements* in the south-west and always spread out our drops across the whole territory. Drops were never more than fifteen containers at a time because we had no maquis. We had about thirty little cells all out in the country. That was Starr's strength. He found places where there were no neighbours; isolated farms and small hamlets. The groups became known as 'les bataillons d'Hilaire'.

The weapons were carefully hidden. The explosives were used for a certain amount of sabotage, but our aim was mostly military training for D-Day. Starr and I taught them how to use their weapons. I helped mostly with grenade training. There were only the two of us until April 1944 when an arms instructor was sent over. My cover was to pose as a district nurse. I went round on a bicycle in a dark blue uniform. Starr posed as a tobacco inspector.

It's not true that I stayed for months in one place. It was Starr who did that, at the village of Castelnau-sur-Auvignon in the Gers, not far from Condom. I moved every three days, to cover my transmissions. I was never refused a meal or a bed. I stayed with very basic peasant farmers and wine-growers. I had difficulty understanding their French. Many could not read or write. Some were Italians who had fled from Mussolini and had settled in the country as tenant farmers. There were quite a few of them in the south-west: very anti-German and anti-fascist.

We never had a maquis, though Starr agreed to help Maurice Parisot who started up a small independent maquis in the Gers. He had about 400 men by D-Day. I got weapons and explosives for him. The other maquis in the south-west tended to be too conspicuous: we kept away from them. They made too much noise.[44] We were never integrated in any way with the French maquis, but by the third week of August we numbered 1,500 when we marched into Toulouse. Our job had been to delay the German troops who were ordered to reinforce the battlefronts in the north.

Most of the peasants were tobacco-growers, and felt nothing but hostility towards Vichy, who requisitioned the tobacco as soon as it was dry. The peasants tried to hide the drying-places, and they kept illicit stills everywhere. Certain villages were pockets of Resistance, like Castelnau-sur-Auvignon where the mayor, Monsieur Larribeau, and the *institutrice* were both involved with us, and Tazan on the verge of the Basses-Pyrénées which is where I got my papers changed in September 1943 when Vichy ordered that the colour of all identity cards was to be changed overnight. There were eight villages called Castelnau in the Gers, and the Germans never found Starr, but they eventually sacked the village, and three villagers were killed. It's important to recognize that our organization was entirely rural. No town was involved. The French peasants were wonderful.

H. M. Despaigne (Harrow, London, 18 August 1979)

In 1940 I was aged 23, was single with an Anglo-Belgian-French background, and was in shipping insurance in London. I was called up into the British army, and then summoned to the War Office in 1941 and asked if I would like to go back to France. I had been at university in Nancy, and I said I was happy to go back. I thought it might be at once, but I was then put through various training stages which lasted nine months. My first SOE trip was in May 1942 when I was smuggled into Cannes by boat from Gibraltar, as wireless operator to Major Bodington whose mission was to inspect all existing SOE agents in France. He got no further than Cannes before problems forced him to return to England. I was left with no brief, no money, and no assured passage back to England. Peter Churchill arrived to take over the local circuit and I made my way by my own means across the Pyrenees to Spain, Portugal, and eventually London.

[44] Shortly after interviewing Yvonne Cormeau I met the SOE agent Tony Brooks, who was an outstanding organizer of railway sabotage across the South of France. He was even more critical of the maquis, saying he avoided any involvement with them, a fact underlined by Maurice Buckmaster who said, 'Tony Brooks had a very low opinion of the maquis. He operated almost entirely with the railway-workers.' Evidence from Maurice Buckmaster, 4 Nov. 1990.

My second trip was in September 1943, again as wireless operator, as part of a team of three with a mission to restart the Detective circuit in the Toulouse region. The leader was Sévenet and the man on the spot was Mompezat. Sévenet went round organizing suitable zones for parachute drops, and we then collected the arms and entrusted them to people we had enlisted, but with strict orders to do nothing until D-Day.

We heard about D-Day a little before and decided to create a proper military unit in the Montagne Noire above Mazamet. The idea was formulated by the three of us, and we had sounded out possible recruits well before D-Day. As it was, far more arrived at the Pic de Nore than we had anticipated and we had to send some back to their homes. Several felt rejected and aggrieved, but at the time we only had arms for about 500, and we were against the idea of being a camp for people just hiding in the mountains. Those whom we accepted expected to be combatants. In fact we had some difficulty restraining them. There was no mention of the word maquis. We were the Corps Franc de la Montagne Noire (CFMN) and had our own uniforms, made by a tailor in the camp. We were a clandestine army.

The *cavaliers*, as we called the men, came from Castres, Mazamet, Albi, and Toulouse. Sergeants in the gendarmerie became many of our company commanders. There was a serious shortage of military experience, and we had only one regular army officer with us, Captain de Kervenoael. There were perhaps some twenty or so men who had come from small maquis groups in the area. One of the recruits was Max Cormouls-Houlez, whose father and grandfather had made a fortune in the wool-cleaning industry at Mazamet. We also had doctors, dentists, chemists, mechanics, students, workers of all sorts. Politics were never discussed, nor religious differences. We were all there to fight.

We stayed only a day or so at the Pic de Nore before taking over a Chantiers de la Jeunesse, which was fully equipped with beds, telephones, and kitchens. We just told them to get out. They did. We didn't ask them to join us. Life in the camp was then organized as if in the regular army, with officers eating and sleeping separately from the men. I received a million francs a month from London, so we paid for most of our food. Special groups in three lorries would set off every day to buy food, often well to the north of Castres. There were only forests in our area, and we had little to do with the local peasantry. We also requisitioned—another word for stealing—German and Chantiers stocks in Toulouse and elsewhere. We lived in something of a world of our own. Every day there was action of some sort, including combats with German forces; we would discuss these and plan others. We never discussed what would happen to France after the war. Nobody in the CFMN was there to further a political career.

The civil Resistance in the area, whatever they called themselves, were jealous of the fact that we had money, arms, and men. We were never short of food or clothing, and discipline was good. Anyone who wanted to leave could do so, without recriminations. We received an order from London that all communists in the CFMN were to leave. We let them do so. The main problem was getting the men to realize that they could not launch actions on their own initiatives. Everything was planned.

The only superior authority we recognized was General Koenig in London. The others in the area were unimportant to us. When the Germans bombed and attacked us in July, a maquis nearby didn't lift a finger to help. I had to move my wireless transmitter, and when I did so the rumour circulated that I was dead. Even when I asserted that I was very much alive they didn't believe me. It was their way of trying to break up the CFMN. They kept saying we were an 'English maquis' run by the British Intelligence Service. I told them I *was* in regular touch with London, but only because Koenig was there. Mompezat particularly resented being called a leader of a 'foreign' maquis. Much of the hostility was what you might expect in a regular war between staff officers and those in the field. We were out there doing the job and we didn't want to be told what to do by those with political aims. We were proud to be the CFMN, as we demonstrated on 14 July in our march through Revel, all in uniform. The population was very impressed. But after the war it was a black mark against you if you had been in the maquis or in a unit like the CFMN.

We were never involved in actions against collaborators. That wasn't our job. Vichy meant nothing to us. There were no Milice in the Montagne Noire. The only Pétainist I remember well was the hotelier where my wife-to-be and I spent much of the winter of 1943–4. He didn't know who I was. I dearly wanted to go back after the war and tell him he had been harbouring a British officer.

Francis Cammaerts (Grane, Drôme, 18 March 1991)

In many ways there has been too much focus on the maquis, as if that was the whole story. It was tiny before 1944; small groups, often just hiding. From March 1943 to March 1944 what I knew were the *sédentaires*. It's a name I dislike; that was the last thing they were. They were living in their homes but it was they who did all the picking up of parachuted material, the hiding of it, the organization of resistance. They were the ones I worked with.

I'd been sent over by SOE, F Section, to have a look at the network Carte in the south-east. What I found was musical comedy stuff: no concept of security whatsoever, and wildly over-ambitious. So in the summer of 1943 I set up on my own with my wireless operator, a Frenchman trained in England, August Floiras. My code-name was Roger and the network became known as Jockey.[45] It extended from Nice to the Loire, and Marseille to the Alps. I didn't have any official link with the movements of French Resistance, but it was just after Jean Moulin's arrest, when other leaders of Combat, Libération, and Franc-Tireur were on the run, so I found many small groups who had belonged to one or other of the movements and were now somewhat adrift. I came along and said, 'All I want is a self-contained cell, with its own parachute ground, a place to hide material, and a place to train. I don't want you to be part of any big movement. If you agree I'll contact London and the material will arrive soon.' The little village of Charols on the Rubiron east of Montélimar was our HQ and from there we built solid cells in Montélimar, Beaurepaire, and Chazelles: they were our three big successes—all smallish towns.

Our network then extended to the Hautes-Alpes where our main task was to sabotage the hydro-electric and bauxite industries, and into the Vercors where I met the maquis for the first time. There were already some 600 in makeshift camps in July 1943. I told Chavant, 'This is not something I can take under my wing, in my network, but I will give you full support.' I heard of the plan by Pierre Dalloz for a base in the Vercors, but the plan has always been misunderstood. It was not a blueprint for a fortress maquis. He believed as much in mobile guerrilla tactics as I did. But neither London nor Algiers ever gave it sufficient attention. By 6 June 1944 there were about 1,500 in the Vercors, and by mid-July some 6,000. The big parachute drops meant they could be armed, but the drops were mainly 14–21 July, too late for the men to be properly trained. On 8 June I was told that I was now attached to the FFI, but I could not simply transfer the arms from my group into the Vercors: it would have destroyed the whole of the organization. Chavant had been to Algiers and had been told to hold the Vercors for three weeks after D-Day, but not a day longer. The aim was to act as a magnet for German troops. It worked sensationally: in the end over 20,000 German troops were tied down in the Vercors.

After the three weeks were up the problem was what would happen next. The Allies and Algiers clearly hadn't made up their minds. There was still the 'grasshopper' notion, which meant holding an area long enough to allow a massive parachute landing, but Algiers thought of the Massif Central as a possible place for that, as well as the Alps, so there was no decision. And

[45] Among the many testimonies to the importance of Francis Cammaerts to the armed Resistance in the south-east of France is the comment in Madeleine Baudoin, *Histoire des Groupes Francs des Bouches-du-Rhône* (PUF, 1962), 22: 'Les sabotages effectués par les Groupes Francs n'auraient jamais pu être réalisés sans les explosifs fournis par le réseau Action Buck "Jockey", dirigé par le lieutenant-colonel Francis Cammaerts, alias Roger.'

then there was the notion of a landing on the Mediterranean coast. A decision in favour of this was probably not made until the end of June or early July. Certainly we didn't know what was being planned, so the Vercors carried on, full of expectations. It *was* an effective operational centre, if only we had had the back-up, plus an air attack on the small airfields in the vicinity. Roger Poyol, one of my main organizers, and myself had seen the little airstrip at Montélimar with gliders ready and parachutes attached to their tails, and we had sent messages to London saying that such airborne forces would be ineffective in front-line battles, but would be ideal against Resistance pockets in the mountains. We had excellent information on what was happening, especially at the airfield of Chabeuil. What made us so angry was that three weeks *after* the defeat in the Vercors the N.7 road in the Rhône valley was bombed like hell, twisted metal everywhere. They could easily have put three little airfields out of action. The final telegram from the Vercors was entirely justified. We felt we had been used. My cables and reports to London said that the names and numbers of the dead in the Vercors should be written in red and pinned on the desks of the High Command. What we really lacked was mortars. Sten guns were fine for hit-and-run operations, or in the towns. But in the mountains you needed to be able to fire over the ridges. But then in Algiers there was an element highly nervous about the armed Resistance. All the men they sent to the Vercors arrived too late.

Going back to my Resistance cells in Jockey, we never used the word 'maquis' until after 6 June 1944. The men were known as 'Company X'—where X was the code-name of the leader. From our point of view it was a hell of a lot more dangerous to work from home in, say, Montélimar and go out and blow up a train at night, then return to work, than to sit in the woods and behave like a boy scout. But that's a hard statement. There was no antagonism, and there was enormous sympathy for those on the run. What has to be realized is that the year spent building up a cell of fifteen so that they could fight well after D-Day was a more dangerous time than the actual period of fighting. Where the maquis had the edge on the *sédentaires* was that they had the space to train in a more realistic way: you could fire weapons in the mountains. In the towns you could learn to strip a weapon down but you couldn't fire it. It's true also that the maquis endured terrible cold in the winter, without adequate clothing.

Here in the Drôme there were long-standing *mentalités* of revolt. The wars of religion had been very important in the area: Montélimar had been at the centre of them, Crest as well, where they are still very proud of having resisted against Richelieu. This anti-authority attitude of the Protestants had survived. In the mountains they all went after the chamois, even though it was forbidden. They needed the meat to feed their families.

Without the women there could have been no Resistance. Because we lived at home we were dependent on them for everything. In my whole time in France I never once slept in a hotel. I stayed only in people's houses, with their families. The women looked after the grandparents, the children, and us. And every day they went off on a bicycle with a trailer in search of food. What needs emphasis is the role of women, and children, in the security of the Resistance. I never heard of a single person who had been put in danger by a child's indiscretion. Take Madame Reynier for example, in Crest, with whom I was staying at one point. She was arrested by the Milice with her three children. They were all stripped naked and questions were fired at them about the whereabouts of her husband and myself. She seemed a timid little woman, but she just kept saying how her husband ran around after other women. She stuck to her story, and eventually they gave her back her clothes and sent her home. Wonderful courage; and it's almost a banal story: it was not an exceptional event.

For food and other necessities we all depended on the goodwill of small shopkeepers and farmers. The Resistance in this area was very tough on those who called themselves maquisards and robbed people. There were a lot of executions by the Resistance for banditry. In suburban areas, though, requisition slips were being signed as early as January 1944. They were never refused. There must have been millions of them for small quantities. I had no authority to sign: they were signed by representatives of Combat, MUR, or FFI. I didn't have a lot of money to dispense either. We were always receiving gifts: a police sergeant gave me his pension once.

I worked a lot with the FTP. They had a strong feeling of getting on with the job. Sometimes we had to discourage them from rather useless actions. They loved explosives. They would much rather blow up a telephone exchange than cut all the wires with a pair of cutters, which was far simpler and more effective. But that was common to everyone, whether communists, French army, or whatever. It's very understandable. The French were dying to do something to wipe out the shame of 1940. They are a very proud nation. My problem with the FTP was that they had very strict rules about structures of command and decision-making. I could never get hold of the real commanders. I had to say, unless I can talk to the ones that make the decision I can't provide the weapons. They didn't like this: they accused me of being very British. But in fact there was very little anti-British feeling. As for socialists, 50 per cent of my friends running our cells were socialists. In the rural areas they were marvellous, very different from the socialists in Marseille, who were the real *attentistes*, planning for an *insurrection nationale* in the town *after* the Germans had left.

In October 1943 we sent a report to London saying that, providing the Germans didn't change their order of battle and providing the Allies armed the Resistance, they could land on the south coast and reach Grenoble in seven days. When the landing happened, the Americans nevertheless expected to spend at least six weeks to attain this destination. But once they started up the Route Napoléon they reached Digne without any opposition. And they went on to Gap without a shot being fired. In Gap 2,000 German soldiers were in the cinema, locked up by an ordinary key, with their weapons piled outside, and two lads on the front and back doors. That was the taking of Gap. The garrison at Digne had surrendered in the same way. By continuous ambushes and sabotage from 6 June to 15 August the Resistance had cleared the Alpine roads. The Germans left in the towns dared not attempt to pass or break out. It was an amazing achievement by the Resistance. It has to be repeated over and over again: when the Allies invaded the Alpine regions *there wasn't any fighting*. It had all been done. In terms of lives saved, both Allied and German, it was an enormous achievement.

Tragically, far more were killed by Allied bombing than by the Germans. Errors were constant after 27 May. It was improper and inaccurate. I tried to explain and alleviate the suffering by suggesting there were military reasons. But there weren't. They always bombed the wrong places. What we had to do was to balance this against the losses and heroism of the pilots who had done the parachute drops and the pick-ups throughout the previous year.

It was astonishing that the Liberation happened as it did. All you hear about is shaving women's heads, personal vendettas, and so on. But I had a lieutenant who came up to me and said, 'I've got 300 German prisoners. What do the international conventions say about how much food and exercise they are entitled to every day?' And those were Germans who had strung up Resisters and their families. There was something extraordinarily civilized about the Liberation. Far too little has been written about it.

Conclusion: Alternatives

IN the museum on Mont Mouchet in the Auvergne, next to the memorial to the maquis, there are familiar photographs of well-known Resistance leaders, and imaginative diagrams of the chains of command and organization which made the FFI a relatively cohesive force in the three liberation months of June, July, and August 1944. This study, this search for the maquis, has barely mentioned the command structures and has certainly shed no new light on their effectiveness or shortcomings. But in the museum alongside the familiar faces and the facts of national organization, there are documents, photographs, and recordings of other people and other structures whose role in the maquis is known only locally and even then by very few. It is towards these that the empirical drive of this particular search has been largely directed. The search has been an attempt to re-member the maquis at its most basic level and to present it as a phenomenon of rural resistance in certain parts of southern France.

The problem of reconstruction at local level is that it raises encyclopaedic expectations. Surely the coverage should have been greater and the omissions fewer? Surely Dortan, a small commune of the Ain, in the valley of Bienne, a few kilometres from Oyonnax, should have been mentioned? On 21 July 1944 the Germans sacked the town as a reprisal for maquis activity, leaving 35 dead, including 16 horrifically massacred in the château. Among them were several maquisards, the local priest, aged 72, and old Monsieur Colnet, aged 80.[1] Surely Valréas, the commune of the Vaucluse, martyred by the Germans after the local FFI had liberated it prematurely on 8 June 1944, should have been analysed to furnish a comparison with the drama of Tulle?[2] Undoubtedly the search could have been wider and deeper, but choices would still have been made that failed to do justice to the locality, the individuality, and the heterogeneity of the maquis.

Enumeration is no less problematic than coverage. The numbers of the maquis were never less than elusive. Size was a reality but also a bluff. The Germans were not the only ones to be deceived. André Pavelet, appointed by Michel Brault to co-ordinate the five *départements* of the Montpellier

[1] Evidence given by M. Morel, mayor of Dortan, to Pierre Luizard, *La Guerre n'était pas leur métier* (Éditeurs français réunis, 1974), 131–42.

[2] Christian Durandet, *Les Maquis de Provence* (France-Empire, 1974), 166–78.

region, credulously believed that he had 5,000 men at his disposal in the autumn of 1943; Brault commented that it was more like 500, and Gilbert de Chambrun, closer to the ground than either of them, mentioned no more than a few hundred at that stage.[3] We know that there were 465 maquisards on the plateau of Glières in March 1944, some 4,700 at Mont Mouchet and la Truyère in June, and at least 4,000 in the Vercors in July. The Corps Franc de la Montagne Noire set a target of 500 but easily exceeded that in the first week following Jour-J, and at that time the maquis of the Lot was about 3,000 strong, having grown from the 250 or so who followed Jean-Jacques Chapou into the FTP three months earlier.[4] Colonel Buckmaster, head of F section of the British SOE, has said that Heslop and Romans-Petit commanded over 5,000 fighters in the Ain and the Haute-Savoie, and Henri Michel, doyen of Resistance studies, gave 22,000 for the whole of the *zone sud* at the beginning of 1944.[5] That figure may well be too high for January, but five times that figure would be a reasonable estimate for FFI troops in the south by the middle of August. It is acknowledged that some 400,000 men were available in the FFI after the Liberation in the whole of France, and of these some 120,000 enrolled in the regular French armies.[6] But none of these putative or confirmed figures give any indication of the numbers of active supporters, carers and providers, *agents de liaison*, or medical personnel. Their Resistance has no statistical representation, not even an elusive one. It can only be written qualitatively, though quantitative judgements of depth and intensity filter through in the telling of their story. It is something of that history of initiatives and response, from isolated achievements of refuge and revolt to the infrastructure of *terrains* and *pays* identified with the maquis presence, that this search has tried to illuminate.

There were other paths to be trodden, other directions to take, other regions to be explored. In his first words of oral evidence Francis Cammaerts moved the focus away from the maquis, and any study of the SOE networks keeps the claims of the maquisards in perspective.[7] That is also the message of excellent books and memoirs on the numerous groupes francs, not least the Groupes Vény in the area of the Lot,[8] and the groupes francs of the Bouches-du-Rhône rigorously portrayed by Madeleine Baudoin. She reminds

[3] AN 72. AJ 63, 'Le Service National du Maquis' report by Commandant Brault, 18 Dec. 1944.

[4] Laborie, *Résistants, Vichyssois et autres*, 310 and 328. He further estimates that the numbers had grown to 6,000 by the Liberation. Jean Lurçat gives a final total of 8,000 in *Les Étoiles du Quercy*, 3 (Jan. 1945).

[5] Evidence from Colonel Maurice Buckmaster, 4 Nov. 1990; Henri Michel, *Histoire de la Résistance en France* (PUF, 1950), 99.

[6] Rioux, *The Fourth Republic 1944–1958*, 11. To the figure of 120,000 should be added 'the 20,000 men of the 27th Alpine Infantry Division, plus the FFI units that concentrated their efforts on the German coastal garrisons', ibid.

[7] See Ch. 7, Oral Memories.

[8] Picard and Chaussade, *Ombres et espérances en Quercy*.

us that the groupes francs in and close to Marseille, 'had no contact with the maquis. In Basse-Provence the maquis were practically non-existent before the Normandy landings. After that date fairly weak units were decimated soon after their formation (massacres of Lambesc, Charleval, and Jouques); other units only took shape shortly before the Liberation (maquis of Allauch, 12 km. from Marseille). If the maquis had been constituted earlier, the groupes francs would have been able to use them to absorb the prisoners from the Chave prison, who escaped on 23 March 1944.'[9] Another timely perspective was provided by the oral evidence of Gérald Suberville and Denise Guillaume, recorded in Paris in 1984, which pointed to the indifference of scholars to the achievements and structures of Action Ouvrière (AO). As head of AO in the Montpellier and Béziers areas, Suberville had a strategic interest in keeping his sabotage teams within the factories, within the goods and shunting yards, within the quarries and power stations. Only there could they enact their Resistance. Taking to the maquis could seem an irrelevance, a distancing of potential saboteurs from the heart of the action. But Action Ouvrière has been marginalized in many local conferences on the Resistance due to suspicions of the anarchic dispositions and behaviour of many of its exponents. The saboteurs of AO worked alongside, but often in discordance with other constituted units of the Resistance, from the AS maquis through to the clandestine Communist Party.[10] Lucien Maury provides good evidence of its considerable successes in the Aude, but other local histories of the region tend to mention it only *en passant.*[11] Another search would be necessary for its implantation to be rightly established. It cannot be subsumed under the maquis.

Much of maquis activity is regarded as no less anarchistic than Action Ouvrière, despite the abundance of maquisard denials. The accusations of anarchical behaviour are rarely based on the facts of anarchist participation in the maquis, but rather on the memory of growing disorder in the countryside as the regime of Vichy disintegrated. A feeling of mounting chaos is frequently expressed in letters intercepted by the Contrôle Technique, and most prefectoral reports at some point in 1943–4 give credence to popular fears of growing anarchy. A hunt for political anarchists was not undertaken by this study, though many of their names have been recorded by the Centre International de Recherche sur l'Anarchisme (CIRA) in

[9] Madeleine Baudoin, *Histoire des Groupes Francs (M.U.R.) des Bouches-du-Rhône* (PUF, 1962), 87. The book is also extremely good on the total organization of Resistance in the *zone sud.* See also evidence from Madeleine Baudoin in Kedward, *Resistance in Vichy France*, 276–8.

[10] Evidence from Gérald Suberville given on 7 Dec. 1984. Some of Denise Guillaume's evidence is quoted above on p. 200, but the full interview with Suberville will feature in a projected future publication.

[11] Maury, *La Résistance audoise*, i. 297–302. Note also that AO and Gérald Suberville are credited with considerable success by Roger Bourderon, *Libération du Languedoc méditerranéen* (Hachette, 1974), 51–3.

Marseille, together with a wide range of *témoignages*. It is evident from these testimonies that many libertarians rallied to the promotion of a tangible liberation of France, to which Spanish anarchists were as dedicated as their counterparts within France, and that general anti-authoritarian attitudes were channelled by the maquis into action against the specific authorities identified with the German presence and the collaboration of Vichy.[12] More widely, even though most maquis memoirs, both written and oral, steer well away from the concept of anarchy, they contain many instances where an anarchic outlook was quick to evaluate the possibilities of alternative actions. The maquis was always an alternative, and there is nothing to be gained by sanitizing its history. It thrived on alternative ways of thinking. This does not make it anarchic, but without a fundamental disrespect for the established authority of Vichy, the story of the *réfractaires* and of the growth and survival of the maquis would not have scored itself on the history of rural France.

This search began with no preconceived idea of how the material discovered *en route* should be patterned and presented. But very soon the recurrence of inversionary acts, attitudes, and aims suggested an underlying pattern which ran through archives and oral interviews and through pamphlets and scholarly local histories, and it is the primacy of inversion that this book has repeatedly affirmed, without any intention to minimize the evidence provided by those who disagree, or who would wish to emphasize quite different themes. Inversion, as an overturning of norms, convention, and authority, has been used more by cultural historians interested in such subjects as the politics of Carnival, than by political historians who set out to explain the culture of revolt. As a concept it should not be constrained by its own normative usage. There were inversions at every turn of the Resistance, and in every act of the maquis. The national and patriotic aim of driving out the occupier, which stood at the forefront of all Resistance motivation, produced more than symbolic inversions of occupation when the maquis 'occupied' Oyonnax, Cajarc, Lasalle, and many other villages and small towns, well in advance of the process of liberation. There was the inversion of the hunt, the tracking down of infiltrators, Miliciens, and other sympathizers of collaboration. Maquisards regularly use inversionary language to describe this process, the 'poacher turned gamekeeper', the 'outlaw prefect', the 'maquis police'. It was a process which involved inverting the regulatory mechanisms of Vichy, including the fixing of agricultural prices and the distribution, or redistribution, of food. The entire maquis discourse, as a distinctive part of wider Resistance assertion, inverted the notion of legality and proclaimed the rightness and legitimacy of revolt. The Chantiers de la Jeunesse were replaced by the 'maquis des jeunes' as the rightful

[12] *Les Anarchistes dans la Résistance*, 2 vols. (CIRA: Marseille, 1985).

uniformed presence of young men in the countryside. Arms were transported by women in prams; messages and pamphlets in school satchels; food and other necessities for the maquis in everyday shopping bags; *curés* used the camouflage of their *soutanes*; *pasteurs* the privacy of their presbyteries: all were usages which exploited the familial and religious susceptibilities of Vichy and inverted their association with innocence and convention. The cult of the venerable Pétain as the 'Chef' with instinctual charisma, was not just abandoned; it was inverted in the oppositional cult of the maquis *chef*, of the instinctual authority of the young leader for whom many maquisards would, and did, give up their lives. As the *réfractaires* and the maquisards took to the farms and the woods, the hills and the mountains, there was an ironic inversion of Vichy's 'retour à la terre'. Communal collusion in the maquis grouped together villagers of all ages and drew on historical *mentalités* of regional pride and independence, the very political values associated with local and regional *libertés* as defined by Maurras. These values were deployed in the protection of refugees, foreigners, Jews, anarchists, and communists, anti-fascists and Resisters on the run, the very categories excoriated by Maurras in the columns of *L'Action française* as un-French or anti-French. It was an inversion which defined the nature of rural patriotism in 1942–4, as many localities and communes of the ancient *pays* identified themselves as integral to Resistance France.

The sense of being welcome within a rural locality cannot be found in all maquis memoirs, nor do local attitudes as recorded at the time allow any generalized identification of rural France and the maquis. There were maquis murders and thefts which some communities will never allow to be justified as the necessities of war, and there were a number of bitter denunciations of maquis ruthlessness which must be taken at their face value and not dismissed as Vichy propaganda. This negative side to the maquis has been well researched over the years, and there is a certain defensiveness in much of the public image of the maquis, as if the unravelling of its actions will inevitably lead to further indictments. Some history, it would seem, is expected to reveal only its darker aspect as depth of enquiry is pursued. This has not, however, been the preoccupation of this study. What has consistently demanded emphasis has been the history of the maquis as an inventive adaptation of everyday lives to new forms of wartime survival and action, in a struggle which breached the frontiers between the home and the fighting front. What has emerged is the recognizable quality of day-to-day creativity which infused the struggle and made it the epitome of communities at war.

The western end of the Monts de Lacaune, near Vabre in the Tarn, saw the survival of Jewish scouts from the local Éclaireurs Israélites de France, who went into hiding in mid-1943 to avoid arrest and deportation, and formed the maquis of la Malquière, one of two mainly Jewish maquis units which eventually made up an effective fighting force within the maquis of the Tarn.[13] Their initial training for the new challenge of military action contrasted with the continued normalcy of their cultural activities: Frédéric Hammel remembers literary readings in the morning and biblical study in the evenings, with courses in Hebrew given by Maurice Horowitz.[14] Lieutenant-Colonel Redon dedicated one of his lively pen-portraits to another unusual maquis grouping in the woods of the Tarn, largely made up in the summer of 1944 of women, and people related to each other, and situated in a farm close to Saint-Jean-de-Jeannes but inaccessible by road. It was known as the Maquis Robur, and included the young Madame Robur, her mother-in-law, Madame Armagnac, Madame Sabatini, the fiancée of a maquis radio operator, and the daughter of Captain Laporte, the head of the Milice in Albi, who was held as a prisoner but did the same work as the others and lived alongside her captors. All slept in the hay in the barn, while the beds in the farm were reserved for the wounded. The collective family atmosphere, according to Redon, gave this maquis a character of its own, quite unlike any other.[15] Further north in the forests of the Ségala not far from Latronquière in the Lot, Lieutenant Marcenac of the FTP ran a maquis printing press from June to August 1944, aided by the painter and tapestry-maker from Aubusson, Jean Lurçat, and employing the skills of typesetters from Figeac. A young Jewish student from Alsace translated FTP tracts into German and left them on roads frequented by the Wehrmacht. The first number of *Partisan* was produced for 14 July 1944, and Lurçat brought works by Éluard, Aragon, and Vercors to be set at the 'imprimerie des bois'. In October 1944 the *Étoiles du Quercy* documented its origin in this maquis press, and stressed the local role of the printed word in transmitting orders from the FTP command to the maquis in the Ségala: 'Totally isolated in the woods,' wrote Noel Ballif, 'and leading the life of pioneering trackers in some saga of the Far-West, the young fighters for freedom were kept constantly informed by the press.'[16] These are three final glimpses of the diversity of the maquis phenomenon, three concluding examples of the ways in which civilian and military identities were fused in a multitude of similar yet singular experiences.

This, then, is where the bulk of the evidence has led; not so much towards the issue of heroism or terrorism, but into the realm of popular inventiveness and creativity. The search for the maquis in 1942–4 resulted in a number of significant new social identities in rural France, not just the *réfractaire*, the

[13] Chaynes and Saulière, *Le Tarn et les tarnais dans la deuxième guerre mondiale*, 11.

[14] Frédéric Chimon Hammel, *Souviens-toi d'Amalek. Témoignage sur la lutte des Juifs en France, 1938–1944* (CLKH, 1982), 219. I owe this reference to André Kaspi's valuable study, *Les Juifs pendant l'occupation* (Seuil, 1991).

[15] AN 72. AJ 198, Redon, 'Souvenirs de la Résistance dans le département du Tarn', 30.

[16] Noel Ballif, 'L'Imprimerie clandestine des F.T.P.F. du Lot', *Étoiles du Quercy*, 2 (Oct. 1944), 37.

maquisard, the *franc-tireur*, the *partisan*, and the *sédentaire*, but also the *curé du maquis*, the *préfet des bois*, the *mère du maquis*, the *agent de liaison*, and the saboteur. It created the opportunity for the *instituteur* and *institutrice*, the gendarme, the *maire*, and other local administrators to forge a social role as sympathizers, supporters, and facilitators, thereby fracturing the local establishment of Vichy and pluralizing its identity. In the collusion of the peasantry there were convergencies of patriotism and economic self-interest, but just as many divergencies, and the same may be said of the aid given by certain proprietors with châteaux in the woods, employers of rural *chantiers*, small-town *commerçants* and *garagistes*. The interweaving of these roles and identities into a particular social fabric followed no regular pattern and was often no more than a rough texture of loose ends and broken threads. But in a number of rural areas a composite product was not only created but sustained, a way of life that made up the culture of the outlaw. Who and what constituted that culture is the main substance of most of the chapters of this book, but the fact that such a culture existed will never be uncontested. For some maquisards the concept of an outlaw culture comes dangerously close to accepting the Vichy stigma of illegality. For others there is a gendered reluctance to face the blurring of home and fighting front which brought the Resistance role of women to the fore and made the infrastructure of the maquis the *sine qua non* of their own combative identity. It will also be contested by alternative local studies which will stress its non-existence in many rural areas or argue that it was never more than marginal in rural France as a whole. It has not, however, been the intention of this book to generalize; on the contrary the naming of persons and places in as much detail as possible has aimed at specificity. It is precisely the very localized nature of the outlaw culture which necessitates a rigorous search.

Metaphorically the search for the maquis was always a search for identity, and perhaps still is. At the time, it created the identity of the Milicien and the infiltrator as well as the maquisard, and among those who pursue its history it still forges the sceptic as well as the enthusiast, the demythologizer as well as the purveyor of myths. Keeping the focus on the South of France, it is clear that the choice or discovery of identity through the maquis has been a continuing dynamic beyond the Liberation. It proclaimed alternatives which have resonances outside the conjunctures of Occupation, Vichy, and the Resistance. It makes considerable historical sense to see the maquis as revealing, or at the very least strengthening, a notion of rural and regional value in the south. It did not need to be enunciated in Occitanist terms, but there is much to support Robert Lafont's contention that post-war Occitanists were orientated by the very existence of the maquis: 'La terre d'Oc a été une terre de maquis. Les combats pour la liberté ont été chantés en oc.'[17] The poetry of Max Allier proclaimed this identity and announced

[17] Robert Lafont, *L'Occitanie* (Seghers, 1971), 195.

the regional thrust of the maquis, a thrust which he himself still readily celebrates as a major dimension of Resistance France when it is analysed in local terms.[18] It carried a strong moral imperative in support of threatened sectors of southern society, miners of Bousquet-d'Orb, Decazeville, Carmaux, and Alès, *vignerons* of the Languedoc plain, textile workers of Mazamet, *bergers* in the sheep-rearing uplands of the plateau de Larzac, some of the many occupations still involved in a long resistance against enforced regional decline, economic neglect, and marginalization. The solidarity behind the miners' strike at Decazeville in 1962 as a struggle for community survival is a forward projection of the maquis: supportive peasants and traders took the local manifestations of the maquis as a *point de départ*.[19] There is an alternative history of the maquis to be written, not as a product of regionalism but as a regionalist incentive and cultural spur.

There is also a wider question of identity in the arguments of maquisards, saboteurs, and SOE agents such as Harry Rée and Francis Cammaerts, that the armed Resistance could harm and destroy German plant and equipment with an immeasurably smaller cost in human lives than the effects of Allied bombing. Only someone who had first been a conscientious objector could have observed, as Cammaerts did, that the success of the FFI on the Route Napoléon from Digne to Grenoble should be measured in the saving of lives, not just Allied and French but also German.[20] It was not a conventional measure of maquis achievement to assess the benefits for the Germans. In similar ways it seems anomalous to find the following appreciation of Léon Eyraud on the wall of the museum at Mont Mouchet. He was a Resister of Huguenot ancestry in le Chambon-sur-Lignon where he ran the Pension des Ombrages, sheltering Jews and *réfractaires* and directing young men into the maquis. He was convivial with an infectious sense of humour, and, we are then told, 'he knew how to moderate the fiery spirit of the maquisards, eager to use their weapons, and how to calm the anger which boiled up against those who were collaborators'. It seems an unlikely epitaph for any Resister, still less one associated with the maquis, until it is realized that a concern to pin-point the humanity and reconciliation within conflict and destruction has played an increasing role in the thinking behind new museums of war. There is an alternative search for the maquis as a

[18] Evidence from Max Allier, 26 Mar. 1982.

[19] Lafont, *L'Occitanie*, 198. See also for excellent analyses of previous workers' struggles in the south, Jean Sagnes, *Le Midi rouge. Mythe et réalité* (Anthropos, 1982).

[20] Evidence from Francis Cammaerts, 18 Mar. 1991. Harry Rée, who was also a conscientious objector before joining SOE, gave the author an interview in 1980 in which he told the story of his involvement in the highly successful sabotage of the Peugeot factory at Montbéliard in the Doubs, after the RAF had killed several nearby inhabitants in an ineffective raid. He commented that the operation, which prevented further loss of life, was an 'ideal job for someone with my attitudes to war'. See also Foot, *SOE in France*, 266 and 287, who stresses the use of sabotage as economical in lives, and who gives a good account of the Montbéliard operation.

minimizer of loss which would start from this perspective, enshrined in the title of the new war museum at Caen, 'Le Mémorial, un musée pour la paix'. In one account after another in the *zone sud*, the ill-informed and futile Allied bombing across the South of France from June to August 1944, which resulted in hundreds of random and incomprehensible civilian deaths, is compared to the frustrated capacity of Resistance groups whose access to military targets was informed and direct.[21] The refrain is a litany of lost opportunities: 'if only the Allies had adequately armed and trusted the saboteurs.' It is difficult to find any maquisard who does not reiterate those words. The controversy is relevant to all issues of guerrilla action and civilian resistance: it is not merely a specific debate about a single theatre of war.

How the history of the maquis might be differently recorded preoccupies much of the popular memory of the Occupation. The search for the maquis at the time, whether by *réfractaires* and Resisters on the run, military planners and visionaries, the AS, the FTP, or the ORA never ceased to reveal a number of alternative actions and strategies. The policies of Vichy played no small part in forcing choices, provoking reactions, and keeping the situation volatile. Crucial decisions still had to be made at the Liberation, and since then there has never been anything less than a lively sense of controversy among ex-maquisards. What might appear to be a simple celebration of an anniversary, or the erection of a monument, reopens a Pandora's box of alternatives. If this study has looked more closely at the structures of refuge and revolt than at the military organization of the FFI, valued women and men of supportive communities as highly as the men in the woods, talked of discourse as well as action, and brought the rural scenarios closer to the centre of the Resistance stage, then it is mainly a response to the inversions that the records, the memoirs, and the oral testimonies have themselves suggested. A sensitivity to ideas of inversion is only one more twist to the process of acknowledging alternatives. At Manigod, close to the Glières in the Haute-Savoie, there is one of the very rare memorials which mark, not the maquis dead and the victims of reprisals who are rightly mourned in a multitude of monuments, but the local role of villagers in the making of the maquis. On the wall of the village school there is a plaque which reads: 'In this commune young Frenchmen in revolt

[21] For comments on the Allied bombing see: evidence from Francis Cammaerts, 18 Mar. 1991; Sagnes, *L'Hérault dans la guerre*, 132–4; Maisonnas, *La Résistance en Ardèche*, 71–4; Guy Dürrenmatt, *Faim de Liberté ou les mémoires d'un jeune résistant ardéchois* (Le Regard du Monde: Aubenas, 1986), 118; Bourderon, *Libération du Languedoc méditerranéen*, 158. Bourderon's book gives a trenchant and lively account of the actions of the maquis and the FFI in this area for most of the spring and summer of 1944. On the bombings he writes, '... les sentiments pro-alliés ne furent pas affectés, car la population accepta les raids comme d'inévitables conséquences de la guerre ... Même s'il était inévitable que certains objectifs soient détruits par des interventions aériennes, on peut penser qu'une meilleure utilisation des capacités de sabotage de la Résistance, par la fourniture de l'armement nécessaire, aurait permis d'éviter d'aussi contestables opérations que celle qui ravagea Nîmes le 27 mai 1944.'

against deportation and forced labour for the enemy found a refuge, thanks to the support of the inhabitants, where they could prepare themselves militarily for the victorious struggles of the Liberation.' It is different. It is not a tombstone. It is an alternative way of remembering what the life of the maquis involved. There should be many more.

Abbreviations and Glossary

AD: Archives Départementales.

AMGOT: Allied Military Government of Occupied Territory. Projected interim government of European territories liberated by the Allies, which was not imposed on France in 1944 due to Allied recognition of the Provisional Government led by General de Gaulle (GPRF).

AN: Archives Nationales.

AO: Action Ouvrière. Initially an extension of the movement Combat into the urban working classes, it became an active instrument of industrial sabotage, maintaining its organizational position within the MUR but working closely with individual syndicalists and socialist and communist workers.

AS: Armée Secrète. The military side of the MUR led from the winter of 1942–3 by General Delestraint until his arrest in June 1943. It was kept theoretically separate from the organization of the maquis under the SNM, though this separation was widely ignored in practice. Under Delestraint the military role of the AS was to form groupes francs who would be armed and trained for all aspects of Resistance action. As the need to provide for *réfractaires* from STO grew more pressing, many local AS groups began to act as the organizers and providers of the maquis, constituting themselves as *sédentaires*, operating from their homes in support of their local maquis groups. Thus any one area could see the co-existence and overlap of groupes francs, *sédentaires*, and maquis, all representing the AS.

BCA: Bataillon de Chasseurs Alpins. Regiments of the French army based in the Alpine regions. From the 27e BCA emerged many of the leaders and men of the Maquis des Glières.

BCRA: Bureau Central de Renseignements et d'Action (Militaire). The intelligence and action network of de Gaulle's France Libre (later France Combattante), run initially from London by Captain (later Colonel) Dewavrin (Passy). It sent French agents to organize Resistance within France, closely allied to RF section of the British SOE which provided the necessary money and arms from the War Office. Both the BCRA and RF section were often intense rivals of the other section of SOE—F section—which sent British agents to France.

CDL: Comité Départemental de Libération. Nominated, often as early as the winter of 1943–4, in each *département*, these Resistance committees formulated local policy at the Liberation and advised and assisted the Liberation prefects throughout the remaining months of the war.

CFL: Corps Francs de la Libération. The AS and the maquis within the MUR were merged into the CFL in May 1944, a reorganization anticipated on the ground by the structural dependence of many maquis units on the local AS. The formal merging did, however, appear to give a boost to those calling for more direct action by AS maquis groups before Jour-J.

CFLN: Comité Français de Libération Nationale. The governing body of France Combattante established in Algiers under both Giraud and de Gaulle. From the spring of 1944 de Gaulle assumed single leadership.

CFMN: Corps Franc de la Montagne Noire. A fighting Resistance unit of over 500 men assembled in the mountains to the south of the Tarn in June 1944, which received a number of *parachutages* and was attacked by a much larger German force in July. It disbanded, but its separate units continued maquis activity in the surrounding area.

CLL: Comité Local de Libération. Committees nominated by the Resistance to take the place of municipal councils at the Liberation until the first post-war local elections of April–May 1945.

CNR: Conseil National de la Résistance. The crowning achievement of Jean Moulin's efforts to unite the Resistance within France under de Gaulle. Unlike the MUR it brought together all the Resistance movements in the south including the Front National, and the first leader after Jean Moulin's arrest in June 1943 was Georges Bidault who came from the internal Resistance and was not an envoy of de Gaulle. The essential role of the CNR was to give shape to the aims of the Resistance for liberated France. This was achieved in the CNR charter of March 1944 to which Resisters calling for social as well as political changes at the Liberation specifically referred as the authoritative and radical voice of Resistance France. The CNR's military organization was the Comité d'Action Militaire (COMAC) which acted as a unifying force in the struggles of the Liberation.

FFI: Forces Françaises de l'Intérieur. The official, and at first largely theoretical, merging of all armed Resistance into one military organization under General Koenig who had led the French against Rommel in the victory of Bir-Hakeim in June 1942. The FFI dated from the end of 1943, but it was not until the spring of 1944 that regional and departmental FFI leaders were in place, and in some southern areas the practical and strategic fusion of groupes francs, maquis, and FTP forces did not happen until July or even August. Even then the grass-roots units retained much of their individuality of leadership and tactical approach. It was said by Montgomery and Eisenhower that the FFI were worth between ten and fifteen divisions to the Allies in the liberation of France.

FN: Front National. The Resistance movement initiated by the Parti Communiste Français in 1941, which operated in both zones and was open to all volunteers whether communist or not. By 1944 several non-communists were on its directing committees. It was both a military and political movement, with the FTP as its main military forces, and it was based on the concept of immediate, direct action, including attacks against individual German personnel. Its organizational links with the Communist Party continued after the Liberation.

FTP (F): Francs-Tireurs et Partisans (Français). The armed forces of the FN, open, like the movement itself, to all volunteers, and equally identified with the Communist Party, though the closeness of that identification varied considerably from unit to unit. The national leader was Charles Tillon, and each FTP unit, whether urban or rural, had a tripartite structure of command: a commissaire aux affaires militaires, effectively the leader in any action, a commissaire aux effectifs, responsible for recruitment, political matters, and the external relations of the group, and a commissaire technique, responsible for all material provisioning, including arms and food. The FTP's chain of military command ran through regional and departmental leaders, and during 1944 every region had its own FTP batallions, each grouping several companies. At its most organized in the summer of 1944, the basic unit was a detachment of twenty-eight men, divided into three groups of eight, together with the three commissaires and an *agent de liaison*. This was more a model than a universal reality, and local FTP units varied considerably in size after the afflux of volunteers in June 1944. Some had their own special corps francs for specific tasks, and all made a distinction between those more or less permanently mobilized away from home and the *sédentaires* or *statiques* who operated from their homes and workplaces as providers, support, and reserve.

FUJP: Front Uni des Jeunesses Patriotiques *or* Forces Unies de la Jeunesse Patriotique. Set up in the autumn of 1943 to mobilize young people in support of maquis groups and the FTP, it derived from an MUR initiative, but in most areas developed its own spontaneous and independent character. Many of those involved were teenagers, who later joined the maquis or made up the milices patriotiques at the Liberation. Tracts promoting resistance to STO were issued by groups of FUJP in most of the southern towns, and there were raids on STO files.

GF: Groupes Francs. Formed as action units within Combat as early as 1941, they became the main military formations of the AS before, and alongside, the maquis. In some areas, such as the Bouches-du-Rhône, they were the main military forces of the Resistance right through to the Liberation, operating from their homes in acts of sabotage, harassment of the enemy, and eventually direct military encounters. Like the AS maquis, the groupes francs received parachuted arms and ammunition organized directly by British or French agents acting individually, or by the Service Atterrissage Parachutage (SAP) which co-ordinated the reconnaissance of possible landing grounds and organized their coding with the BCRA and the SOE.

GMR: Groupes Mobiles de Réserve. Vichy paramilitary police organized in regional brigades whose main function became the hunt for the maquis.

GPRF: Gouvernement provisoire de la République Française. Developing from the CFLN, and led by General de Gaulle, it established itself in Paris at the Liberation and continued the war against Germany. Its success, and de Gaulle's right to represent the French nation, was symbolized by the presence of France at the signing of Germany's surrender.

JOUR-J: D-Day. Also referred to as 'le débarquement'. Both terms were used in expectation of the Allied landing and were current throughout 1943 as well as the first five months of 1944.

MOI: Main d'Œuvre Immigrée. Pre-war organization set up by the PCF to defend the rights of immigrant workers in France. It continued as a force within the work camps set up by Vichy and in the rural *chantiers* which employed large amounts of foreign labour (TE). It worked with local Resistance leaders to create maquis and FTP units when its workers were threatened with arrest or deportation.

MUR: Mouvements Unis de la Résistance. The unified organization of Resistance made up of three movements of the *zone sud*, Combat, Libération (sud), and Franc-Tireur. The MUR dated from January 1943 and was one of the products of Jean Moulin's unificatory missions to France on behalf of General de Gaulle. It had been hoped to include the Front National and the FTP but such a fusion only took place within the CNR and eventually the FFI.

NAP: Noyautage des Administrations Publiques. A branch of Combat in 1942 aimed at infiltrating and destabilizing the public administrative sectors, it grew under the MUR into a powerful source of Resistance activity, particularly in the postal and telephone services and the railways.

ORA: Organisation de Résistance de l'Armée. An extension of Resistance already started within the Armistice Army, but effectively relaunched after the latter's dissolution following the German occupation of the *zone sud*. Its organization was on professional military lines, with career officers in charge, and initially it looked to Giraud as a Resistance leader rather than to de Gaulle. Its aim was to train and prepare for Jour-J, without political involvement, and its maquis formations during the Liberation period were independent of the AS and the FTP, though they were officially part of the FFI. Before 6 June 1944 the ORA made contacts and distributed arms, but it was not until the mobilization orders at Jour-J that the ORA maquis were firmly established. At that point the Toulouse area (R4) saw the emergence of some 3,000 armed men, grouped in small units under professional officers, and in the Marseille area (R2) the numbers were estimated as 2,000. There were ORA groupings in all the other areas of the south and their numbers grew like all other combat organizations during July and August: they played a considerable role in the military encounters of the Liberation.

OSS: Office of Strategic Services. American secret services sending agents into France, though far fewer than those from SOE. Many arrived after Jour-J on Jedburgh missions, uniformed teams of British, French, and Americans trained in guerrilla tactics who brought arms and leadership to local French Resistance particularly in the west of the *zone sud*.

OT: Organisation Todt. German-run organization constructing fortifications within France particularly on the coasts. It carried the name of the German engineer Todt who had originally made his reputation in autobahn construction, and it conscripted thousands of French and immigrant labour, often in rivalry with the German and Vichy efforts to maximize the sending of workers to Germany under STO.

PCF: Parti Communiste Français.

PPF: Parti Populaire Français, the pre-war party of Jacques Doriot, closely involved in acts of collaboration, notably the recruitment of the Légion des Volontaires Français contre le Bolchévisme (LVF) which fought for Germany on the Russian front.

PTT: Postes, Télégraphes, Téléphones.

R1, R2, R3, etc.: the twelve military regions of Resistance France, six of which were in the *zone sud*, i.e. the regions centred on Lyon (R1), Marseille (R2), Montpellier (R3), Toulouse (R4), Limoges (R5), and Clermont-Ferrand (R6). In the organization of both the SNM and the FFI regional military leaders varied enormously in the degree of co-ordination and control that they exercised over the combative units on the ground. The difficulties of maintaining regular contact and responding to the unpredictability of Vichy and German movements left many essential decisions to be taken at the level of the local maquis leaders. Regional estimates on numbers and material effectiveness were often wildly inaccurate and historians will always be reluctant to give precise figures for the regional strength of the armed Resistance.

Résistance-Fer: A highly successful area of sabotage operations organized among railway workers. It had its own organization within the MUR but all Resistance bodies—FTP, maquis, SOE, groupes francs, AO, etc.—

worked closely with railway saboteurs and intelligence networks within the SNCF.

SCT: Service du Contrôle Technique. The Vichy mechanisms of postal censorship and telephone tapping, under which thousands of letters were intercepted in every *département* every week, and evidence drawn from them on subjects designated by Vichy as the most important and sensitive areas of policy and public opinion. Most of the letters were then sent on to their destinations as if they had not been opened, and reports and findings from the interceptions were sent to the Prefect and the Ministry of the Interior. The system became more and more of a political surveillance operation and was subject to increasingly direct control from Vichy.

SNCF: Société Nationale des Chemins de Fer français. The French railway network.

SNM: Service National Maquis. Organization set up by the MUR in April 1943 to promote and co-ordinate the creation of the maquis as a separate form of Resistance from the AS. Its head was Michel Brault (see Note on the SNM, p. 297).

SOE: Special Operations Executive. Secret British organization set up to wage war against Germany within Occupied Europe. F Section under Major (later Colonel) Maurice Buckmaster was the main body which sent British agents into France, building close to one hundred independent circuits, and recruiting French Resisters on the ground. There was the less extensive RF Section which also operated in France with French agents, and RF worked more closely with the Gaullist BCRA.

SS: Schutzstaffeln. Originally Hitler's protection squads with their distinctive black shirts, organized by Heinrich Himmler, they made up several armoured divisions within France and were the most determined in their actions against the maquis. SS divisions, such as Das Reich, were sent to the *zone sud* to recuperate from service on the Eastern Front.

SSR: Service de Santé de la Résistance. Resistance medical service, constituted at national and local level within the MUR from 1943 onwards.

STO: Service du Travail Obligatoire. A successor to the *Relève* scheme to meet Sauckel's demands for labour in Germany, it was promulgated on 13 February 1943 and made labour service obligatory for most young Frenchmen aged between 20 and 23. Numerous refinements, extensions, and a complexity of exemptions followed with each new demand from Sauckel for ever-increasing numbers. After a break in departures for Germany in the last months of 1943, the whole process of STO was finally suspended by Laval on 23 June 1944. By then the Germans, under the pressure of the Allied landings, had ceased to insist on its implementation.

TE: Travail Étranger. Vichy's organization of immigrant workers into camps and *chantiers*, mostly in forestry and agriculture.

UFF: Union des Femmes Françaises. A broad-based Resistance movement of women, recalling the movement which had been prominent during the Paris Commune of 1871. It was re-formed in mid 1944, continuing the work of the 'comités féminins', and like them closely linked to the communist Resistance. At the Liberation many women became members of the CDLs or CLLs as representatives of the UFF.

Note on the operation of the Service National Maquis (SNM)

ESSENTIALLY the role of the SNM was to turn *réfractaires* into military combatants, as set out in Michel Brault's first two circulars of April–May 1943. Brault envisaged three large natural maquis regions in the *zone sud*: the northern Alps, the southern Alps, and the Massif Central, but accepted the administrative structure adopted by both Vichy and the Resistance of military regions (R1, R2, R3, etc.). In all the six regions of the south the initiative in forming the first maquis groups was taken locally, before the SNM was fully operational, and Brault's first need was to discover the number of groups already in existence, or rather to scale down the estimates which came in from over-optimistic, or over-credulous, organizers. The Montpellier region (R3), according to Brault, was poorly organized from the start, and the Toulouse region (R4) he described as 'catastrophic' in the late summer of 1943. His judgements reflect, not the wealth of initiatives which had created the first maquis in these areas, but his estimation of administrative coherence.[1] The SNM was always one step behind, trying to locate, enumerate, and structure the groups formed by others, but it was not therefore irrelevant to the development of the maquis. It was on the basis of Brault's calculations that money, made available from the BCRA, was handed out to the regions, and many of his organizers painstakingly investigated the forests and hills of their region, bringing groups into closer contact and providing a much-needed financial impetus at a crucial stage in their growth.

It was, for example, the eulogistic appraisal of the maquis organized by Romans-Petit in the Ain which brought an Anglo-French mission to the area together with a succession of *parachutages*. In the south-west of France an army captain Sarda de Caumont (Rosette), appointed by Brault to bring coherence to R4, claimed to have organized 71 different maquis groups in

[1] AN 72. AJ. 63, report by Michel Brault, 18 Dec. 1944, p. 4. See also his interview with Marie Granet in 1949, p. 2.

the region from his base in Toulouse. By February 1944 he estimated total maquis strength in the area to have reached 2,800. His leading *agent de liaison* was a Parisienne, Thérèse Armand-Duclos (Antoinette), who brought money from Brault and distributed it to different groups.[2] Equivalent responsibility for R5 (Limoges) was vested in Georgette Gérard, who had earlier been given the job by Combat of setting up the AS in the Dordogne from November 1942 to March 1943. Originally from Lorraine she met large numbers of refugees from her home region, exiled by the war in the Limousin area, who gave her a sense of belonging, even though she had no prior knowledge of the Dordogne. When she moved from the AS to the SNM she travelled ceaselessly by train and bicycle across R5, reporting her discoveries and achievements to meetings in Paris and Lyon. By November 1943 she estimated the number of maquisards as 5,000 in a multitude of small camps, totalling a maximum of 120 men in each, with the Corrèze most heavily implanted. Her numbers included the FTP who 'made up half the effective force', and with whom, she asserted, she personally always had good relations. Her difficulties, she stated, lay first in disguising the fact that a woman was effectively in charge, and secondly in dealing with political susceptibilities.[3] Brault was ambivalent towards her, respectful of her capabilities, but ultimately deciding that 'her sex and her political sympathies' disqualified her from running such a difficult region. He held her to be both very pious and very anti-communist.[4] She was replaced in January 1944, a decision she herself ascribed to the fact that she was too closely pursued by the Gestapo. Her sideways move into the network Andalousie was deemed a sensible precaution by Georges Rebattet (Cheval), Brault's second in command.[5]

Both Georgette Gérard and Sarda de Caumont emerge in their own reports as 'organizers' of the maquis, but local accounts hardly, if ever, mention them as organizers and refer rarely to any initiative by the SNM. It would seem more accurate to describe them as co-ordinators, and as one part of the provisioning structure from above. Indeed Georgette Gérard refers to the diffuse nature of this structure in her post-war testimony. Arms, she said, in the Limousin, came from parachute drops organized by a British agent, clothes came, at times, from Paris, and money from Brault and Rebattet.[6]

Policy and personality differences within the MUR are overtly mentioned in the SNM reports, particularly in respect of relationships with the parallel

[2] Ibid., evidence given to Marie Granet by Sarda de Caumont in 1955.
[3] Ibid., evidence given to Marie Granet by Madame Georgette Gérard, 31 Jan. 1950.
[4] Ibid., Brault's report, 18 Dec. 1944, p. 5.
[5] Ibid., Georgette Gérard's evidence, p. 9. Georgette Gérard was arrested by the Gestapo in May 1944 and held in Limoges until the town was liberated by the FFI in August.
[6] Ibid. 7–8.

structures of the AS. General Delestraint, leader of the AS, was unresponsive to the popular and *ad hoc* origins and activities of the maquis, and Jean Moulin shared his concern that the maquis should be controlled and trained as a potential army under Allied command, leaving the AS to organize direct action such as sabotage. Shortly after the decision to situate the SNM within the political wing of the MUR the budget allotted to that section was cut by the BCRA. The meaning was clear. The maquis were not to be equipped to engage in an outbreak of immediate action: sabotage and other such acts were to remain the province of the AS and its groupes francs, Résistance-Fer, and Action Ouvrière. The maquis, according to this design, were to receive the *réfractaires* and concentrate on long-term military training.

The arrest and death of Jean Moulin and the deportation of General Delestraint were the major events at the top which threw this strategy into disarray. But at the grass roots the rolling effect of maquis *coups de main* carried the whole strategic arguments beyond the control of the national leaders of the MUR. On 1 September 1943 Brault's SNM met in Lyon to co-ordinate the organization of both major zones. In the *zone sud* the number of maquisards in camps was put at 22,000, with a further 8,000–10,000 men in individual hiding-places. The penury in arms was widely noted, but the expectation of an imminent Allied landing led the SNM to look forward to 'des parachutages massifs'. But of all the results of the meeting the most revealing was the acceptance that the maquis could be held together and could survive the winter only if they launched war on Vichy institutions such as 'dépôts de secours national' and the Chantiers de la Jeunesse, and trained not just as combatants but also as saboteurs. From that moment, Brault affirms that guerrilla warfare was officially approved by the MUR maquis,[7] though he himself declared at an SNM meeting in October that he would call the maquisards 'militaires' but not 'combattants' because they would not be thrown into combat until the Allied invasion (Jour-J).[8]

It is this distinction which informed the MUR or AS maquis throughout the winter of 1943–4 and led to the FTP accusations of 'attentisme'. *Coups de main* and acts of sabotage were endorsed, but any engagement with the enemy was to depend on the instructions and strategy of the Allied command at the moment of the *débarquement*. At the level of practicality it was neither a clear nor a consistent distinction, and it was blurred by the generic word 'action' as used, for example, by Henri Jaboulay, the leader of R1, who reported at the end of October 1943 that 'One of the surest means, in fact an indispensable means, of creating cohesion and team spirit within the camps, and keeping morale high, is through action.'[9] The word could, and did, indicate an indeterminate number of maquis activities, but it continued

7 Ibid., Brault's report, 18 Dec. 1944, p. 7.
8 Quoted in Henri Noguères, *Histoire de la Résistance* (Laffont, 1967–81), iv. 59–60.
9 Quoted by F. Marcot in 'Les Maquis dans la Résistance', in *Colloque sur les maquis*, 21.

to be argued within the SNM that even discriminate attacks on the occupying forces were to be discouraged, not least because of the insufficiency of arms. Brault was eloquent in putting his case to London that the maquis could not even be termed *militaires*, let alone *combattants*, without the requisite arms and ammunition. He also signalled a dearth of military personnel ready to be appointed by the SNM to the role of officers in the maquis.

By the end of 1943 the separate status of the SNM was being progressively eroded by the close structural relationships between AS groups and the local maquis, and by early 1944 its role was defunct. The integration of all military aspects of the MUR into the Corps Francs de la Libération (CFL) in late May 1944 was a long-overdue recognition of the widespread reality on the ground. But the CFL were more a name than a coherent force, and the potent symbol of a co-ordinated armed Resistance was soon the FFI.

Sources and Bibliography

1. National and Local Archives

Archives Nationales, Paris (AN)

F1C III, Rapports des Préfets au Ministère de l'Intérieur

F1C III. 1135, Ain
F1C III. 1143, Bouches-du-Rhône
F1C III. 1147, Corrèze
F1C III. 1148, Côte-d'Or (*zone occupée*)
F1C III. 1151, Dordogne
F1C III. 1153, Gard
F1C III. 1158, Isère
F1C III. 1163, Lot
F1C III. 1165, Lozère
F1C III. 1186, Savoie
F1C III. 1187, Haute-Savoie
F1C III. 1193, Tarn
F1C III. 1194, Var
F1C III. 1195, Vaucluse
F1C III. 1197, Haute-Vienne

F7 Police

F7. 14610, Bulletins hebdomadaires des Renseignements Généraux
F7. 14880, Menées antinationales
F7. 14881, Répression des menées antinationales
F7. 14887, Utilisation des détenus
F7. 14888, Communistes, terroristes
F7. 14889, Personnel de la police et lois sur le STO
F7. 14892, Cours martiales
F7. 14893, Gendarmerie
F7. 14894, GMR
F7. 14895, Notes allemandes sur les Renseignements Généraux
F7. 14897, Grèves, septembre 1943–août 1944
F7. 14898, Sécurité des troupes d'occupation

F7. 14900, Milice avril–août 1944
F7. 14904, Activité terroriste
F7. 14908, Circulaires 1943
F7. 14909, Circulaires 1944
F7. 14912, Gardes des communications
F7. 14924–F7. 14934, Services des Contrôles Techniques
F7. 15312, Attentats 1944

397 AP 12–14, Papiers Marie Granet

72. AJ, Archives de la Commission d'Histoire de l'Occupation et de la Libération de la France et Archives du Comité d'Histoire de la Deuxième Guerre Mondiale

72. AJ 9, STO 1943–4
72. AJ 63, Maquis
72. AJ 80, Union des femmes françaises
72. AJ 112, Corrèze
72. AJ 124, Gard
72. AJ 157, Lot
72. AJ 159, Lozère
72. AJ 198, Tarn
72. AJ 512–517, Papiers Galimand. Histoire des FFI

F 60 Premier Ministre

F 60. 514, Service des Contrôles Techniques (SCT), 1941–6; Milice française

Archives Départementales (AD)

AD Aude, Carcassonne

M 2575, Militaires disparus dans les maquis
M 2585, Propagande régionaliste
M 2609, Tracts divers
M 2641–M 2647, Activité des maquis, par communes A–V
M 2648, Journées de la Libération
M 2656, Contrôle Technique
M 2740, Sabotages, attentats, rafles, 1943–4

AD Gard, Nîmes

CA 300, Communistes, 1940–3
CA 311, Affaires, cabinet du Maréchal
CA 314, Rapports mensuels, 1944–5
CA 317, Presse, censure, 1944–5
CA 328, Tracts divers
CA 367, Rapports avec les autorités occupantes
CA 413, Attentats, 1943
CA 483, CDL Résistance et maquis

CA 511, Gaullisme
CA 572, Rapport moral, 1944
CA 573, Messages sur la situation de différentes localités
CA 661–CA 670, Terrorisme, attentats, 1941–4
CA 763, STO Réfractaires, 1942–4
CA 764, Ilôts de résistance
CA 777, Rapport moral, 1943
CA 993, STO Réfractaires. Enquêtes, 1953–5
CA 1294, Mouvements de Résistance clandestine, 1944–50
CA 1482, Textes législatifs du gouvernement de Vichy, 1940–3
CA 1483, Images de propagande du gouvernement de Vichy
CA 1510–CA 1516, Documents divers, 1940–4
CA 1861, Attitudes de certains fonctionnaires

AD Haute-Garonne, Toulouse

1769/4, STO Défaillants
1769/5, STO
1831/98, Départs STO. Incidents
1867/166, Arrestations par la police allemande
1867/268, STO. Circulaires, instructions
1960/6, Réfractaires. Opérations de police
1960/116, Israélites
1945/74, Répression des activités anti-gouvernementales
2008/88, Réfractaires. Recherches, 1943–4
M 1526^{1}, Renseignements Généraux. Synthèses, jan.–mars. 1944
M 1526^{2}, ditto, avril–juin 1944
M 1526^{4}, Rapports de l'Intendance de Police

AD Hérault, Montpellier

13W AC 183, Circulaires sur le STO
13W AC 184, STO Listes
13W AC 226, Jeunes chômeurs
15W 169, Main d'Œuvre étrangère
15W 237, Main d'Œuvre
17W 1–17W 14, STO divers
17W 157, Défaillants. SNCF
17W 163–17W 168, Défaillants
17W 231, Défaillants. Agriculteurs
18W 8–18W 10, Noms à rechercher
18W 13, Chantiers de la Jeunesse. Tracts divers
18W 14, Communistes 1940–3
18W 15, Gardes communications
18W 18, Attentats, vols
18W 19, Terrorisme. Listes S et S^{1}
18W 25, Incidents. Intendant de police, rapports
18W 63, STO mai–novembre 1943

18W 64, STO 1943–4
18W 65, Travail Étranger (TE)
136W 1, Rapports du préfet au Commissaire de la Rép.
136W 9, Procès-verbal. CDL du Gard
136W 22, Groupement national de réfractaires
136W 25, CRL Languedoc-Roussillon
138W 17, Séances du CDL de l'Hérault, 1944
138W 18, ditto, 1945
159W 35, Commissariat Général aux Questions Juives
159W 42, Rapports divers. Capestang 6/7 juin 1944
159W 44, Incidents mai–juillet 1944
161W 51, Organisation Todt
161W 69, Relève et STO, 1942–3
172W 4, Bulletins hebdomadaires de Renseignements
172W 35, Journaux clandestins et tracts divers
172W 49, Attentats, dommages
Journaux divers:
L'Information du Languedoc
Le Volontaire
La Voix de la Patrie
Midi libre
Le Travailleur du Languedoc
Languedoc ouvrier
Libération
Défense de la France

AD Lozère, Mende

R 5902, Attentats, réfractaires, 1944
R 5941, Maquis d'Aire-de-Côte
R 7049, Répression de dissidence, Haute-Lozère
R 7060, Tracts divers
R 7244, Propagande paysanne
VI. M2. 19, Contrôle postal. Synthèses, rapports
VI. M2. 21, Contrôle postal concernant menées anti-nationales
VI. M2. 23, Contrôle postal concernant STO, jeunesse
M 11973, Recherches étrangers, 1942–4
T 5880 Cévennes, mémoires

2. Oral Evidence, Now in Author's Archives in Recorded or Noted Form

(Note: the first three interviews were recorded for my earlier volume, *Resistance in Vichy France* (1978), but have been mentioned in the text or footnotes above)

Romain Baz, Annemasse (10 May 1969)

JEAN VITTOZ, Annemasse (19 May 1969)
Abbé ALVITRE, Brive (21 Sept. 1972)
H. M. DESPAIGNE, London (18 Aug. 1979)
HENRI PRADES and Madame PRADES, Lattes (4 Feb. 1982)
FRANÇOIS ROUAN, Montpellier (25 Feb. 1982)
ROBERT BONNAFOUS, Saint-Geniès-des-Mourgues (26 Feb. 1982)
JEAN-PIERRE CHABROL, Génolhac (2 Mar. 1982)
HENRI CORDESSE, Montpellier (22 Mar. and 5 Apr. 1982)
RAYMOND FOURNIER, Rodès (23 Mar. 1982)
MAX ALLIER and Madame ALLIER, Montpellier (26 Mar. 1982)
MAURICE POUGET and BERTHE POUGET, Montpellier (24 May 1982)
GILBERT DE CHAMBRUN, Marvejols (25 May 1982)
ÉTIENNE BOUTES and OLGA BOUTES, Montpellier (21 June 1982)
LUCIEN MAURY and FRANÇOISE MAURY, Quillan (24 June 1982)
MICHEL BANCILHON, Aubenas (5 July 1982)
ÉDOUARD MONTCOUQUIOL and JEAN PUJADAS, Aubenas (6 July 1982)
GÉRALD SUBERVILLE and DENISE GUILLAUME, Paris (7 Dec. 1984)
MAURICE BUCKMASTER, Forest Row (4 Nov. 1990)
YVONNE CORMEAU (Mrs J. Farrow), Kegworth (22 Jan. 1991)
ANDRÉ POUGET, ÉLISE JOUCLAS, and ALBERT MÉLIX, Arcambal (5 Mar. 1991)
MICHELINE BISMES, Aujols (5 Mar. 1991)
IRÈNE MARTY, Piboulède (6 Mar. 1991)
MAURICE DARNAULT, Cahors (7 Mar. 1991)
CHARLES SIMON, Monteils (7 Mar. 1991)
GABRIELLE BOUDET, Marcilhac (7 Mar. 1991)
AIMÉ NOËL, Figeac (9 Mar. 1991)
FRANÇOIS TAYRAC and LUCIENNE TAYRAC, Saint-Perdoux (9 Mar. 1991)
PIERRE LABIE and REINE LABIE, Lalbenque (11 Mar. 1991)
PIERRE COUDERQ and BERTHE COUDERQ, Gramat (12 Mar. 1991)
Abbé GAUCH, Cahors (15 Mar. 1991)
Abbé TOULZE, Trespoux (15 Mar. 1991)
FRANCIS CAMMAERTS, Grane (18 Mar. 1991)
SIMONE CONQUET, Cahors (15 Mar. 1991)
PIERRE COMBES, Cahors (27 Mar. 1991)
JOSEPH NODARI, Cahors (28 Mar. 1991)
JOSEPH ROHR, Labastide-Murat (3 Apr. 1991)
JEAN QUESTA, Lauzès (3 Apr. 1991)
Abbé SOUIRY, Prendeignes (4 Apr. 1991)
Dr JOSEPH BEC, Saint-Pons (18 June 1991)
ARMAND CALAS, Saint-Pons (18 June 1991)
PIERRE BOYER, Saint-Affrique (24 June 1991)

3. UNPUBLISHED THESES AND PAPERS

ABRAHAMS, PAUL, 'Haute-Savoie at War, 1939–1945' (Ph.D., University of Cambridge, 1992).

ATKIN, N. J., 'Catholics and Schools in Vichy France, 1940–44' (Ph.D., University of London, 1988).

AUSTIN, ROGER, 'The Educational and Youth Policies of the Vichy Government in the Department of Hérault, 1940–1944' (Ph.D., University of Manchester, 1981).

CARRIER, RENÉ, 'Récit du combat de Montchal, 19 mars 1944' (Lyon, n.d.).

COMBES, PIERRE, 'Récit d'un coup de main: destruction par les FUJP des archives du STO à Cahors, le 3 février 1944' (Cahors, 1989).

CONRAD, BARBARA, H., 'Politics of the Resistance and the Political and Administrative Reconstruction of the Côte-d'Or' (D.Phil., University of Sussex, 1991).

DIAMOND, HANNA, 'Women's Experience During and After World War Two in the Haute-Garonne, 1939–1948' (D.Phil., University of Sussex, 1992).

POCHARD, COLONEL, 'La Résistance en Savoie, synthèse explicative' (1973) (in my possession).

POLLARD, MIRANDA, J., 'Femme, Famille, France: Vichy and the Politics of Gender, 1940–1944' (Ph.D., Trinity College, Dublin, 1989).

VISTE, JEAN, 'Le Maquis Latourette' (1990) (in my possession).

4. BOOKS

Place of publication is Paris unless otherwise stated.

AMOUROUX, HENRI, *La Grande Histoire des français sous l'occupation*, 8 vols. (Laffont, 1976–88).

Les Anarchistes dans la Résistance, 2 vols. (CIRA: Marseille, 1985).

ARAGON, CHARLES D', *La Résistance sans héroïsme* (Seuil, 1977).

ARNOULT, PIERRE, *Les Finances de la France et l'occupation allemande* (PUF, 1951).

AZÉMA, J-P., *From Munich to the Liberation 1938–1944* (CUP: Cambridge, 1984).

BART, JEAN, *Histoire d'un groupe franc du maquis de Dordogne* (Pierre Fanlac: Périgueux, 1945).

BARTHES, HENRI, *Moïse ne savait pas nager. De Roquefort à Montpellier. Histoire de l'Armée Secrète du Sud-Aveyron et le Maquis Paul Claie* (Bardou: Espéraza, 1988).

BAUDOIN, MADELEINE, *Histoire des Groupes Francs (M.U.R.) des Bouches-du-Rhône* (PUF, 1962).

BENAZECH, YVES, *Les Terroristes de l'espérance: chronique de la Résistance dans le Tarn* (Benazech: Albi, 1985).

BERTAUX, PIERRE, *Libération de Toulouse et de sa région* (Hachette, 1973).

BILLAT, PAUL, *Levés à l'aube de la Résistance dauphinoise* (Les Imprimeurs réunis: Sassenage, 1978).

BOLLE, PIERRE (ed.), *Grenoble et le Vercors. De la résistance à la libération* (La Manufacture: Lyon, 1985).

BONTE, FLORIMOND, *Les Antifascistes allemands dans la Résistance française* (Éditions sociales, 1969).

BOULADOU, GÉRARD, *Les Maquis du massif central méridional* (Service de reproduction de thèses: Lille, 1975).

BOUNIN, JACQUES, *Beaucoup d'imprudences* (Stock, 1974).

BOURDERON, ROGER, *Libération du Languedoc méditerranéen* (Hachette, 1974).

BRÈS, ÉVELINE and YVAN, *Un Maquis d'antifascistes allemands en France, 1942–1944* (Presses du Languedoc: Montpellier, 1987).

BUCKMASTER, MAURICE, *They Fought Alone: The Story of British Agents in France* (Odhams: London, 1958).

CANAUD, JACQUES, *Les Maquis du Morvan* (Académie de Morvan: Château-Chinon, 1981).

CAZARD, GEORGES, *Capitaine Philippe, ou l'histoire du maquis du Lot au travers de la biographie de J. J. Chapou* (Coueslant: Cahors, 1950).

CHABROL, JEAN-PIERRE, *Un homme de trop* (Gallimard, 1958).

CHAMBRUN, GILBERT DE, *Journal d'un militaire d'occasion* (Aubanel: Avignon, 1982).

CHAUDIER, ALBERT, *Limoges 1944–1947. Capitale du maquis* (Lavauzelle, 1980).

CHAYNES, FERNAND, and SAULIÈRE, ÉMILE, *Le Tarn et les tarnais dans la deuxième guerre mondiale* (Éditions de la Revue du Tarn: Albi, n.d.).

CHIPIER, Abbé ÉTIENNE, *Souffrances et gloires du maquis chablaisien* (Reflets de notre temps: Thonon-les-Bains, 1946).

Les Clandestins de Dieu, CIMADE 1939–1944 (Le Signe Fayard, 1968).

Colloque sur les maquis 22/23 novembre 1984 (Institut d'Histoire des Conflits Contemporains, 1986).

CORDESSE, HENRI, *Histoire de la Résistance en Lozère 1940–44* (Cordesse: n.p., 1974).

—— *La Libération en Lozère 1944–1945* (Cordesse: n.p., 1977).

—— and PIERREL, M., *La Lozère de 1940 à 1944* (Marvejols, n.d.).

COURTOIS, STÉPHANE, PESCHANSKI, DENIS, and RAYSKI, ADAM, *Le Sang de l'étranger. Les immigrés de la MOI dans la Résistance* (Fayard, 1989).

CURTIS, JEAN-LOUIS, *Les Forêts de la nuit* (Julliard, 1947).

DALLOZ, PIERRE, *Vérités sur le drame du Vercors* (Fernand Lanore, 1979).

Dossiers noirs d'une certaine résistance: trajectoires du fascisme rouge, 1944 (Éditions du CES: Perpignan, 1984).

DREYFUS, PAUL, *Vercors, citadelle de liberté* (Arthaud, 1969).

DURANDET, CHRISTIAN, *Les Maquis de Provence* (France-Empire, 1974).

DÜRRENMATT, GUY, *Faim de liberté ou les mémoires d'un jeune résistant ardéchois* (Le Regard du Monde: Aubenas, 1986).

ÉRIGNAC, LOUIS, *La Révolte des Croates de Villefranche-de-Rouergue* (Érignac: Villefranche-de-Rouergue, 1988).

ÉVRARD, RENÉ, and VIELZEUF, AIMÉ, *Comme le scorpion sous la laùze* (Évrard et Vielzeuf: Nîmes, 1980).

EYCHENNE, ÉMILIENNE, *Les Portes de la liberté: le franchissement clandestin de la frontière espagnole dans les Pyrénées-Orientales* (Privat: Toulouse, 1985).

FOOT, M. R. D., *SOE in France: An Account of the Work of the British Special Operations Executive in France 1940–1944* (HMSO: London, 1966).

—— *Resistance* (Eyre Methuen: London, 1976).

FOOTITT, HILARY, and SIMMONDS, JOHN, *France 1943–1945* (University Press: Leicester, 1988).

FOULON, C.-L., *Le Pouvoir en province à la Libération: les Commissaires de la République 1943–1946* (Presses de la Fondation Nationale des Sciences Politiques, 1975).

FOURNIER, RAYMOND, *Terre de combat: récits sur la Résistance* (Maury: Millau, 1973).

FREIRE, JEAN, *Les Maquis au combat, textes et témoignages* (Julliard, 1970).

GAMBIEZ, Général, *Libération de la Corse* (Hachette, 1973).

GERMAIN, MICHEL, *Les Maquis de l'espoir: l'occupation italienne en Haute-Savoie (novembre 1942–septembre 1943)* (Cercles d'Or: Sables d'Olonne, 1990).
GILBERT, CHARLES, *La Montagne héroïque* (Cercle d'Or: Sables d'Olonne, 1980).
—— *La Montagne libérée* (Cercle d'Or: Sables d'Olonne, 1981).
GILLIER, GEORGES, *Les Corsaires* (Éditions du Hublot: Toulouse, 1945).
GOUBET, MICHEL, and DEBAUGES, PAUL, *Histoire de la Résistance dans la Haute-Garonne* (Éditions Milan: Toulouse, 1986).
GUINGOUIN, GEORGES, *Quatre ans de lutte sur le sol limousin* (Hachette, 1974).
GUIRAL, PIERRE, *Libération de Marseille* (Hachette, 1974).
GUTTIÈRES, JACQUES, *Le Chemin des maquis: journal de marche d'un médecin* (Piazza: Alfortville, 1972).
HALLS, W. D., *The Youth of Vichy France* (Clarendon Press: Oxford, 1981).
HAON, GABRIEL, *Régionalisme. Esquisse d'une organisation régionaliste et corporative* (Haon: Alès, 1941).
HENRIOT, PHILIPPE, *Et s'ils débarquaient?* (Inter-France, 1944).
HOFFMANN, STANLEY, *Decline or Renewal? France Since the 1930s* (Viking Press: New York, 1974).
INGRAND, HENRY, *Libération de l'Auvergne* (Hachette, 1974).
Jean Moulin et le Conseil national de la Résistance (CNRS, 1983).
JOURDAN, LOUIS, HELFGOTT, JULIEN, and GOLLIET, PIERRE, *Glières, Haute-Savoie, 31 janvier–26 mars 1944. Première bataille de la Résistance* (Association des rescapés des Glières: Annecy, 1946).
JOUTARD, PHILIPPE, *La Légende des Camisards; une sensibilité au passé* (Gallimard, 1977).
—— POUJOL, JACQUES, and CABANEL, PATRICK, *Cévennes, terre de refuge 1940–1944* (Presses du Languedoc: Montpellier, 1987).
KASPI, ANDRÉ, *Les Juifs pendant l'occupation* (Seuil, 1991).
KEDWARD, H. R., *Resistance in Vichy France* (OUP: Oxford, 1978).
—— and AUSTIN, R. (eds.), *Vichy France and the Resistance: Culture and Ideology* (Croom Helm: London, 1985).
LABORIE, PIERRE, *Résistants, Vichyssois et autres: l'évolution de l'opinion et des comportements dans le Lot 1939 à 1944* (CNRS, 1980).
—— *L'Opinion française sous Vichy* (Seuil, 1990).
LACHAPELLE, GEORGES, *Élections législatives, 26 avril et 3 mai 1936. Résultats officiels* (Le Temps, 1936).
LAFONT, ROBERT, *L'Occitanie* (Seghers, 1971).
LE MOIGNE, LOUIS, and BARBANCEYS, MARCEL, *Sédentaires, réfractaires et maquisards. Armée secrète en Haute-Corrèze 1942–1944* (Amicale des Maquis de Haute-Corrèze, 1980).
LEBRUN, FRANÇOIS, and DUPUY, ROGER, *Les Résistances à la révolution* (Imago, 1987).
LÉVY, GILLES, and CORDET, FRANÇOIS, *A nous Auvergne. La vérité sur la Résistance en Auvergne 1940–1944* (Presses de la Cité, 1981).
LEWIS, GWYNNE, and LUCAS, COLIN, *Beyond the Terror: Essays in French Regional and Social History, 1794–1815* (CUP: Cambridge, 1983).
LUIZARD, PIERRE, *La Guerre n'était pas leur métier* (Éditeurs français réunis, 1974).
MAISONNAS, RENÉ, *La Résistance en Ardèche* (Éditions Le Regard du Monde: Aubenas, 1984).
Maquis de Corrèze par 120 témoins et combattants (Éditions sociales, 1971).

MARUÉJOL, RENÉ, and VIELZEUF, AIMÉ, *Le Maquis Bir-Hakeim* (Maruéjol et Vielzeuf: Nîmes, 1947).
MAURY, LUCIEN, *La Résistance audoise*, 2 vols. (Comité d'Histoire de la Résistance du Département de l'Aude: Quillan, 1980).
—— *Le Maquis de Picaussel* (Maury: Quillan, 1980).
Mémorial de la Résistance en Haute-Savoie (Maison du Combattant: Annecy, 1970).
MICHEL, HENRI, *Histoire de la Résistance en France* (PUF, 1950).
MILLAR, GEORGE, *Maquis* (Heinemann: London, 1947).
MOMPEZAT, GEORGES, *Le Corps Franc de la Montagne Noire. Journal de marche* (Mompezat: Albi, 1963).
MUSARD, FRANÇOIS, *Les Glières* (Éditions de Crémille, 1971).
NOËL, AIMÉ, *Figeac d'hier et d'aujourd'hui* (Noël: Figeac, 1984).
NOIREAU, ROBERT (Colonel Georges), *Le Temps des partisans* (Flammarion, 1978).
NOVICK, PETER, *The Resistance Versus Vichy: The Purge of Collaborators in Liberated France* (Columbia University Press: New York, 1968).
OPHULS, MARCEL, *Le Chagrin et la pitié* (Télévision Rencontre, 1969).
PAULHAN, JEAN, *Lettre aux directeurs de la Résistance* (Éditions de Minuit, 1952).
PAXTON, ROBERT, *Vichy France: Old Guard and New Order 1940–1944* (Barrie & Jenkins: London, 1972).
PICARD, RAYMOND, and CHAUSSADE, JEAN, *Ombres et espérances en Quercy. Les Groupes Armée secrète Vény dans les secteurs du Lot 1940–45* (Privat: Toulouse, 1980).
PIERREL, MARCEL, *La Lozère sous l'occupation allemande* (Pierrel: Marvejols, n.d.).
Le Plateau et l'accueil des Juifs réfugiés, 1940–45 (Chambon-sur-Lignon, 1981).
PLOTON, Abbé, *Quatre années de Résistance à Albertville* (Ploton: Albertville, 1946).
POUJOL, ROBERT, *Le Maquis d'Ardaillès* (Poujol: Sumène, 1984).
PRADES, HENRI, *Le Commandant Demarne dans la Résistance* (Prades: Montpellier, n.d.).
R.1.3. Francs-Tireurs et Partisans de la Haute-Savoie (France d'Abord, 1946).
RETOURNÉ, JACQUELINE, *Quelques aspects du service de santé en campagne dans le maquis* (Imprimerie la Charité: Montpellier, 1945).
RIOUX, JEAN-PIERRE, *The Fourth Republic 1944–1958* (CUP: Cambridge, 1987).
ROMANS-PETIT, HENRI, *Les Maquis de l'Ain* (Hachette, 1974).
ROUSSO, HENRY, *Le Syndrome de Vichy 1944–198 . . .* (Seuil, 1987).
RUDE, F., *Libération de Lyon et de sa région* (Hachette, 1974).
SAGNES, JEAN, *Le Midi rouge. Mythe et réalité* (Anthropos, 1982).
—— in collaboration with MAURIN, JULES, *L'Hérault dans la guerre 1939/1945* (Éditions Horvath: Saint-Étienne, 1986).
SENTIS, GEORGES, *Les Communistes et la Résistance dans les Pyrénées-Orientales (1939–1947)*, 2 vols. (Institut des recherches marxistes, Comité d'Histoire de la Résistance catalane: Perpignan, 1985).
—— *Le Maquis FTPF Henri Barbusse* (Comité d'Histoire de la Résistance catalane: Perpignan, 1988).
SHENNAN, ANDREW, *Rethinking France: Plans for Renewal 1940–1946* (Clarendon Press: Oxford, 1989).
SWEETS, J. F., *Choices in Vichy France: The French under Nazi Occupation* (OUP: Oxford, 1986).
TANANT, PIERRE, *Vercors, haut-lieu de France* (Arthaud, 1951).

TEISSIER DU CROS, JANET, *Divided Loyalties: A Scotswoman in Occupied France* (Canongate: Edinburgh, 1992).
TILLON, CHARLES, *Les FTP* (Julliard, 1962).
La Vallée de Thônes et Glières pendant la 2e guerre mondiale, 2 vols. (Amis du Val de Thônes: Thônes, 1984).
La Vie d'un maquis d'Auxois (Association du souvenir de la Résistance: Dijon, n.d.).
VIELZEUF, AIMÉ, . . . *et la Cévenne s'embrasa* (1965; Éditions le Camariguo: Nîmes, 1981).
—— *On les appelait 'les bandits'* (1967; Éditions de Crémille: Geneva, 1972).
—— *Épopée en Cévenne* (Vielzeuf: Nîmes, 1976).
—— *La Résistance dans le Gard* (Vielzeuf: Nîmes, 1979).
VINEN, RICHARD, *The Politics of French Business* (CUP: Cambridge, 1991).

5. ARTICLES

Abbreviations
RHDGM *Revue d'histoire de la deuxième guerre mondiale*
GMCC *Guerres mondiales et conflits contemporains*

AUSTIN, ROGER, 'The Chantiers de la Jeunesse in Languedoc, 1940–44', *French Historical Studies*, 13/1 (Spring 1983).
—— 'Surveillance and Intelligence under the Vichy Regime: The Service du Contrôle Technique, 1939–45', *Intelligence and National Security*, 1/1 (1986).
AZÉMA, J.-P., 'La Milice', *Vingtième siècle*, 28 (1990).
BOULADOU, G., 'Les Maquis du Languedoc', *RHDGM*, 55 (1964).
—— 'Les Maquis de la région de Montpellier', *RHDGM*, 112 (1978).
BOURDERON, R., 'Mouvement de la main d'œuvre et STO dans les mines du Gard', *RHDGM*, 112 (1978).
—— 'Les Maquis FTP: la mise en œuvre particulière d'une conception globale du combat clandestin', in *Colloque sur les maquis* (see above).
CALMETTE, A., 'Les Équipes Jedburgh dans la bataille de France', *RHDGM*, 61 (1966).
COMBES, G., 'La Mobilisation vers le Mont Mouchet', *RHDGM*, 49 (1963).
CRÉMIEUX-BRILHAC, J.-L., 'La Bataille des Glières et "la guerre psychologique" ', *RHDGM*, 99 (1975).
—— 'Radio et information au maquis', in *Colloque sur les maquis*.
DELMAS, JEAN, 'Libération et insurrection nationale (France 1944)', *Revue historique des armées* (1984).
—— 'Les maquis: action immédiate ou action à terme', in *Colloque sur les maquis*.
FARMER, SARAH, 'The Communist Resistance in the Haute-Vienne', *French Historical Studies*, 14/1 (1985).
GRANET, MARIE, 'Dessin général des maquis', *RHDGM*, 1 (1950).
Le Journal de la France. Les Années 40 (1972), 54, 'Les Maquis'; 57, 'Les Glières'; 64, 'L'heure des maquis'; 66, 'Oradour'; 67, 'Le Vercors'.

KEDWARD, H. R., 'Patriots and Patriotism in Vichy France', *Transactions of the Royal Historical Society*, 32 (1982).

—— 'The Maquis and the Culture of the Outlaw', in R. Kedward and R. Austin (eds.), *Vichy France and the Resistance* (1985).

—— 'The Vichy of the other Philippe', in G. Hirschfeld and P. Marsh (eds.), *Collaboration in France* (Berg: Oxford, 1989).

—— 'The Maquis. Whose history?', in M. Scriven and P. Wagstaff (eds.), *War and Society in Twentieth-Century France* (Berg: Oxford, 1991).

LABORIE, P., 'Opinion et représentations: la Libération et l'image de la Résistance', *RHDGM*, 131 (1983).

—— 'Les Maquis dans la population', in *Colloque sur les maquis.*

LAURENS, A., 'Le STO dans le département de l'Ariège', *RHDGM*, 95 (1974).

LÉVY, CLAUDE, 'La Résistance juive en France', *Vingtième siècle*, 22 (1989).

LÉVY, G. M., 'La Concentration des maquis d'Auvergne', *Revue historique de l'armée* (1968).

LOMBARD, M., 'Notes sur quelques aspects financiers de la vie d'un maquis bourguignon', *RHDGM*, 49 (1963).

MANRY, A. G., 'Auvergne premier haut-lieu de la Résistance nationale', *Revue historique de l'armée*, 3 (1968).

MARCOT, F., 'Les Maquis dans la Résistance', in *Colloque sur les maquis.*

—— 'La Résistance et la population, Jura 1944', *GMCC*, 146 (1987).

MARTRES, E., 'La "République de Mauriac" ', *RHDGM*, 99 (1975).

—— 'Un exemple de concentration: le Mont Mouchet', in *Colloque sur les maquis.*

MICHEL, H., 'Bibliographie sur les maquis', *RHDGM*, 49 (1963).

—— 'Les Maquis au-delà de la légende', *Le Monde* (30 décembre 1984).

MOIZET, H., and FONT, C., 'A propos du questionnaire "Sauvegardons la mémoire" ', *La Résistance en Rouergue*, 84 (1990).

PIKE, D. W., 'Les Forces allemandes dans le sud-ouest de la France mai–juillet 1944', *GMCC*, 152 (1988).

POUJOL, JACQUES, 'Histoire abrégée des maquis cévenols 1943–1944', *Causses et Cévennes. Revue du Club cévenol*, 4 (1980).

Revue historique de l'armée, no. spécial, 'Ve Région militaire' (1980).

ROIDOT, GEORGES, 'Les Maquis de l'Organisation de Résistance de l'Armée', in *Colloque sur les maquis.*

SCHWARTZ, PAULA, 'Partisanes and Gender Politics in Vichy France', *French Historical Studies*, 16/1 (1989).

SILVESTRE, PAUL, 'STO, maquis et guérilla dans l'Isère', *RHDGM*, 130 (1983).

Vingtième Siècle, 'Les Guerres franco-françaises', 5 (1985).

VITTE, MARCEL, 'Un été 44 à Mâcon. Occupation et libération', *Annales de l'Académie de Mâcon*, 3e série, 60 (1984).

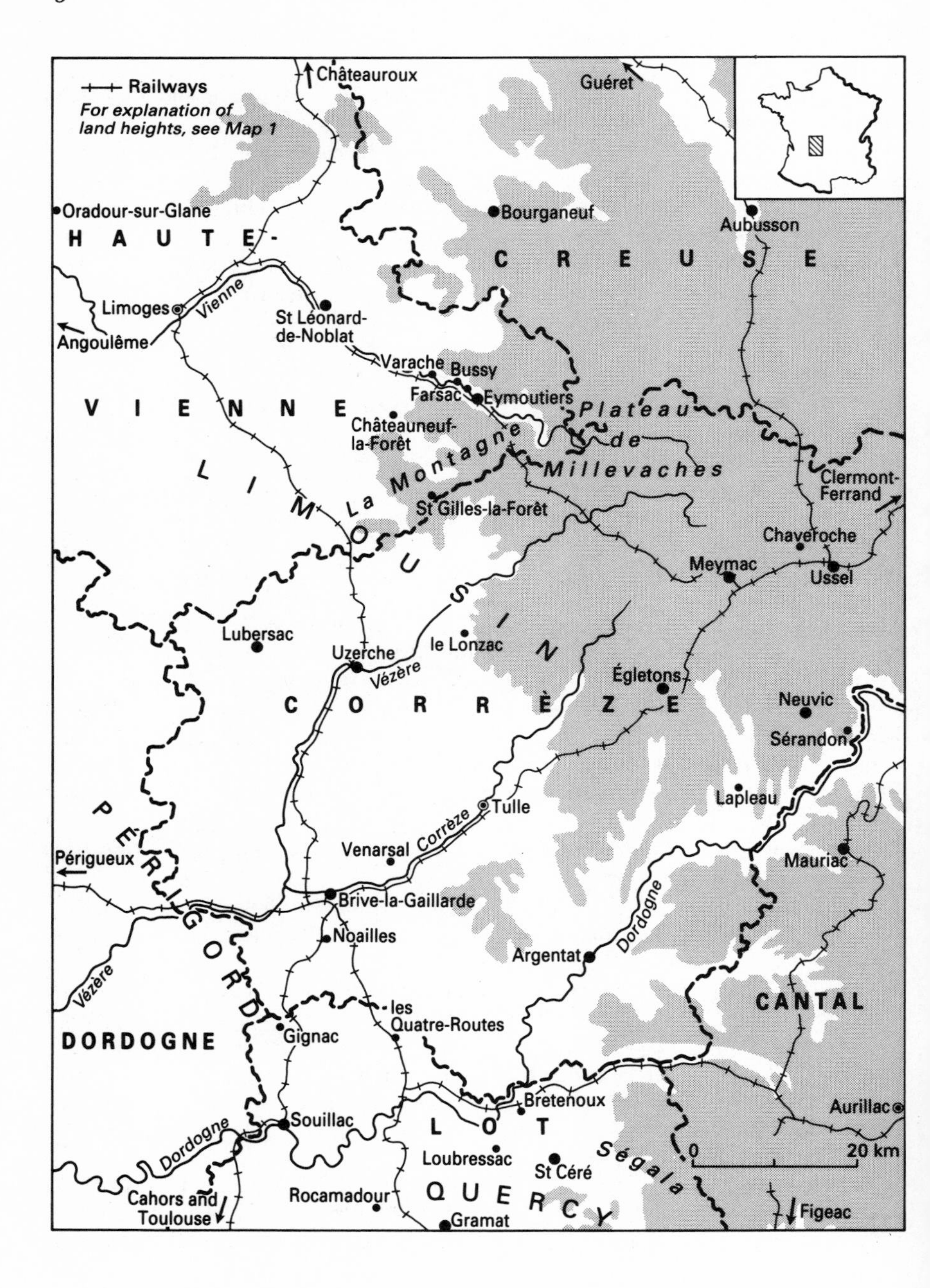

2. The Limousin

3. The Lot and the Tarn

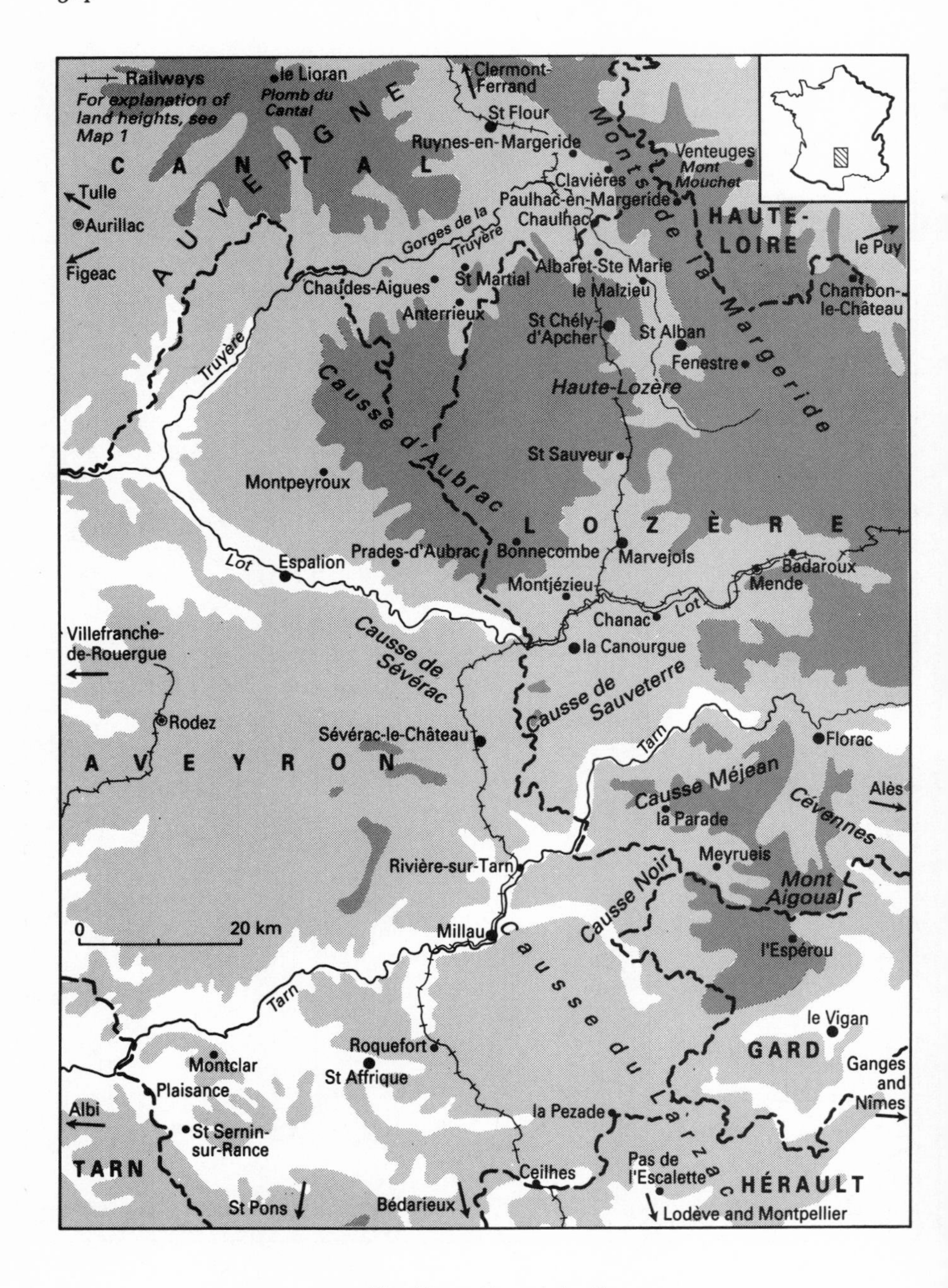

4. The Margeride and the Causses

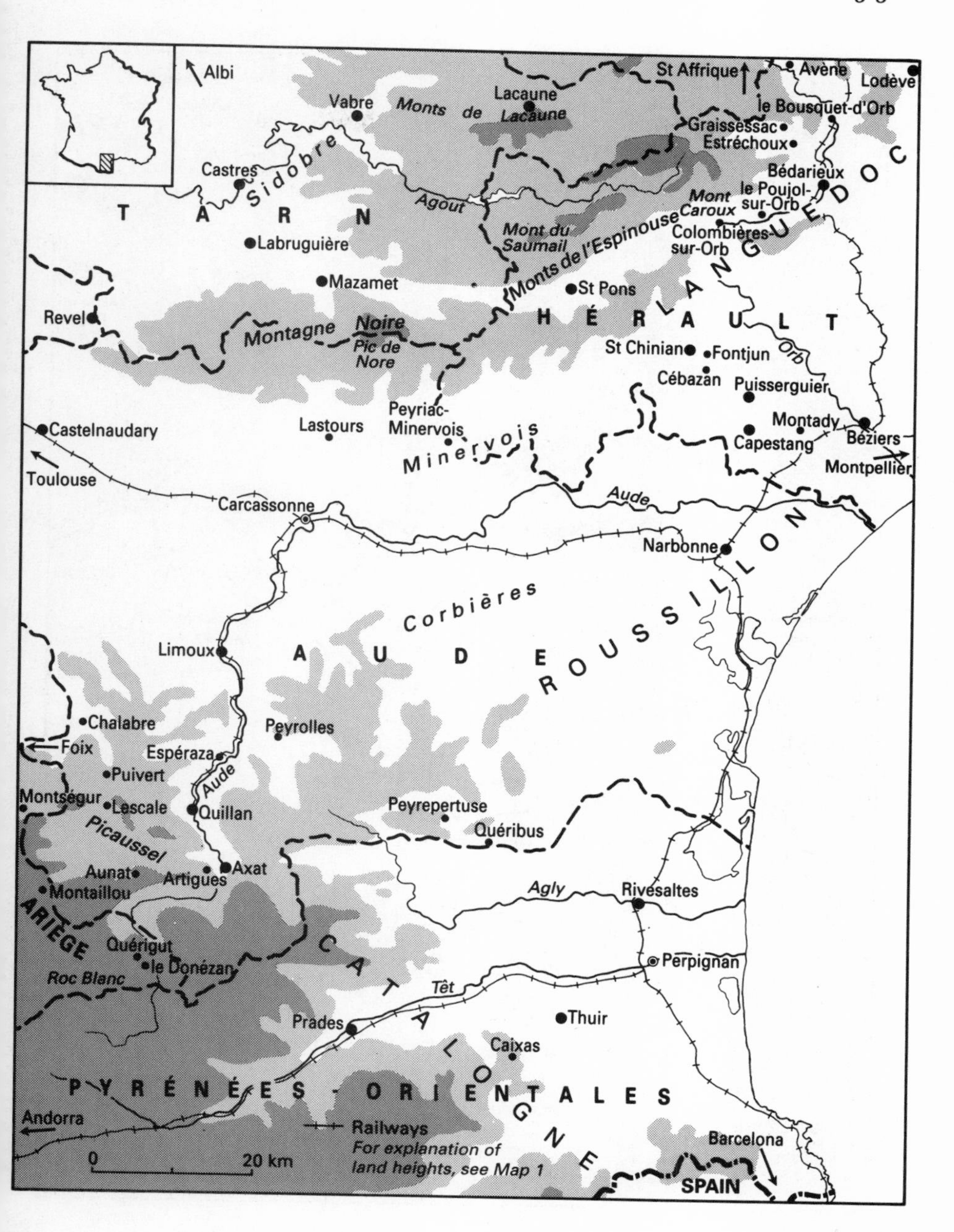

5. The Montagne Noire and the Aude

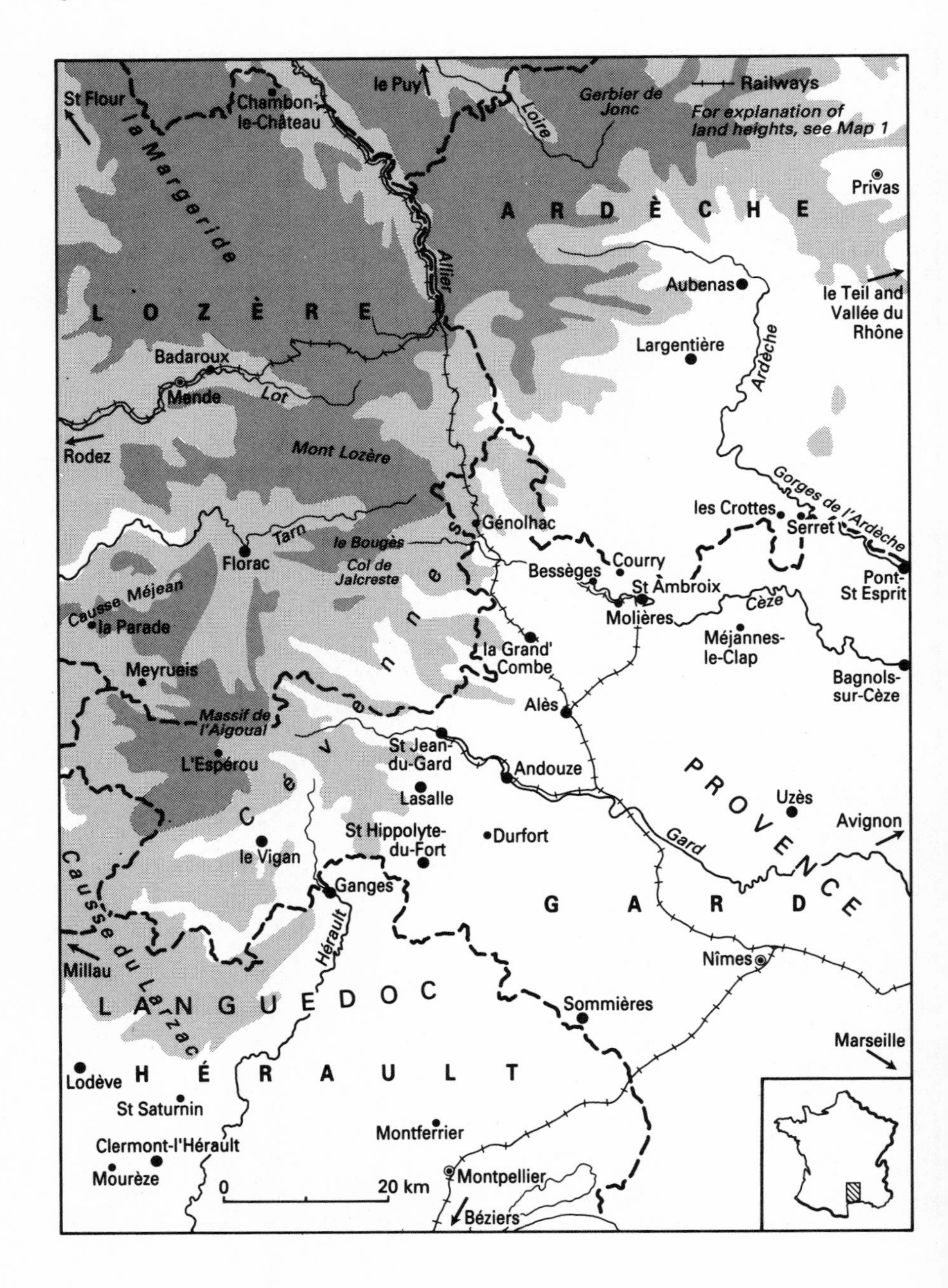

6. The Lozère and the Gard

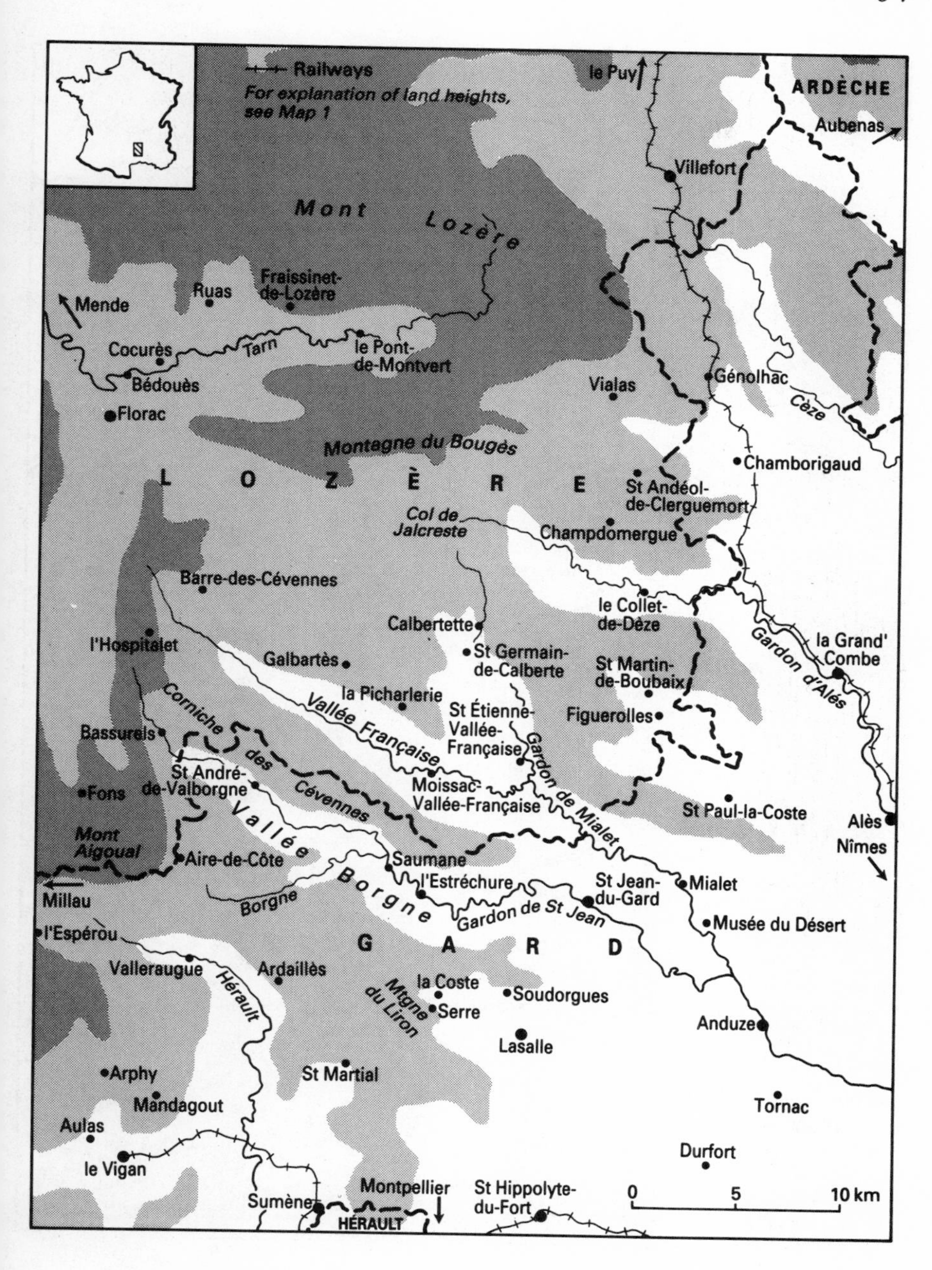

7. The Cévennes

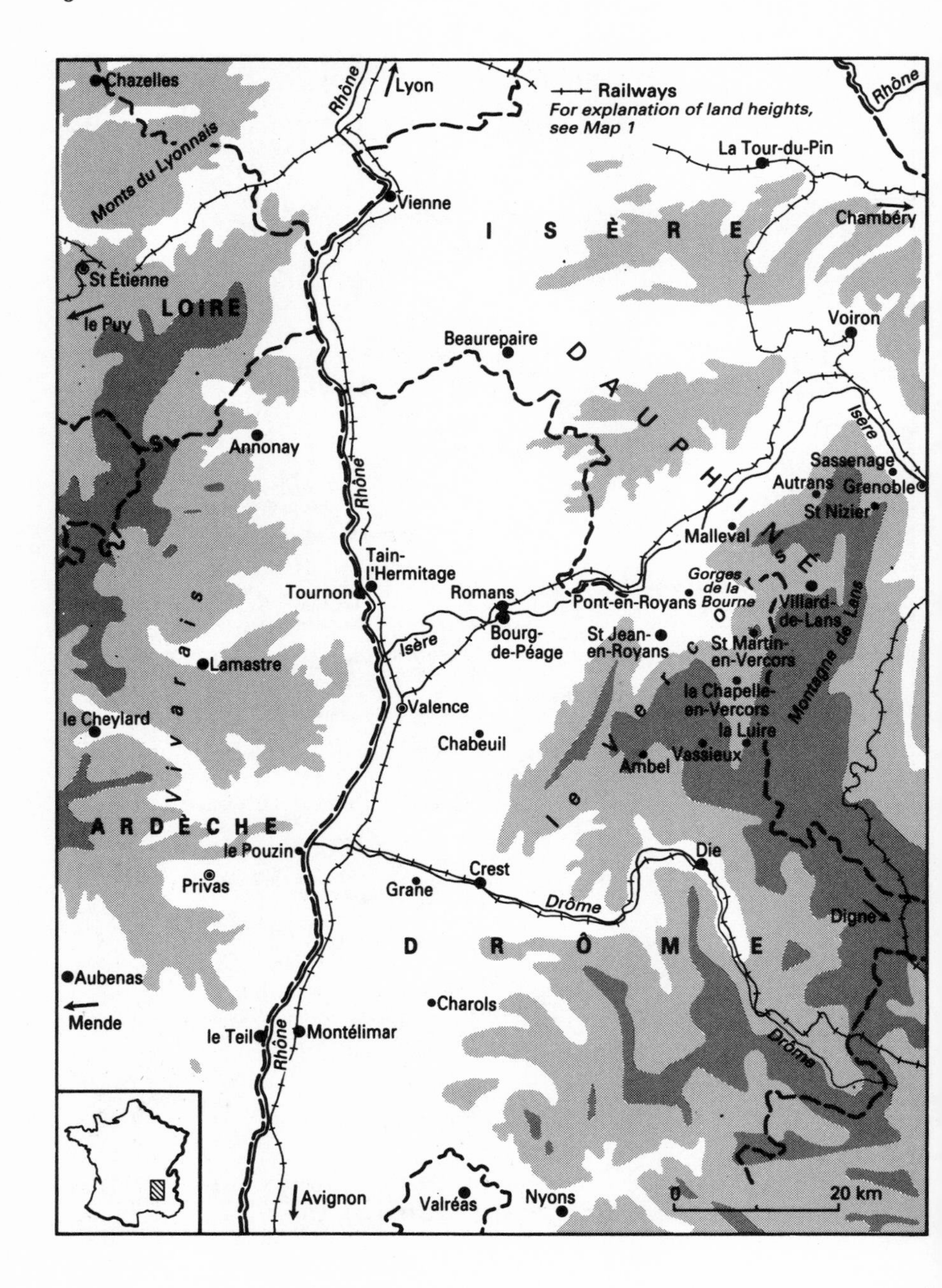

8. The Vercors

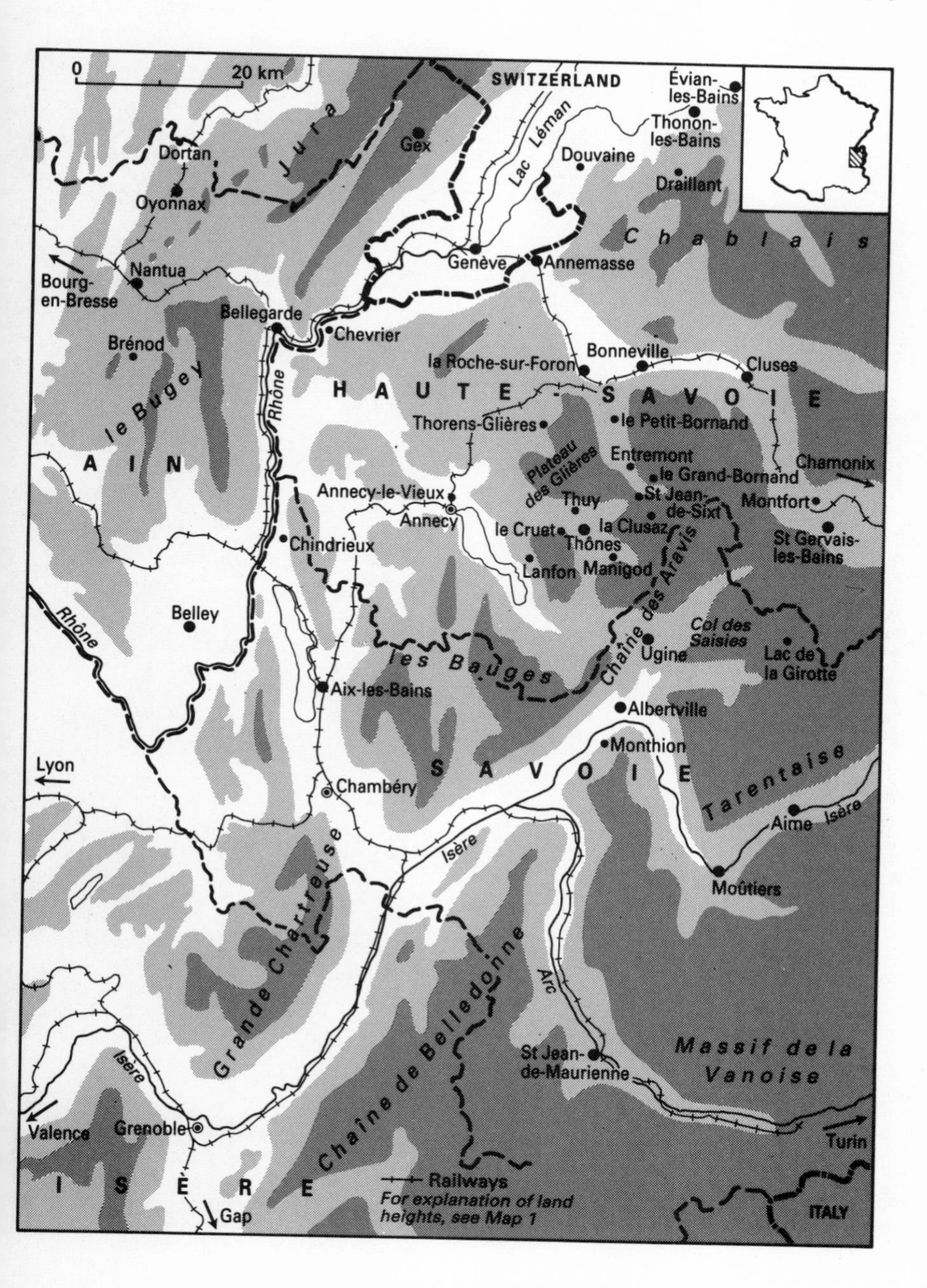

9. The Savoyard Alps and les Glières

Index of Place-Names

Map numbers are indicated in **bold** type

General Index

Galinier (Armagnac) 230
Gallimard 263